The Complete Cigar Box Guitar Chord Book

3-String Cigar Box Guitar Chords in GDG Tuning

By Brent Robitaille

www.brentrobitaille.com
www.kalymimusic.com

KALYMI PUBLISHING

Copyright © 2020 by Brent Robitaille
All Rights Reserved

Unauthorized copying, arranging, adapting is an infringemnet of copyright.

OTHER BOOKS BY BRENT ROBITAILLE

The Complete Cigar Box Guitar 4-String Chord Book
Cigar Box Guitar - Jazz & Blues Unlimited Book One & Two
Cigar Box Guitar Blues Overload
101 Riffs for Cigar Box Guitar
3 - 4 String Cigar Box Guitar Tablature Reference Books
Celtic Collection for Cigar Box Guitar
The Ultimate Collection – How to Play Cigar Box Guitar Vol. 1 & 2
Cigar Box Guitar - The Technique Book
The Pop Rock Looper Pedal Book
The Blues Guitar Looper Pedal Book
Standard Guitar Tuning - Celtic Collection
Open D Guitar Tuning - Celtic Collection
Open G Guitar Tuning - Celtic Collection
Improve Your Guitar Chord Playing
Slide Guitar Collection
Celtic Collection Fiddle - Tab & Notes
Holiday Collection for Fiddle - Tab & Notes
Traditional Collection Fiddle - Tab & Notes
Fiddle Tab - Celtic Collection
Celtic Collection for Mandolin
Celtic Collection for Ukulele
Holiday Collection for Cigar Box Guitar

Audio - Ebooks - Sheet Music - Lessons
Available at:

www.brentrobitaille.com
kalymimusic.com

KALYMI PUBLISHING

PUBLISHED BY KALYMI PUBLISHING
©2020 Kalymi Publishing

Although the author and publisher have made every effort to ensure that the information in this book is in public domain at press time, the author and publisher do not assume and hereby disclaim any liability to any party. Any copying of this material whole or in part with the express written permission of Kalymi Publishing is a violation of copyright law.

Contents: The Complete Cigar Box Guitar Chord Book

Introduction 4
Playing Chords on the Cigar Box Guitar 5
How to Read Tablature and Chords 6

Beginner Chords and Moveable Shapes
Beginner Chords on the Cigar Box Guitar 8
Moveable Chords on the Cigar Box Guitar 20
Diatonic Chords in all Keys 22

Complete Chord Library
A Chords 24
B♭ (A♯) Chords 32
B Chords 40
C Chords 48
C♯ - D♭ Chords 56
D Chords 64
E♭ (D♯) Chords 72
E Chords 80
F Chords 88
F♯ - G♭ Chords 96
G Chords 104
A♭ (G♯) Chords 112

Theory and Chord Progressions
Chord Progressions and Theory 120
Chord Numbering Systems 122
Understanding Chord Formulas 124
Cigar Box Fingerboard and Interval Chart 126

Strumming and Fingerpicking Patterns
Strumming and Picking Techniques 128
Strumming Pattern Practice 130
Strumming and Fingerpicking Patterns 132

Chord Progressions
Tips for Accompanying on Cigar Box Guitar 135
Chord Progressions - Blues 136
Chord Progressions - Pop 148
Chord Progressions - Rock 164

Introduction

The *Complete Cigar Box Guitar Chord Book* is the most extensive library of chords ever assembled for the 3-string cigar box guitar. Incredibly, there are hundreds of possible chords with only three strings in GDG tuning. Of course, there are many "possible" chords with some more practical and easier to play, but this extensive library will cover most chords required to perform all styles of music.

I have included as many chords possible in each of the 12 keys in music, as well as multiple voicings of each chord, providing lots of chord choices. While there is an extensive library, I have also included the most commonly played and user-friendly chords for the majority of players — a convenient summary of easier chords and common chord shapes for beginners.

Learning your favourite chords is the first step, followed by learning to switch between chords to play songs and chord progressions. Improve your chords by playing through some of the chord progressions that are taken directly from some of the most popular songs ever written. There is a good selection of blues chord progressions that cover many of the standard blues changes in all keys. Also, take some time to study some of the standard strumming and fingerpicking patterns. Here you will see these familiar rhythm patterns in many of your favourite songs. If you need to brush up on your chord theory, you will find several pages explaining how chords are formed, the chord numbering system, chord formulas, and understanding chord progressions.

Visit my website for more information and audio tracks:

www.brentrobitaille.com/cbg-chord-book

www.brentrobitaille.com

Playing Chords on the Cigar Box Guitar

Playing chords on the cigar box guitar poses several challenges for most players. First, there are only three strings, and many chords require four notes to produce the full chord. Second, since there are only three strings, and it is often difficult for the fingers to reach the notes of some chords. Fortunately, there are workarounds for these two issues.

The solution to the first challenge is to omit notes from chords requiring four or more notes. Four note chords are all the 7th, 9th, 11th, and 13th type chords. In these chords, the most important notes are the 3rd and 7th of the chord. These two notes are enough to determine the quality of the chord though you still need to add other notes that give the chord its name. For example, a G9 chord has five notes: G B D F A. To achieve the sound and function of a G9 chord, you would need at a minimum the 3rd, 7th and 9th. So that is B, F and A. These three notes are the most important, especially if you are playing solo. If other instruments are accompanying you and playing some of the additional notes like the root of the chord (G), then you will have more options. Either way, use your ear to determine what works best for each situation.

Here is a checklist when figuring out what notes to play in a chord:

1) Always try to include the 3rd of the chord. The 3rd determines if the chord is major/minor.

2) Include the 7th of the chord for 7ths, 9ths, 11ths, and 13ths.

3) Include the extension note that is in the chord name. For example, the 9th of G9 is A.

4) Omit the 5th of the chord.

5) Omit the root of the chord.

Here are a few suggestions for the second issue mentioned about reaching notes in chords.

1) Play hard to reach chords down the neck where the frets are closer.

2) Learn several chord shapes or voicings for each chord in lower and upper positions.

3) Use open strings where possible, so only two fingers are needed.

4) If you are in the standard cigar box tuning (GDG), then you have two G strings. This tuning can be useful for learning variations of the same chord:

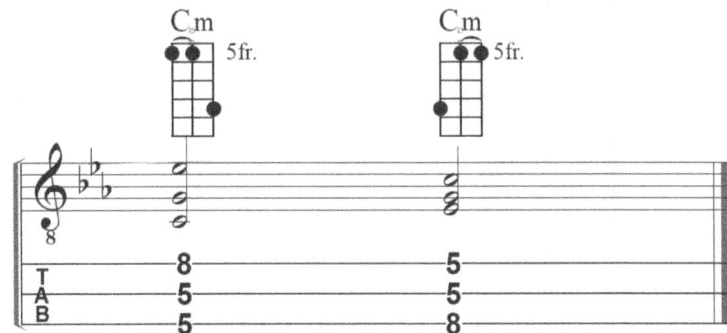

How to Read Chord Diagrams

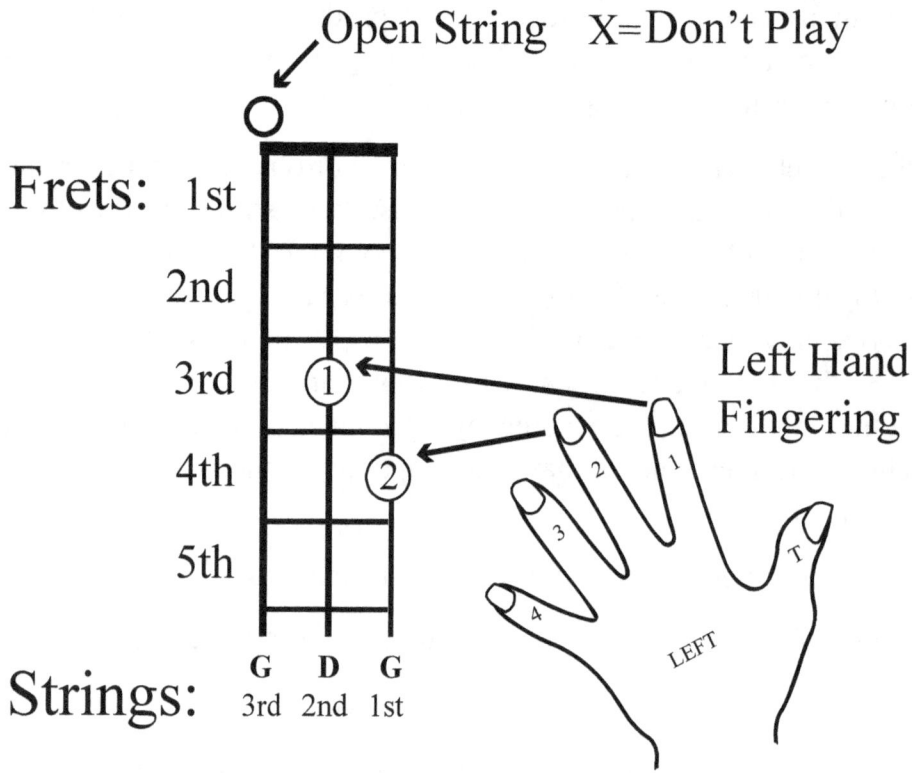

Barre Chords

Barre chords require covering several strings with one finger. In this example, place your 1st finger on strings 1 to 3 then add the 4th finger to form the A minor chord.

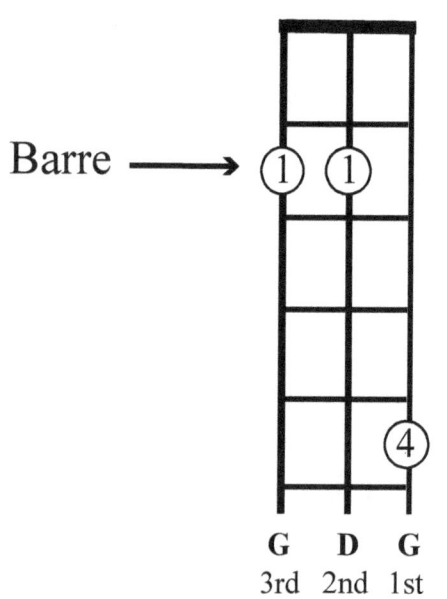

Same chord written in tablature and notation.

How to Read Tablature (TAB)

To read tablature, you need to know four things:

1) What string is the note on? - Strings are thin (1st) to thick (3rd).
2) What fret is the note on? - Fret numbers are left to right.
3) Which finger do I use? - Keep all fingers in position (1-2-3-4) where possible when playing single notes, and most comfortable fingerings for chords.
4) How long to let the note ring? - Based on the song's rhythm but generally keep fingers on fretboard as long as possible to let notes ring throughout.

Fingerboard Chart:

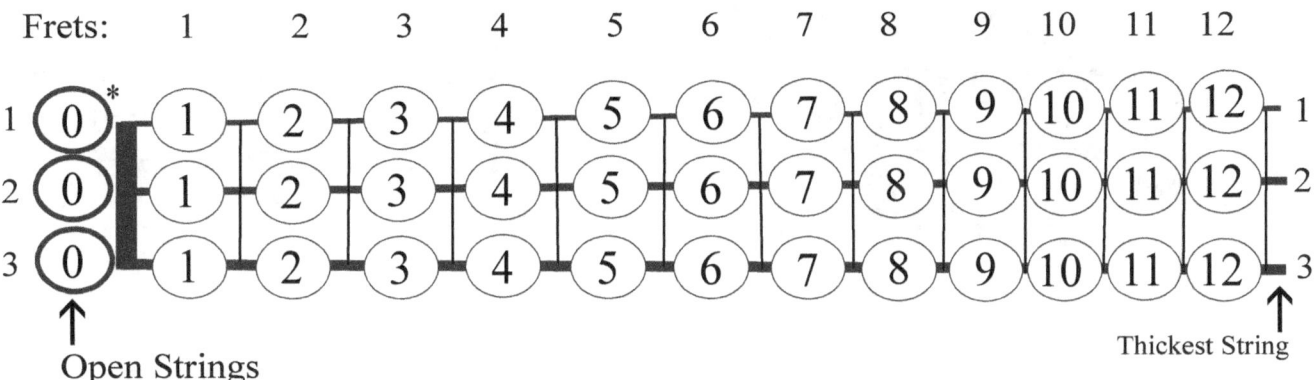

Tablature Examples:

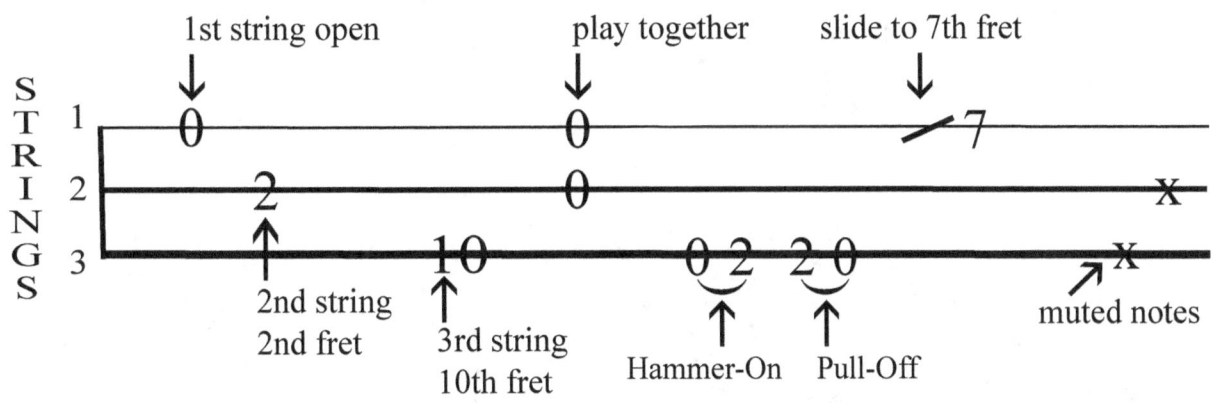

Beginner Chords - Major

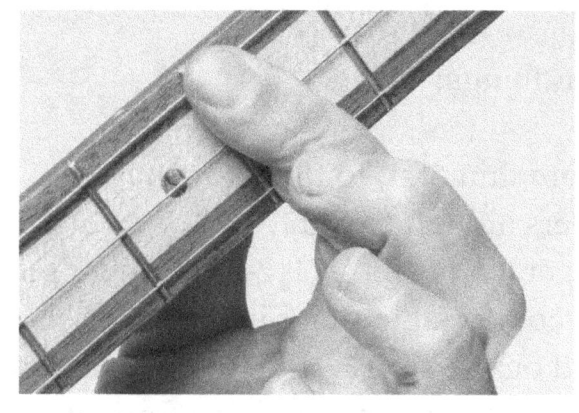  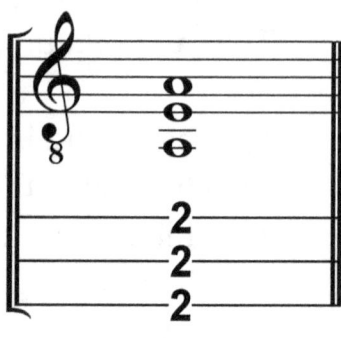

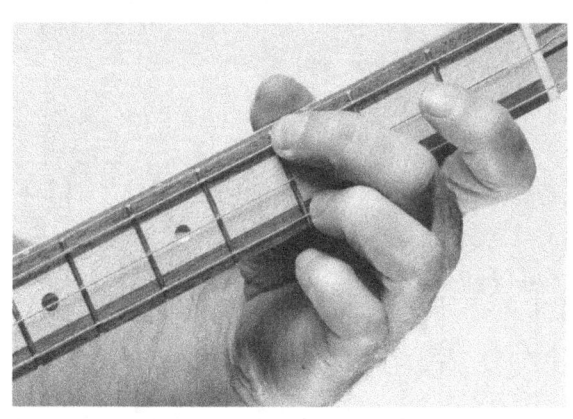 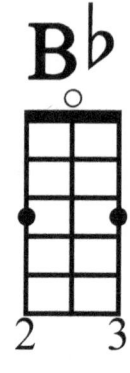 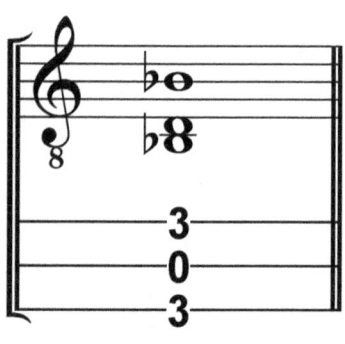

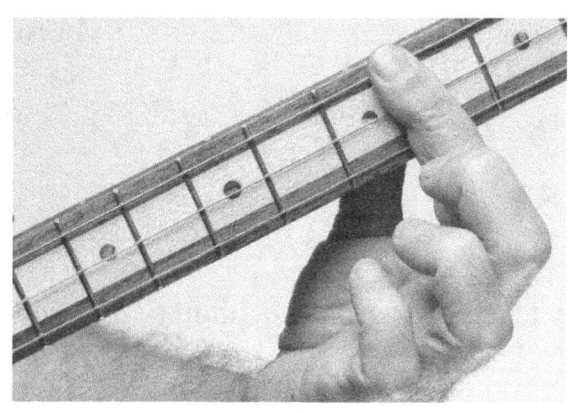 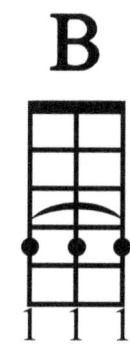 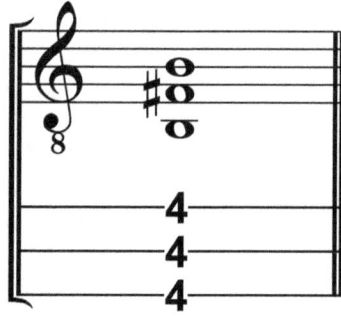

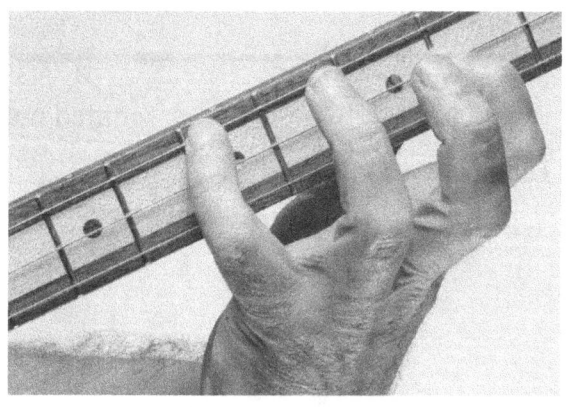 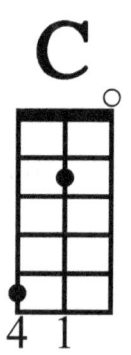 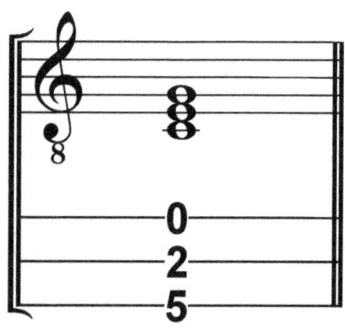

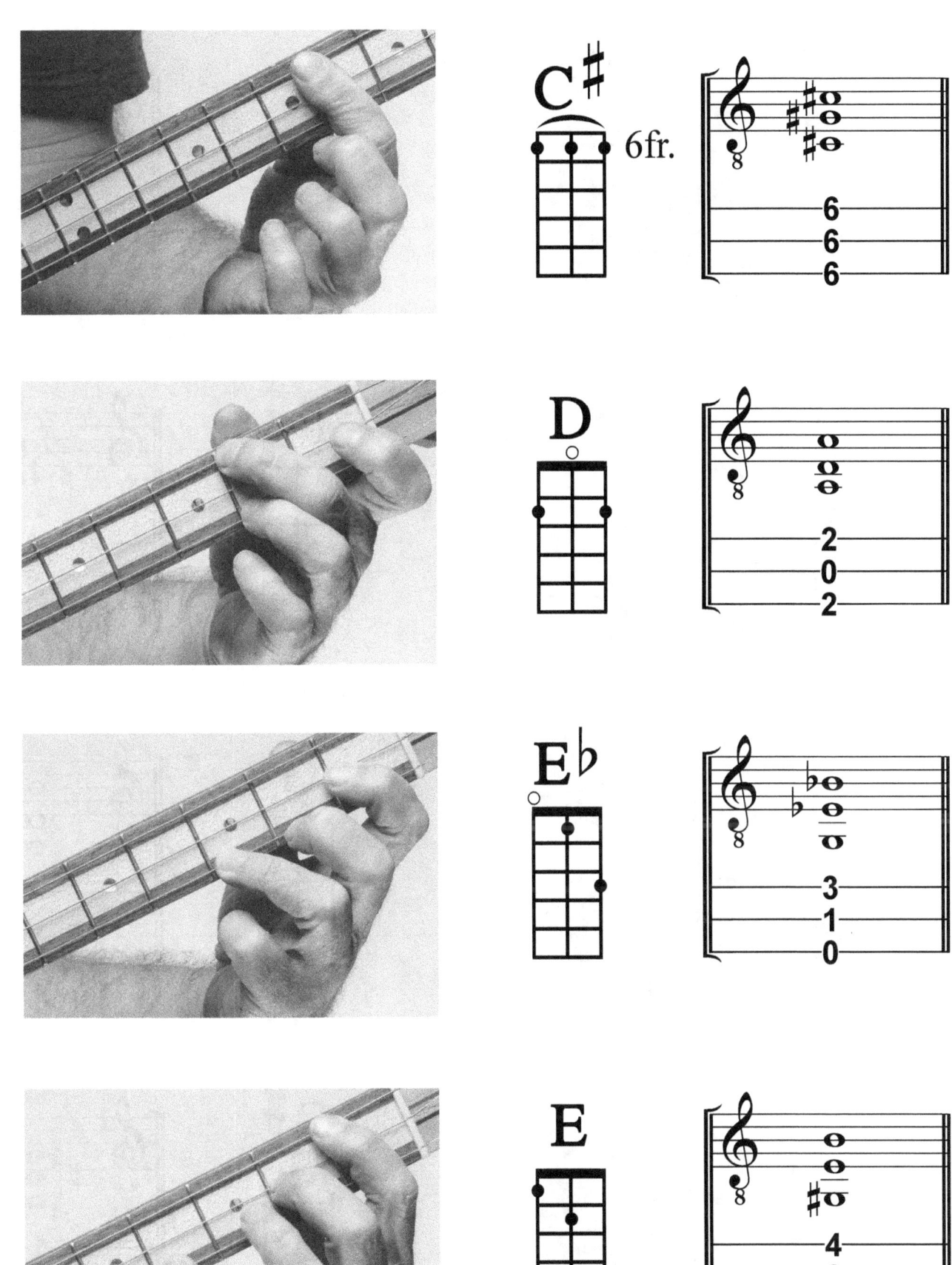

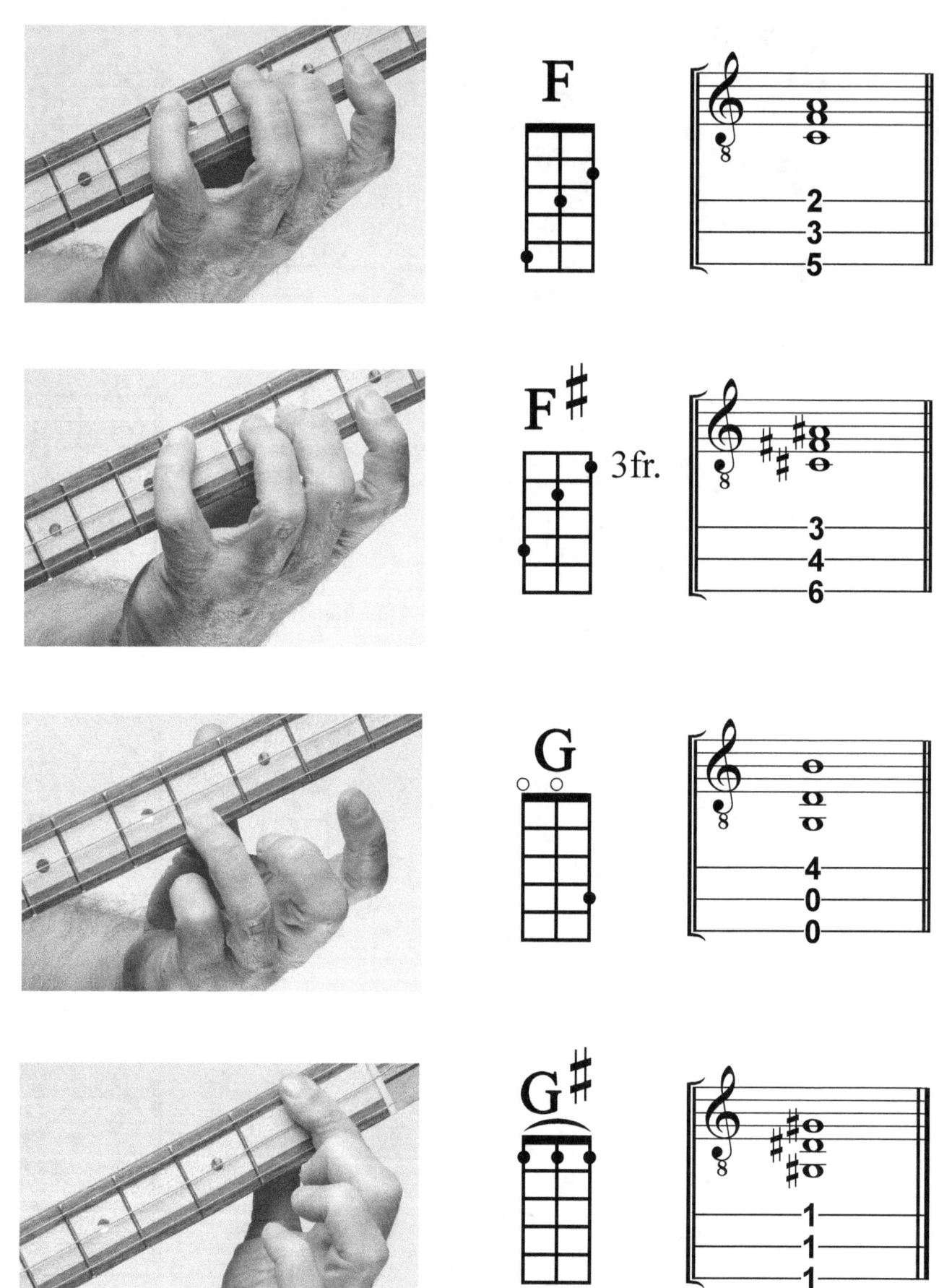

Beginner Chords - Minor

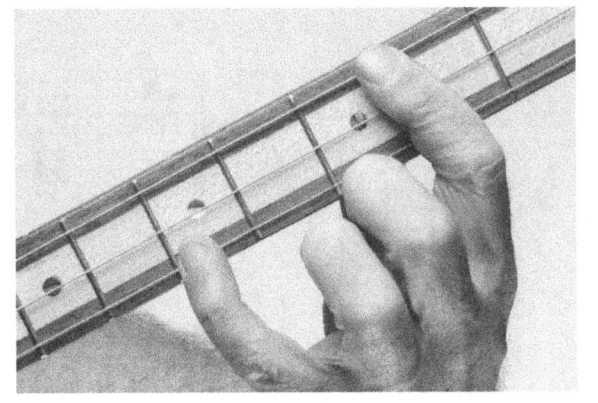

Am
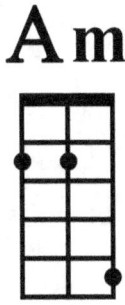 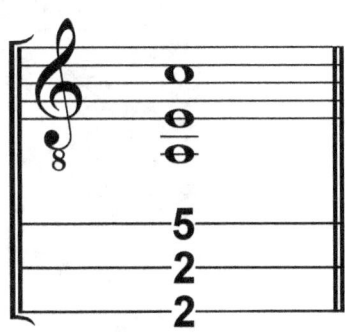

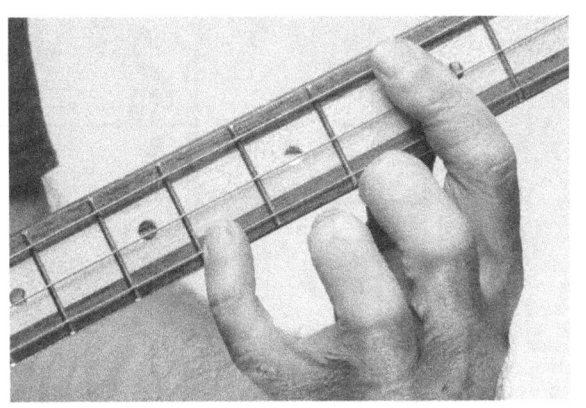

B♭m
 3 fr.
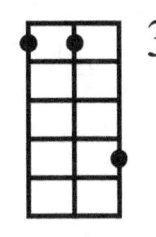 

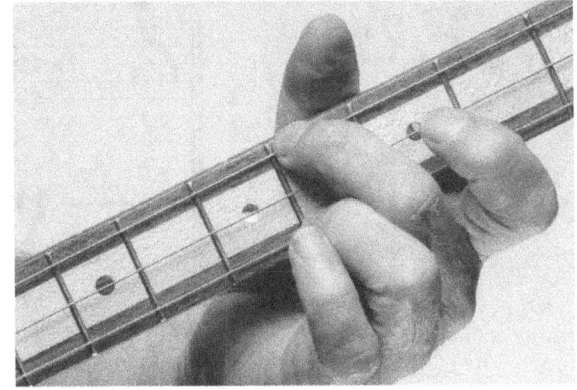

Bm

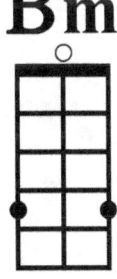 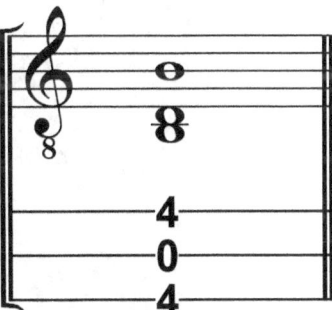

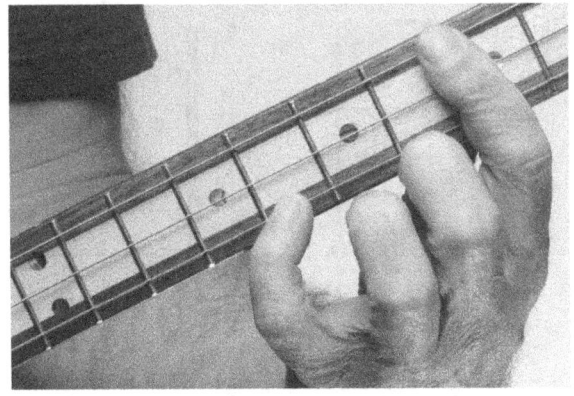

Cm
5 fr.
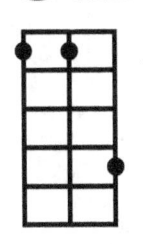 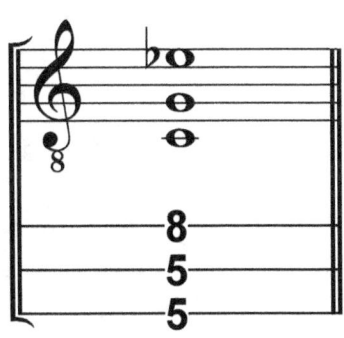

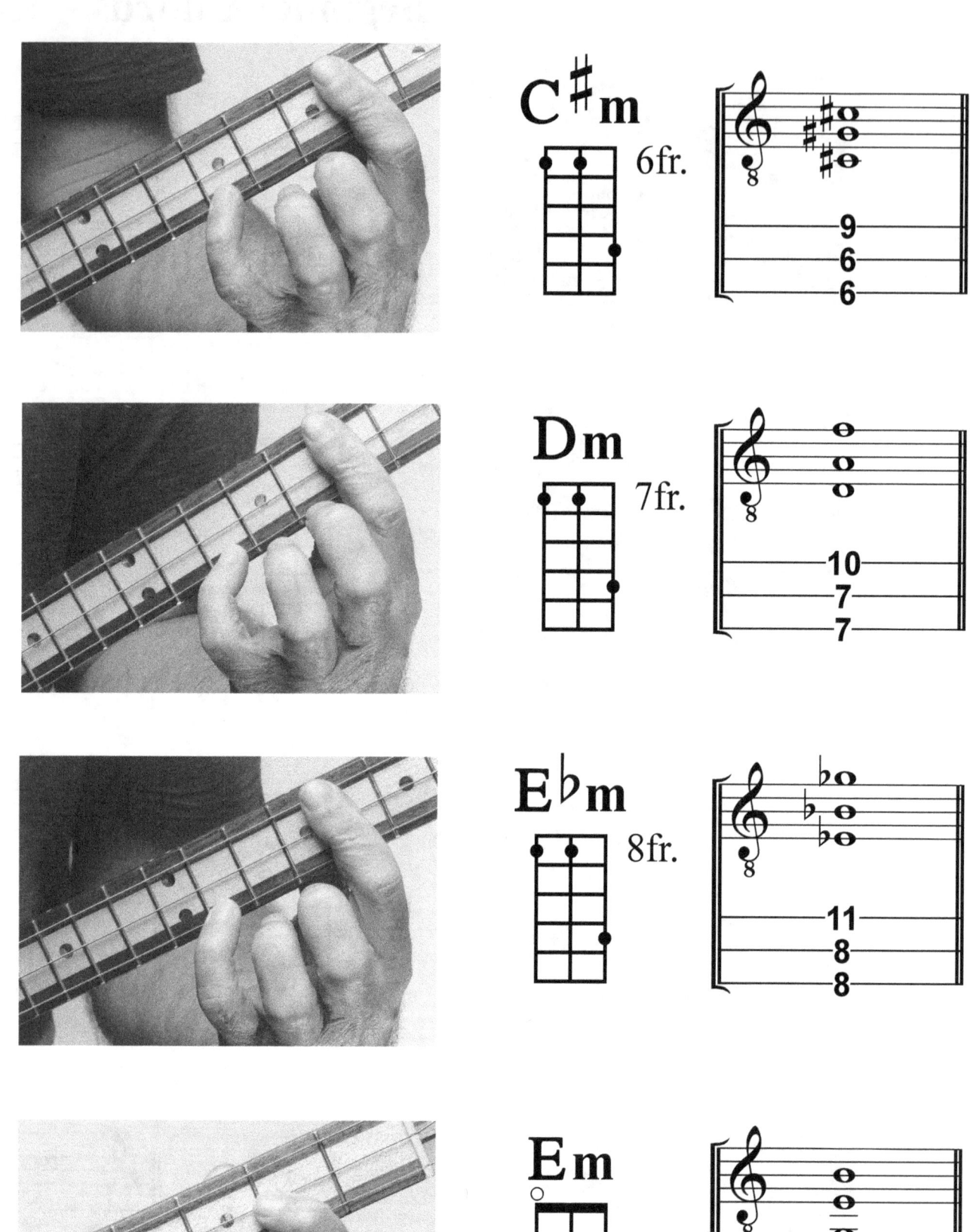

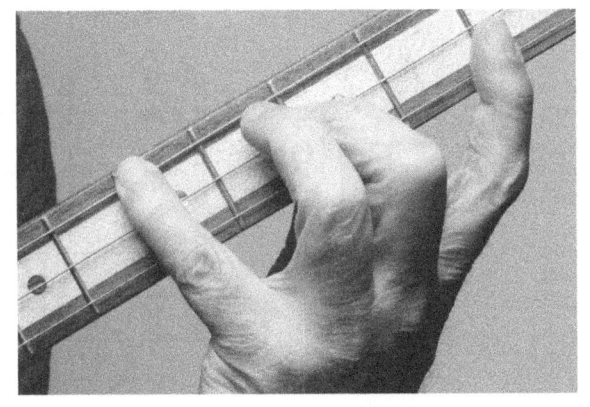 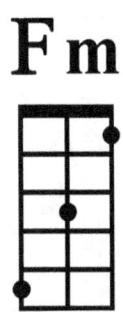 Fm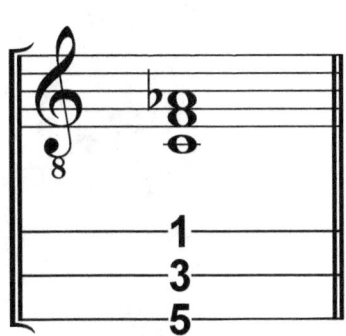

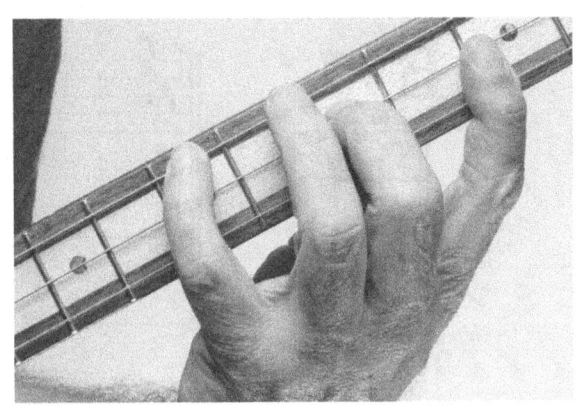  F#m

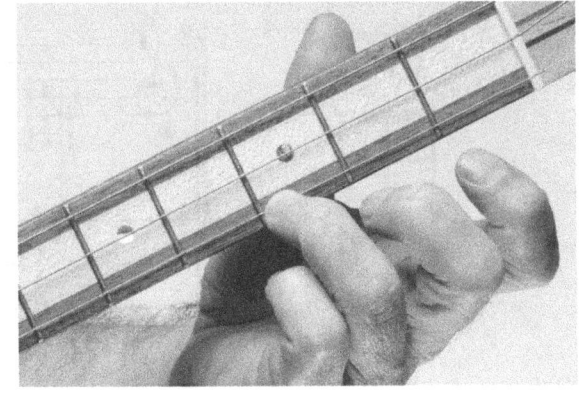 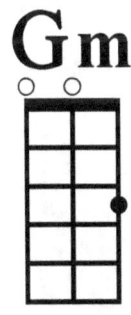 Gm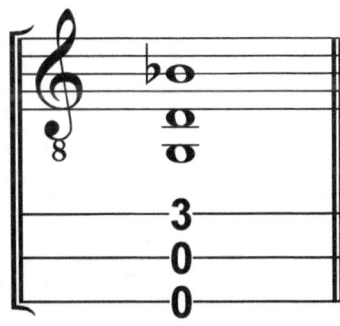

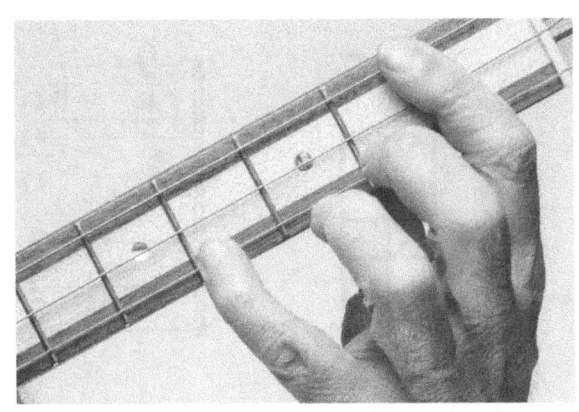 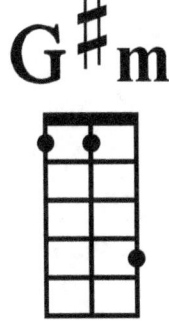 G#m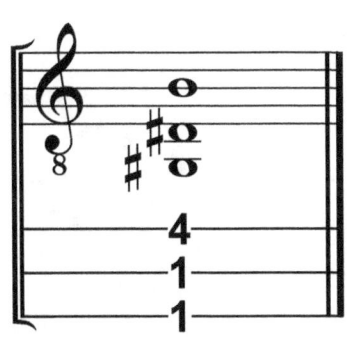

Beginner Chords - Dominant 7

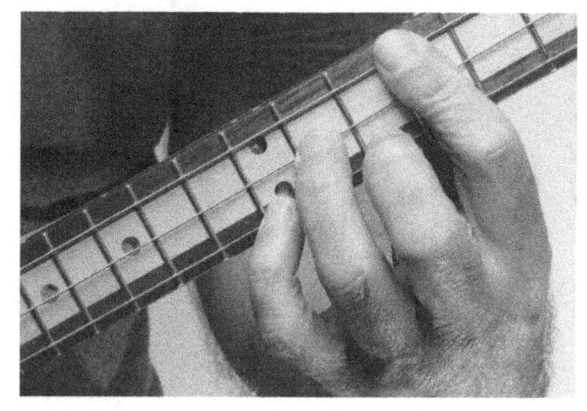
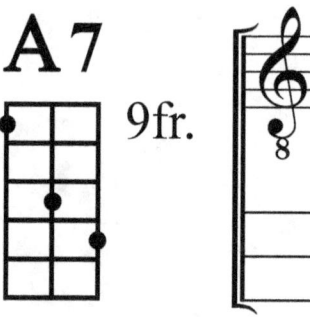
A7 9fr.
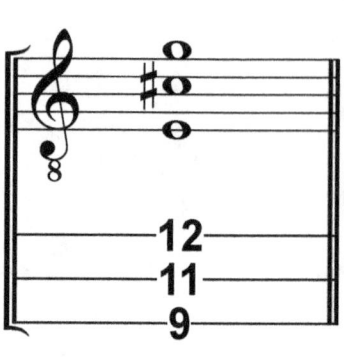

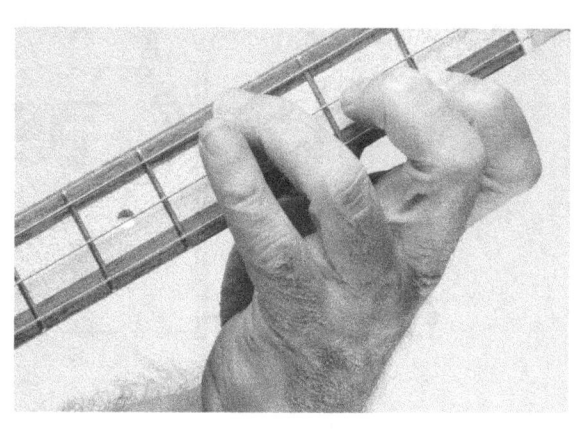
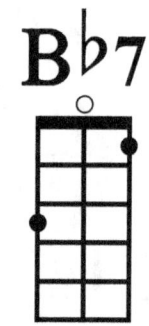
B♭7
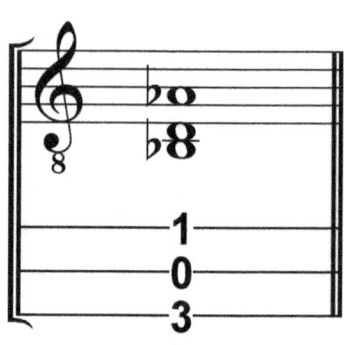

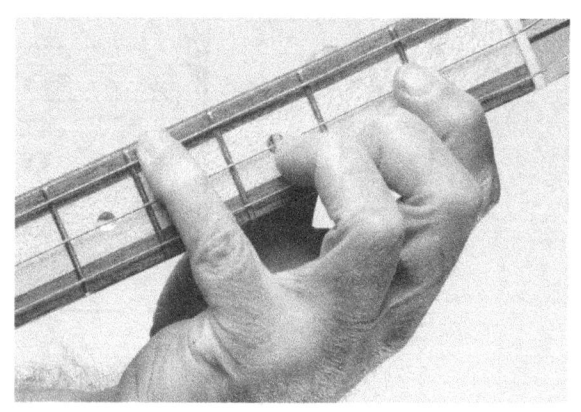
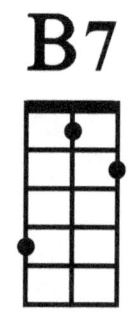
B7
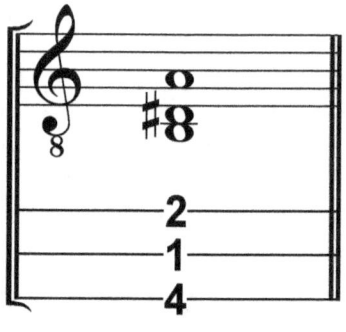

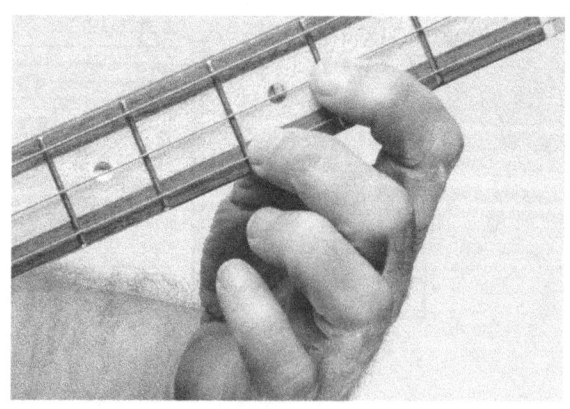
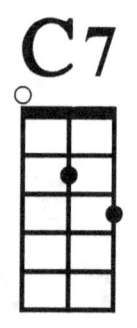
C7
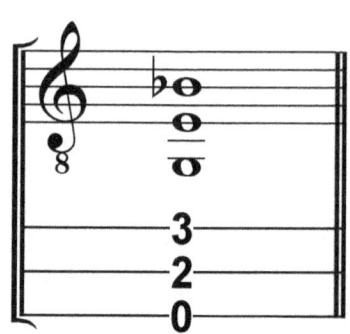

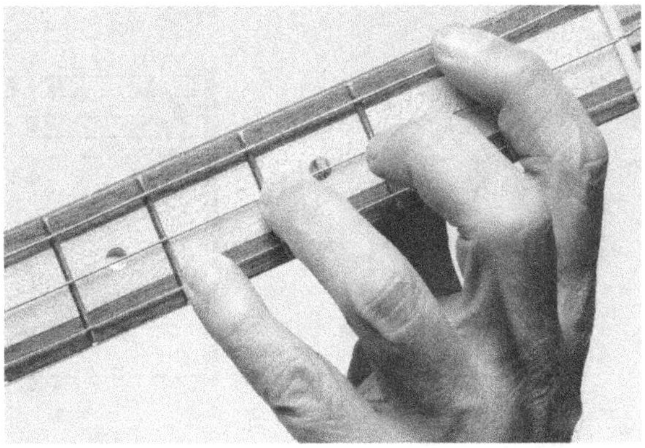

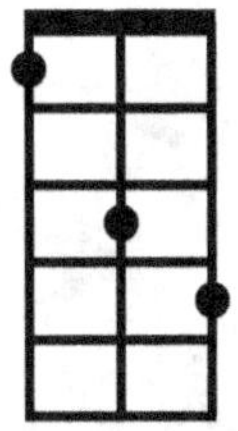

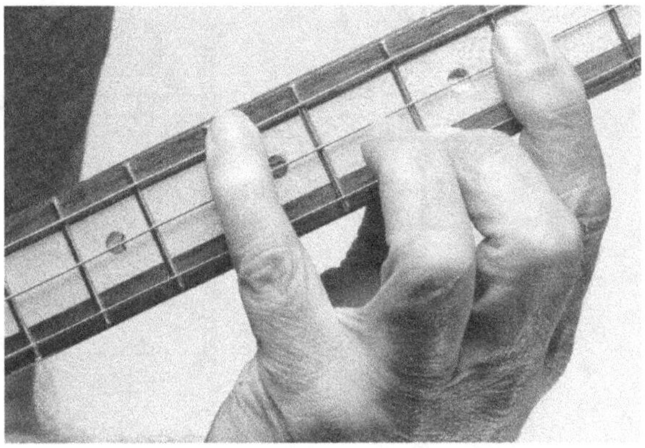

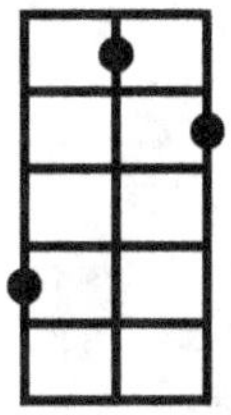

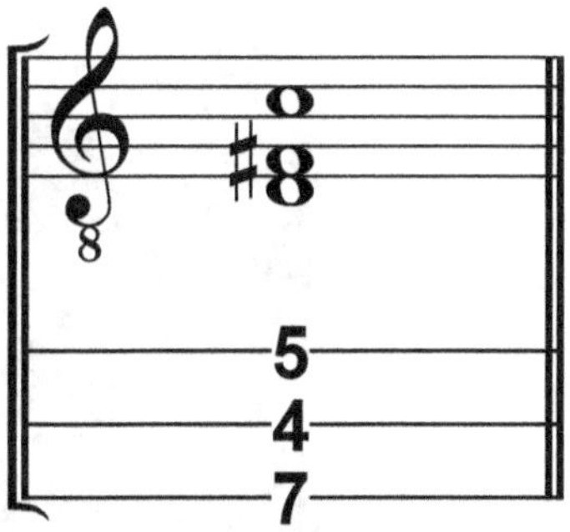

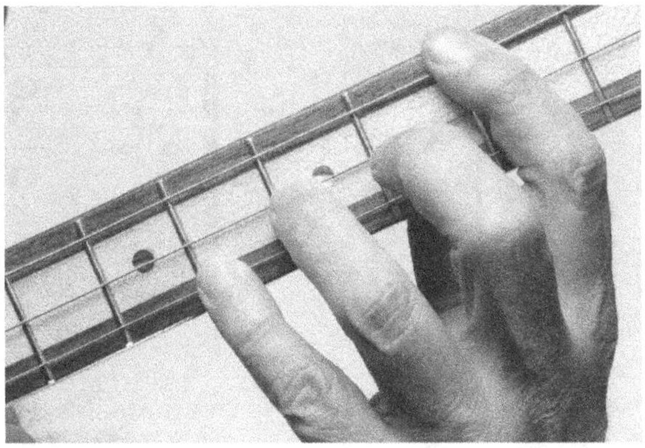

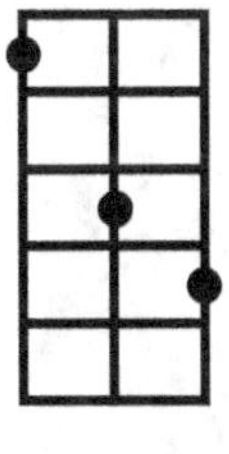

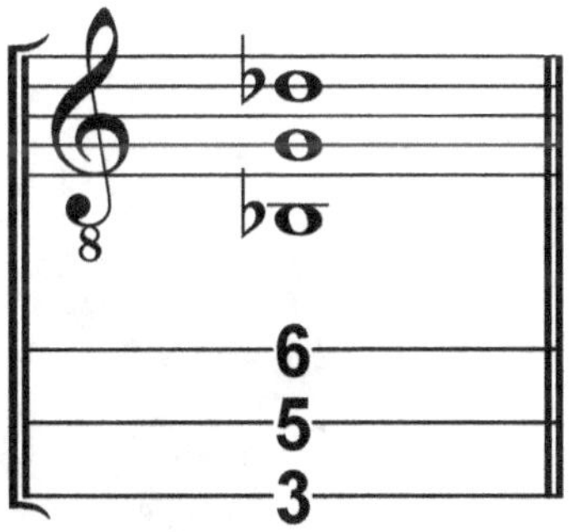

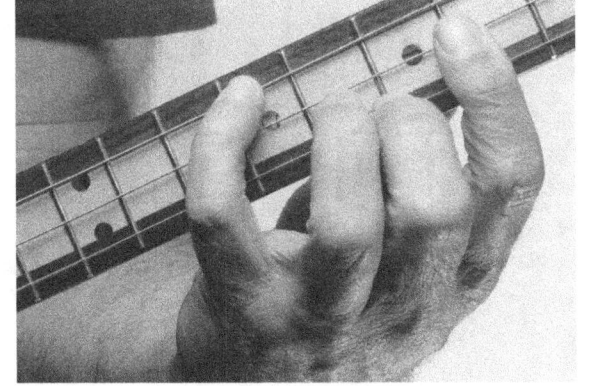
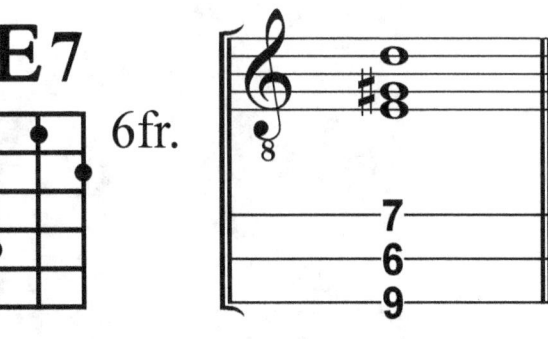

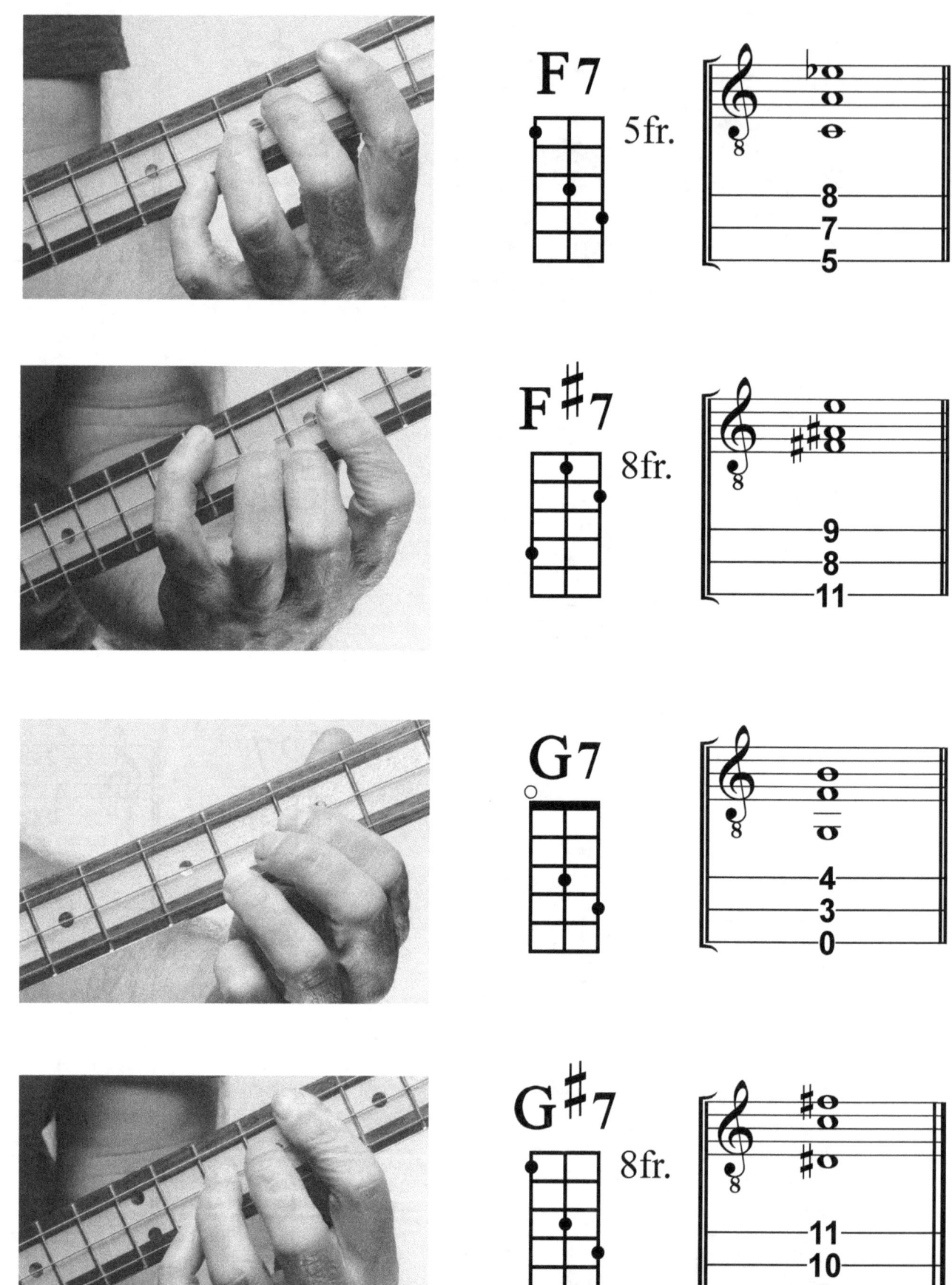

Blank Chord Sheet - 3-String

BEGINNER CHORDS - REFERENCE

MAJOR CHORDS

A | A#/Bb | B | C | C#/Db | D

D#/Eb | E | F | F#/Gb | G | G#/Ab

MINOR CHORDS

Am | A#m/Bbm | Bm | Cm | C#m/Dbm | Dm

D#m/Ebm | Em | Fm | F#m/Gbm | Gm | G#m/Abm

BEGINNER CHORDS - REFERENCE

DOMINANT 7th CHORDS

OTHER USEFULL CHORD SHAPES

5th

5th chords can function as both major "or" minor. They can also substitute for dominant 7th chords.

= Root (*R*)

Sus4 and add9 have the same chord shape but different roots.

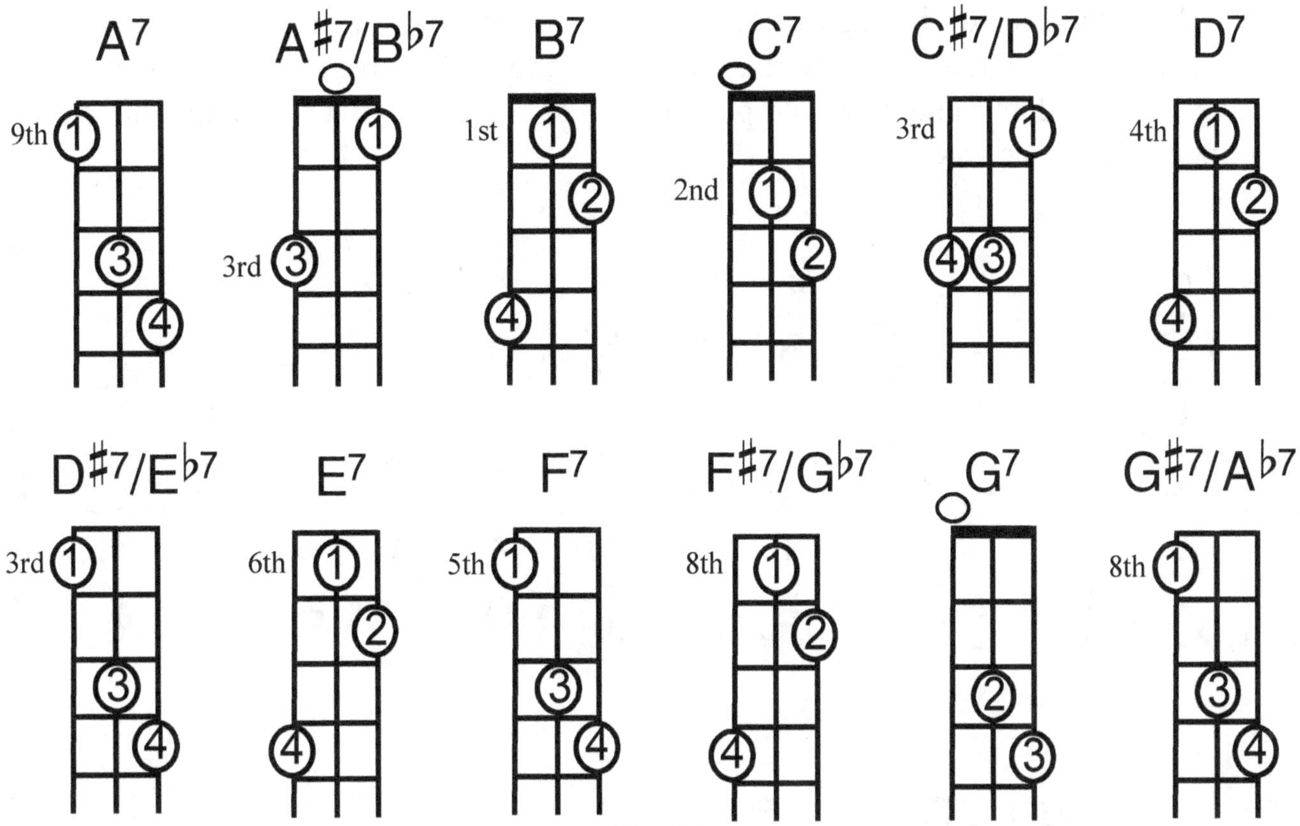

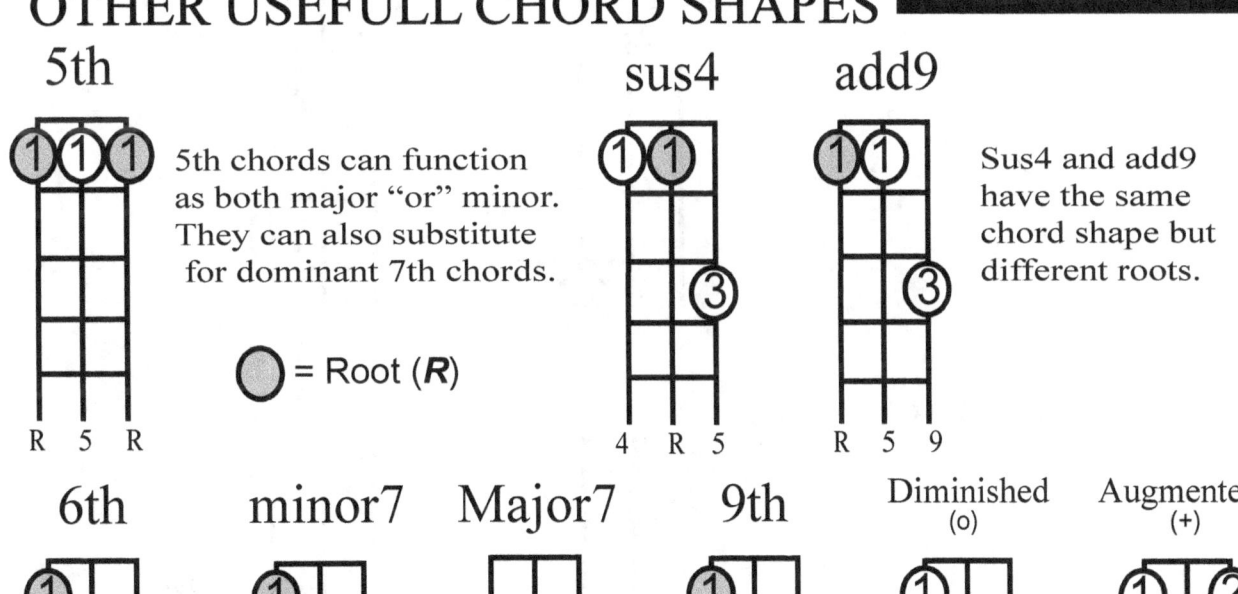

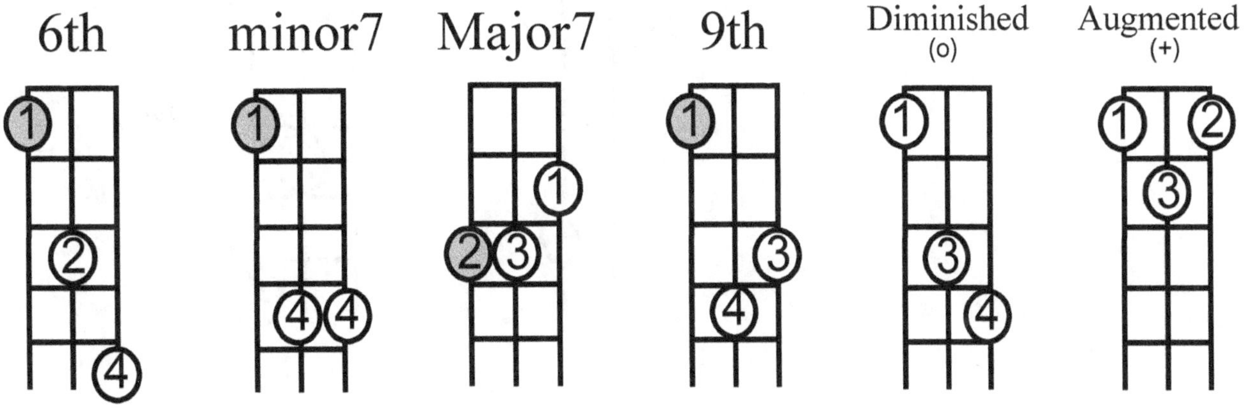

Moveable Chord Shapes

Here are a few of the most commonly used chords in GDG tuning that are moveable up and down the neck of the cigar box guitar. Try to memorize the names of the notes on the 2nd and 3rd string to locate the root of the chord. The root is the letter note that gives the chord its name. For example, the root of a G chord is "G," and the root of a G minor chord is also a G.

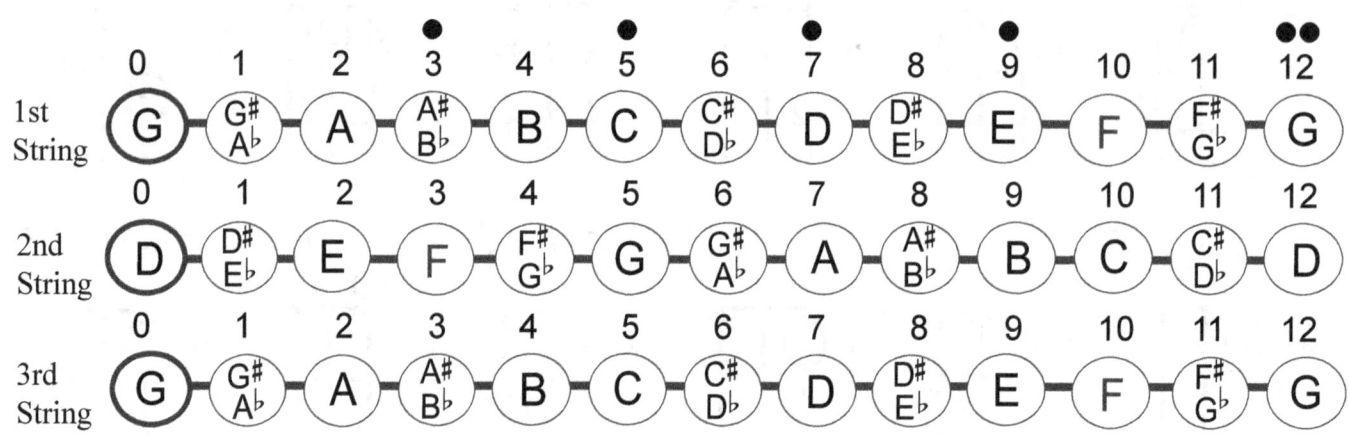

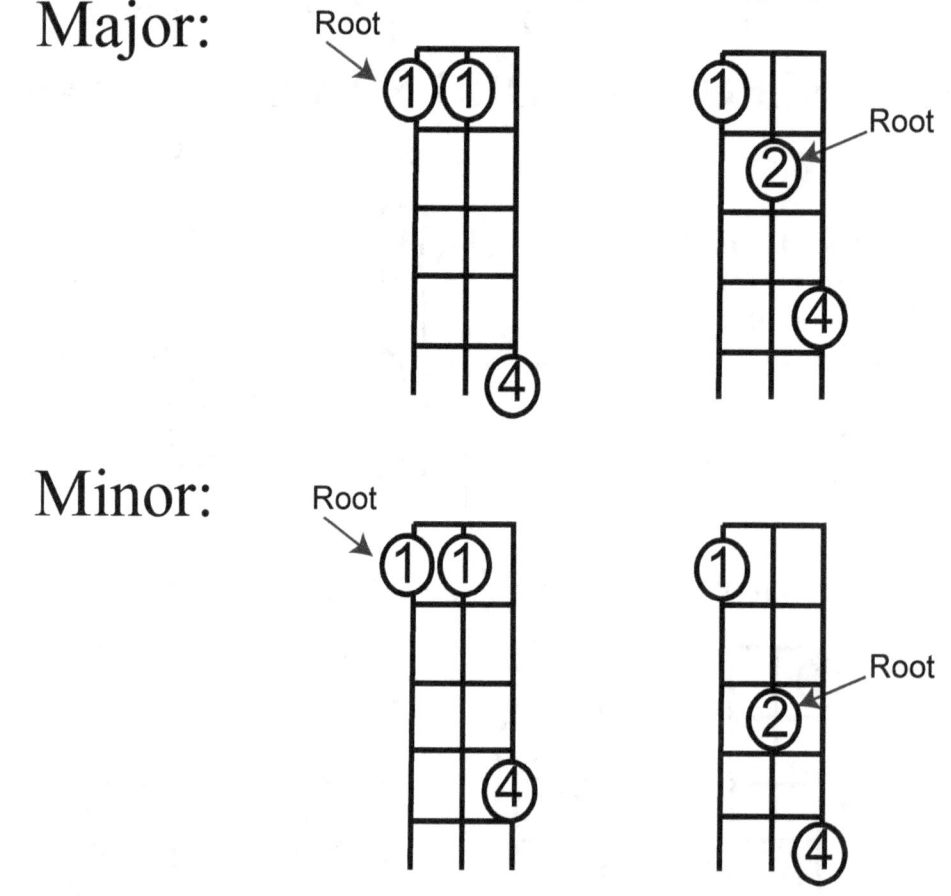

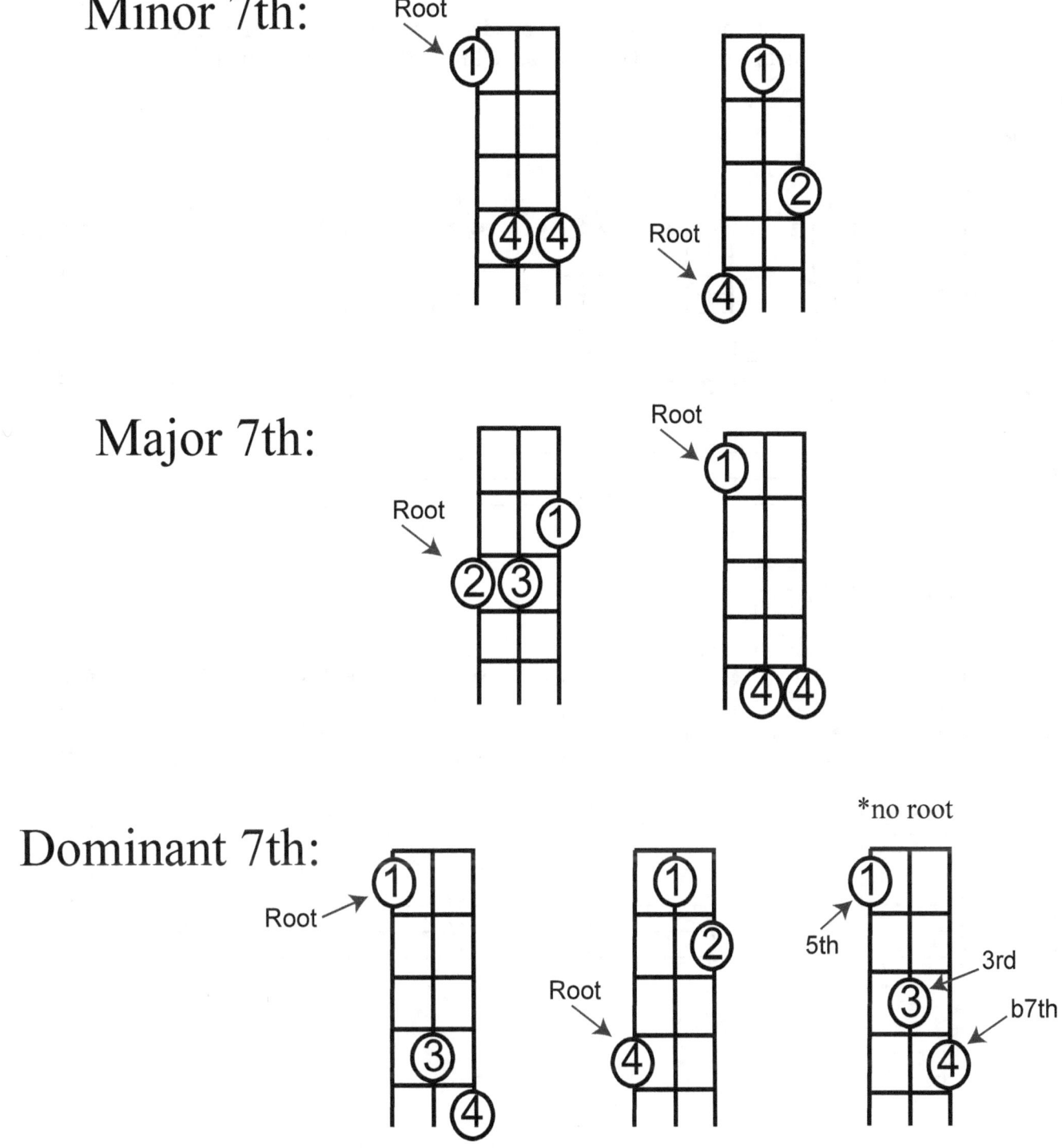

*Sometimes it is necessary to omit the root with only three strings. Generally, the 3rd and 7th are only needed to define the chord, so the root and 5th can be omitted where fingering is an issue.

Practice moving the following chords around the neck to a song or chord progression you know. Here's a sample progression in the key of G and C:

G | B7 | E7 | Am7 | C | Cm | G7 F#7 F7 | E7 | Am7 | D7 | G ||
C | E7 | A7 | Dm7 | F | Fm | C7 B7 Bb7 | A7 | Dm7 | G7 | C ||

Diatonic Chords in G and C

Diatonic chords are when you build a chord on each note of a scale.
In the examples below, the chords are all from the major keys of G, C, and D.

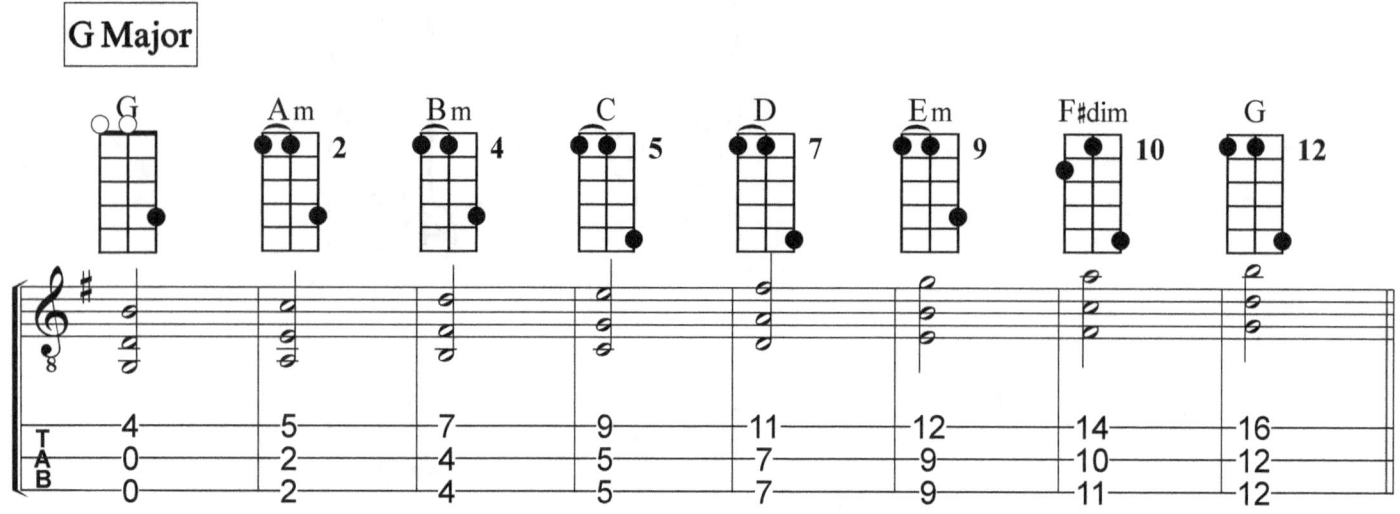

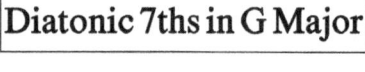

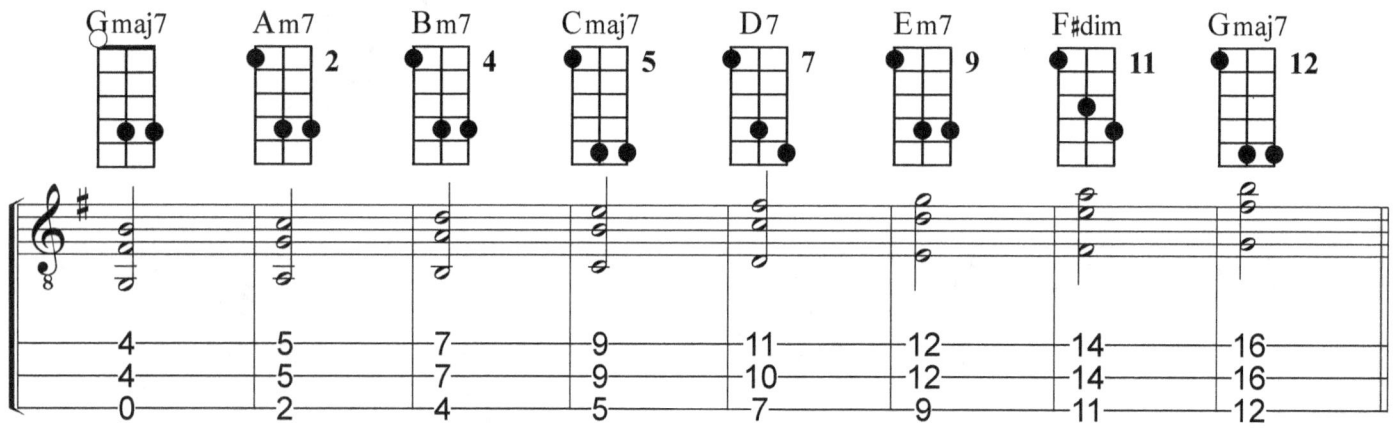

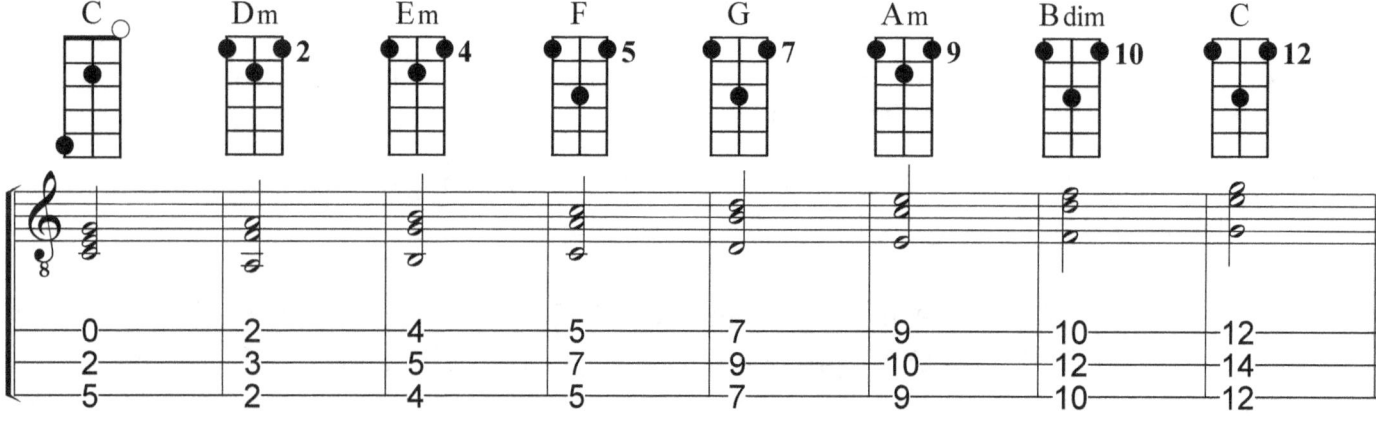

Diatonic 7ths in C Major

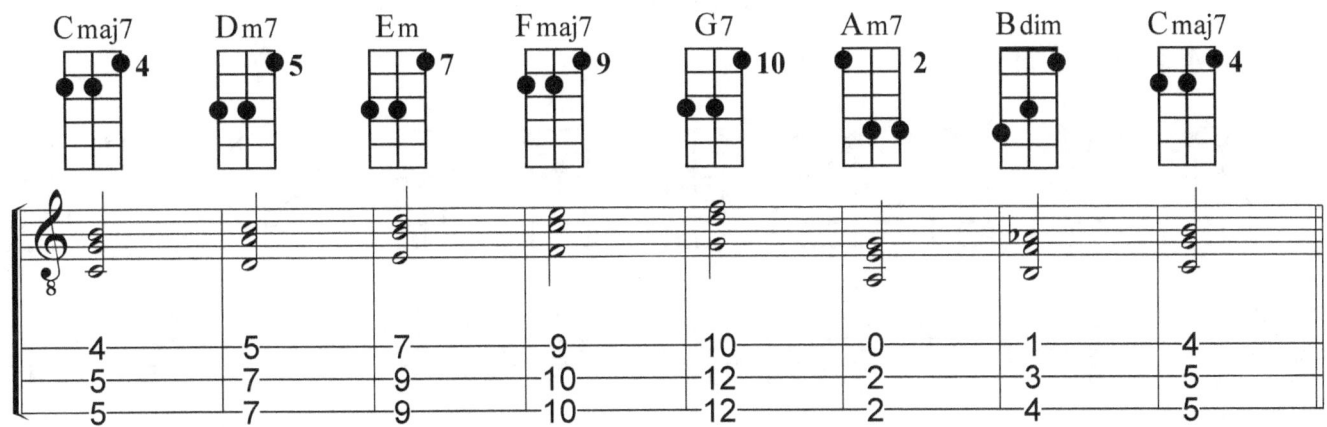

D Major

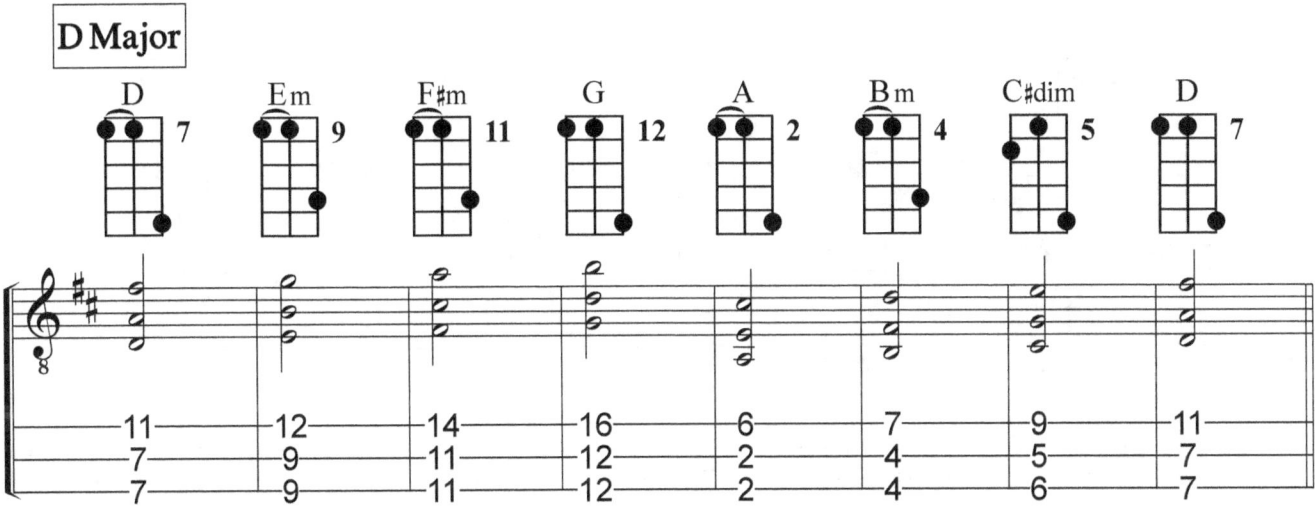

Diatonic 7ths in D Major

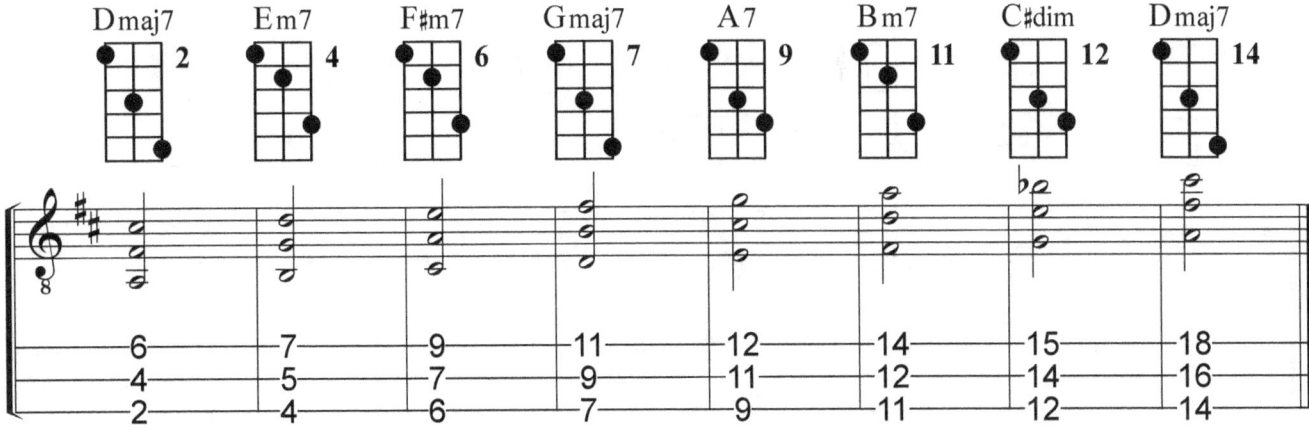

CHORD LIBRARY
A - A6 - Amaj7

Some notes have been omitted from the chords to facilitate playability.
The notes that form the chord are in brackets.

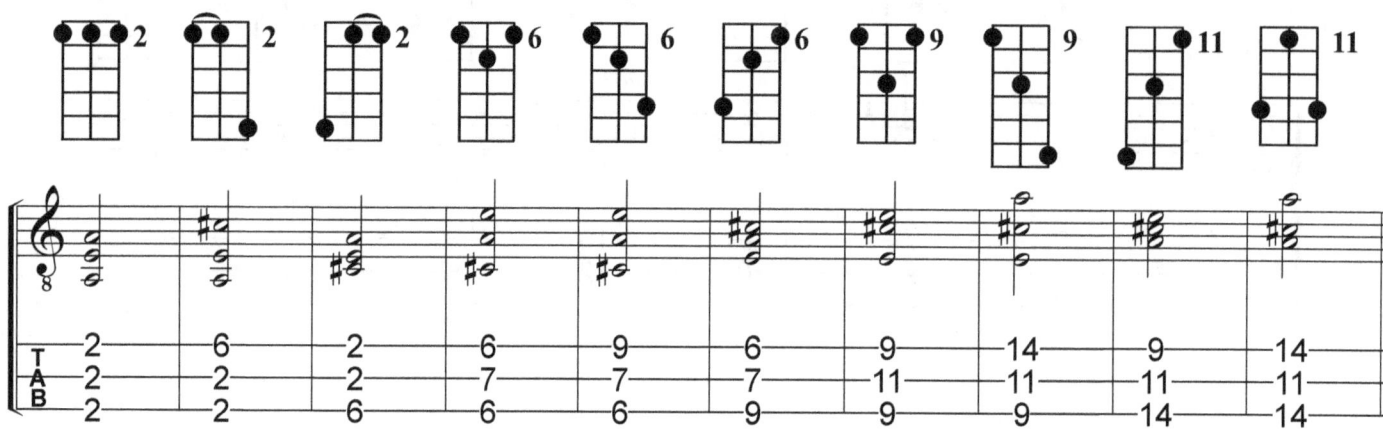

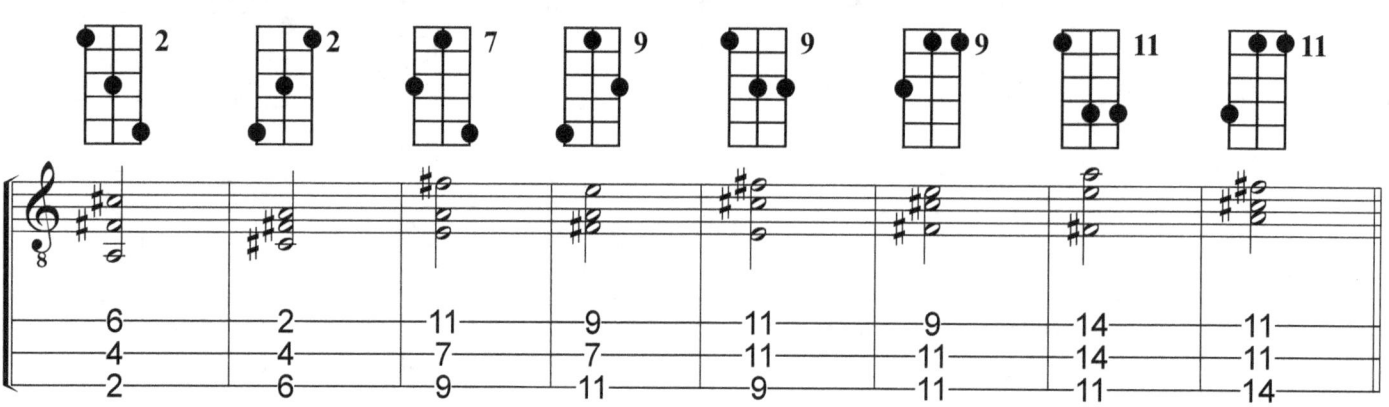

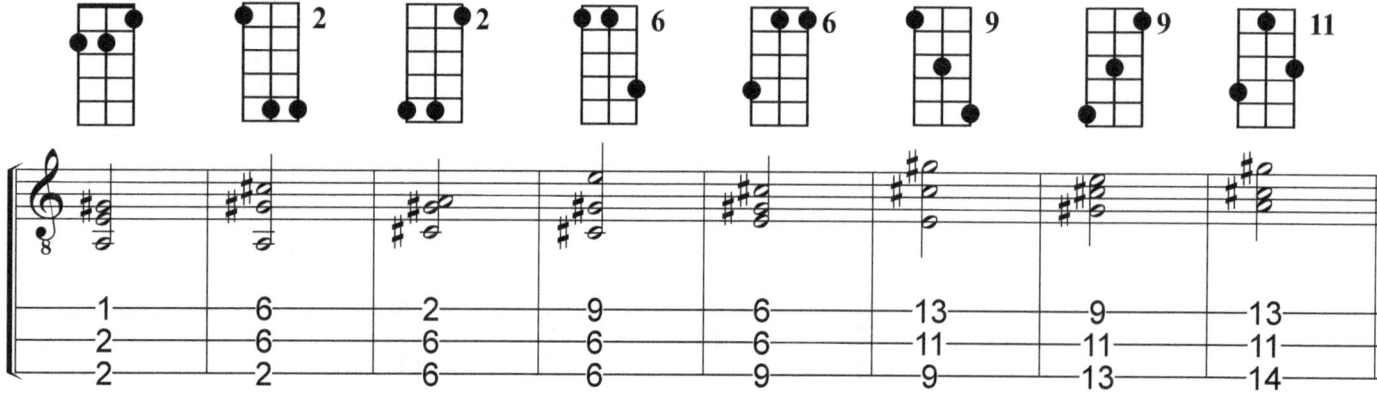

Amaj9 - A6/9 - A+

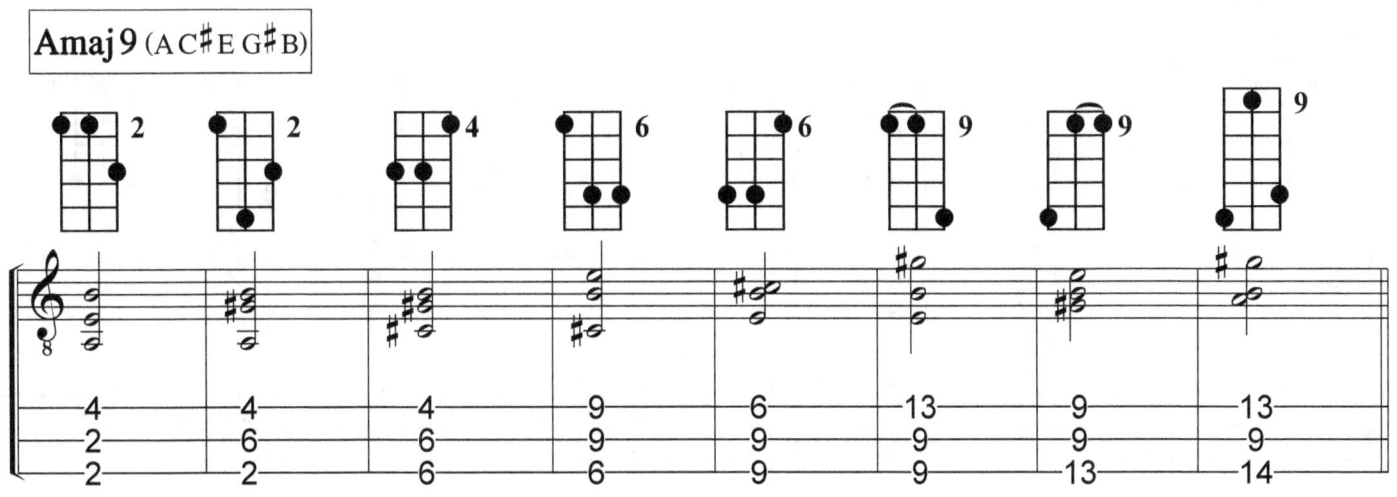

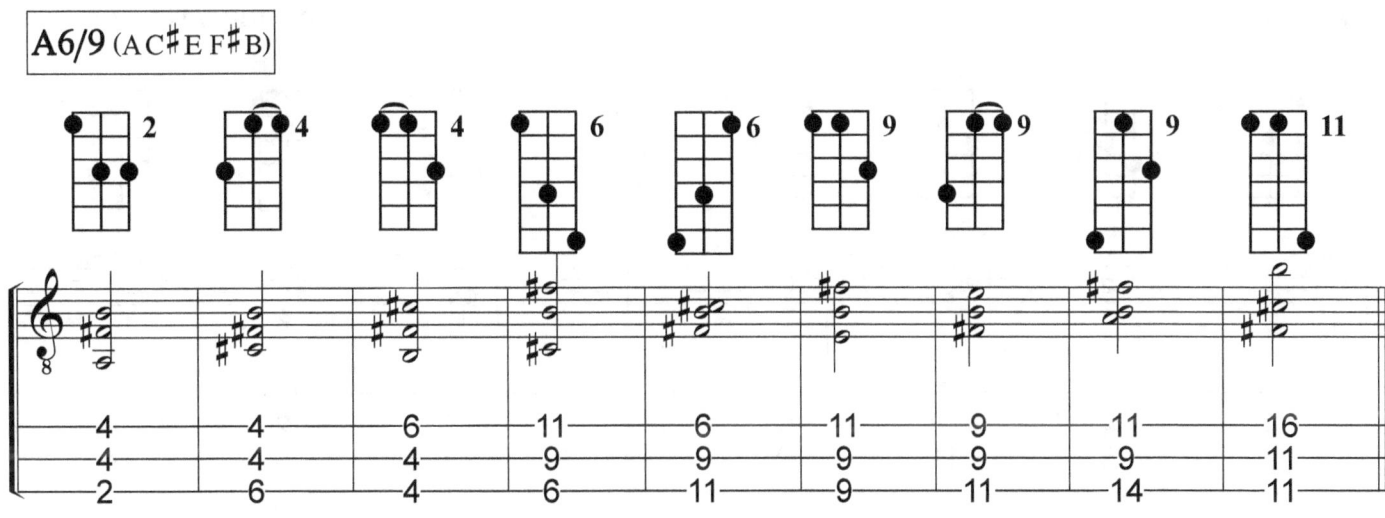

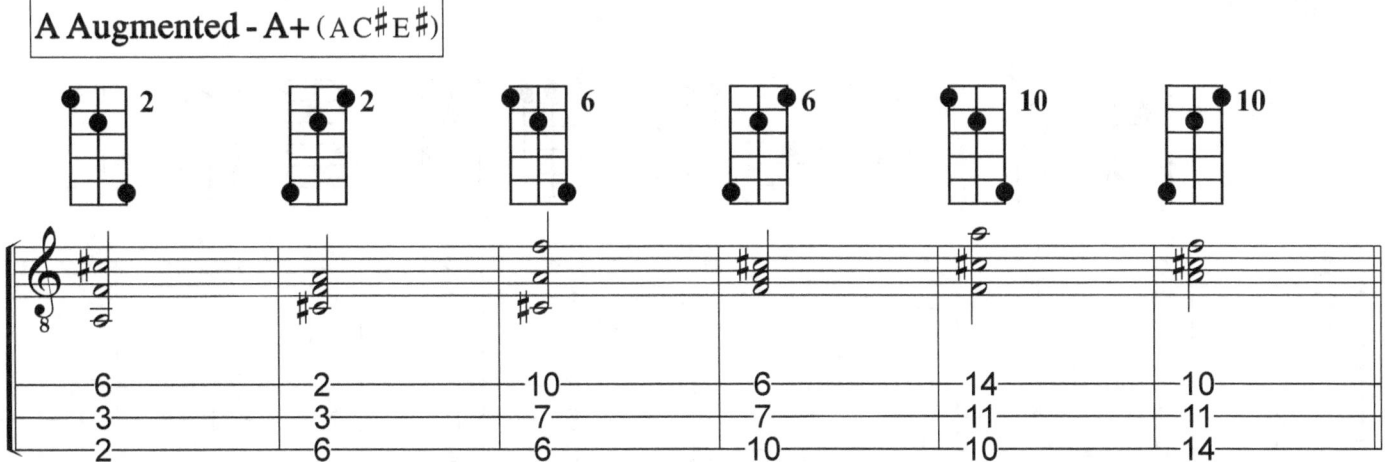

Am - Am6 - Am(maj7) - Am7

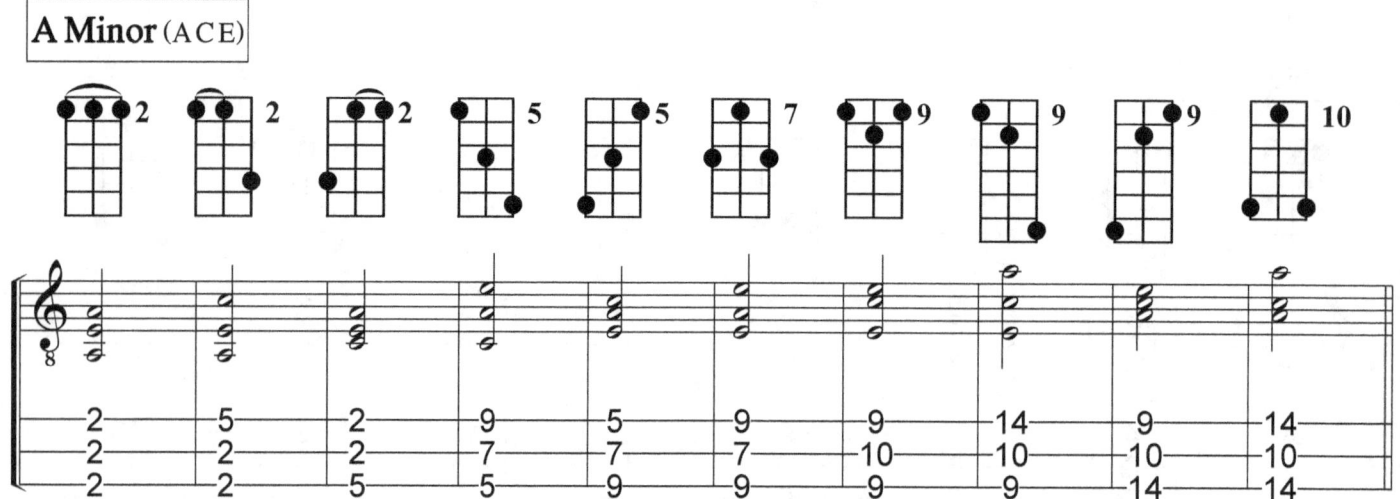

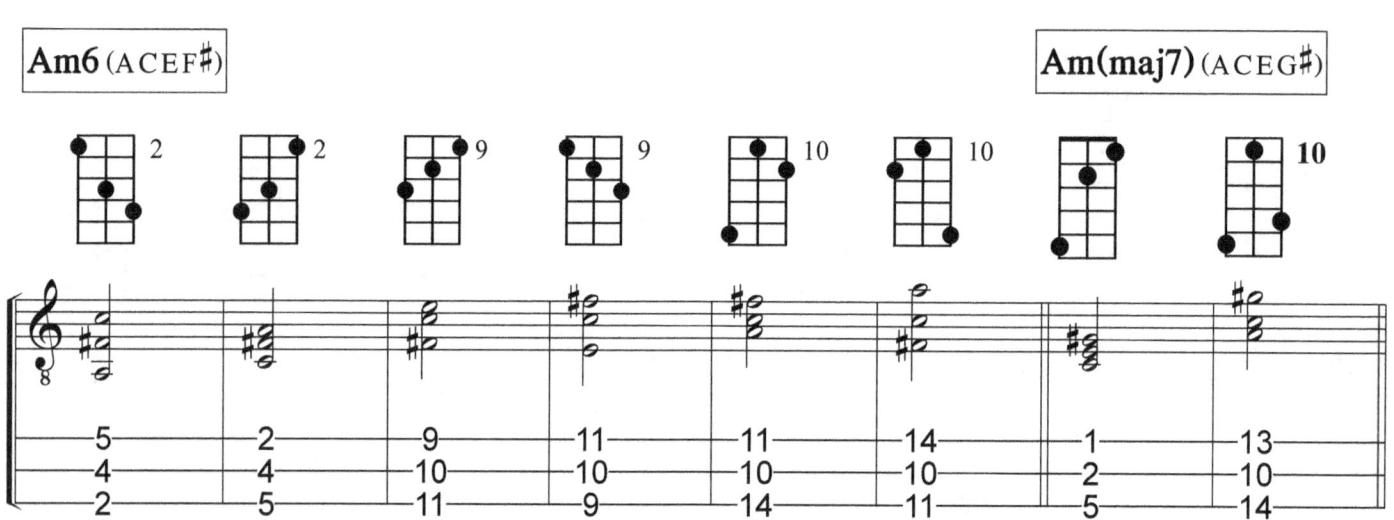

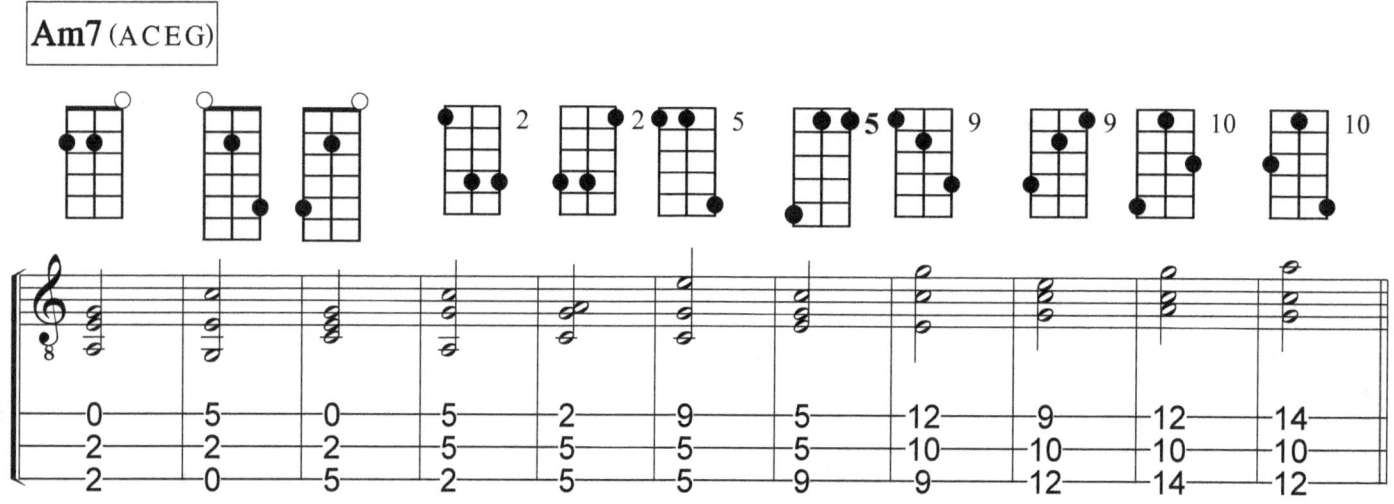

Am7♭5 - Am9 - Am11

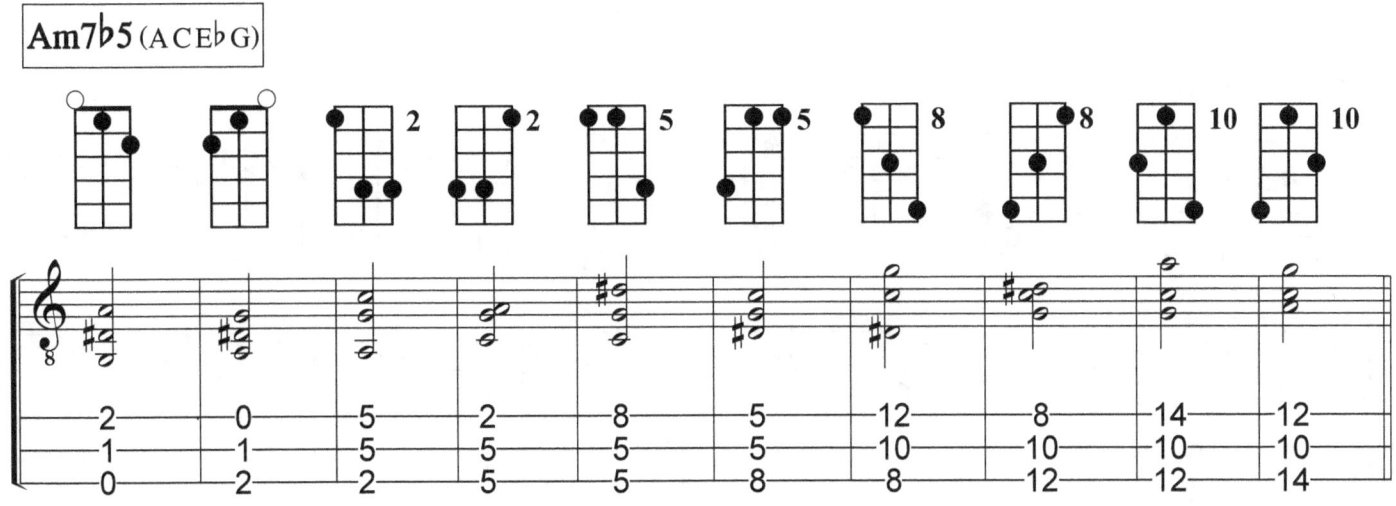

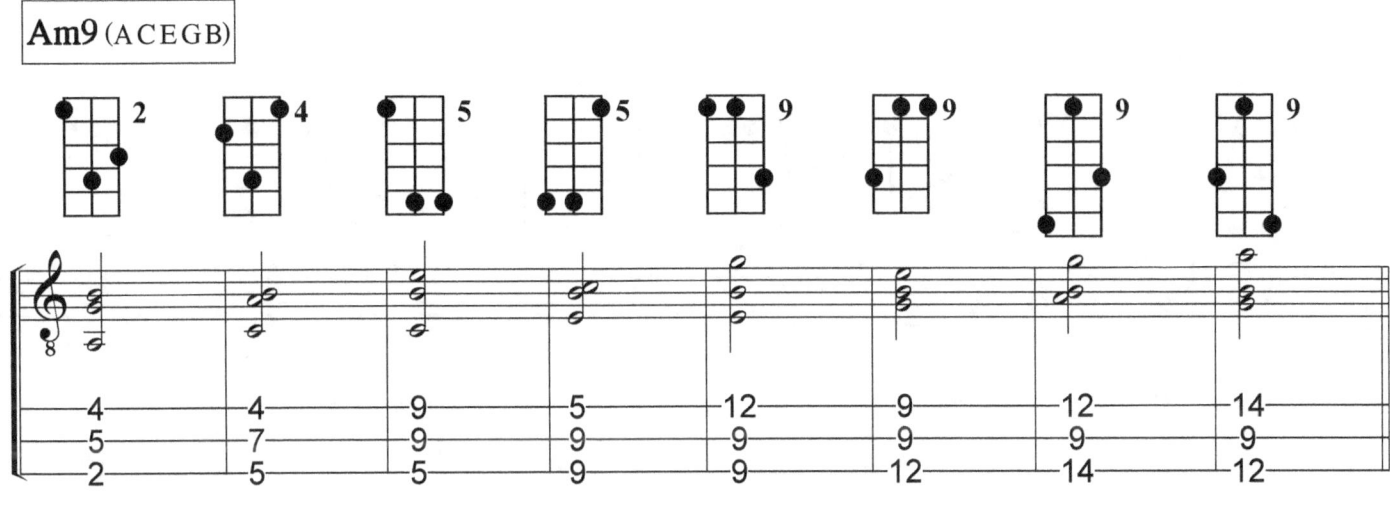

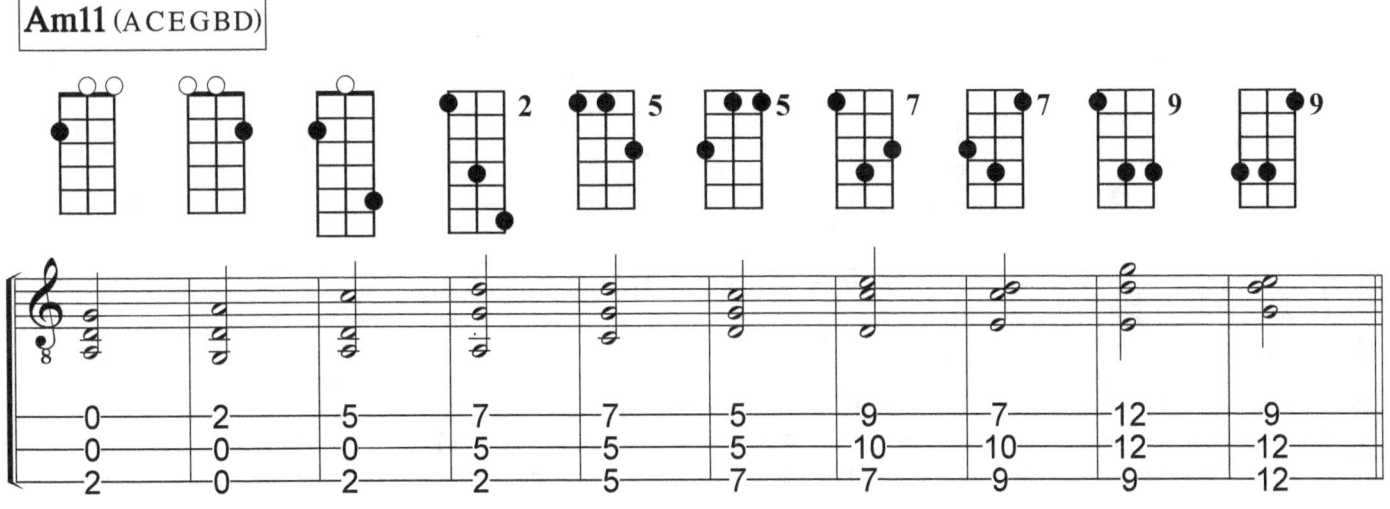

A7 - A9 - A13

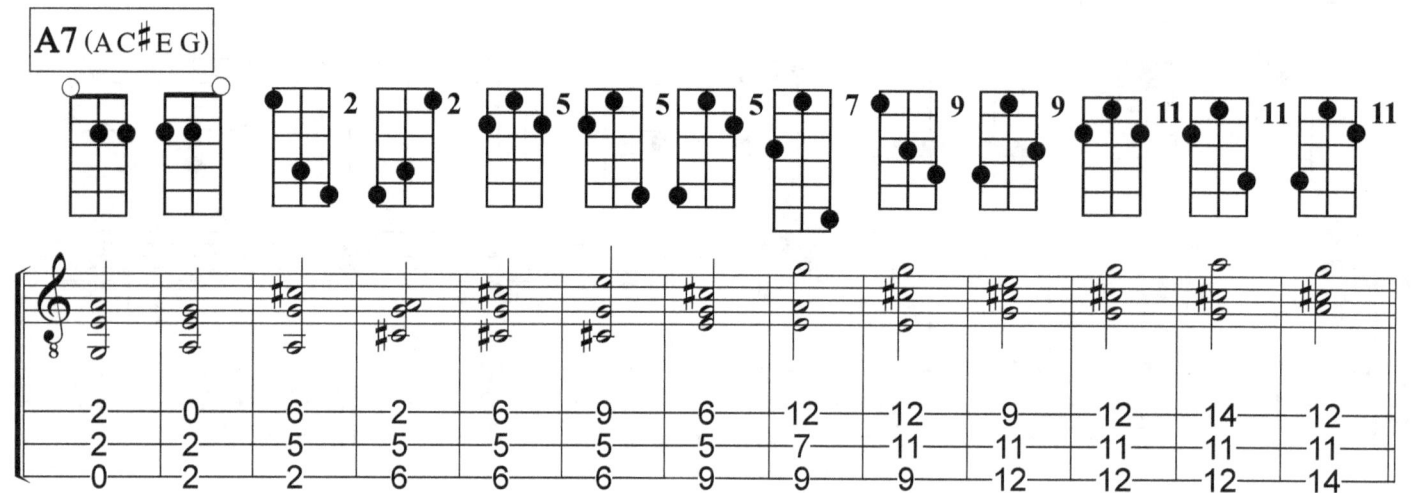

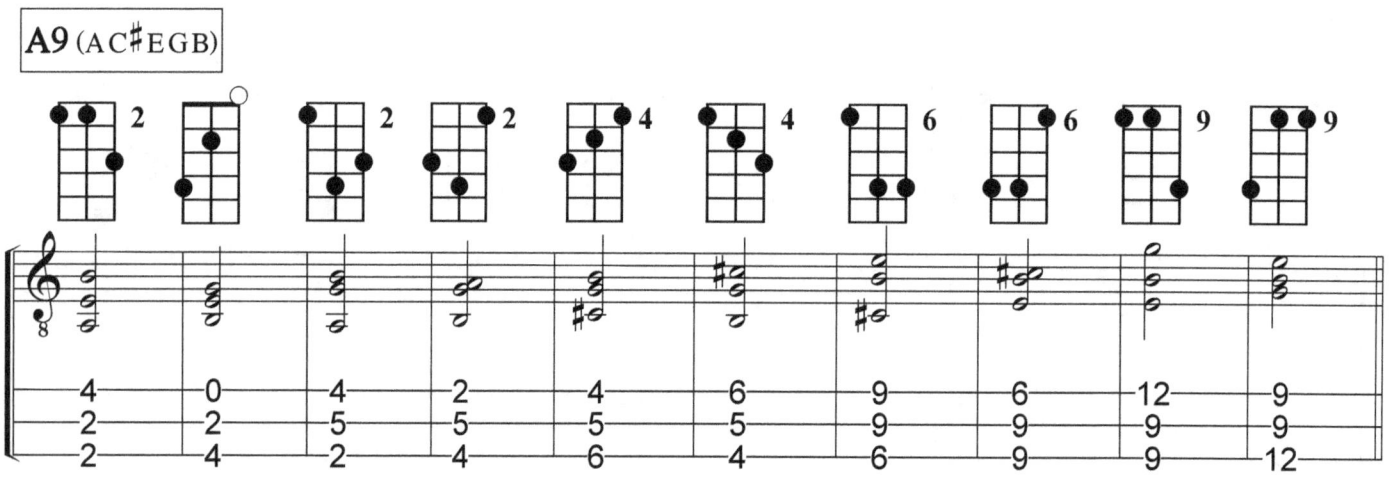

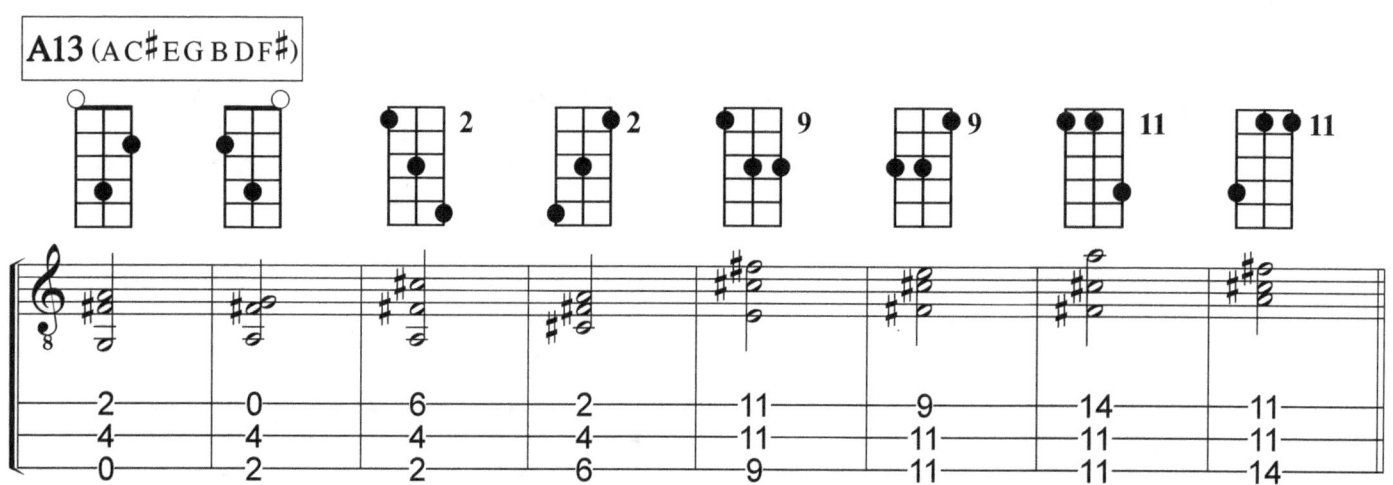

A7b5 - A7#5 - A7#9

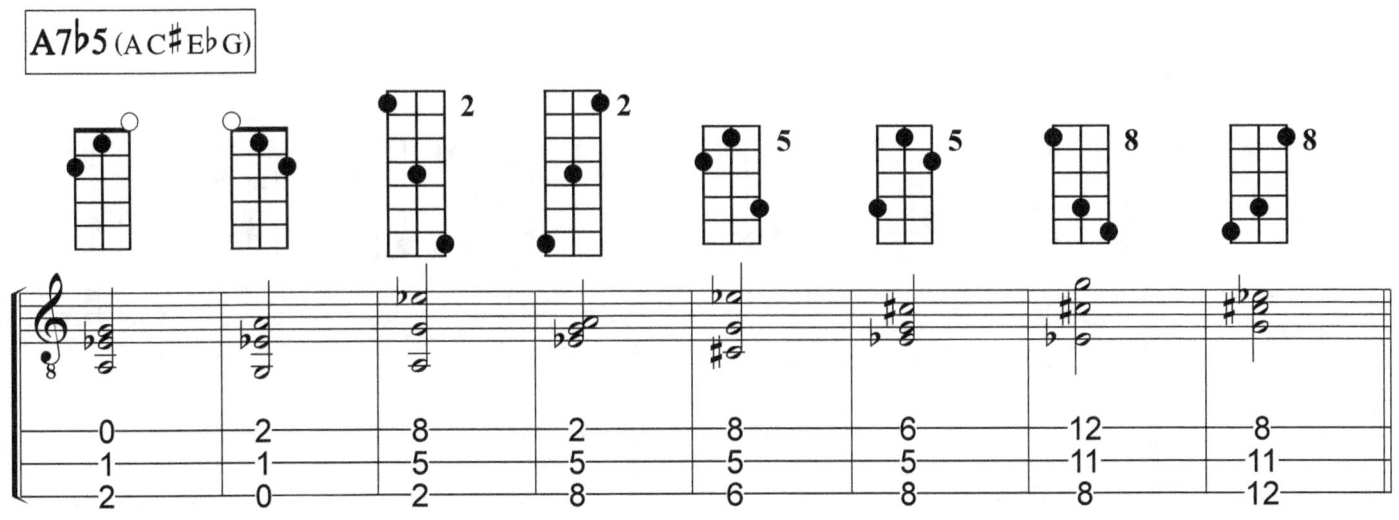

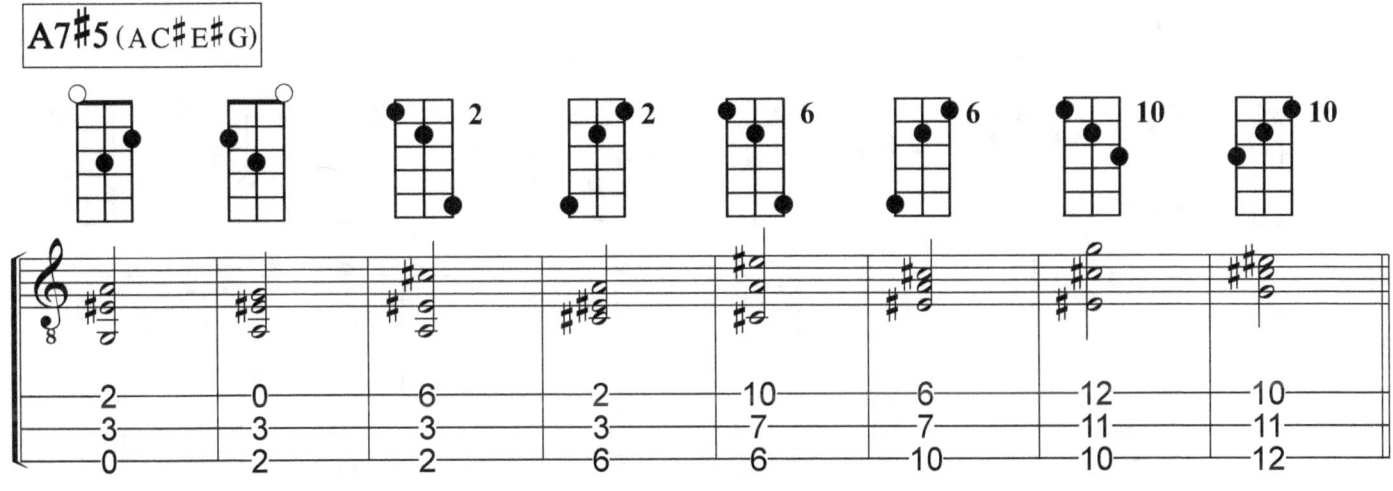

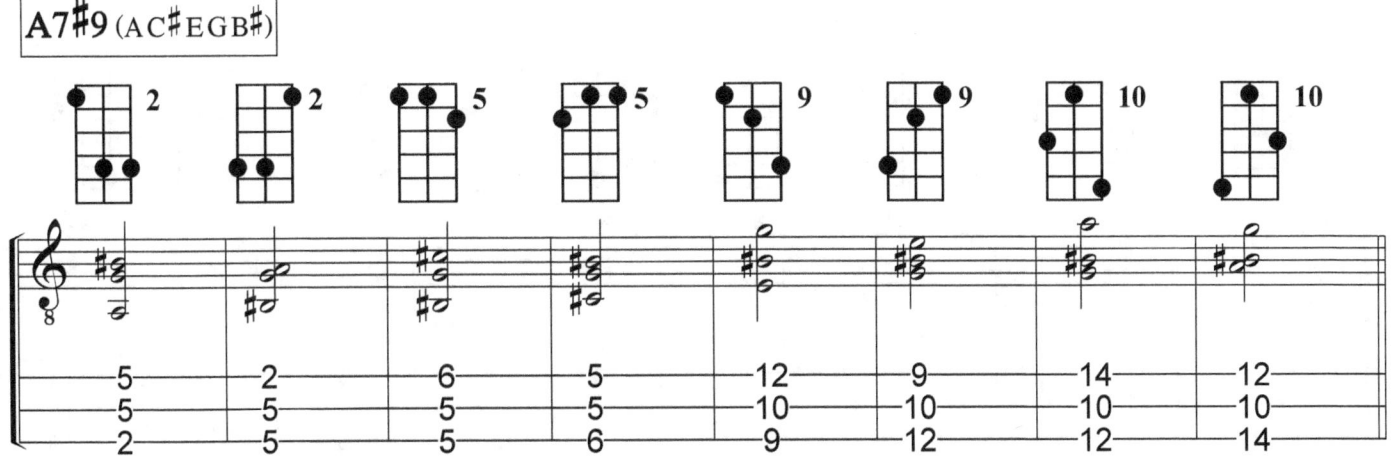

A7♭9 - A diminished - A°7

A7♭9 (A C♯ E G B♭)

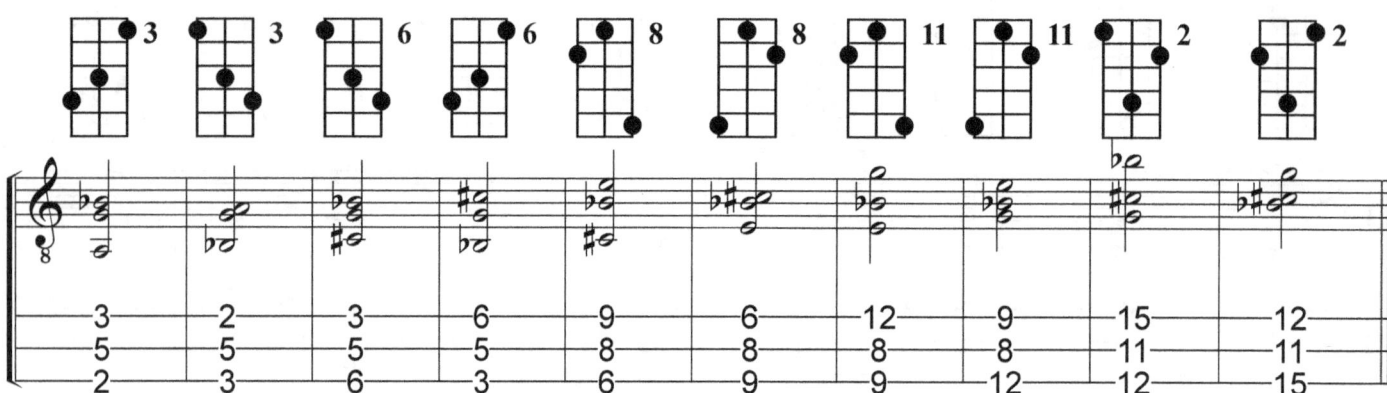

A diminished - A°7 (A C E♭ G♭)

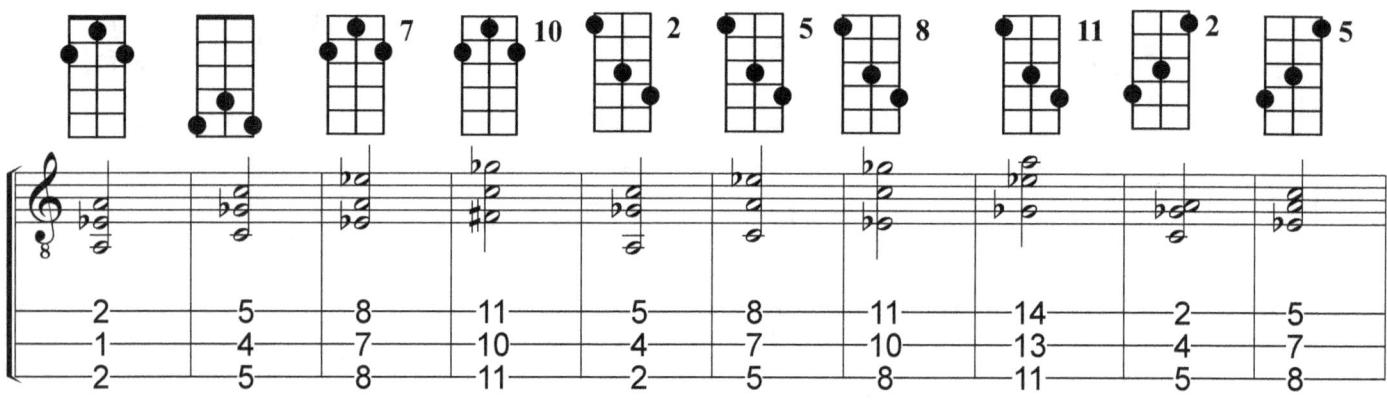

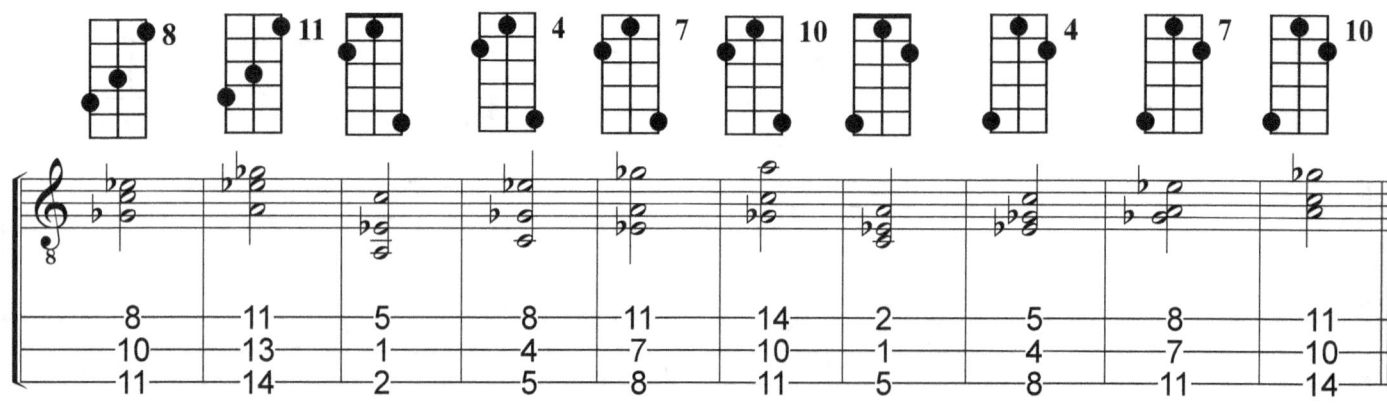

Asus4 - Asus2 - A7sus - Aadd9 - A5

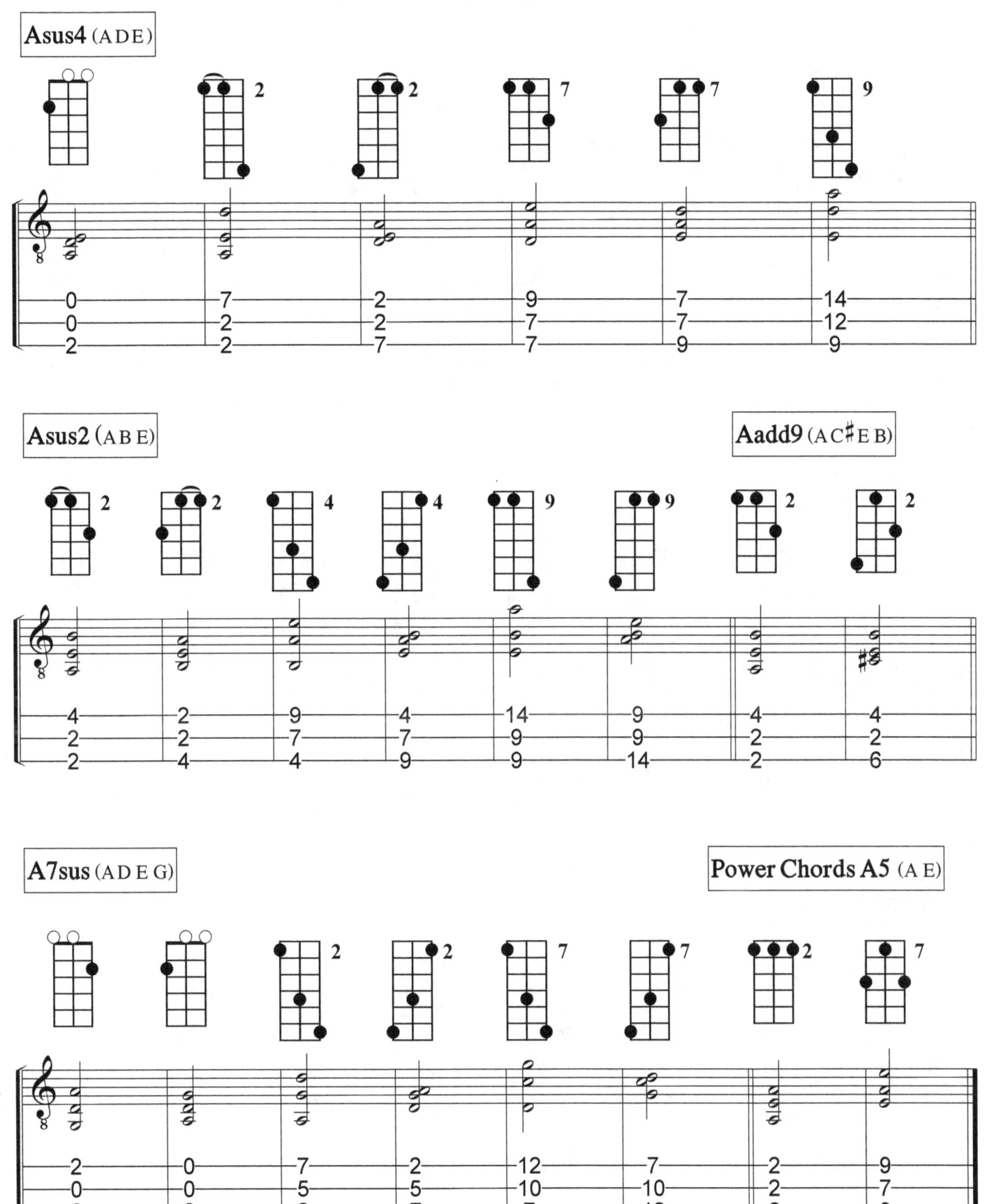

B♭ - B♭6 - B♭maj7

Some notes have been omitted from the chords to facilitate playability.
The notes that form the chord are in brackets.

B♭ Major (B♭ D F)

B♭6 (B♭ D F G)

B♭maj7 (B♭ D F A)

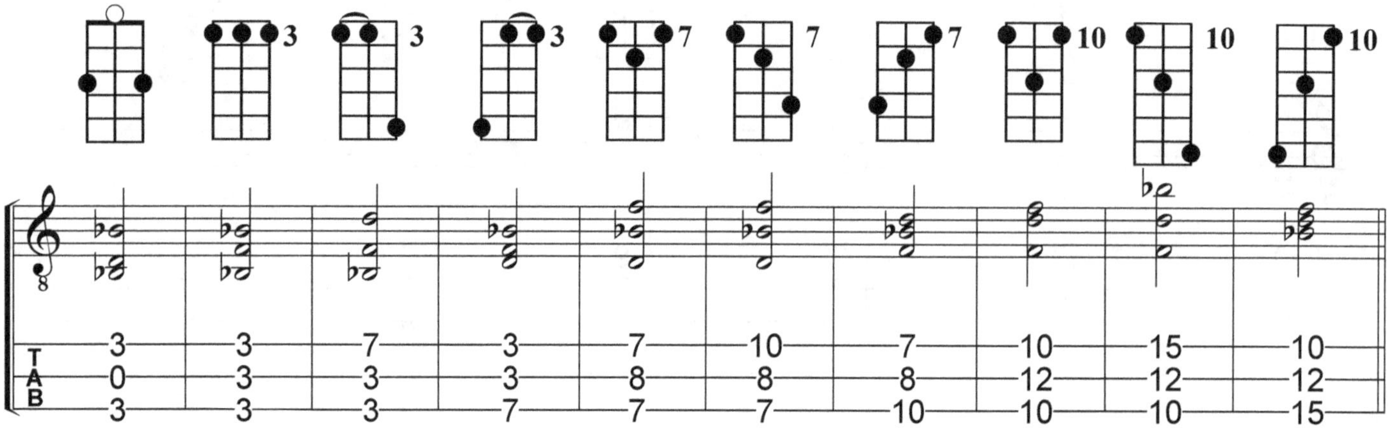

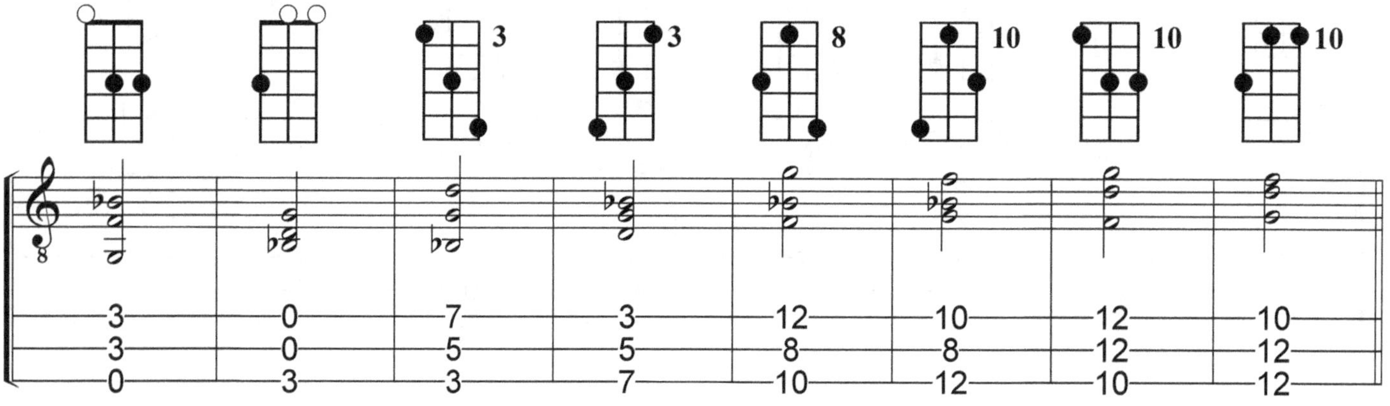

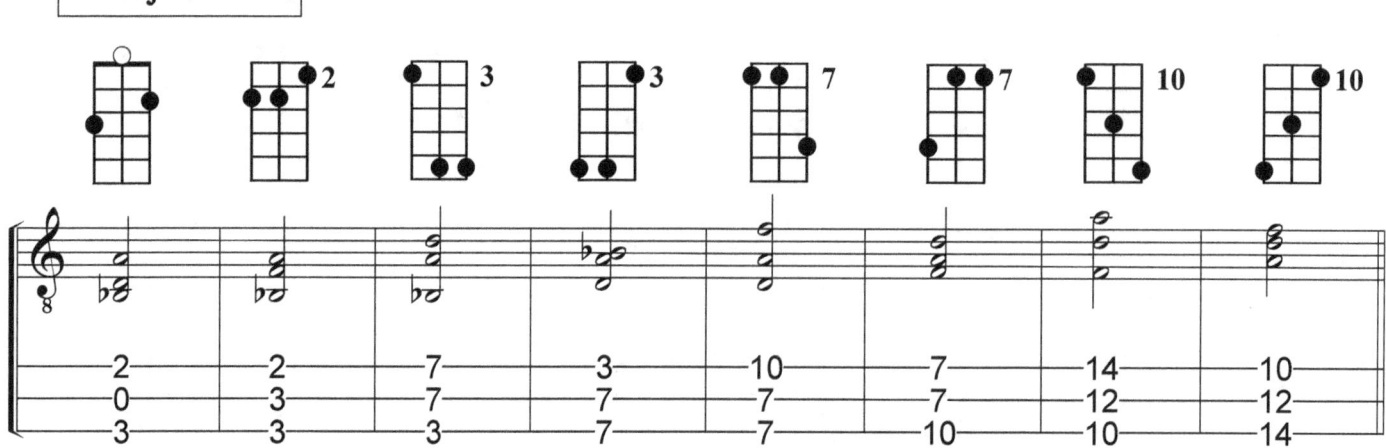

B♭maj9 - B♭6/9 - B♭+

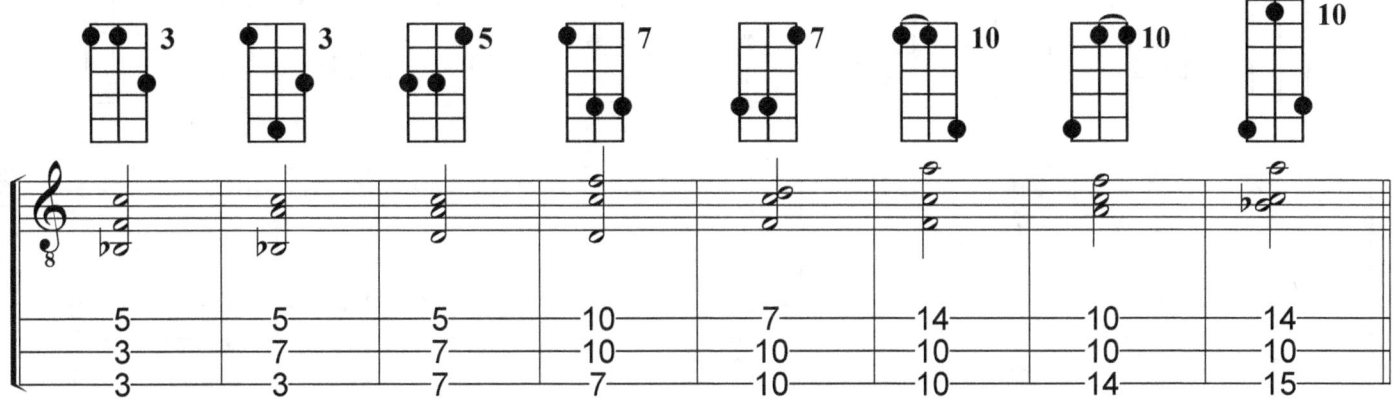

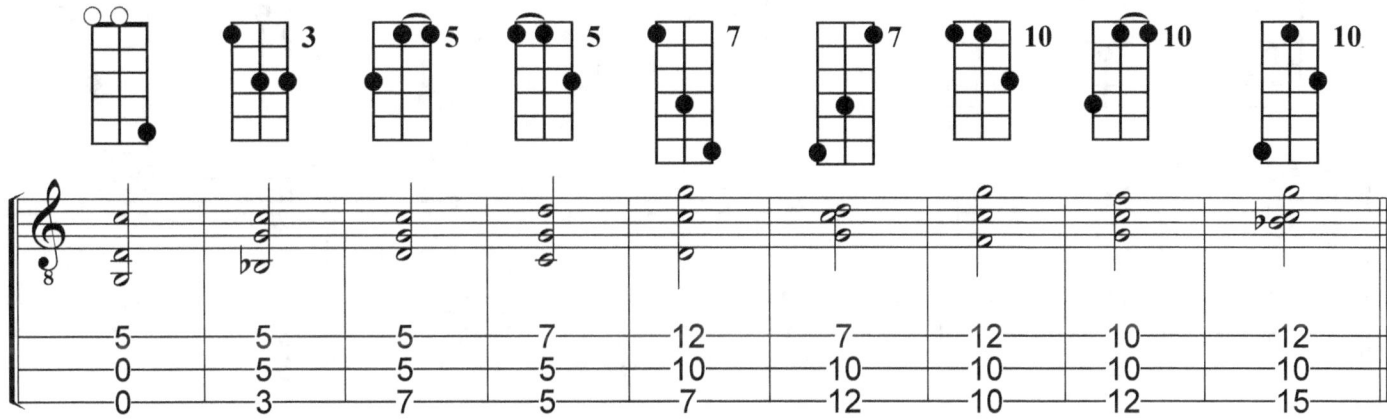

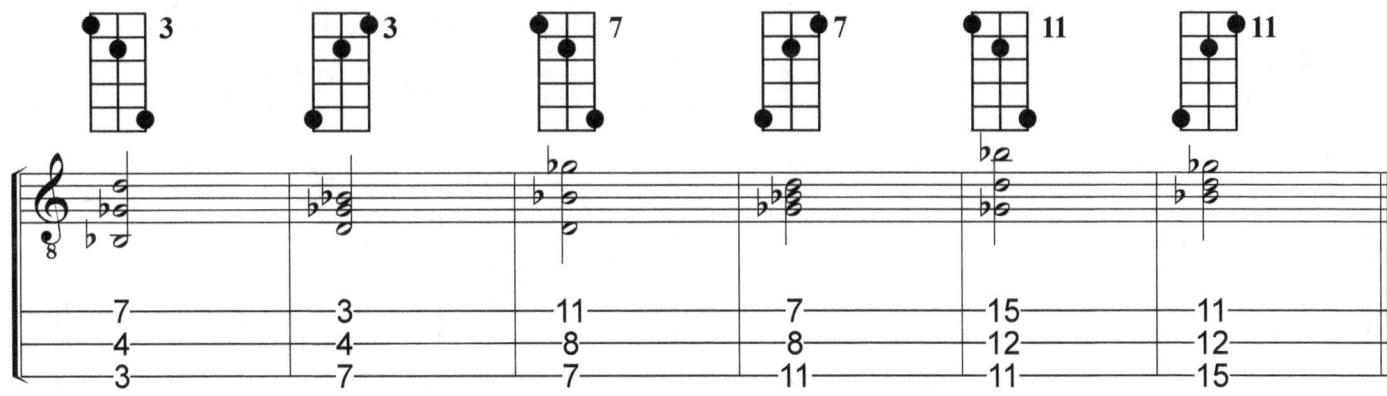

B♭m - B♭m6 - B♭m(maj7) - B♭m7

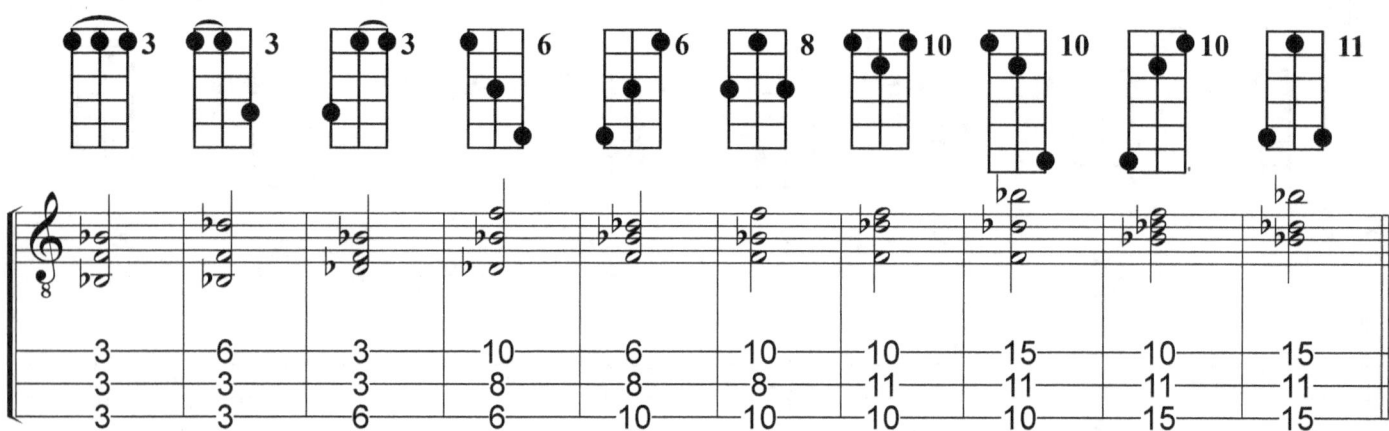

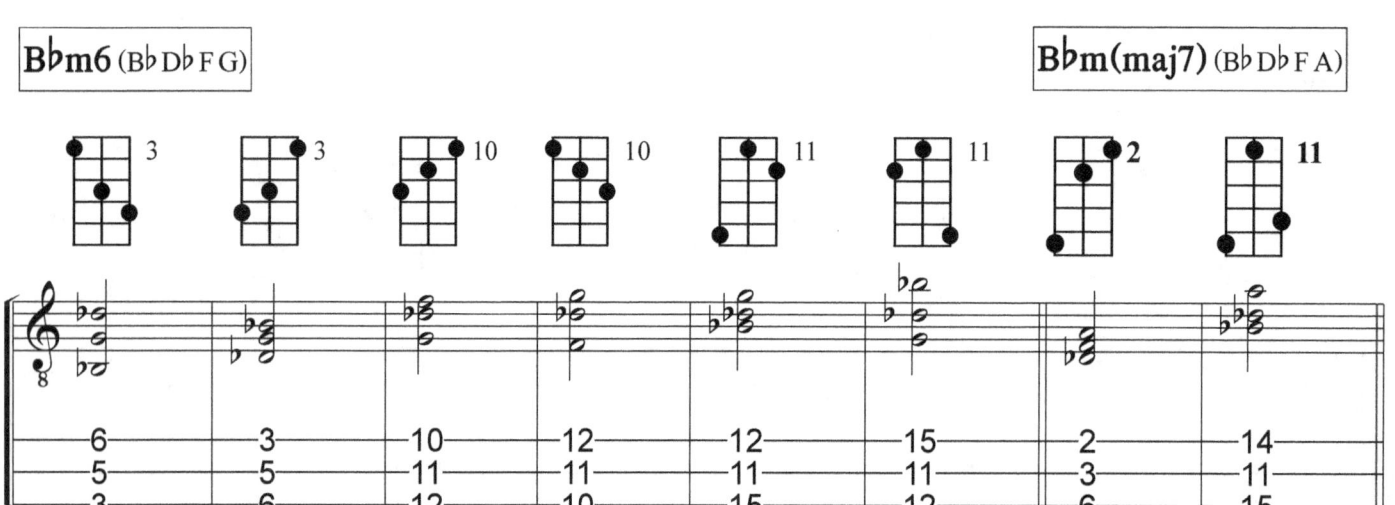

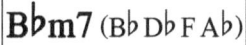

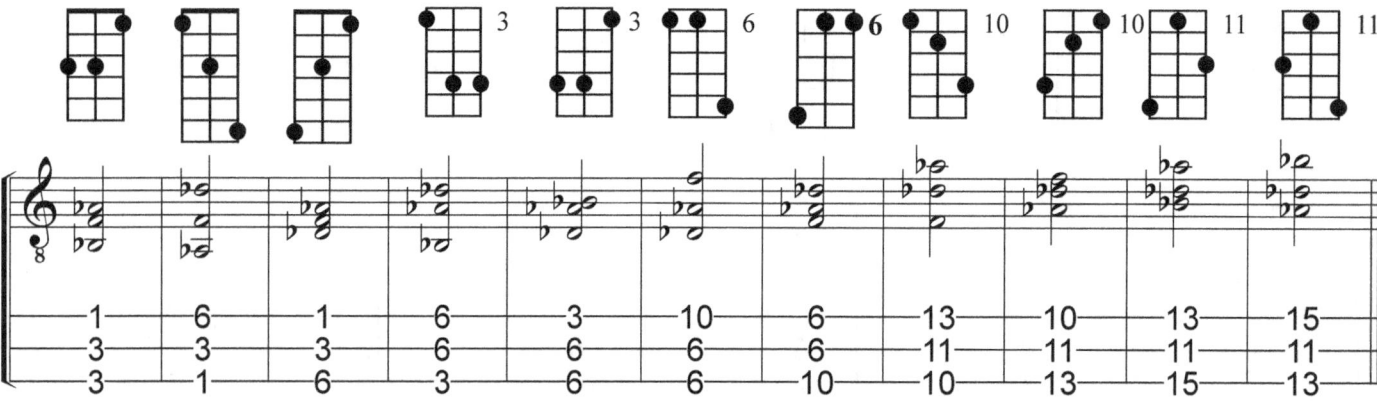

Bbm7b5 - Bbm9 - Bbm11

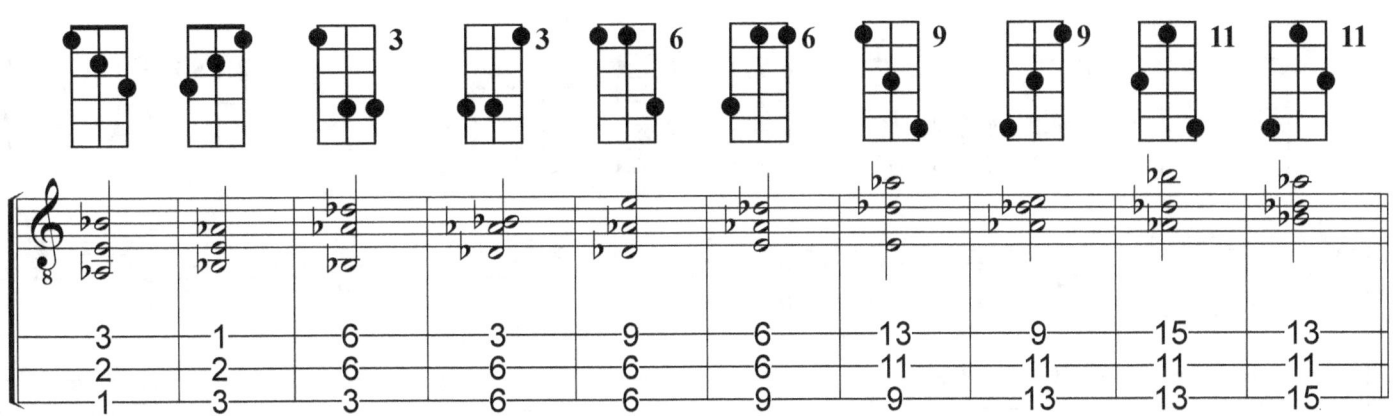

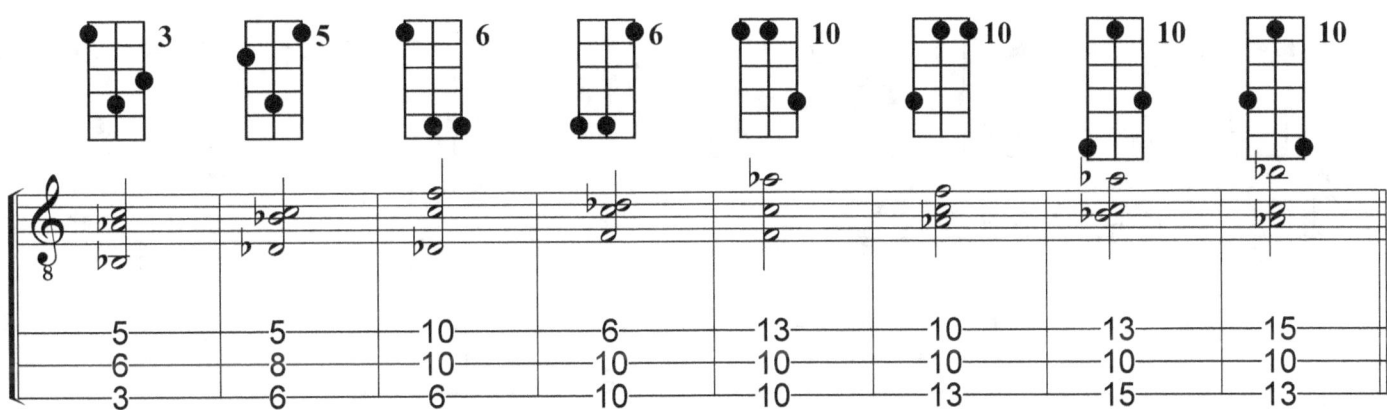

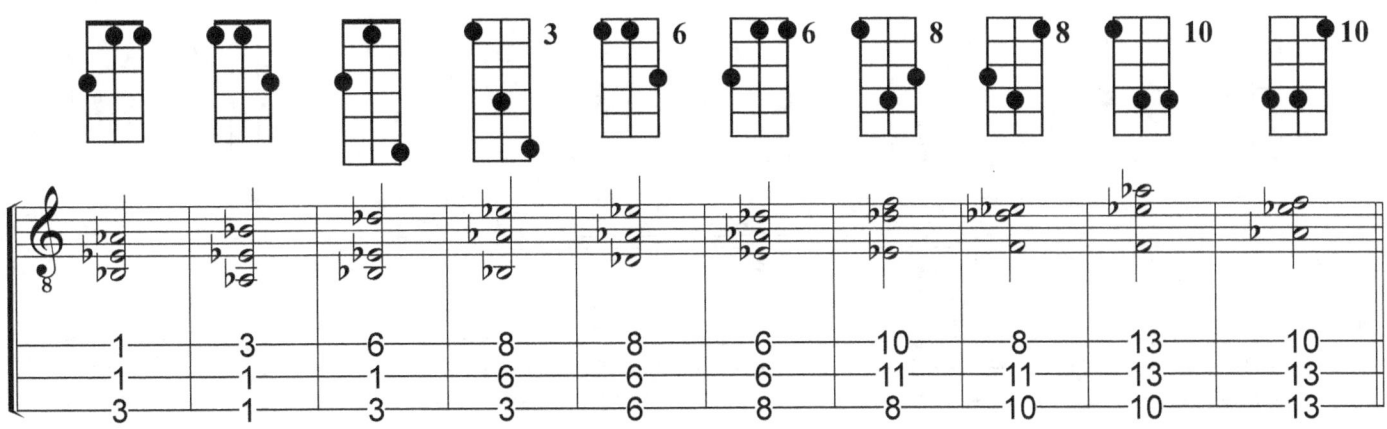

Bb7 - Bb9 - Bb13

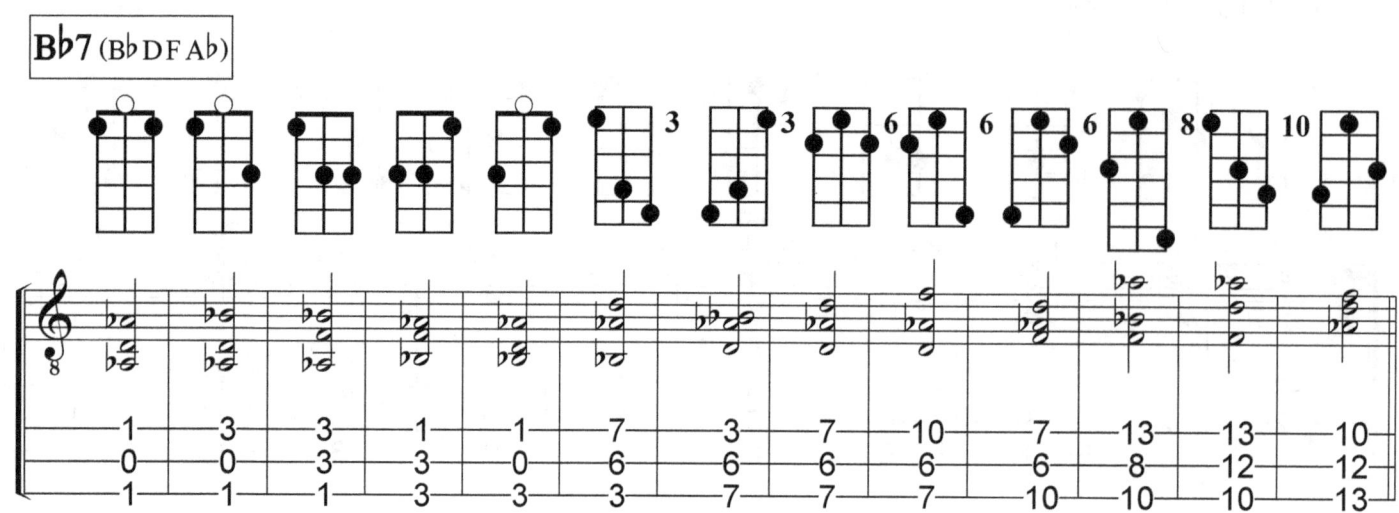

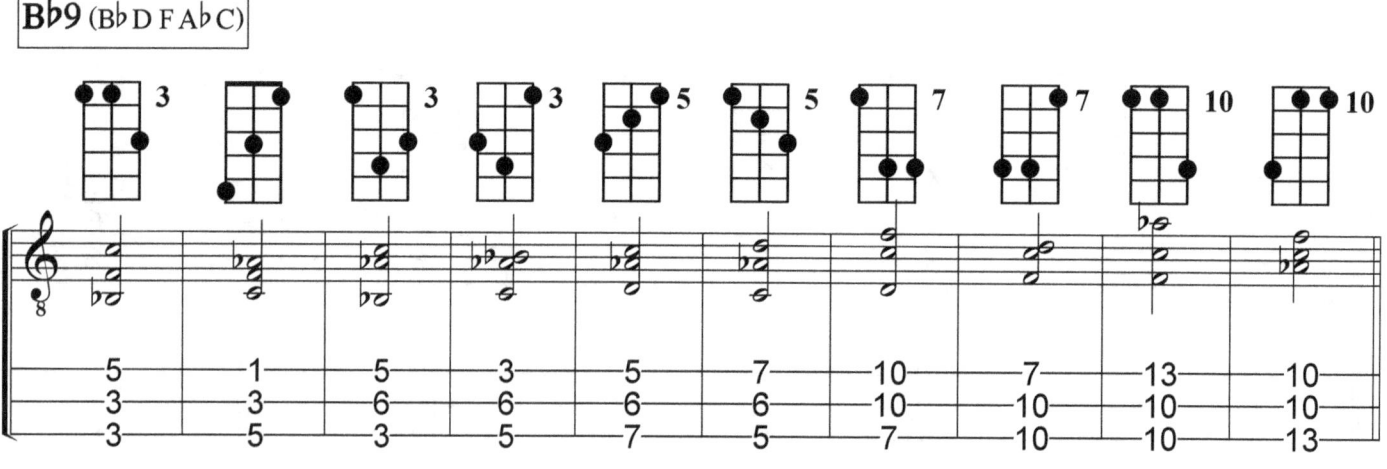

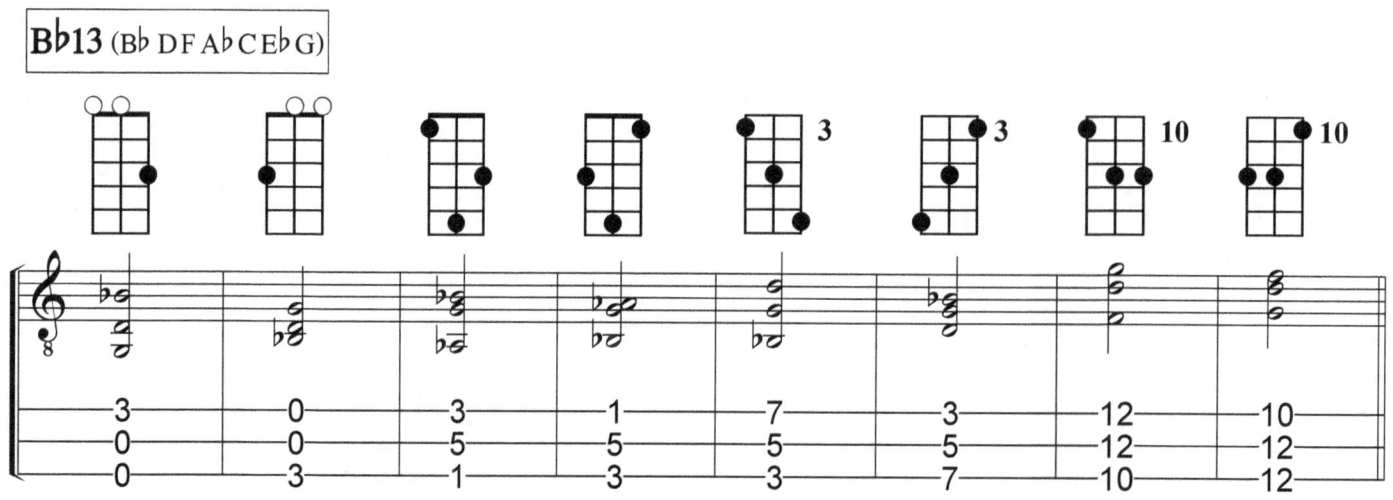

Bb7b5 - Bb7#5 - Bb7#9

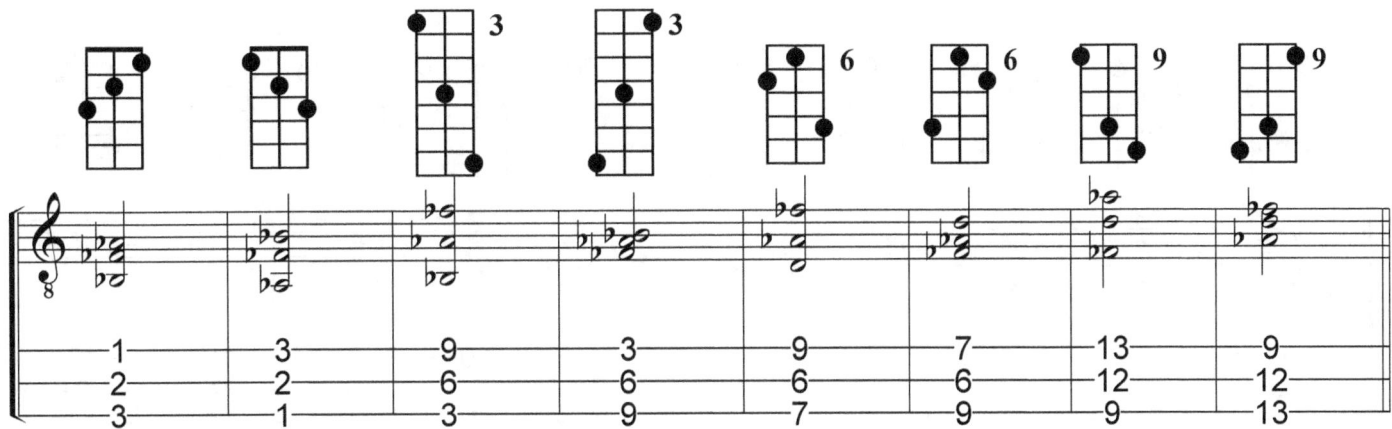

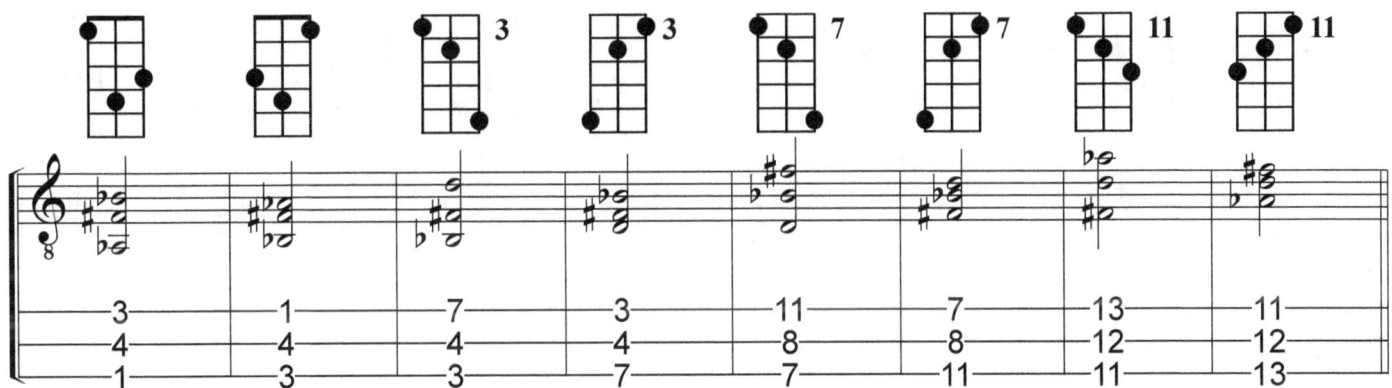

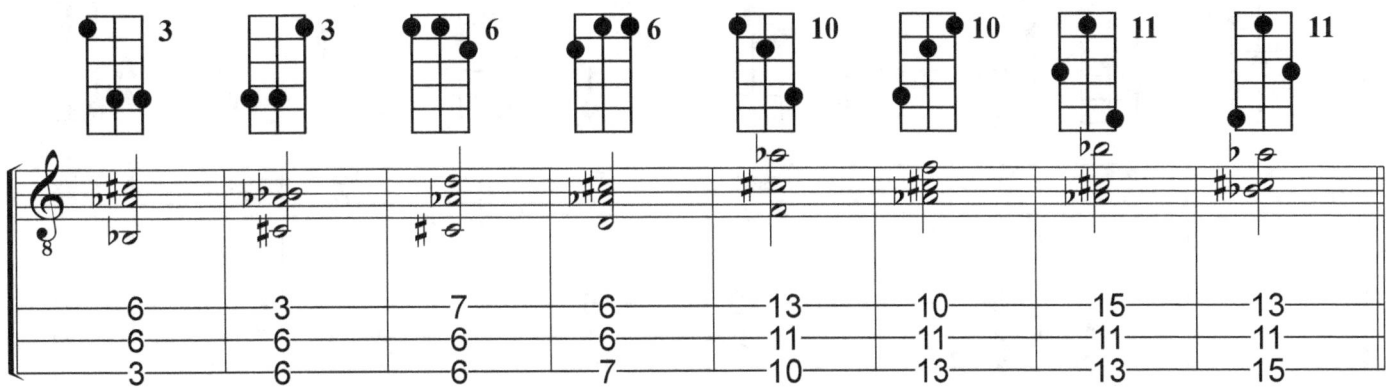

Bb7b9 - Bb diminished - Bb°7

Bb7b9 (Bb D F Ab Cb)

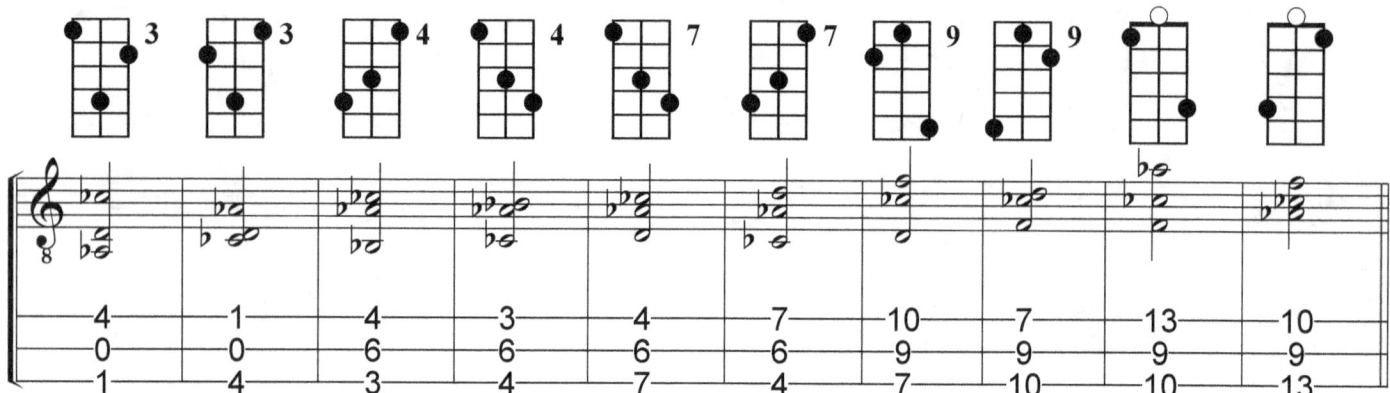

Bb diminished - Bb°7 (Bb Db Fb Abb)

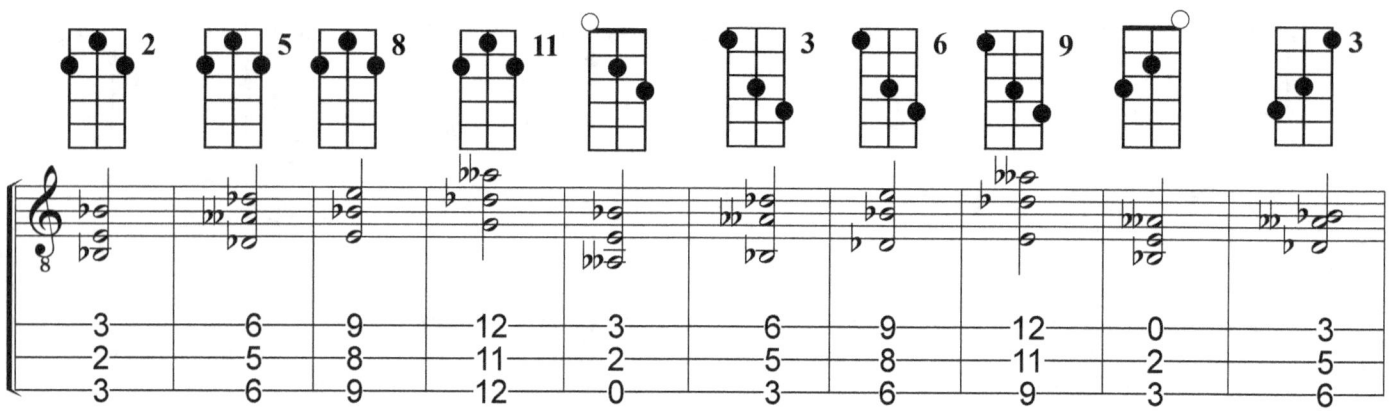

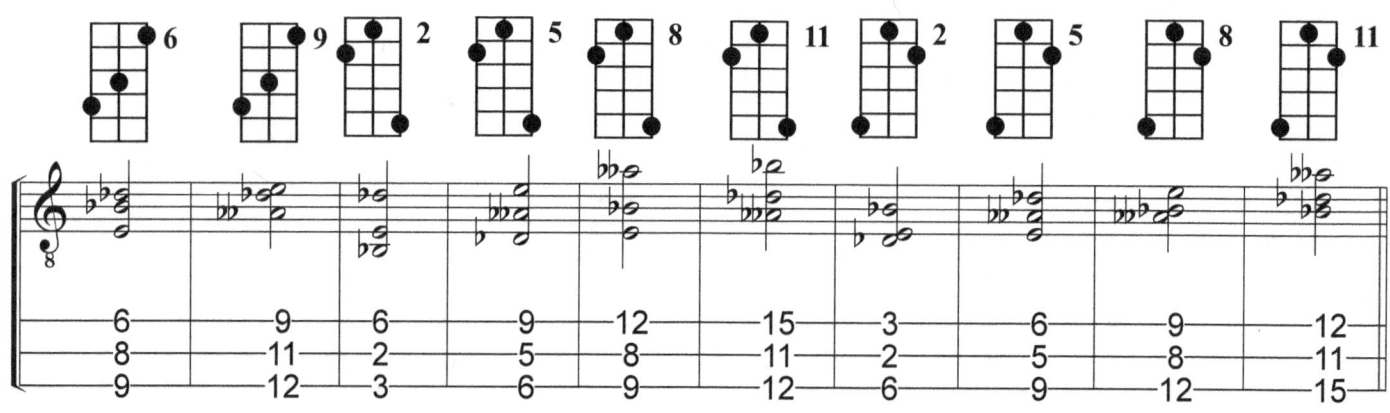

Bbsus4 - Bbsus2 - Bb7sus - Bbadd9 - Bb5

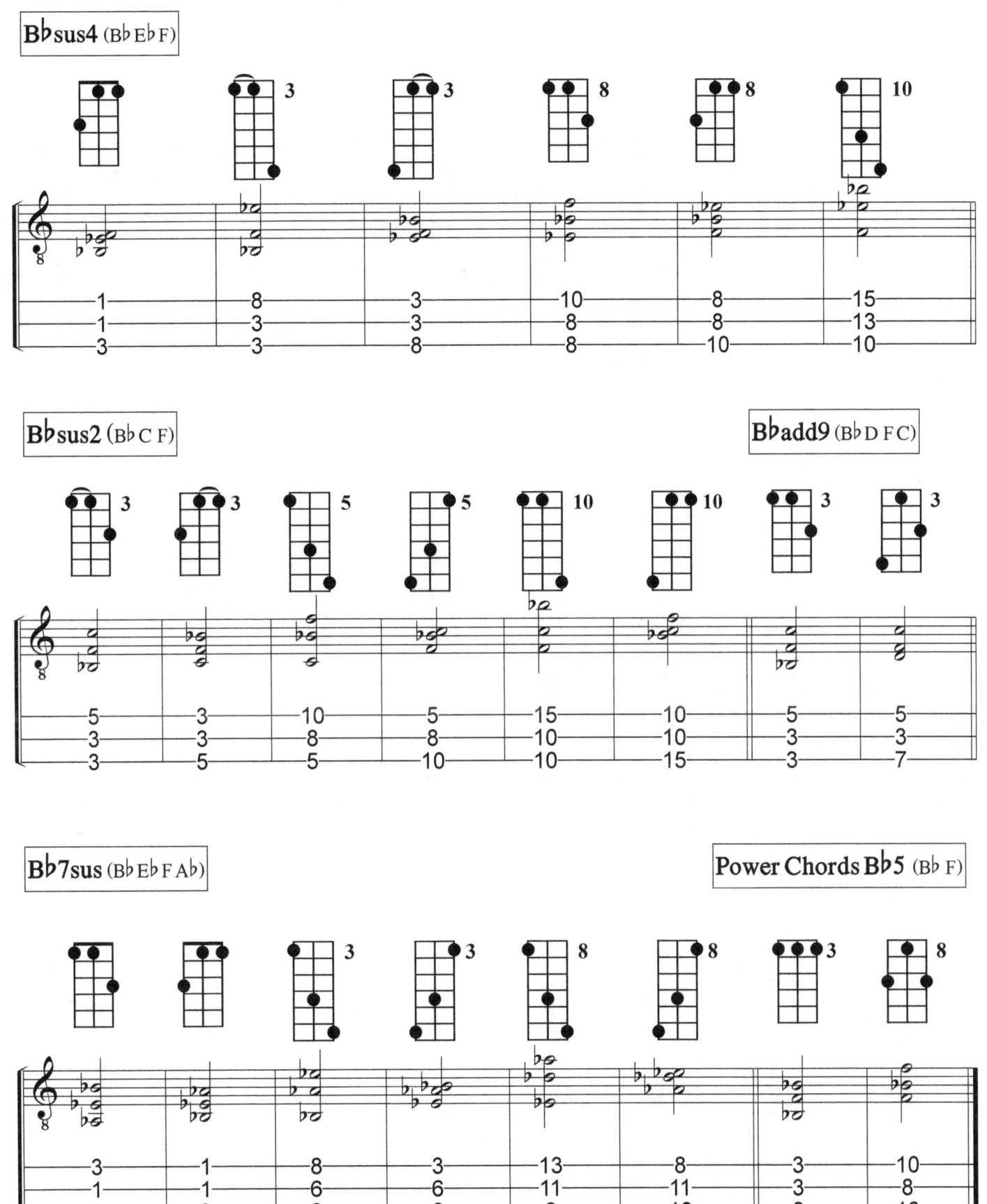

B - B6 - Bmaj7

Some notes have been omitted from the chords to facilitate playability.
The notes that form the chord are in brackets.

B Major (B D# F#)

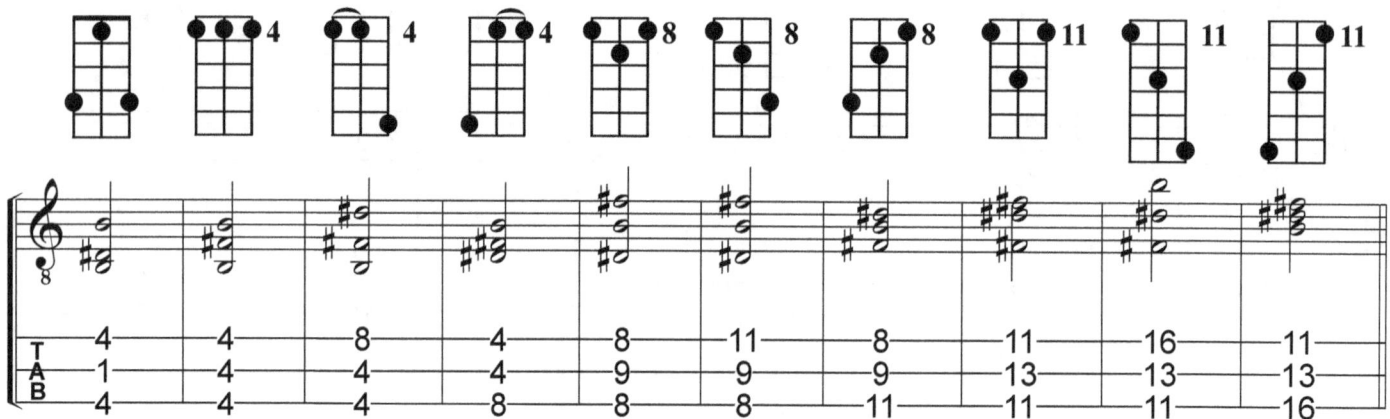

B6 (B D# F# G#)

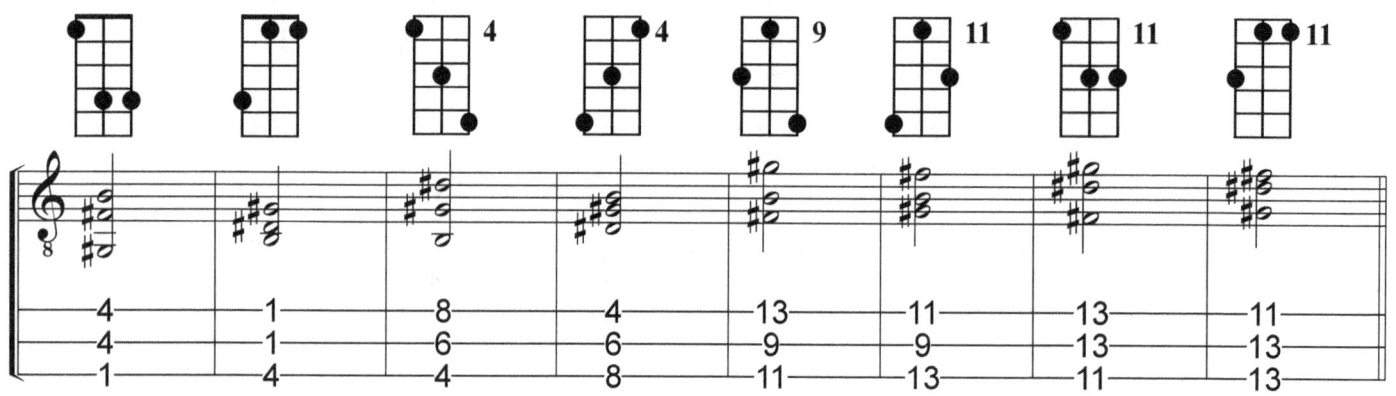

Bmaj7 (B D# F# A#)

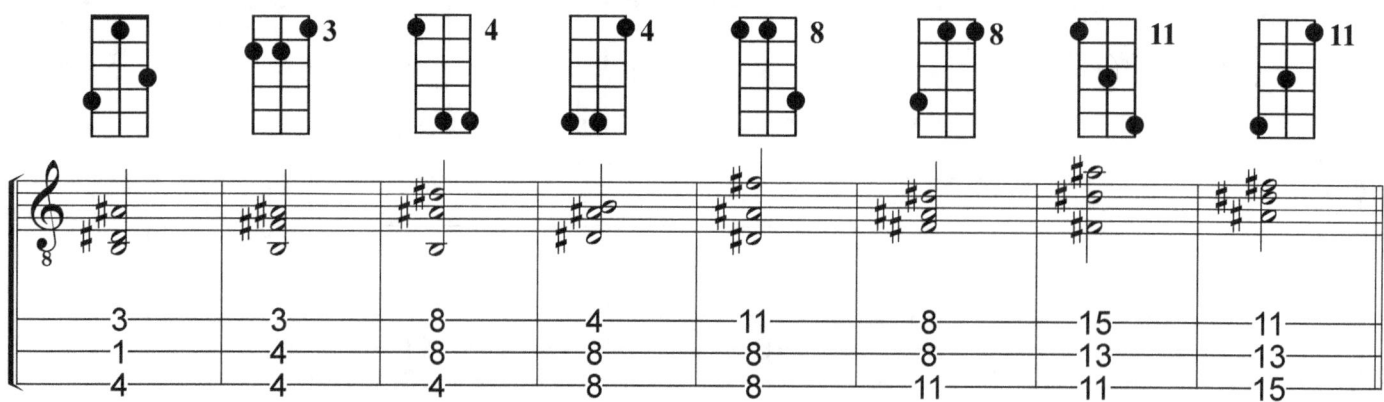

Bmaj9 - B6/9 - B+

Bmaj 9 (B D♯ F♯ A♯ C♯)

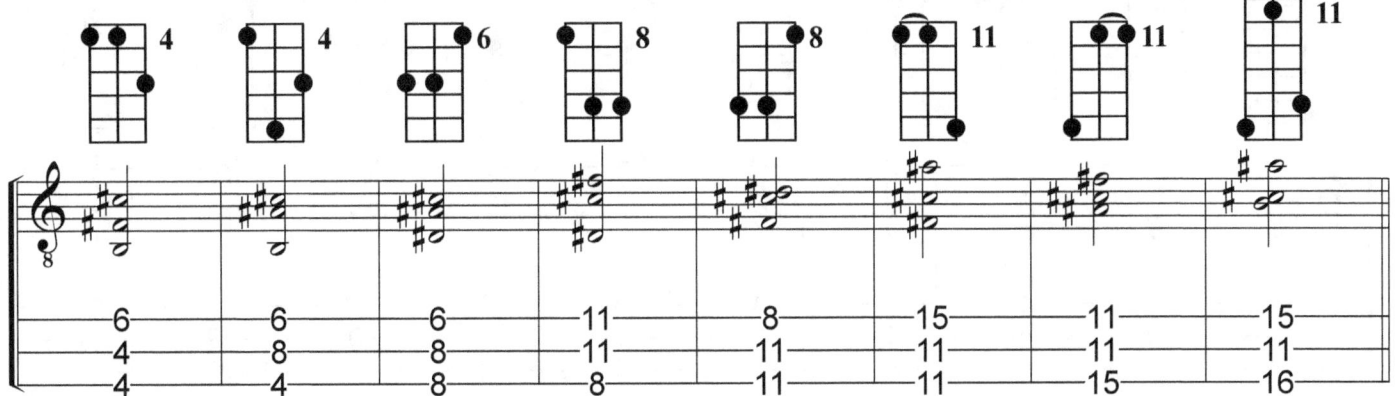

B6/9 (B D♯ F♯ G♯ C♯)

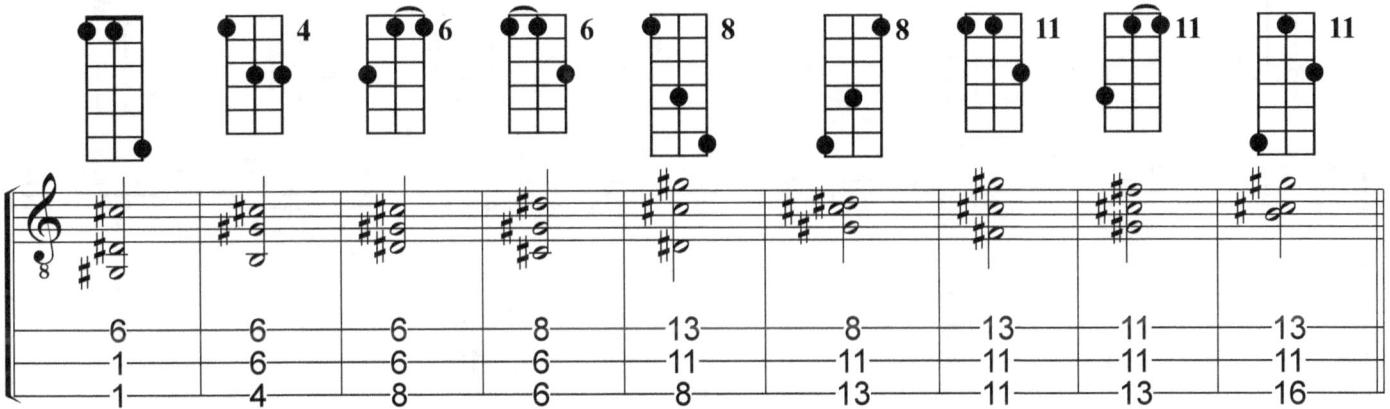

B Augmented - B+ (B D♯ F𝄪)

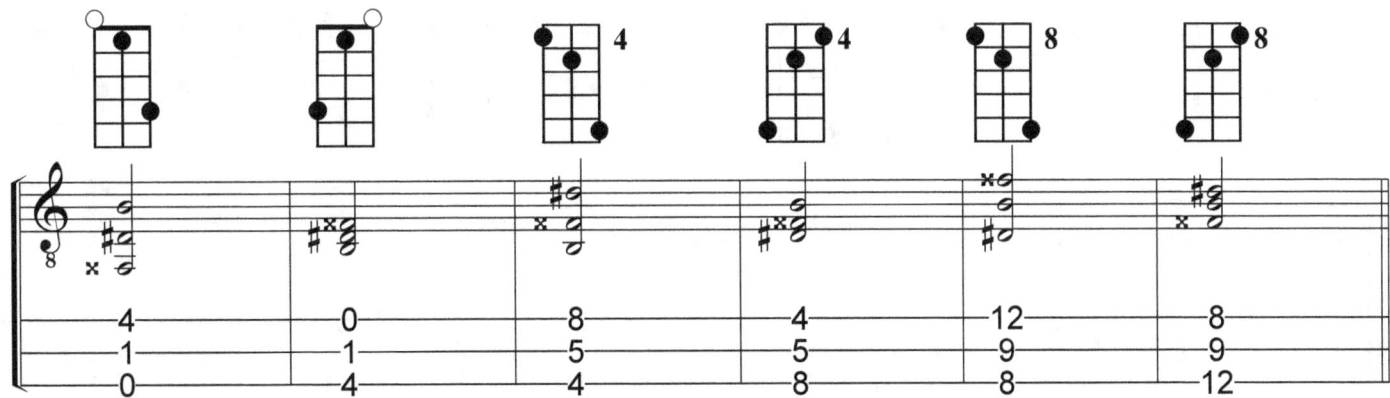

Bm - Bm6 - Bm(maj7) - Bm7

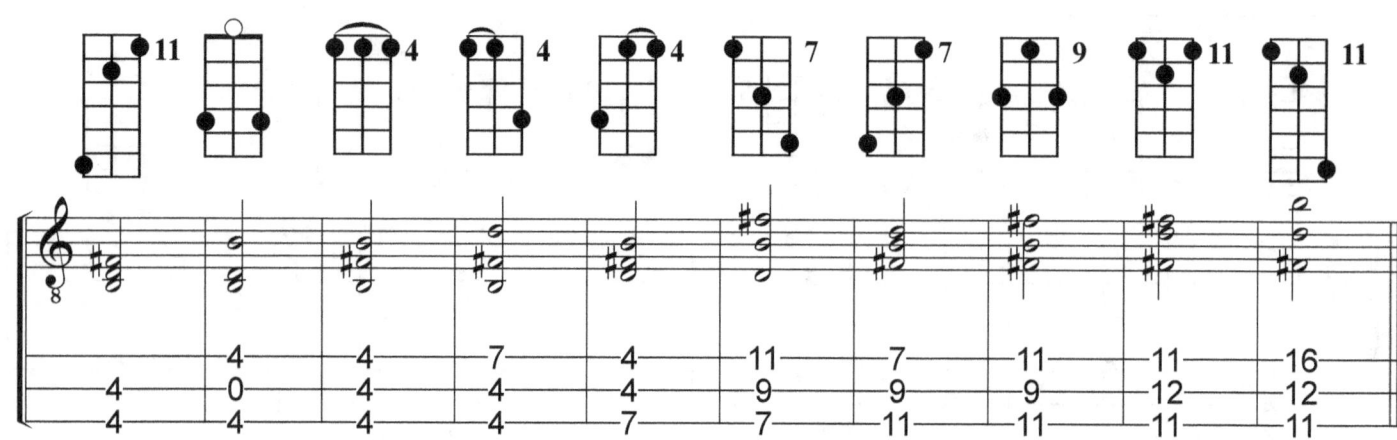

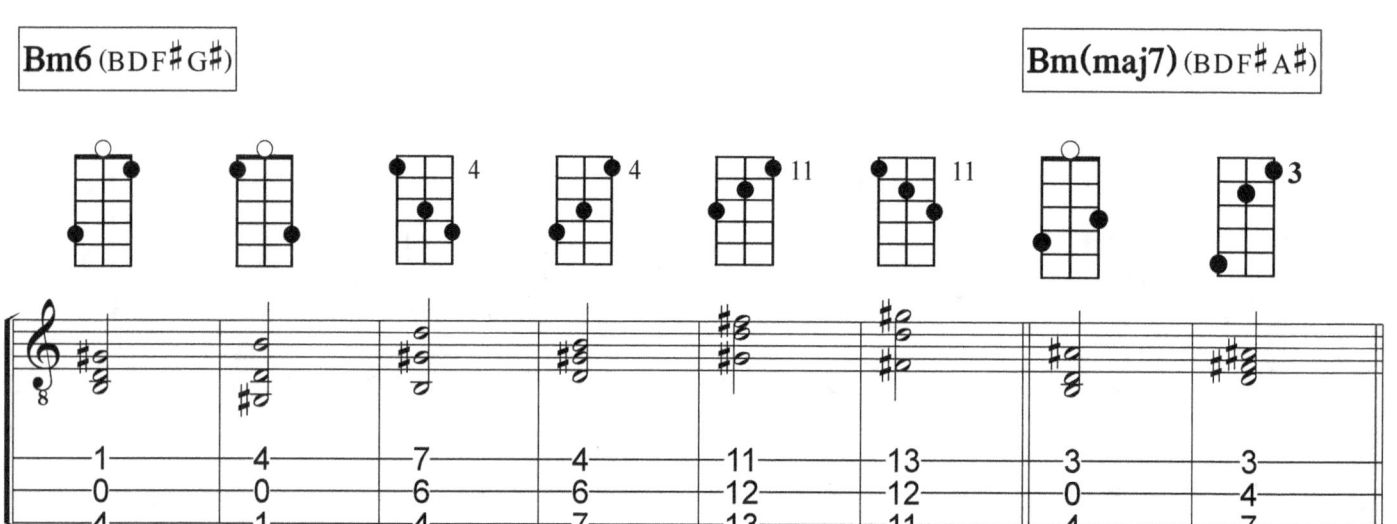

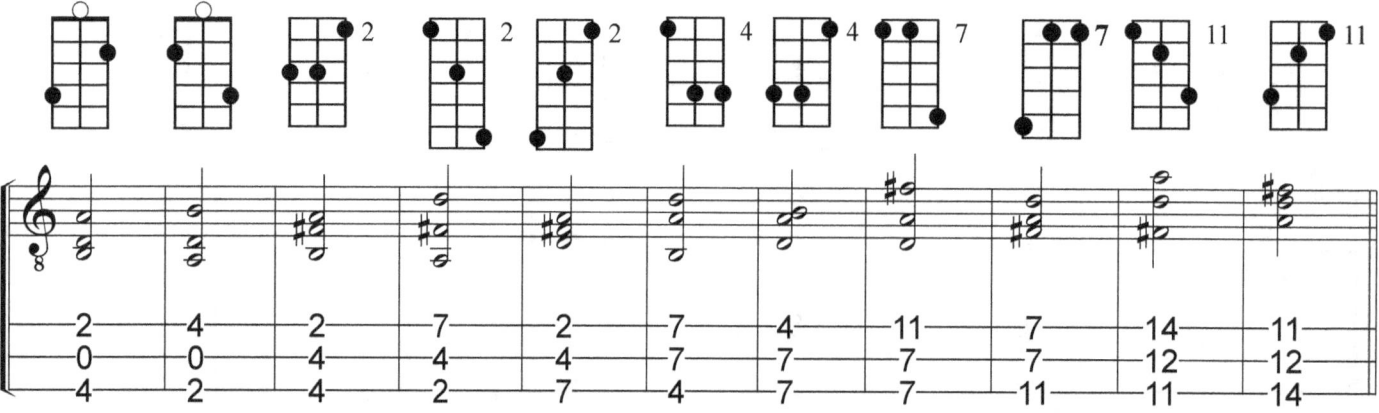

Bm7♭5 - Bm9 - Bm11

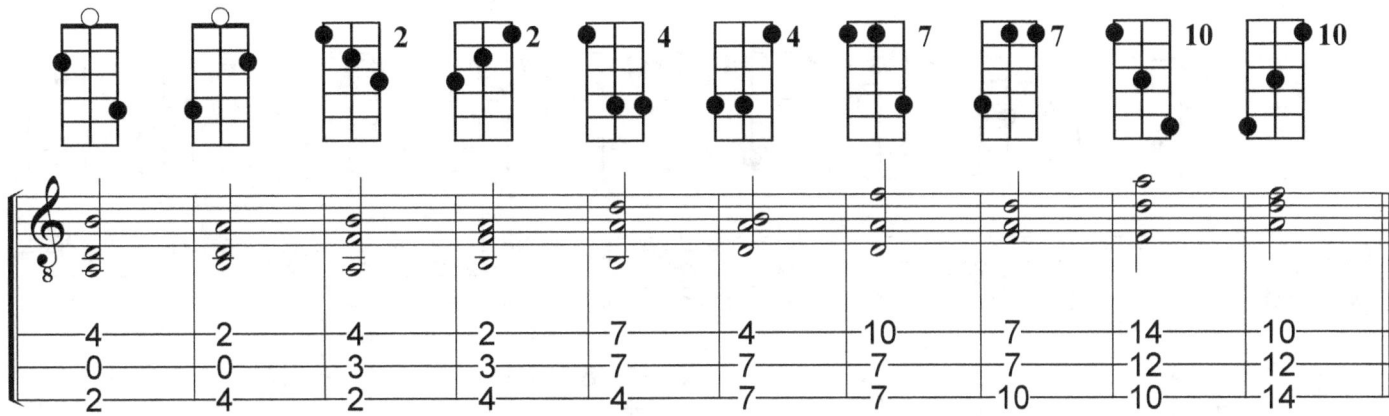

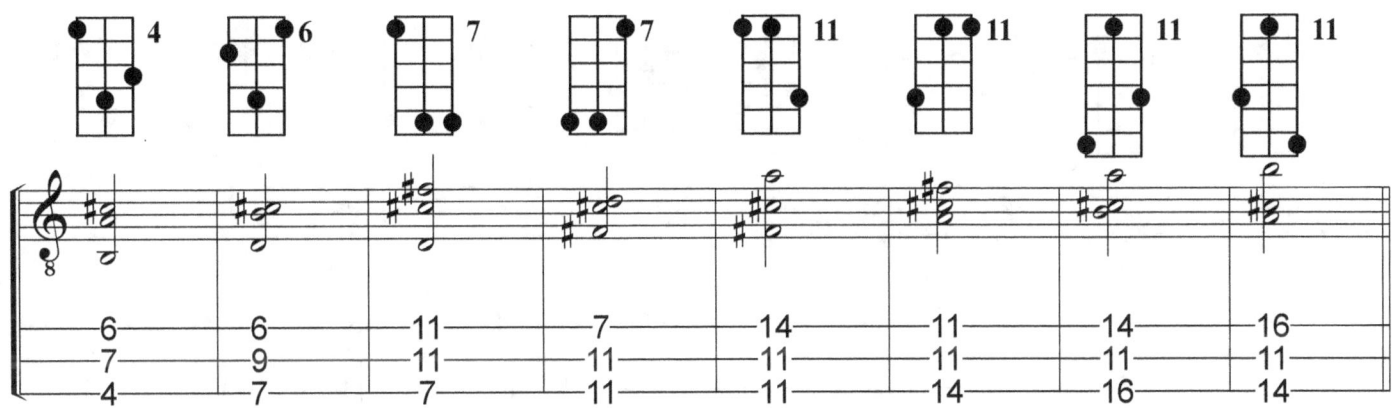

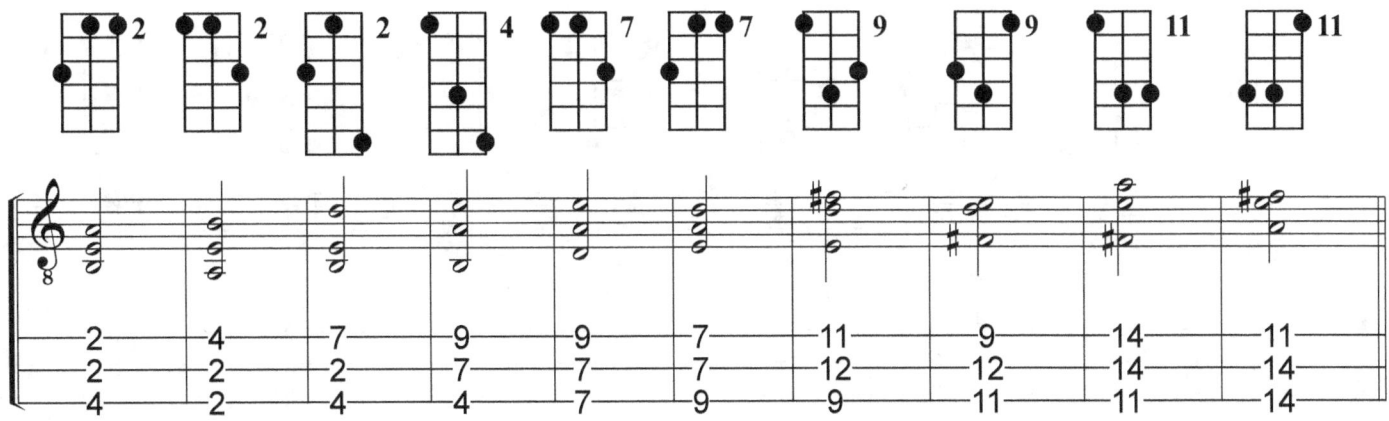

B7 - B9 - B13

B7 (B D# F# A)

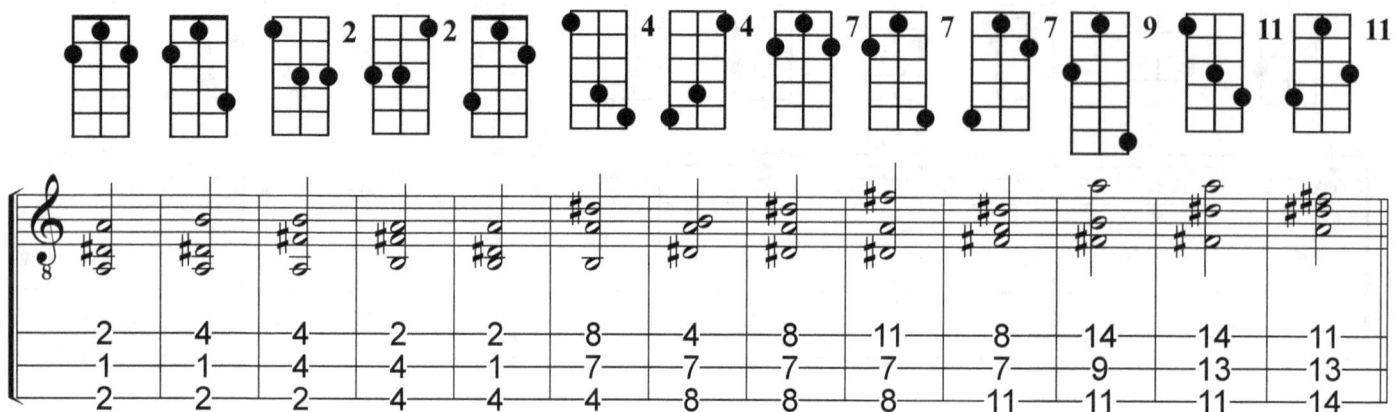

B9 (B D# F# A C#)

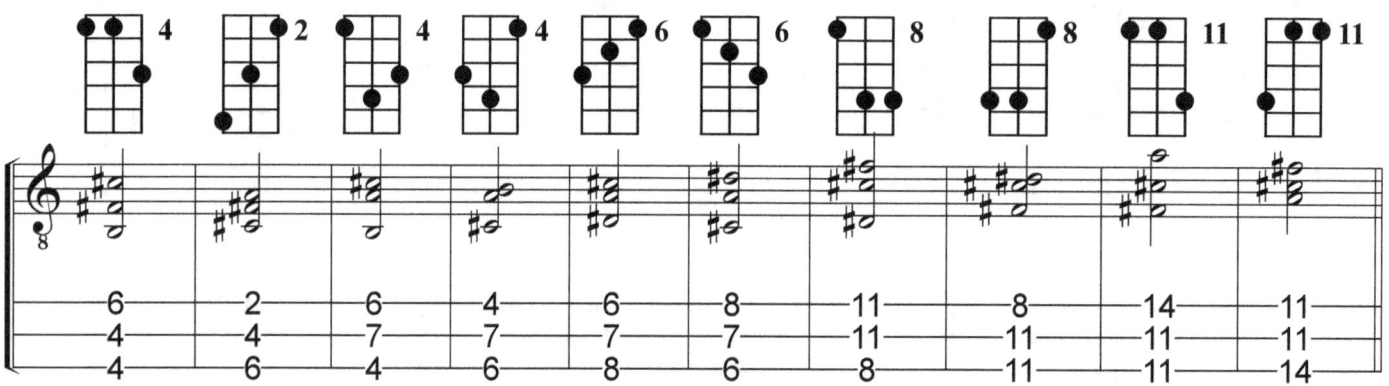

B13 (B D# F# A C# E G#)

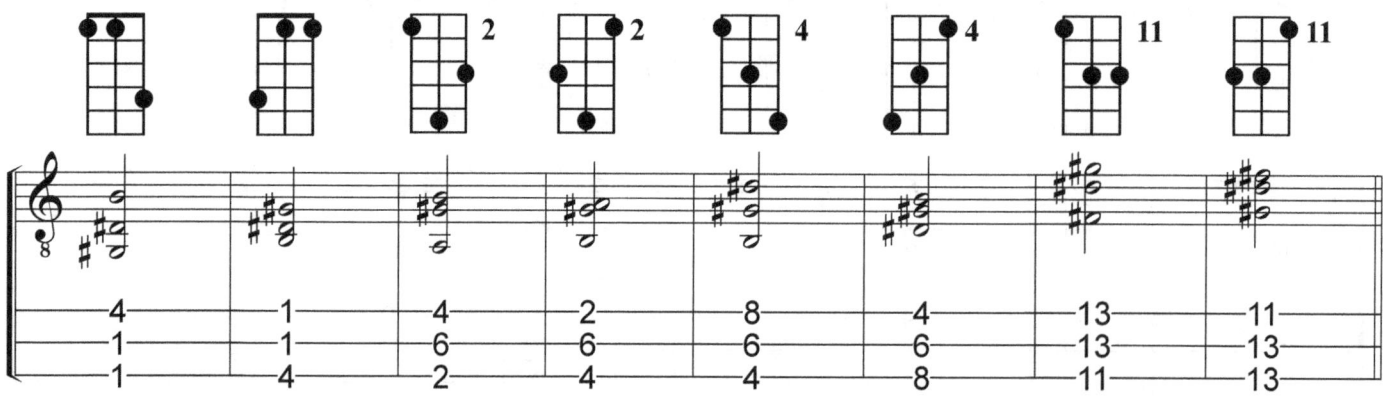

B7♭5 - B7♯5 - B7♯9

B7♭5 (B D♯ F A)

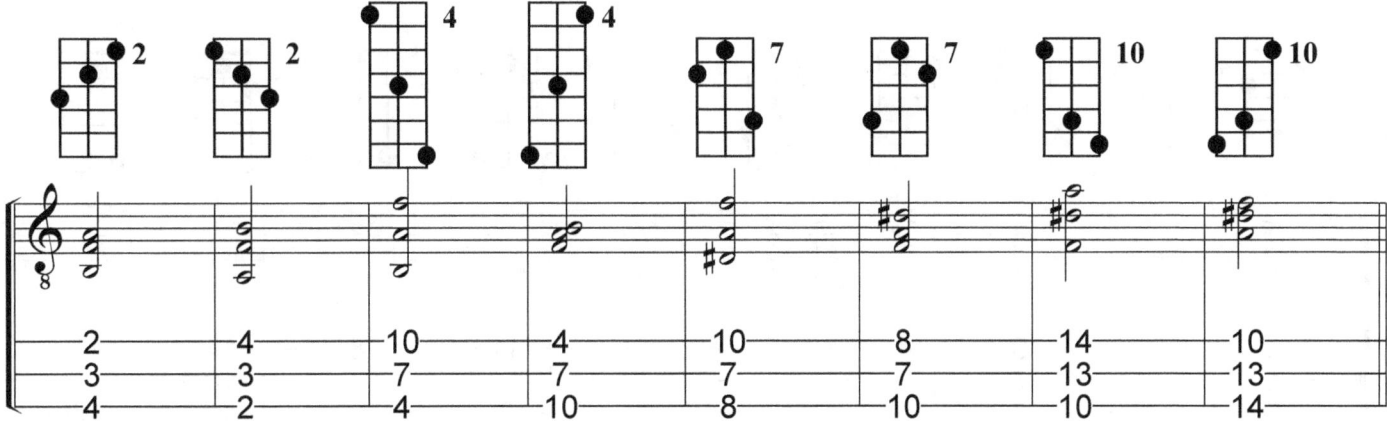

B7♯5 (B D♯ F× A)

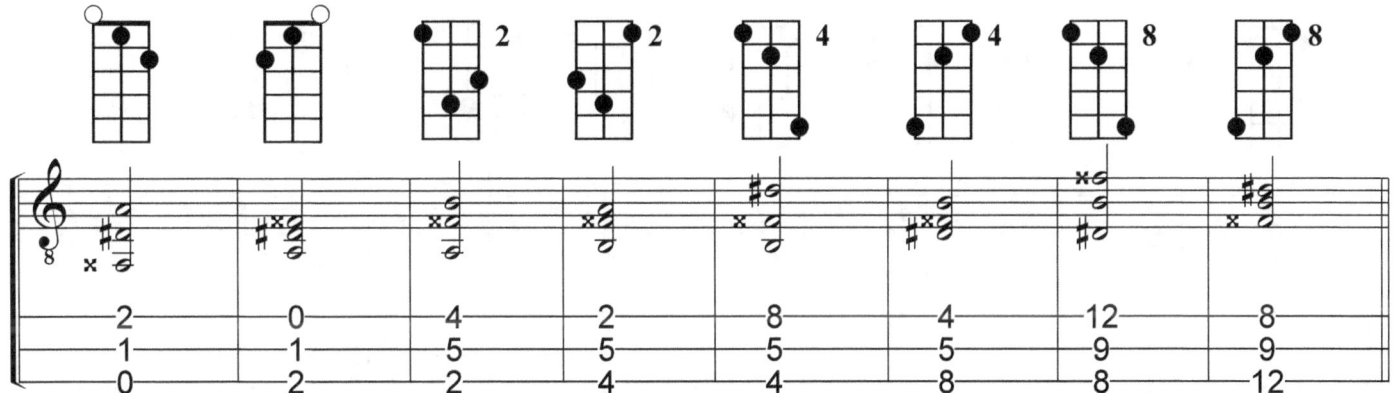

B7♯9 (B D♯ F♯ A C×)

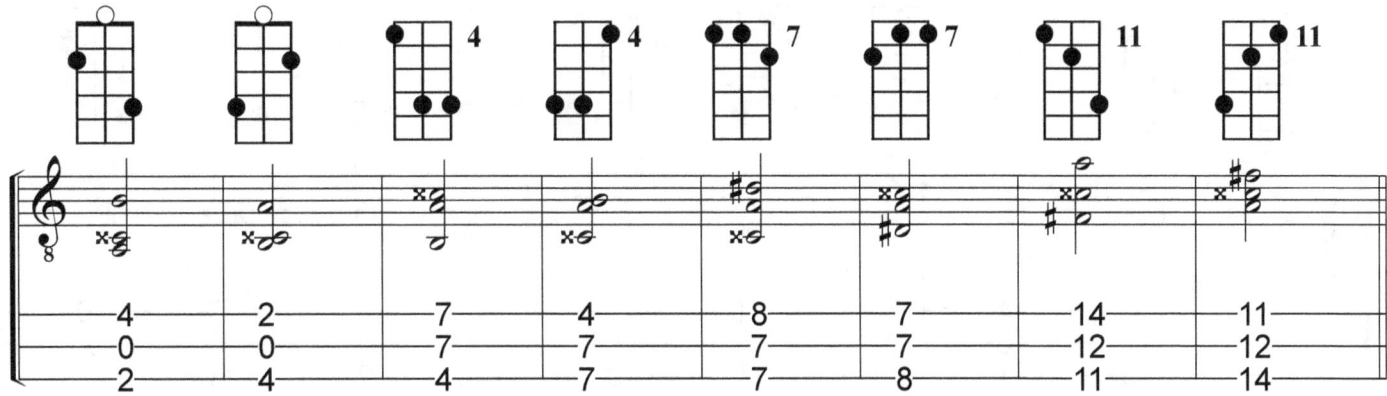

B7♭9 - B diminished - B°7

B7♭9 (B D# F# A C)

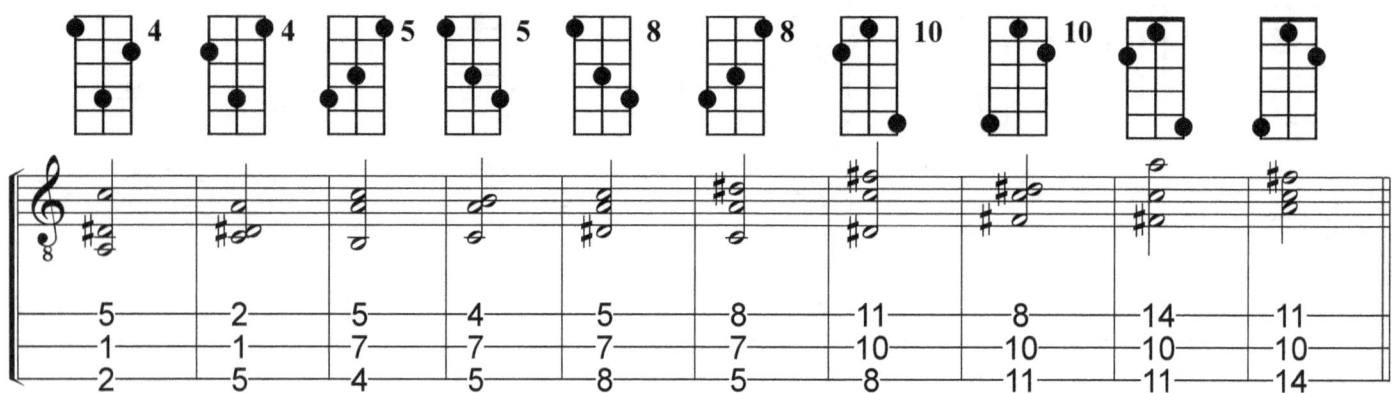

B diminished - B°7 (B D F A♭)

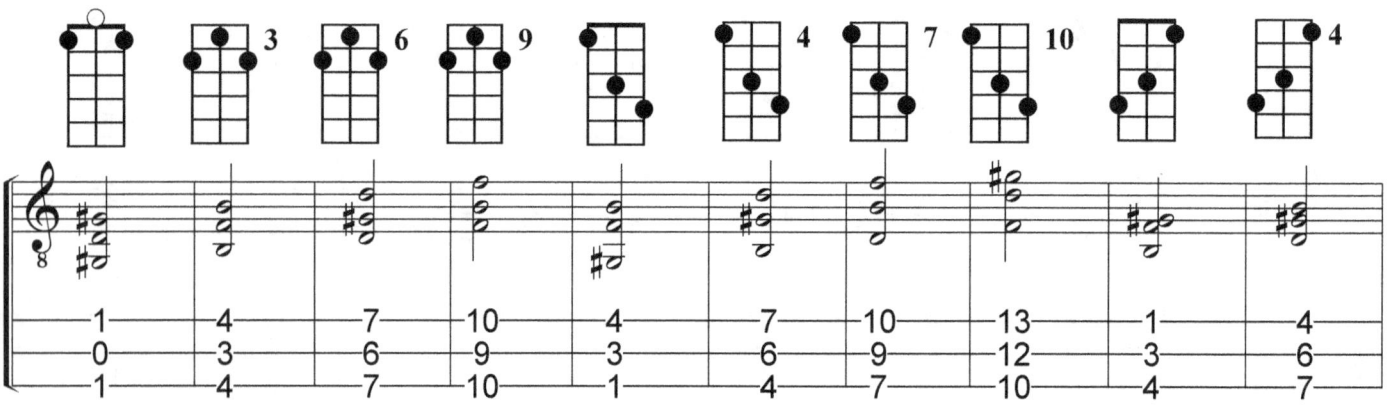

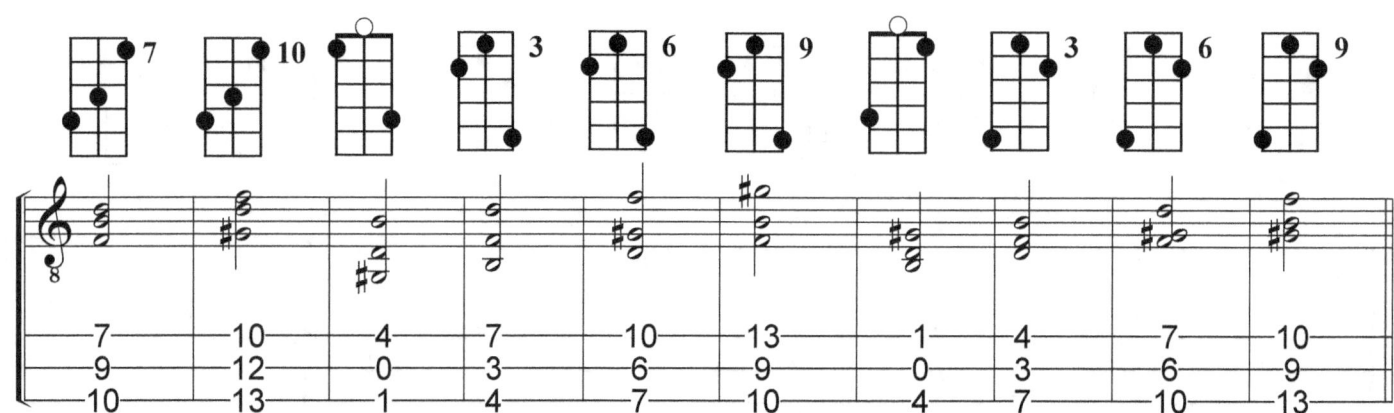

Bsus4 - Bsus2 - B7sus - Badd9 - B5

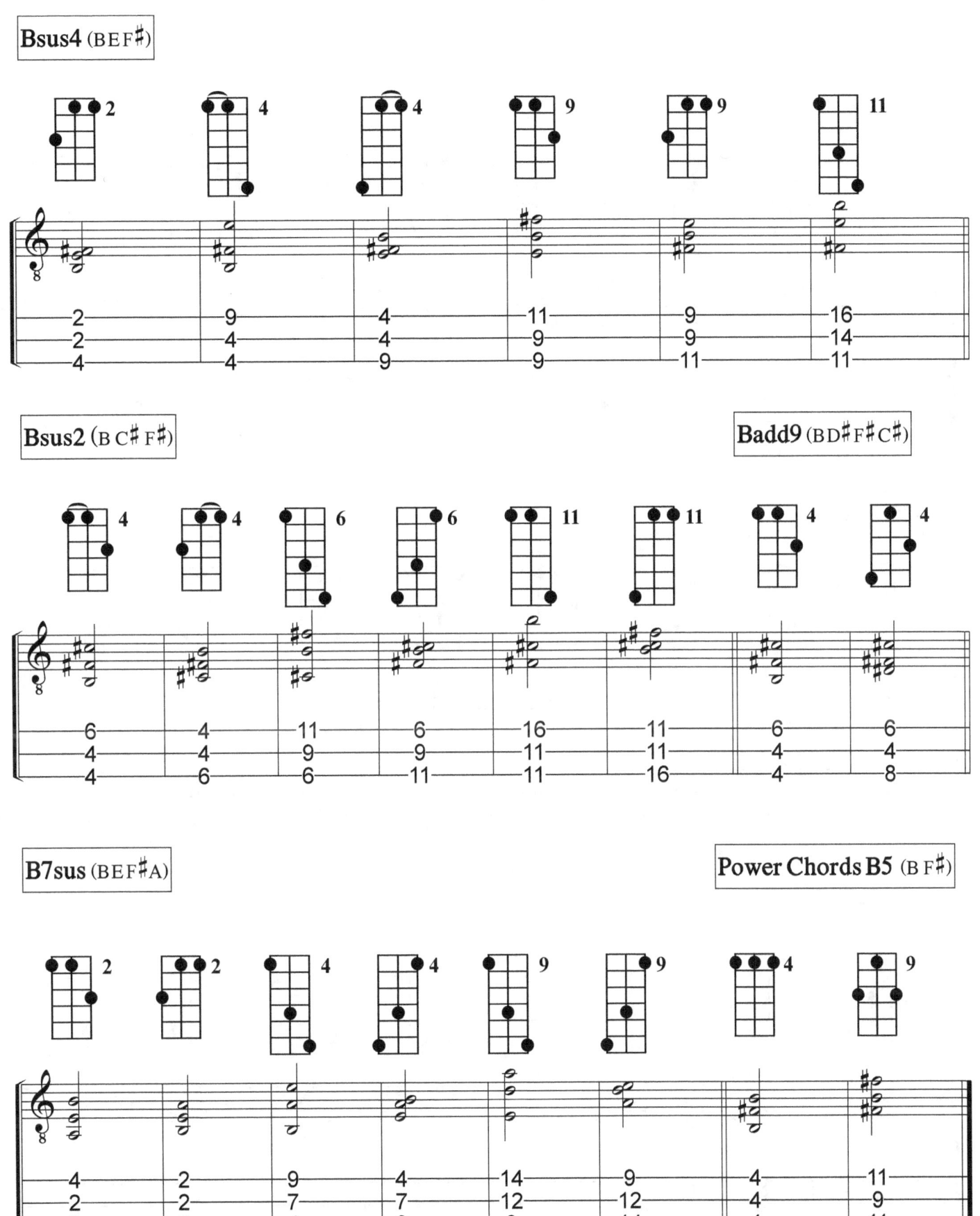

C - C6 - Cmaj7

Some notes have been omitted from the chords to facilitate playability.
The notes that form the chord are in brackets.

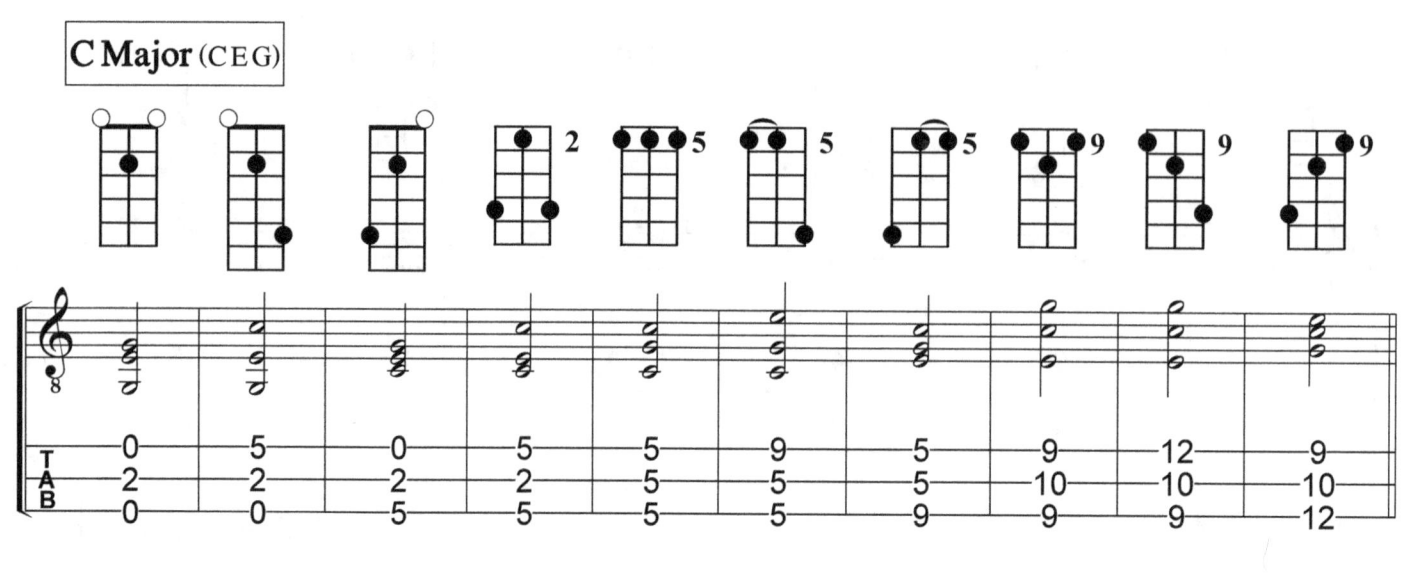

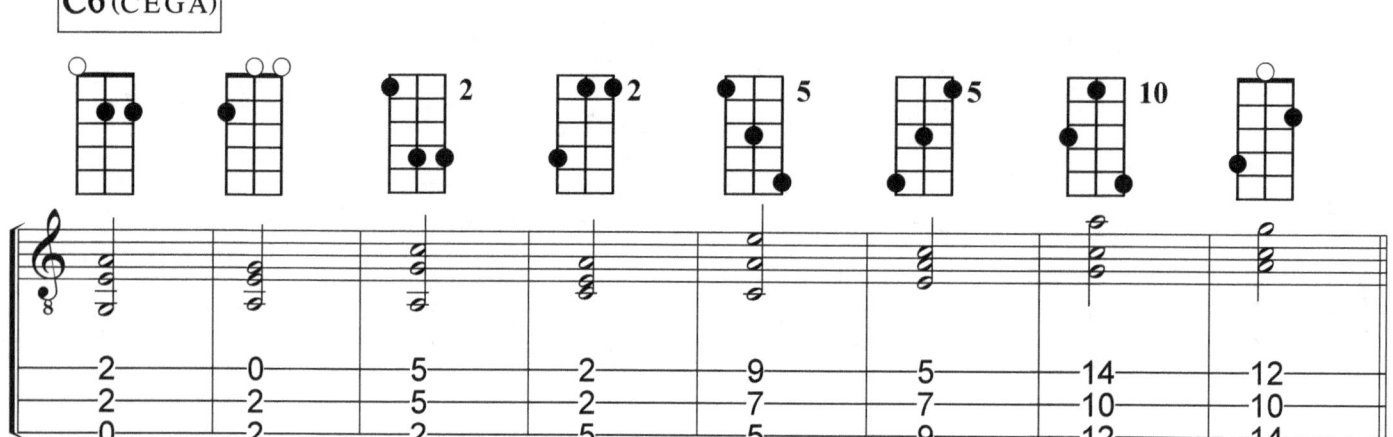

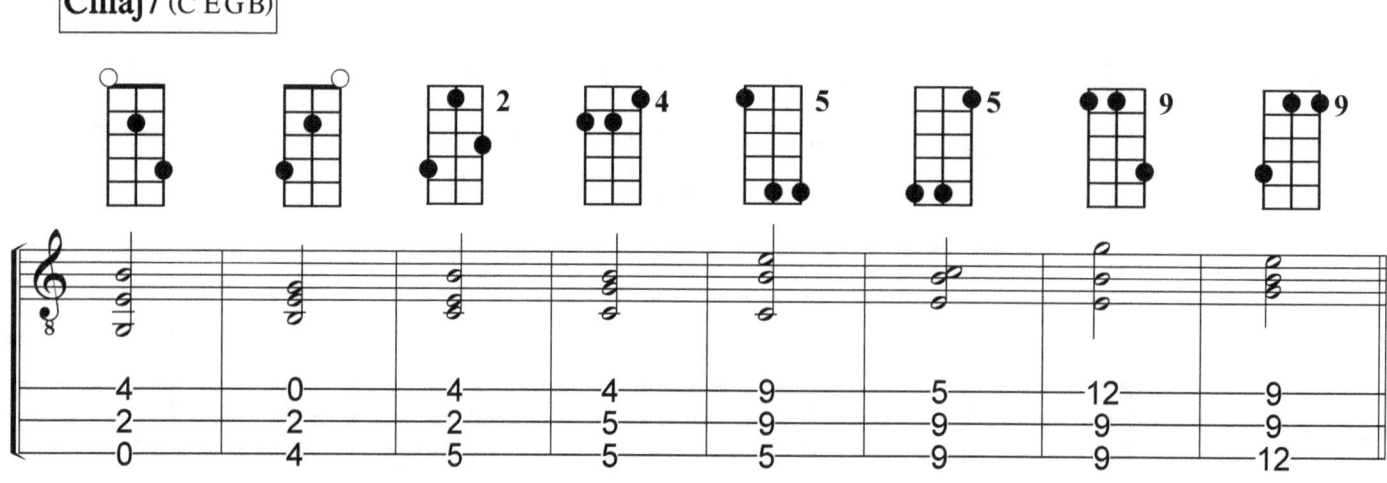

Cmaj9 - C6/9 - C+

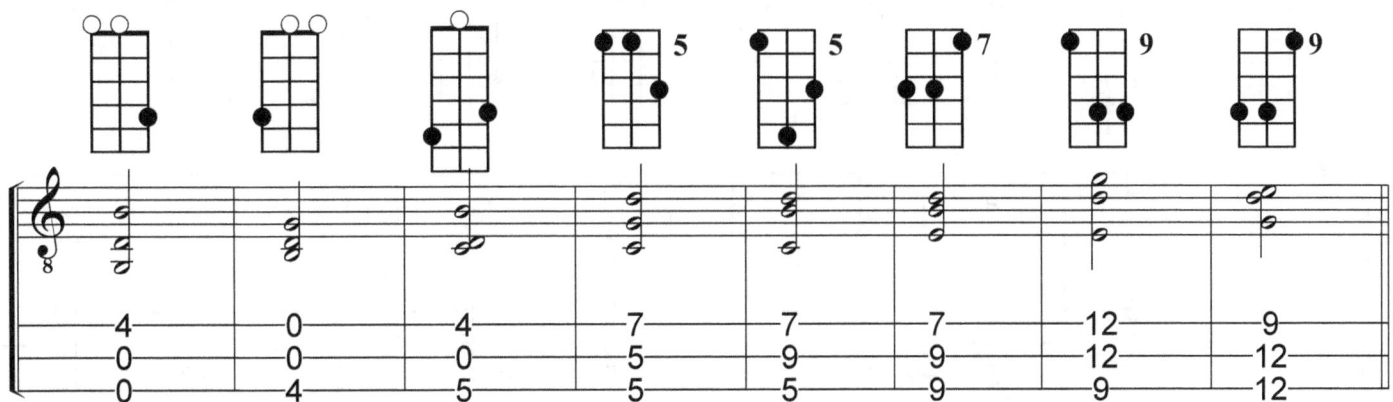

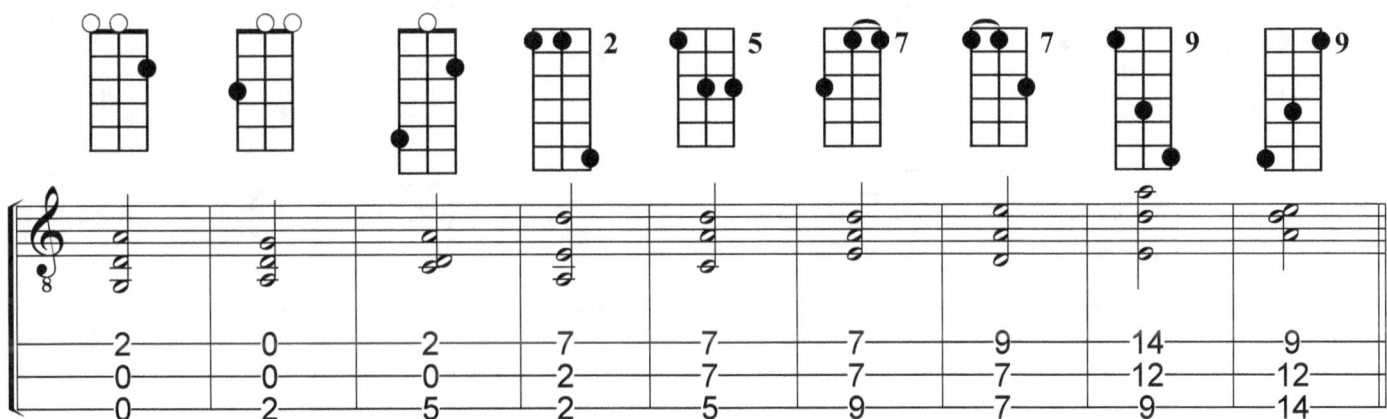

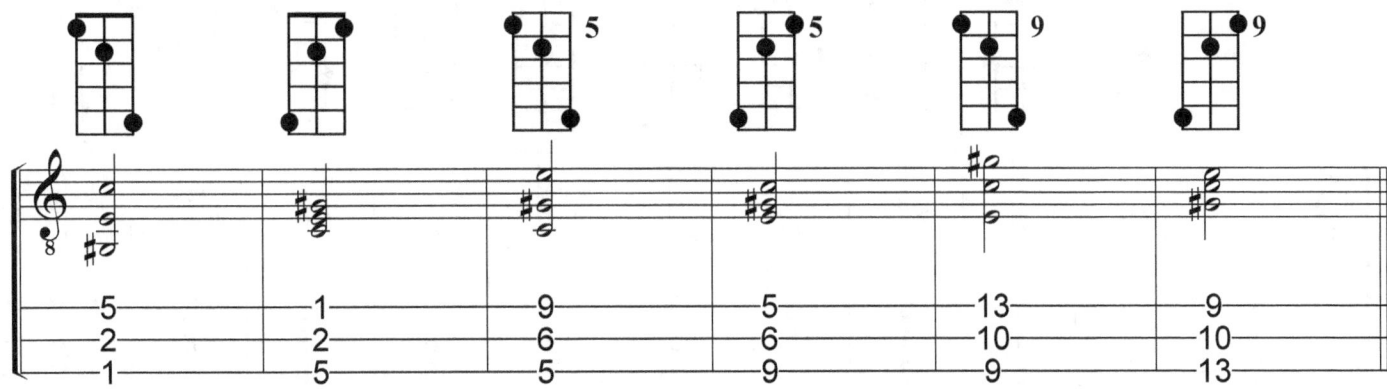

Cm - Cm6 - Cm(maj7) - Cm7

C Minor (C E♭ G)

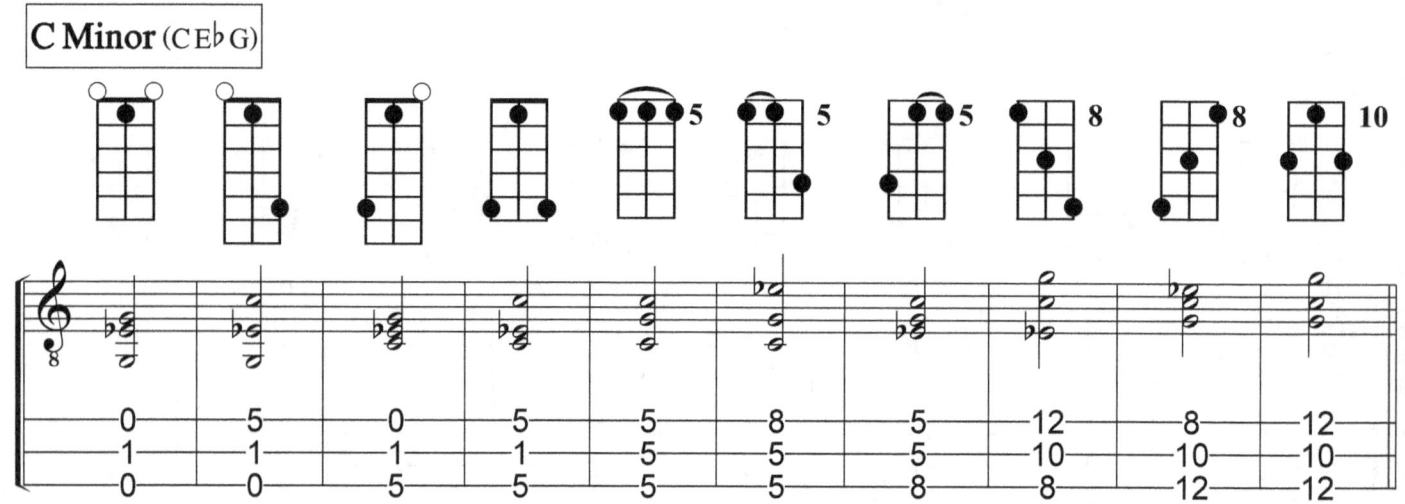

Cm6 (C E♭ G A) **Cm(maj7)** (C-E♭-G-B)

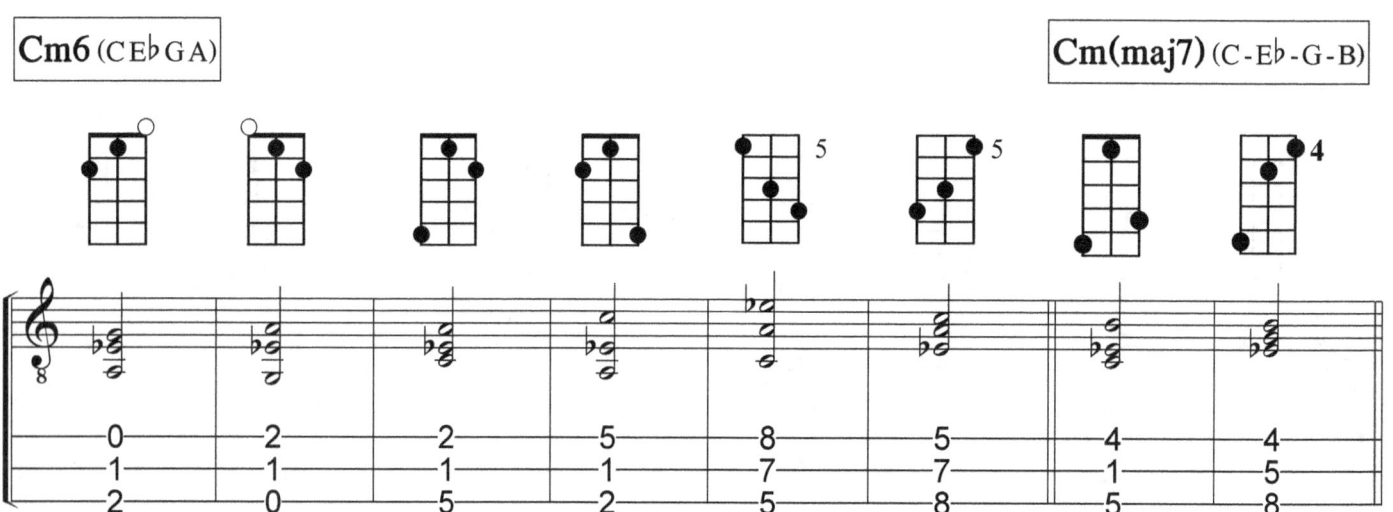

Cm7 (C E♭ G B♭)

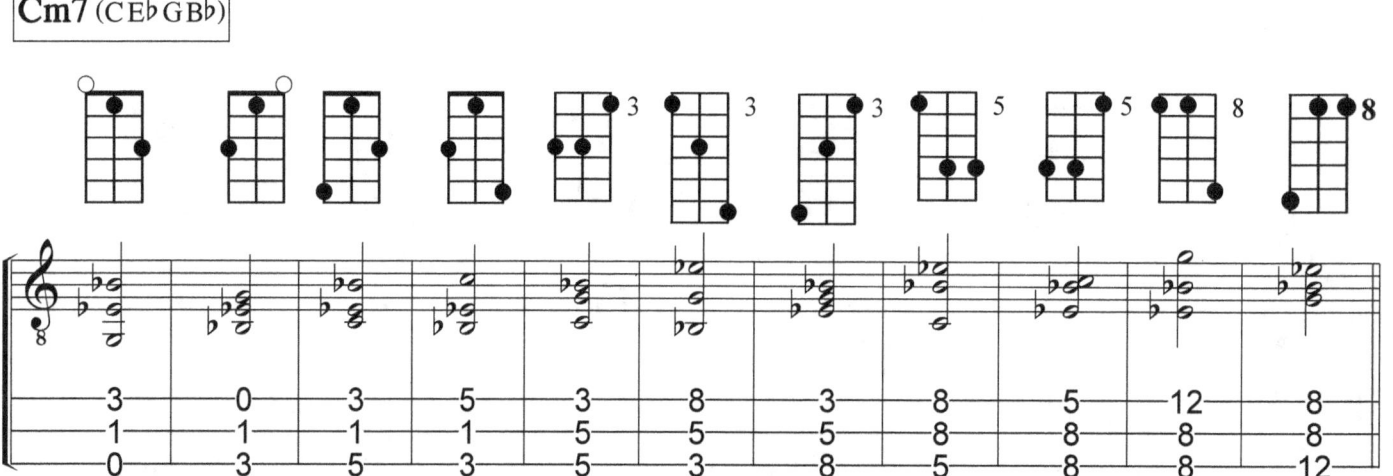

Cm7♭5 - Cm9 - Cm11

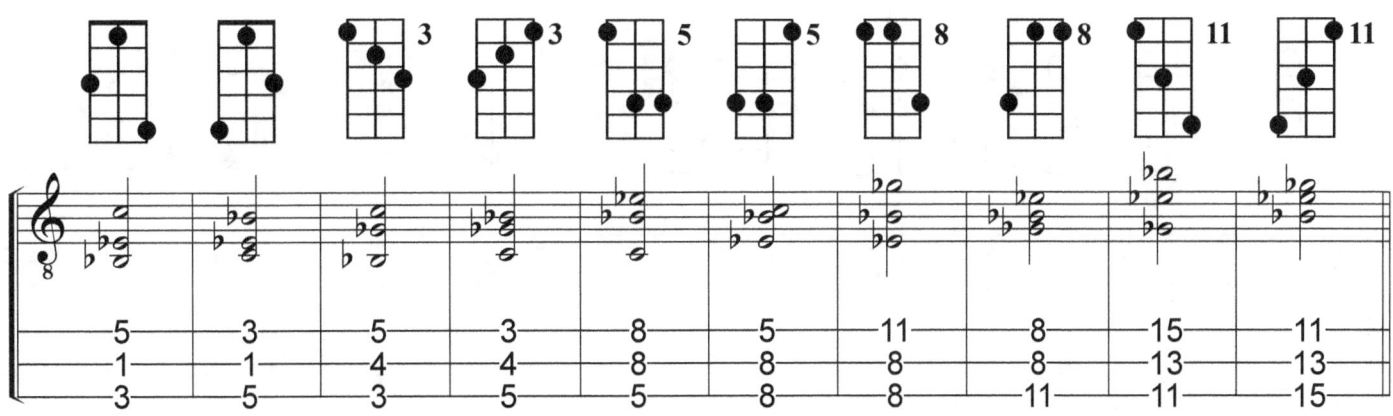

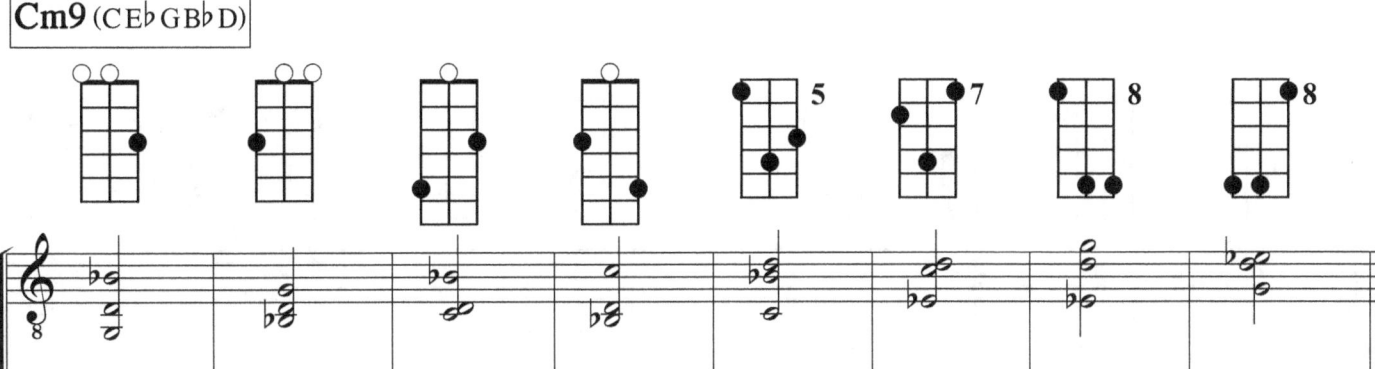

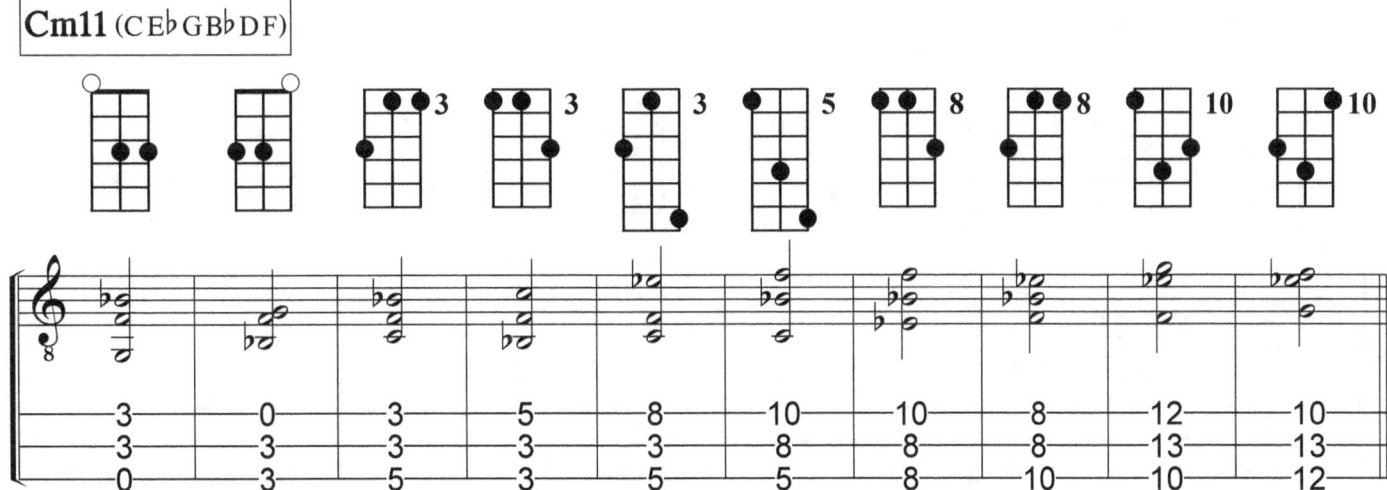

C7 - C9 - C13

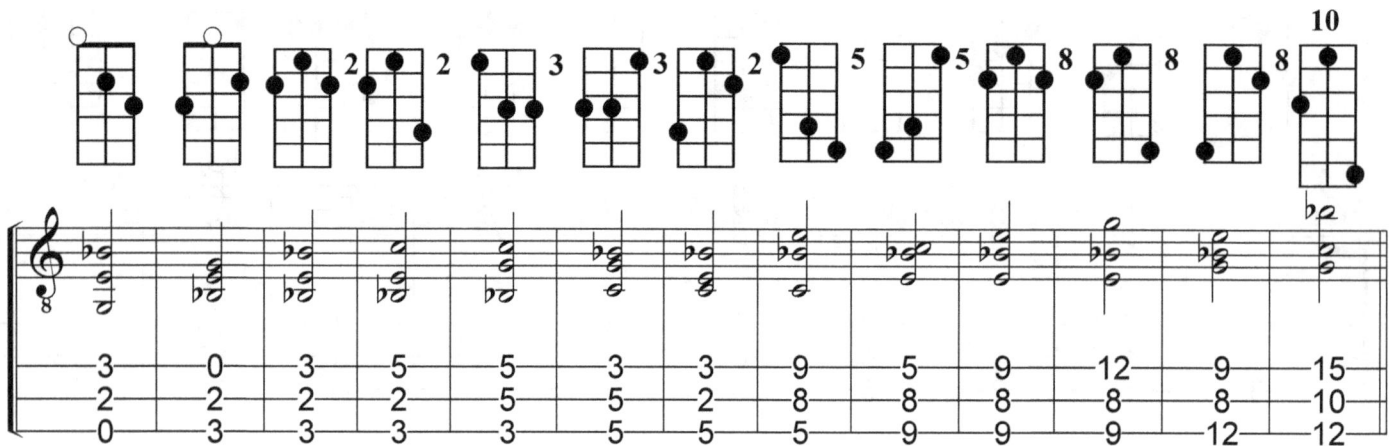

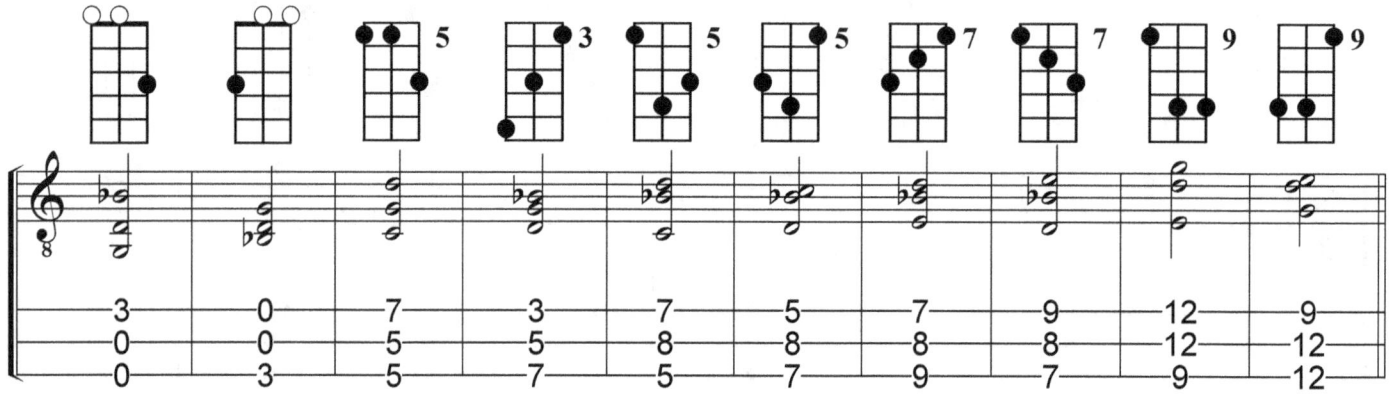

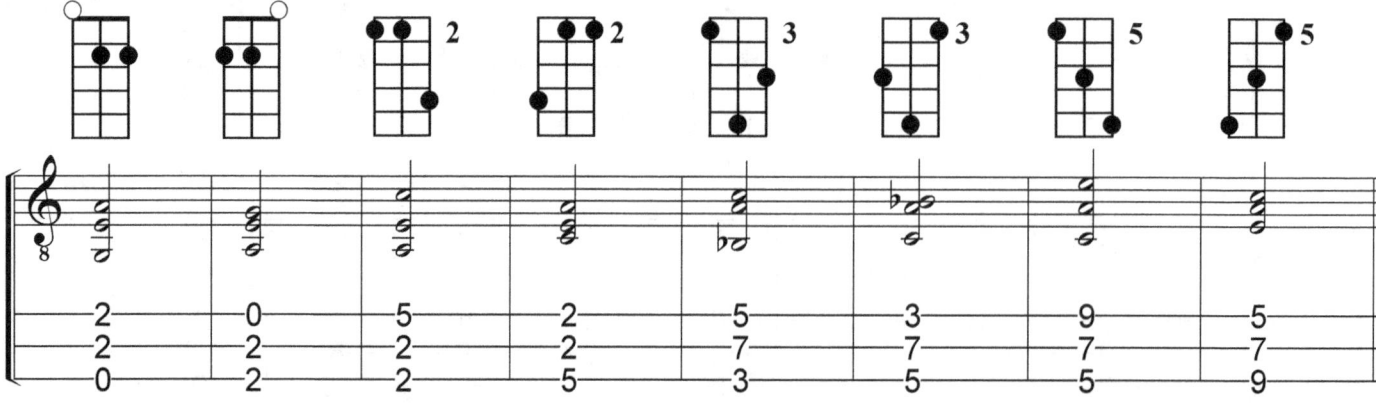

C7♭5 - C7#5 - C7#9

C7♭5 (C E G♭ B♭)

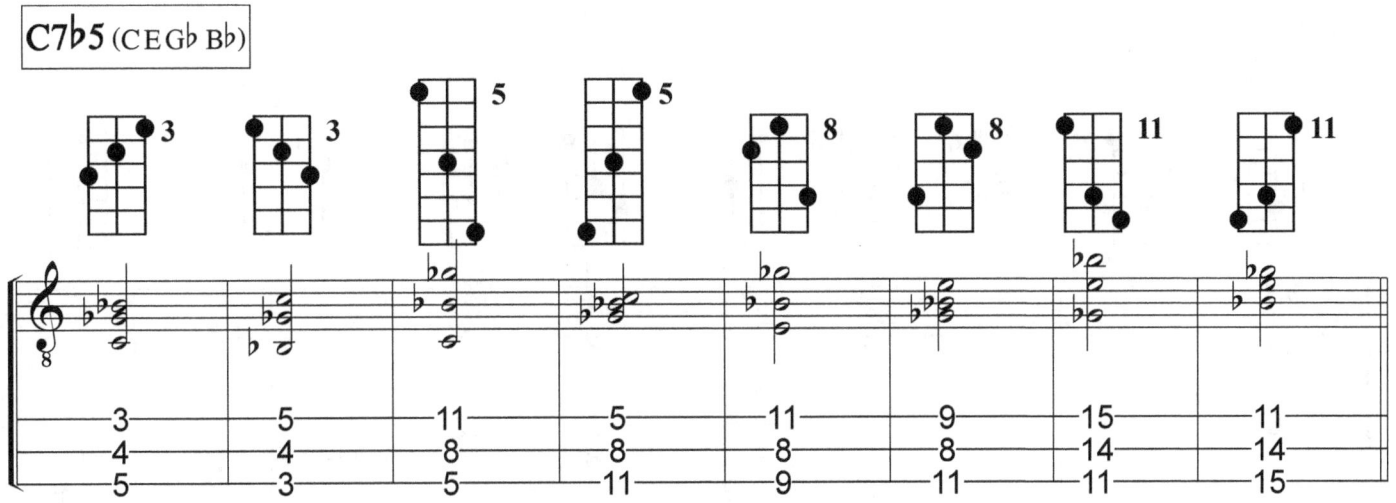

C7#5 (C E G# B♭)

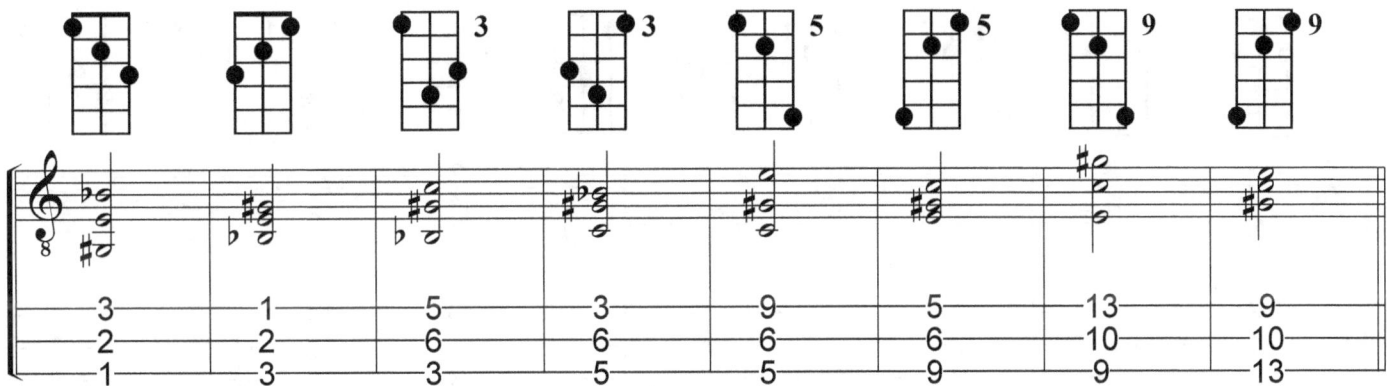

C7#9 (C E G B♭ D#)

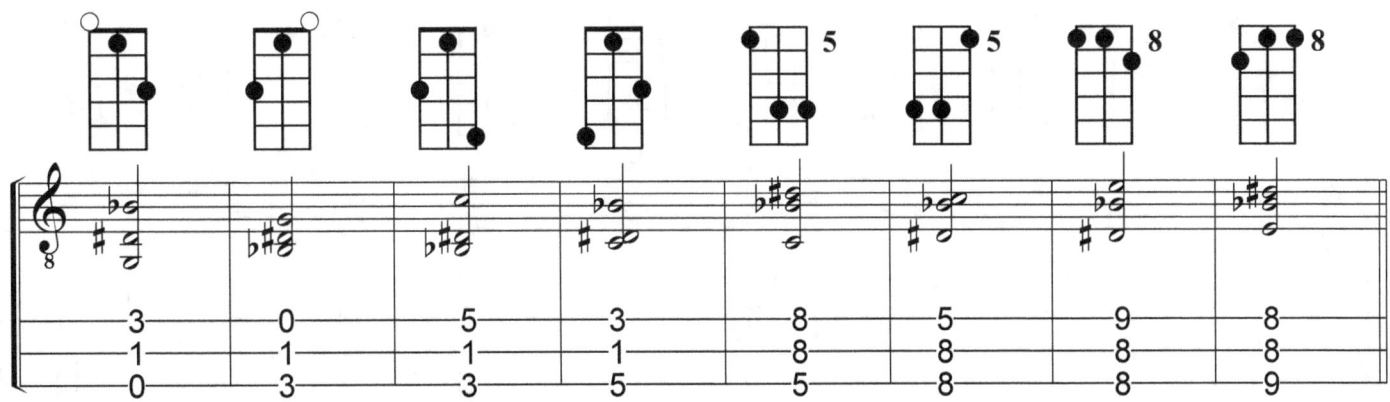

C7♭9 - C diminished - C°7

C7♭9 (C E G B♭ D♭)

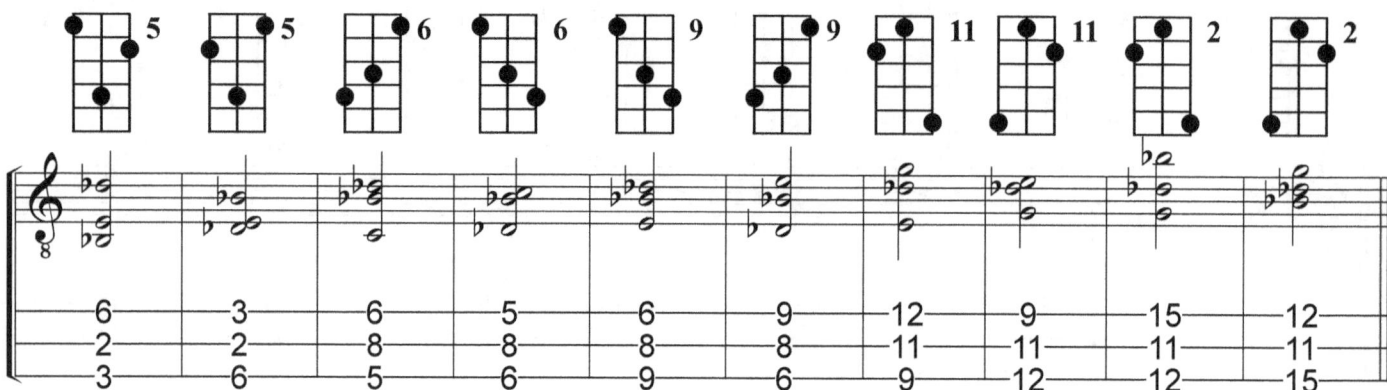

C diminished - C°7 (C E♭ G♭ B♭♭)

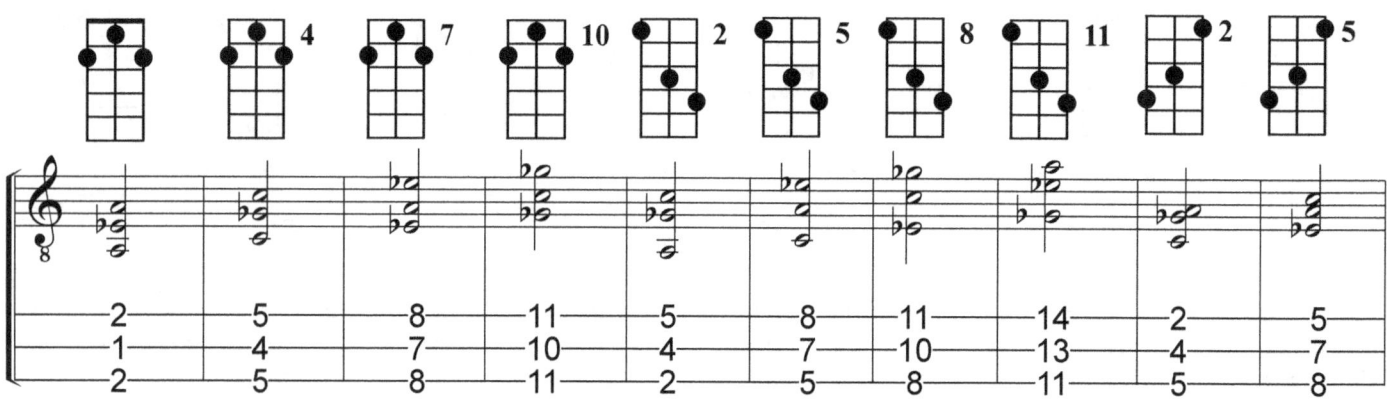

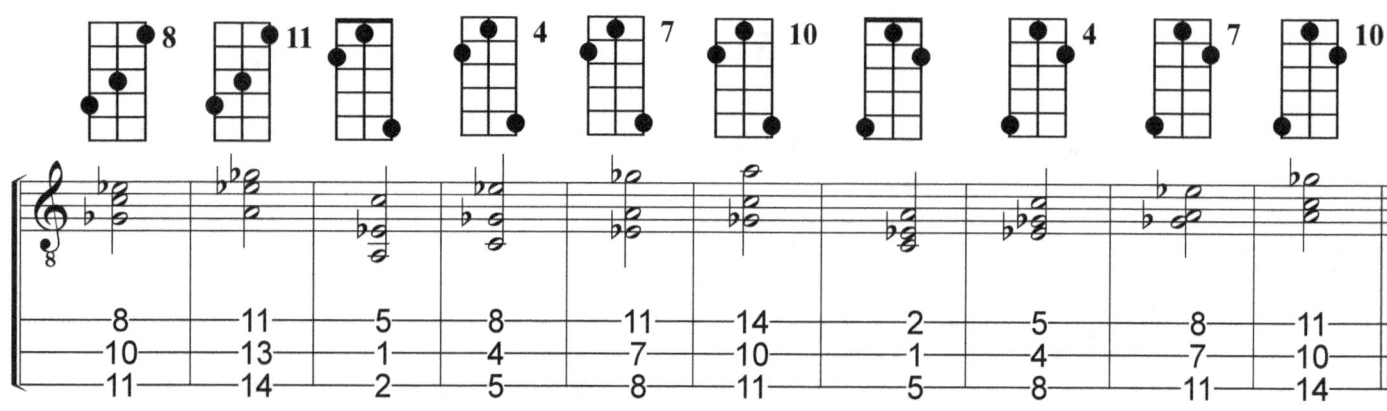

Csus4 - Csus2 - C7sus - Cadd9 - C5

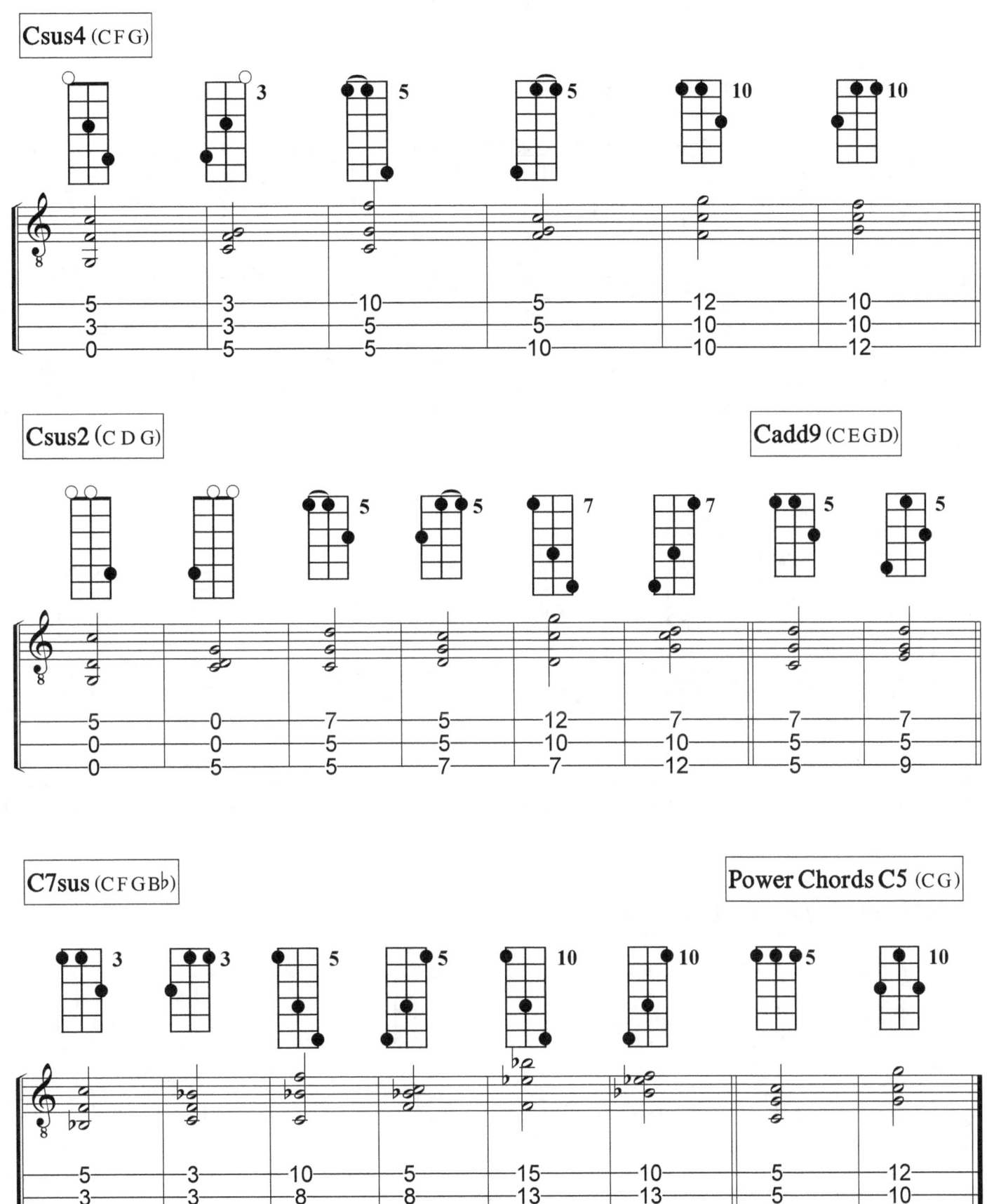

C# - C#6 - C#maj7 / D♭ - D♭6 - D♭maj7

Some notes have been omitted from the chords to facilitate playability.
C# and D♭ are the same note. C# notes are showing in notation.

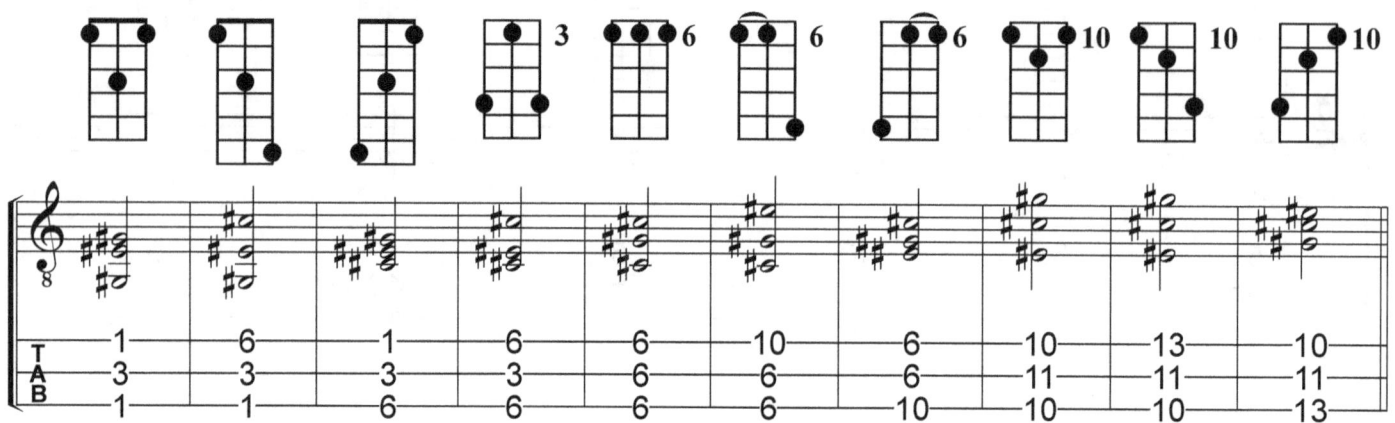

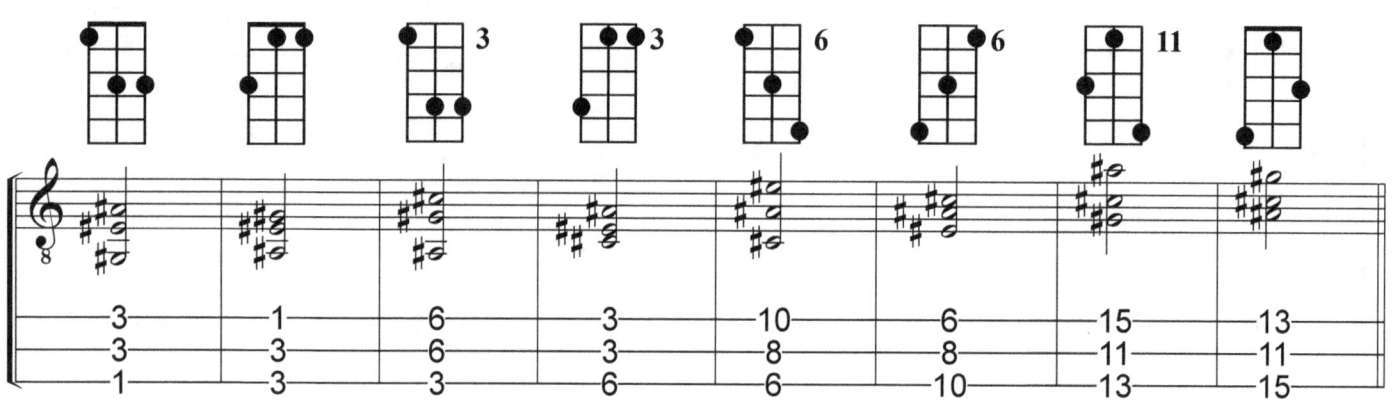

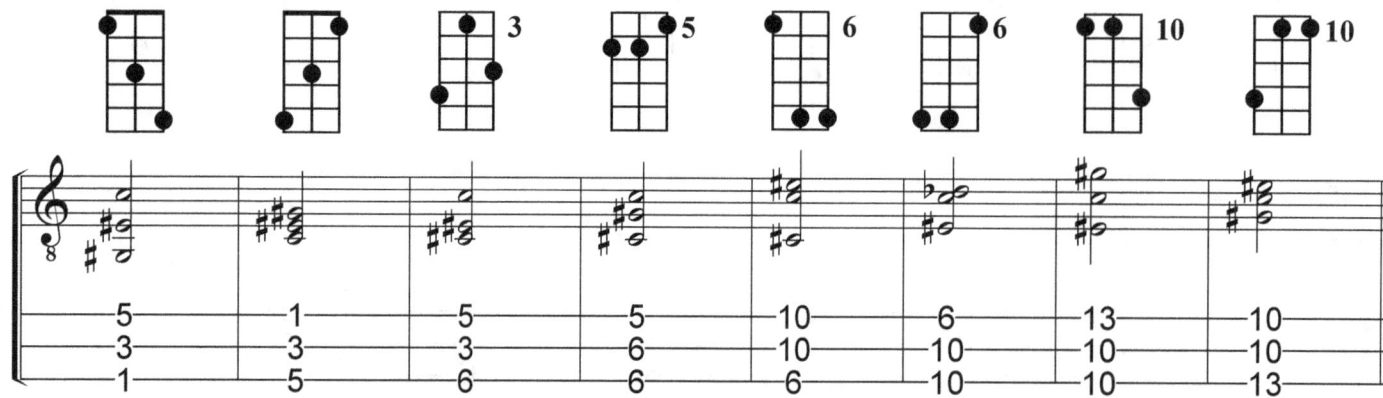

C♯maj9 - C♯6/9 - C♯+ / D♭maj9 - D♭6/9 - D♭+

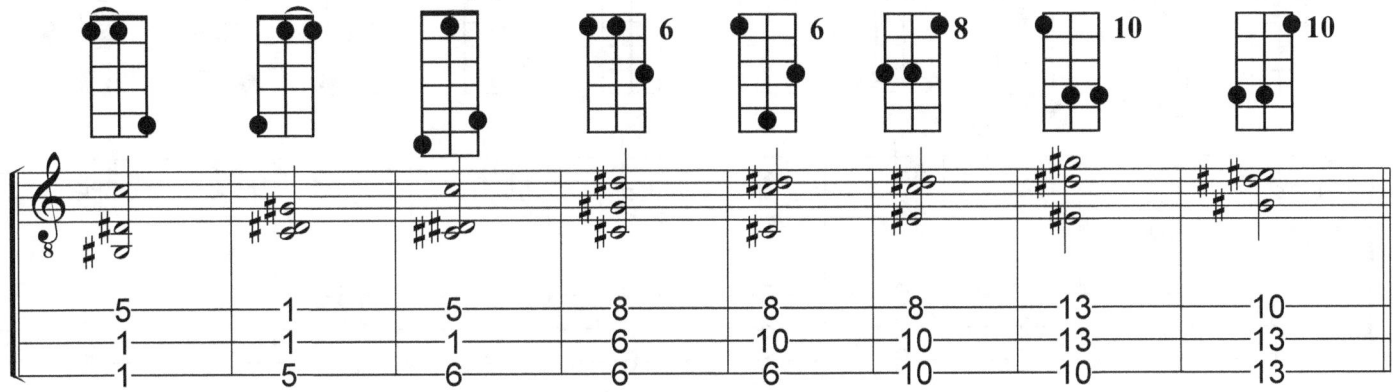

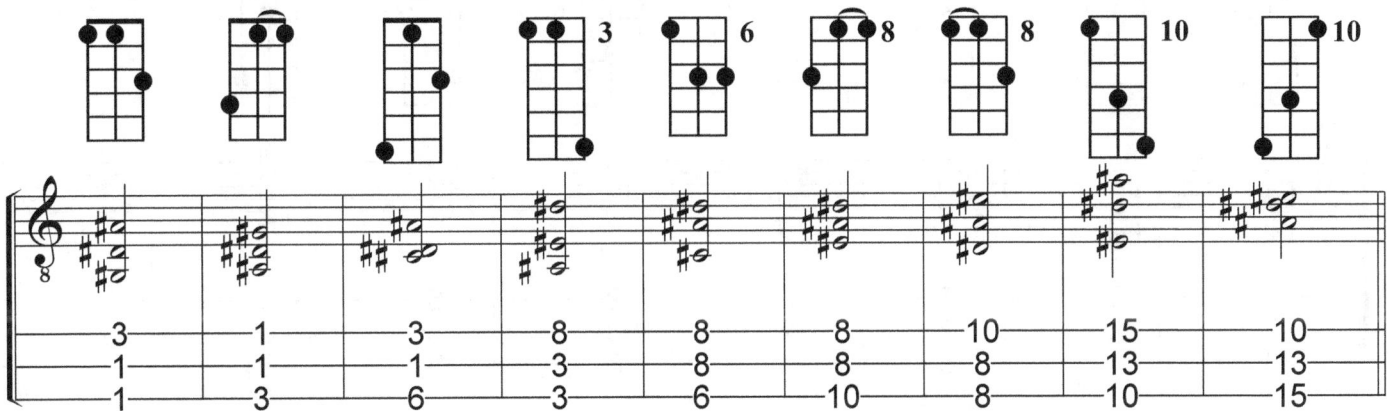

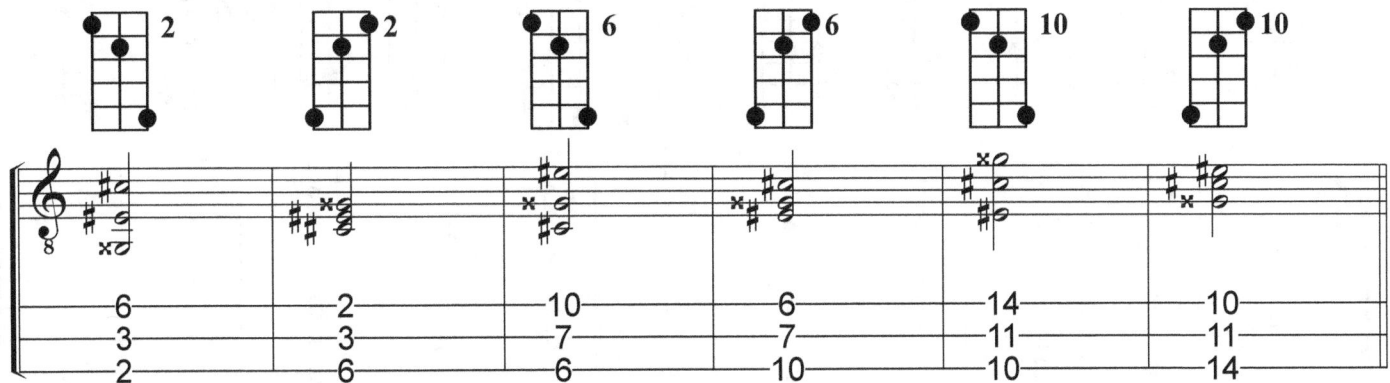

C#m-C#m6-C#m(maj7)-C#m7 / D♭m-D♭m6-D♭m(maj7)-D♭m7

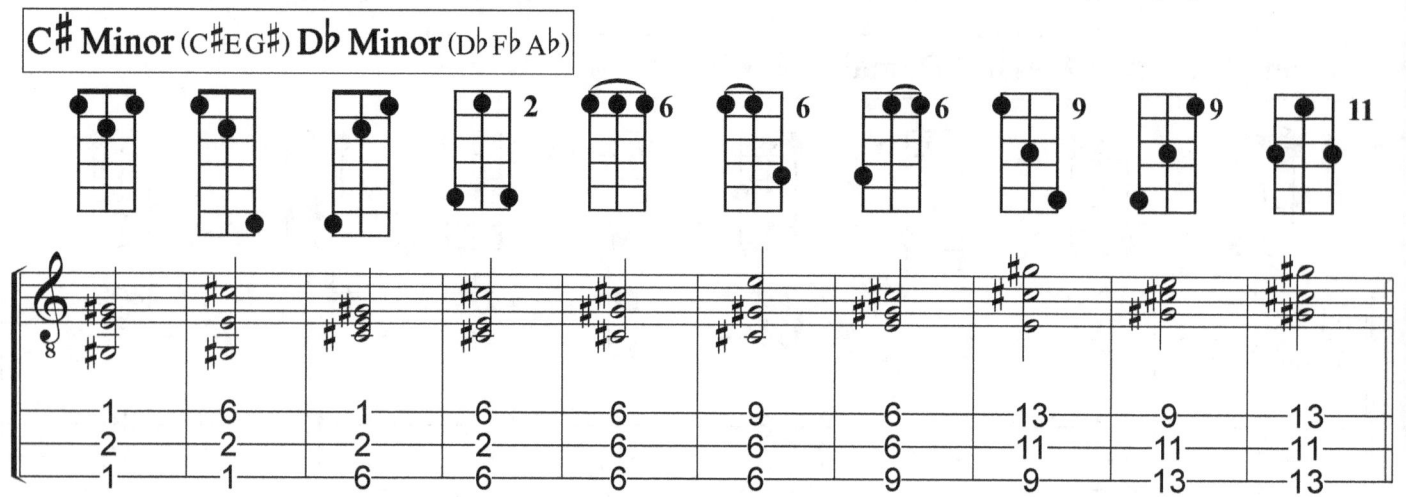

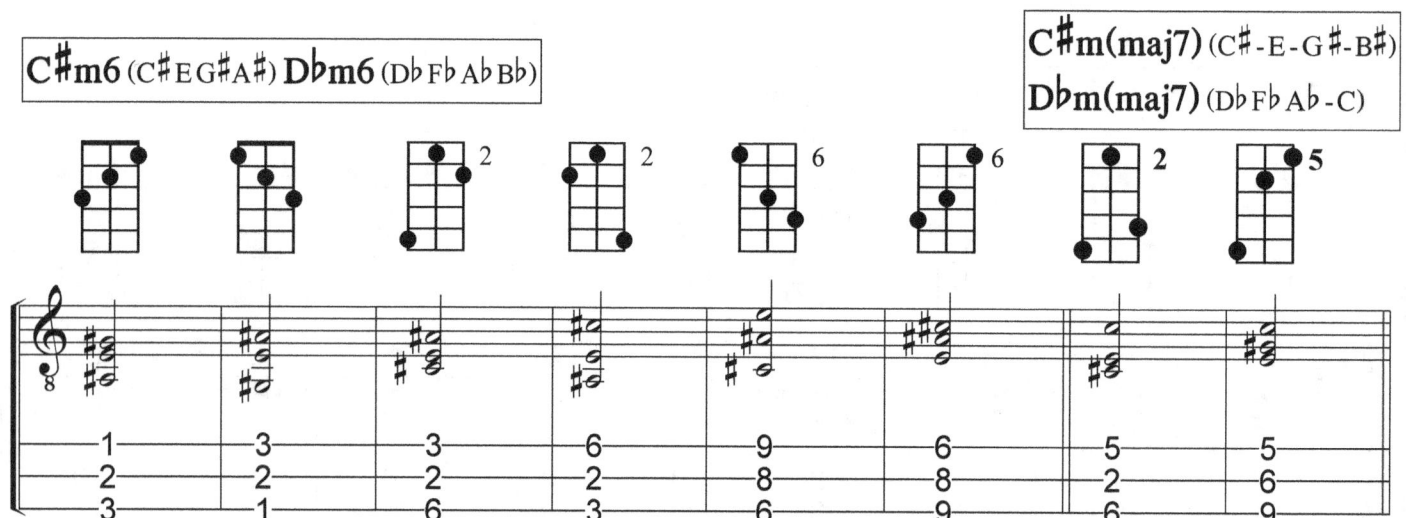

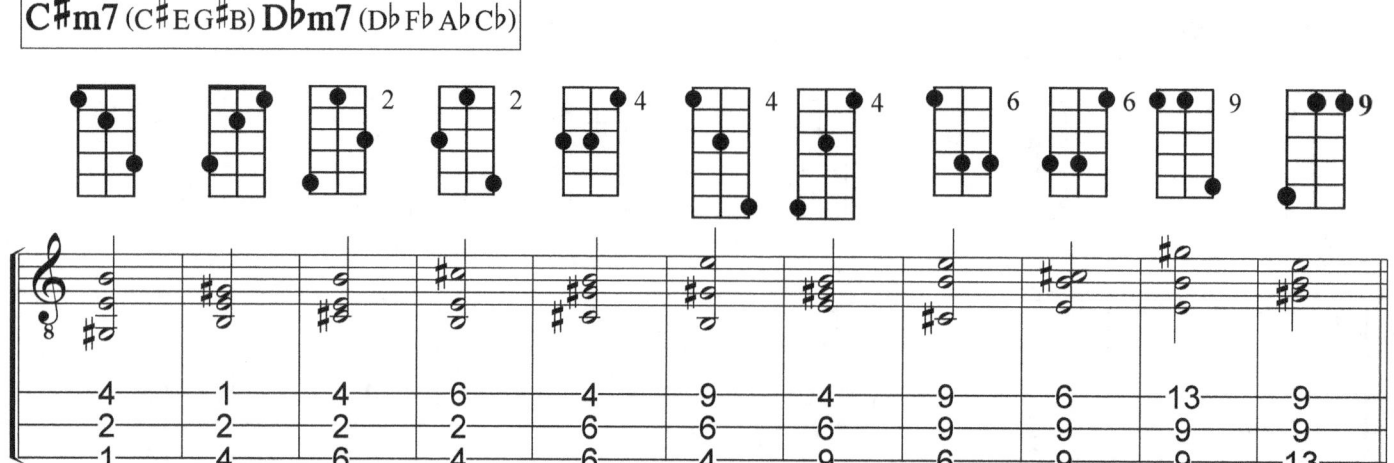

C#m7b5 - C#m9 - C#m11 / Dbm7b5 - Dbm9 - Dbm11

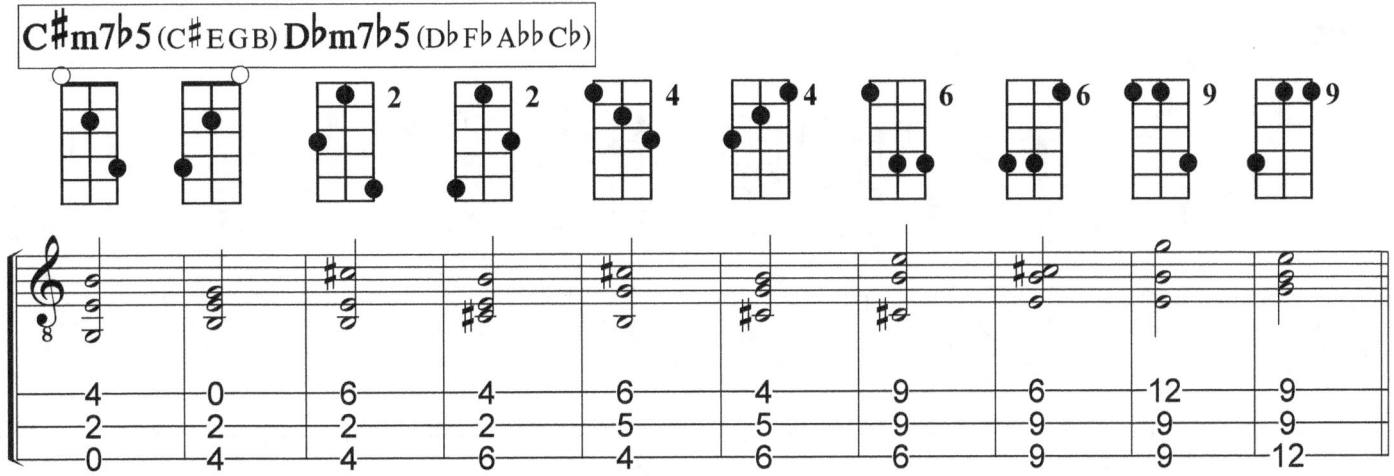

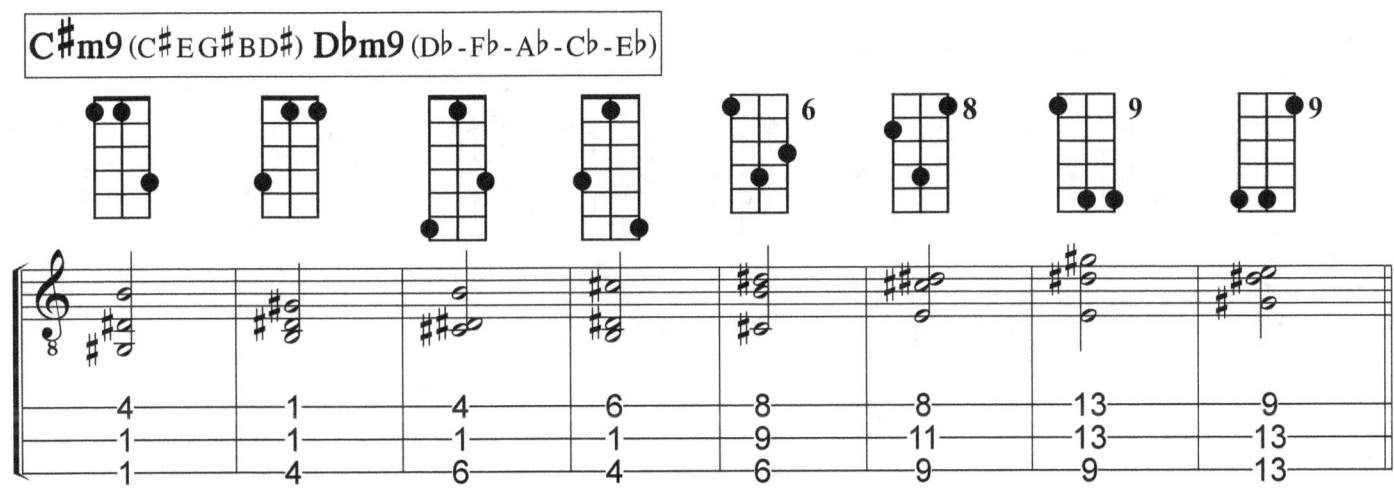

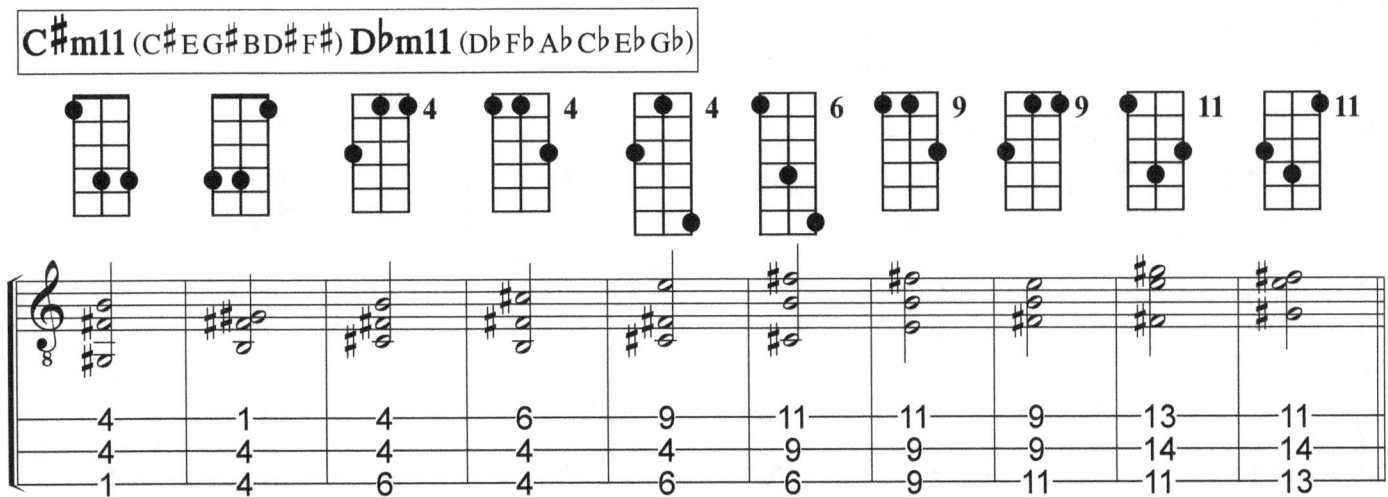

C#7 - C#9 - C#13 / Db7 - Db9 - Db13

C#7 (C# E# G# B) **Db7** (Db F Ab Cb)

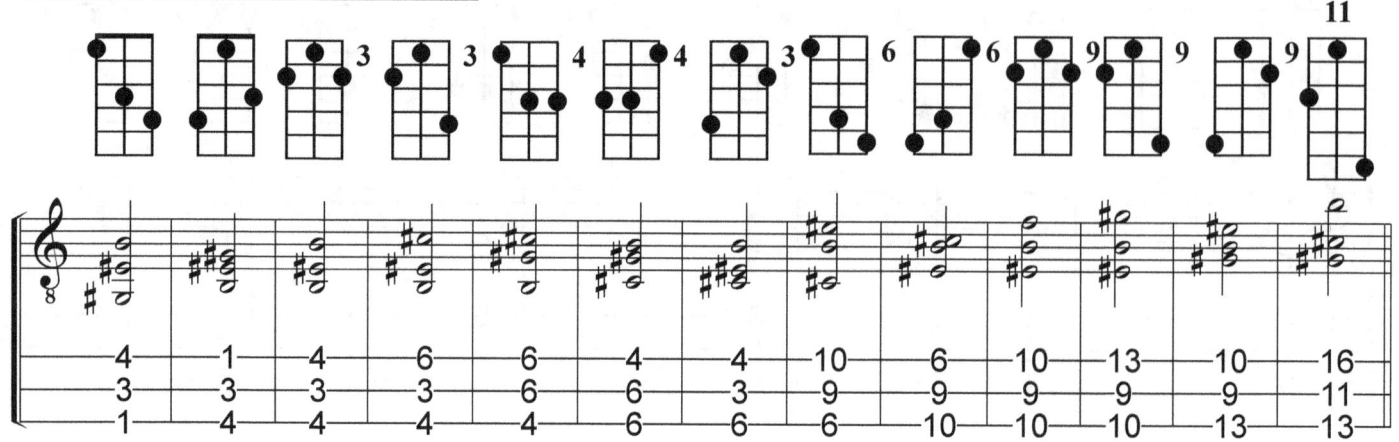

C#9 (C# E# G# B D#) **Db9** (Db F Ab Cb Eb)

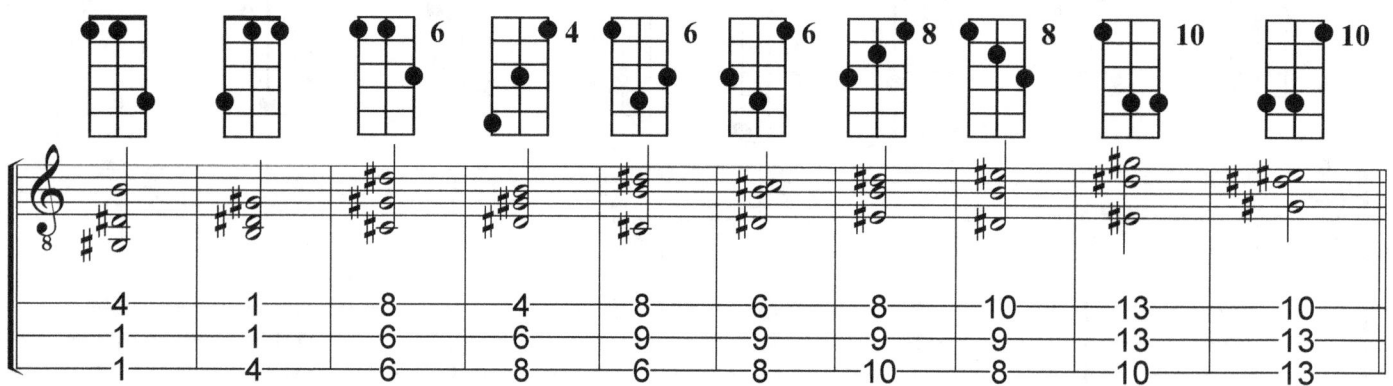

C#13 (C# E# G# B D# F# A#) **Db13** (Db F Ab Cb Eb Gb Bb)

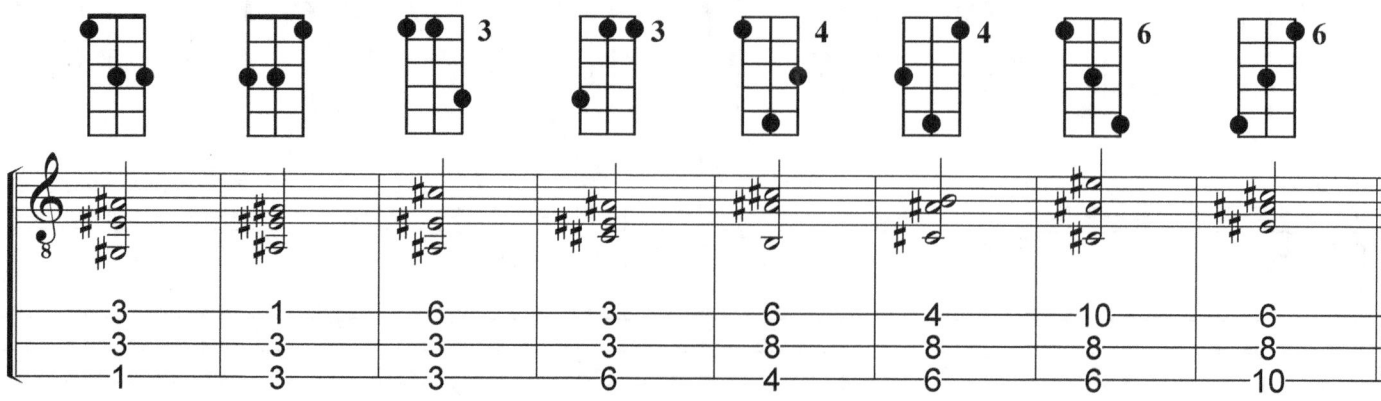

C#7b5 - C#7#5 - C#7#9 / Db7b5 - Db7#5 - Db7#9

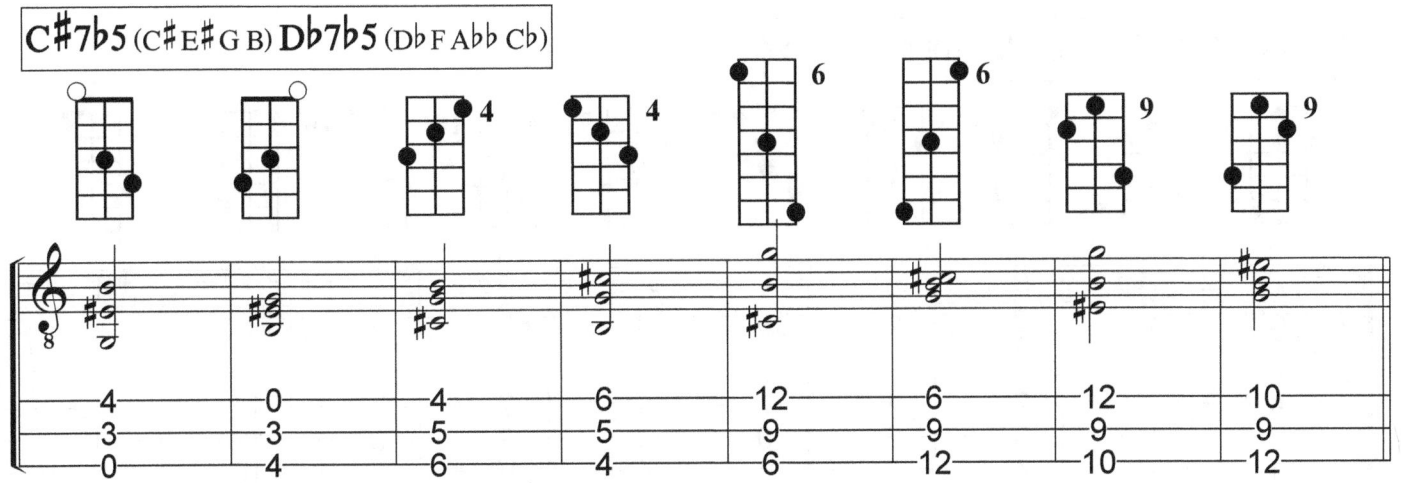

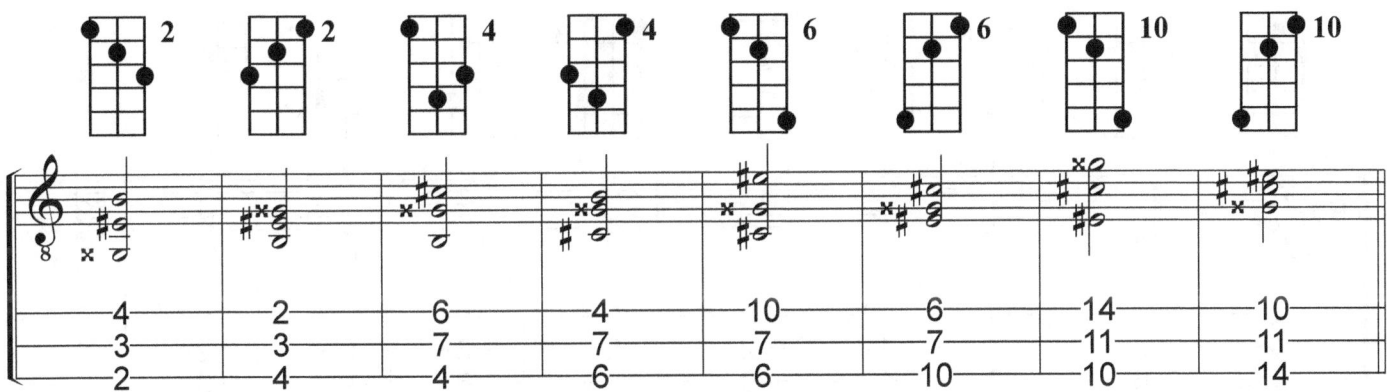

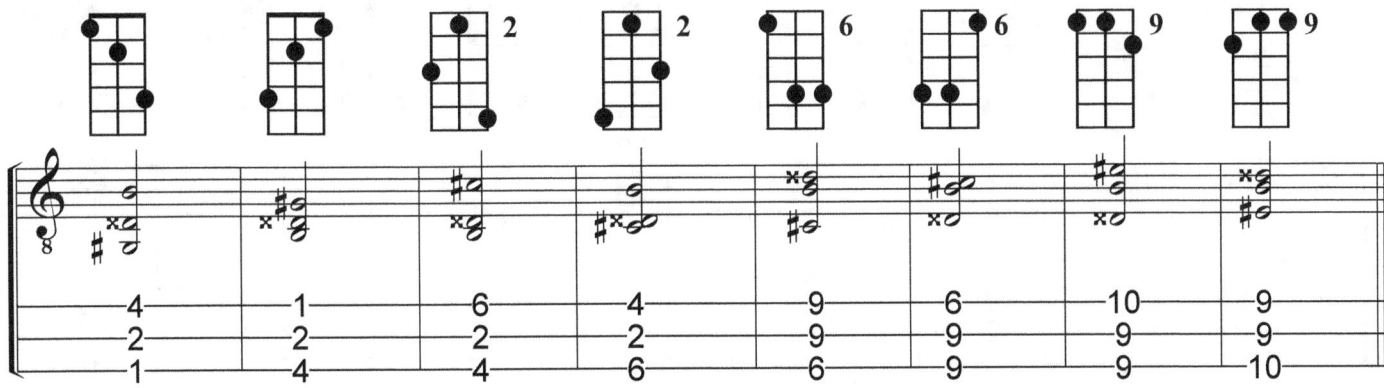

C#7♭9 - C#diminished - C#°7 / D♭7♭9 - D♭ diminished - D♭°7

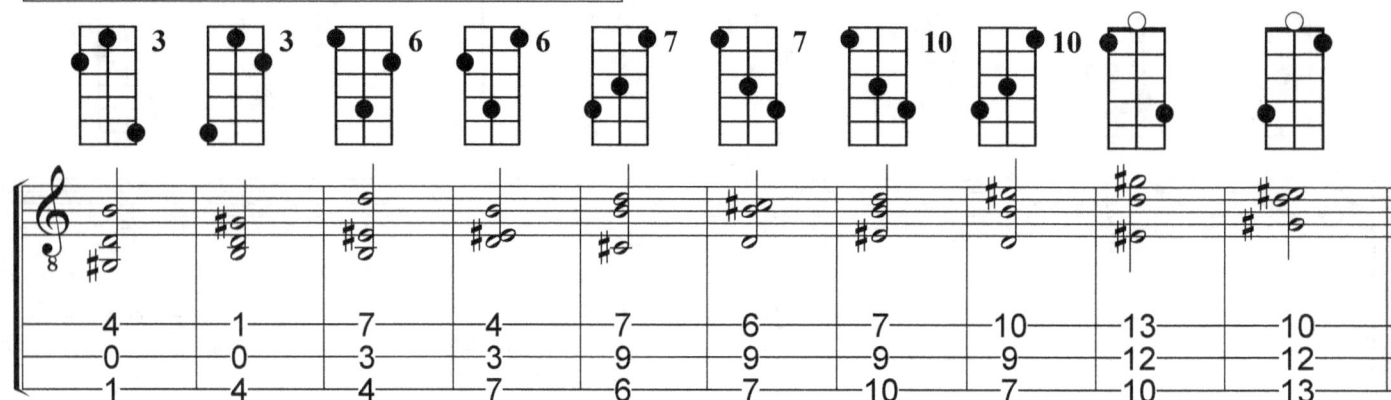

C#7♭9 (C# E# G# B D) D♭7♭9 (D♭ F A♭ C♭ E♭♭)

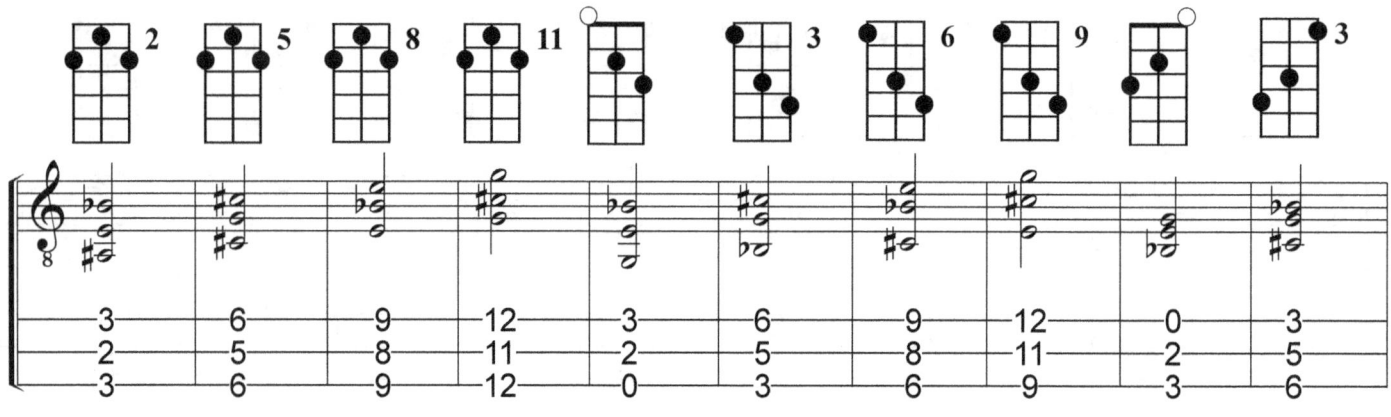

C# diminished - C#°7 (C# E G B♭) D♭ diminished - D♭°7 (D♭ F♭ A♭♭ C♭♭)

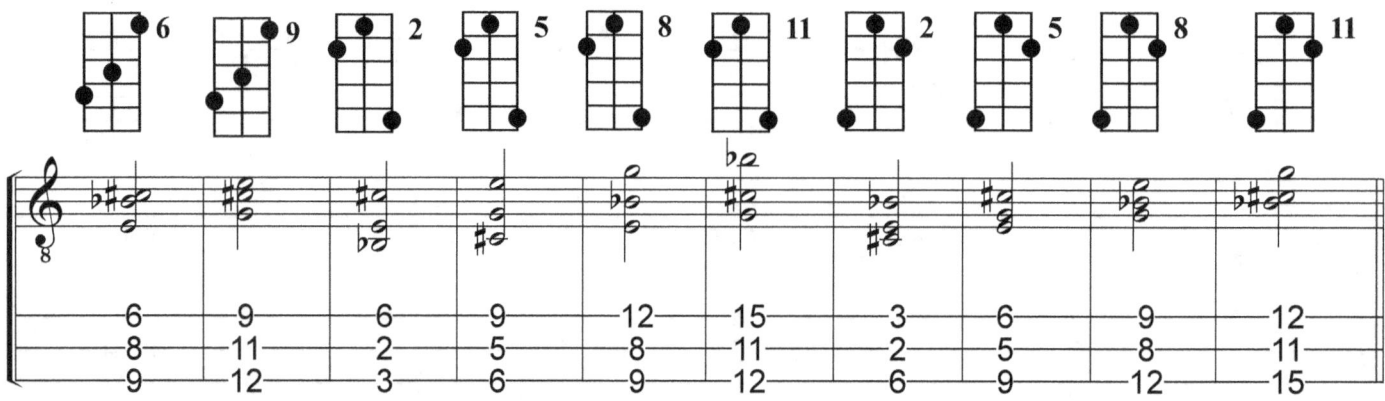

C#sus4 - C#sus2 - C#7sus - C#add9 - C#5 /
Dbsus4 - Dbsus2 - Db7sus - Dbadd9 - Db5

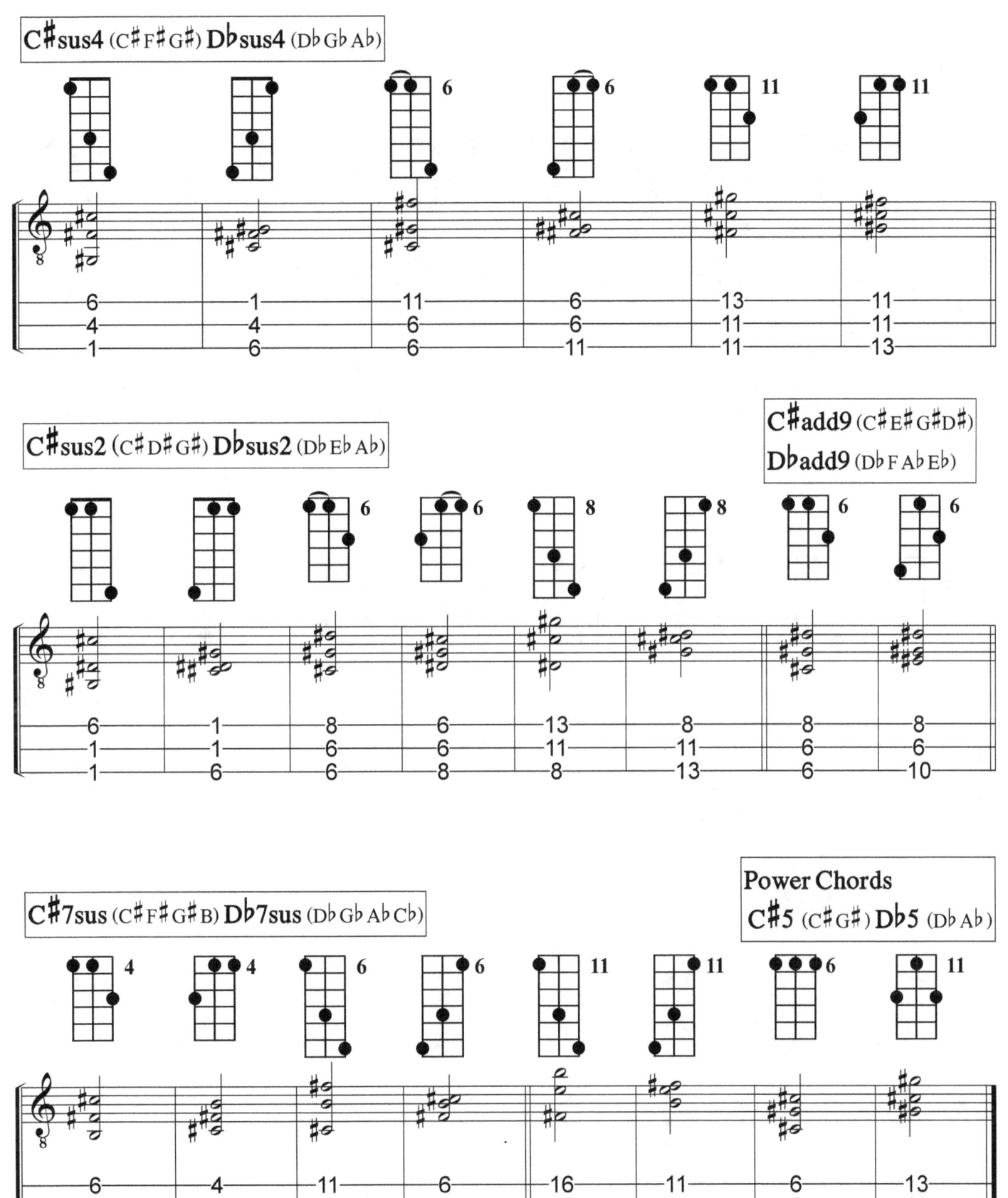

D - D6 - Dmaj7

Some notes have been omitted from the chords to facilitate playability.
Notes in the chord are in brackets.

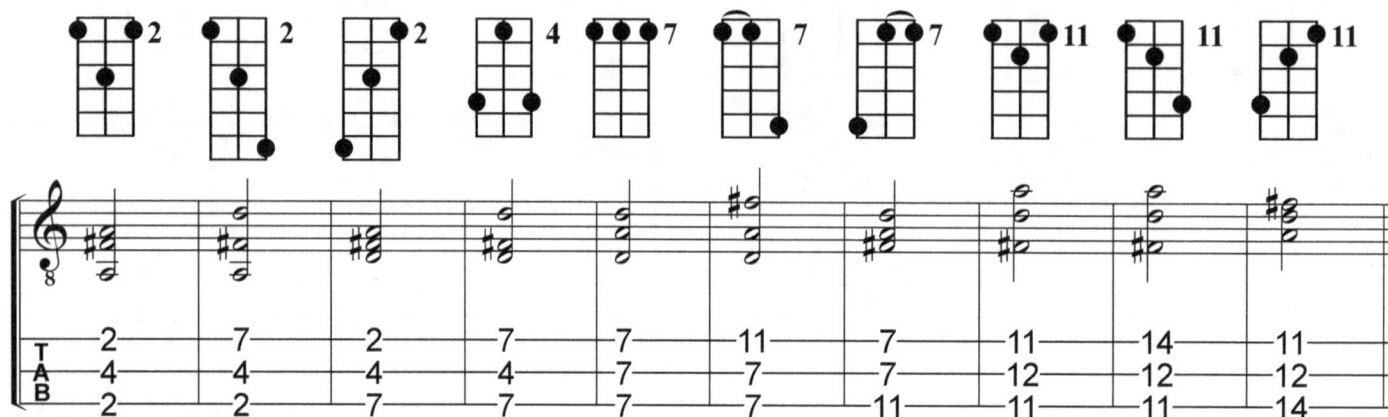

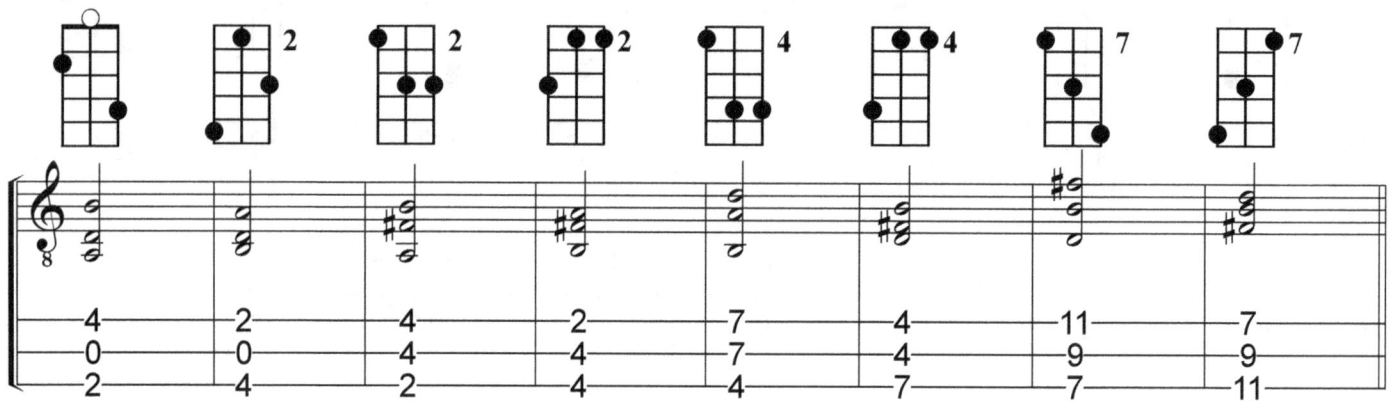

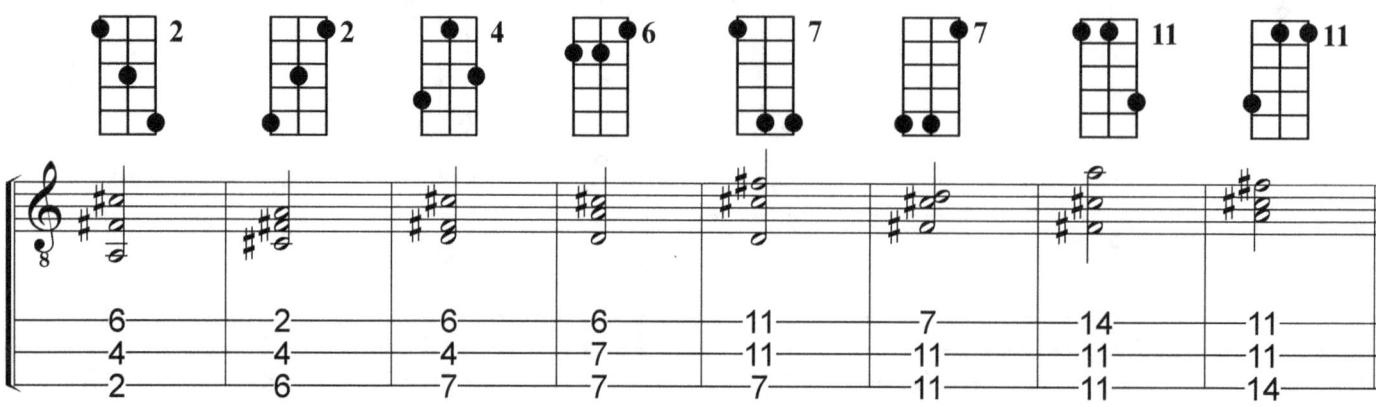

Dmaj9 - D6/9 - D+

Dmaj9 (D F# A C# E)

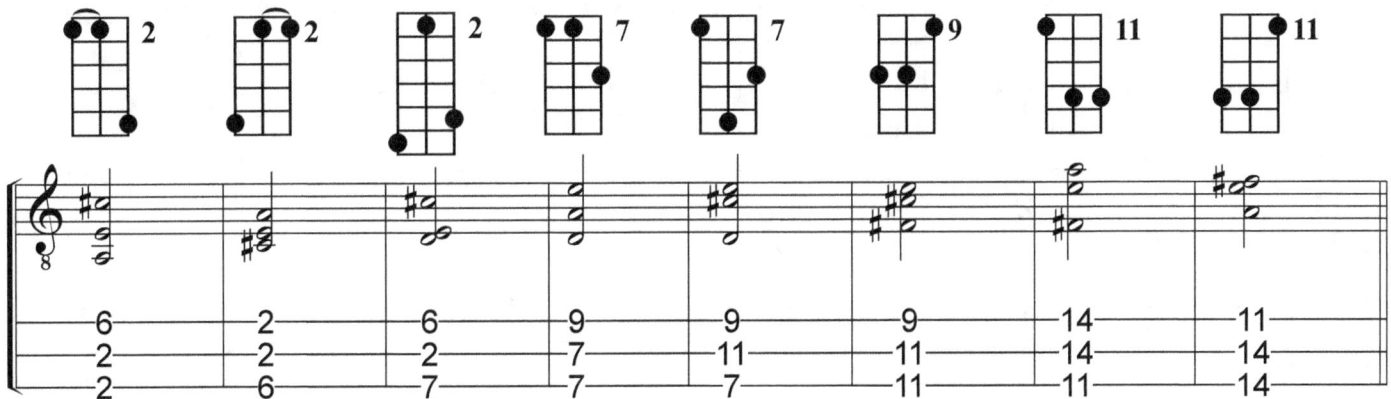

D6/9 (D F# A B E)

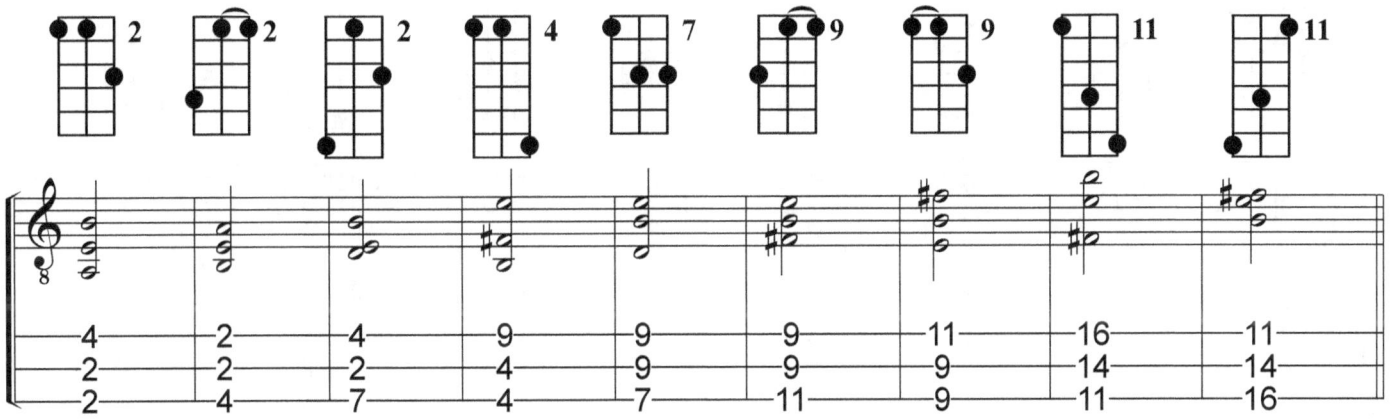

D Augmented - D+ (D F# A#)

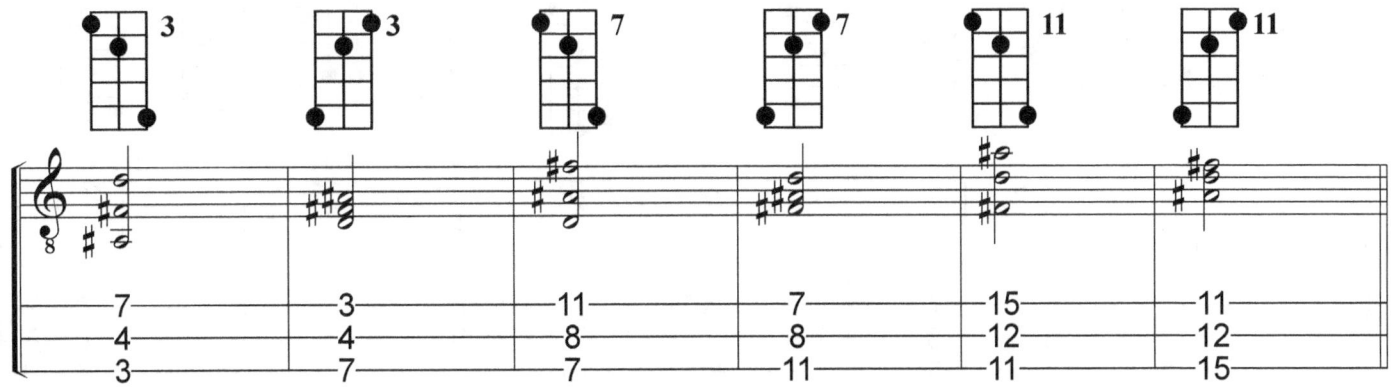

Dm - Dm6 - Dm(maj7) - Dm7

D Minor (D F A)

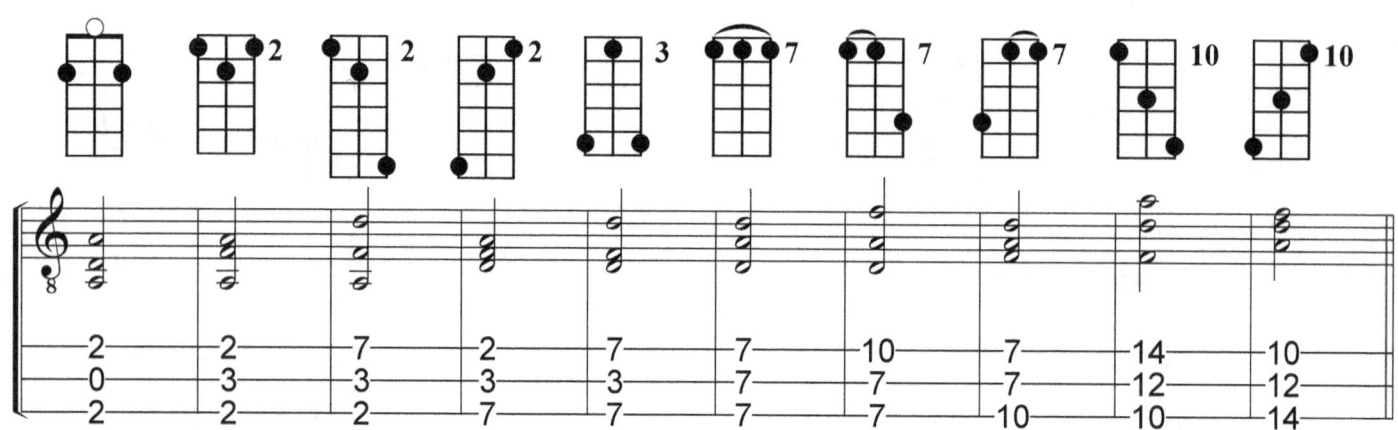

Dm6 (D F A B)   **Dm(maj7)** (D F A C#)

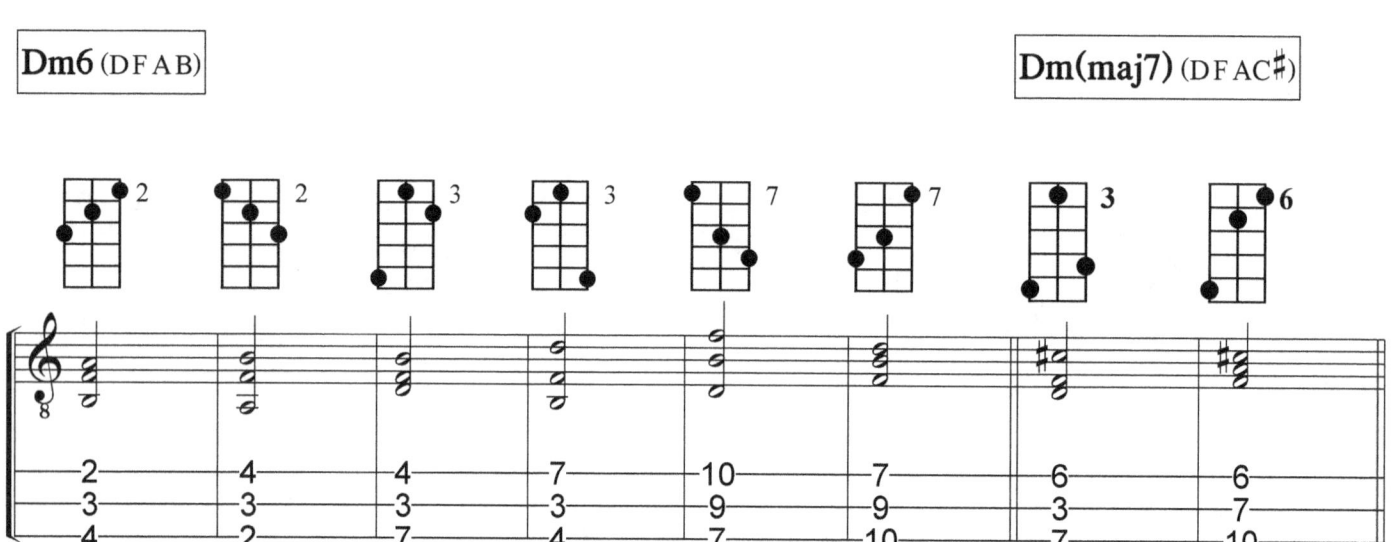

Dm7 (D F A C)

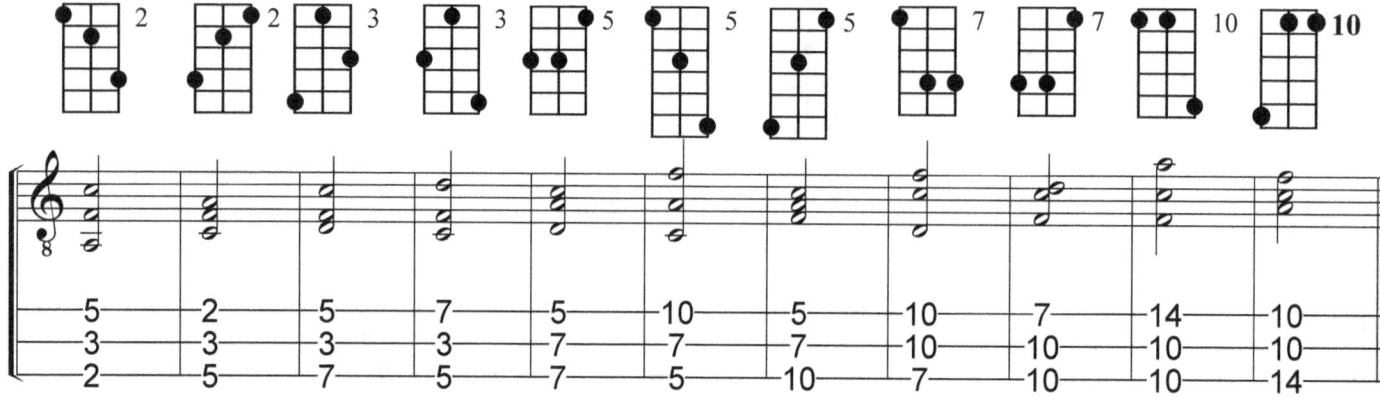

Dm7♭5 - Dm9 - Dm11

Dm7♭5 (D F A♭ C)

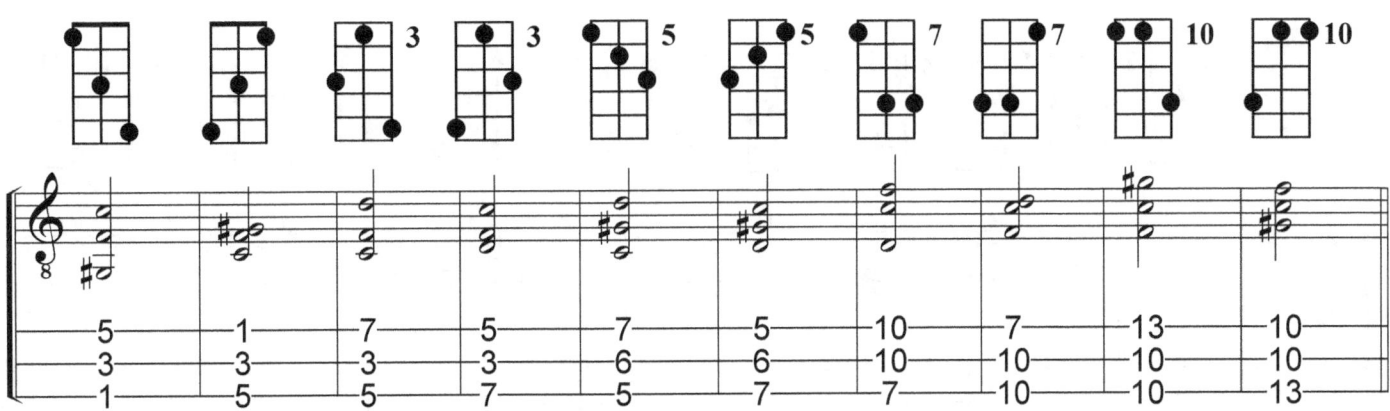

Dm9 (D F A C E)

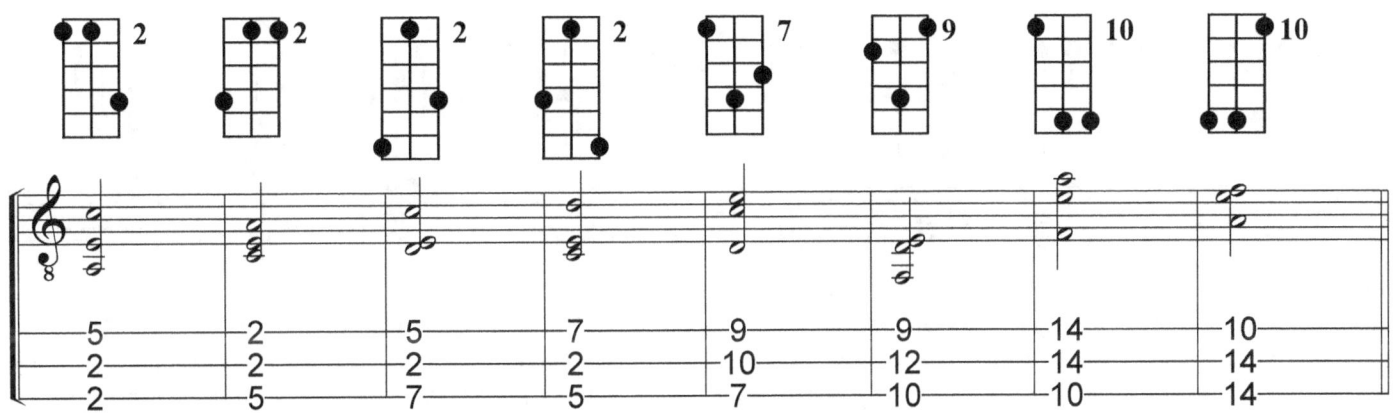

Dm11 (D F A C E G)

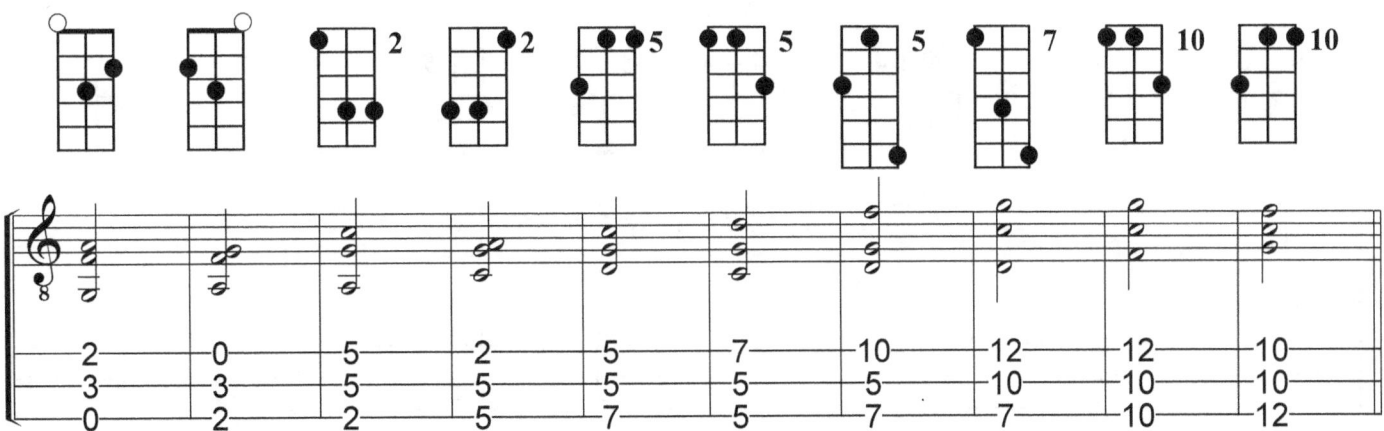

D7 - D9 - D13

D7 (D F# A C)

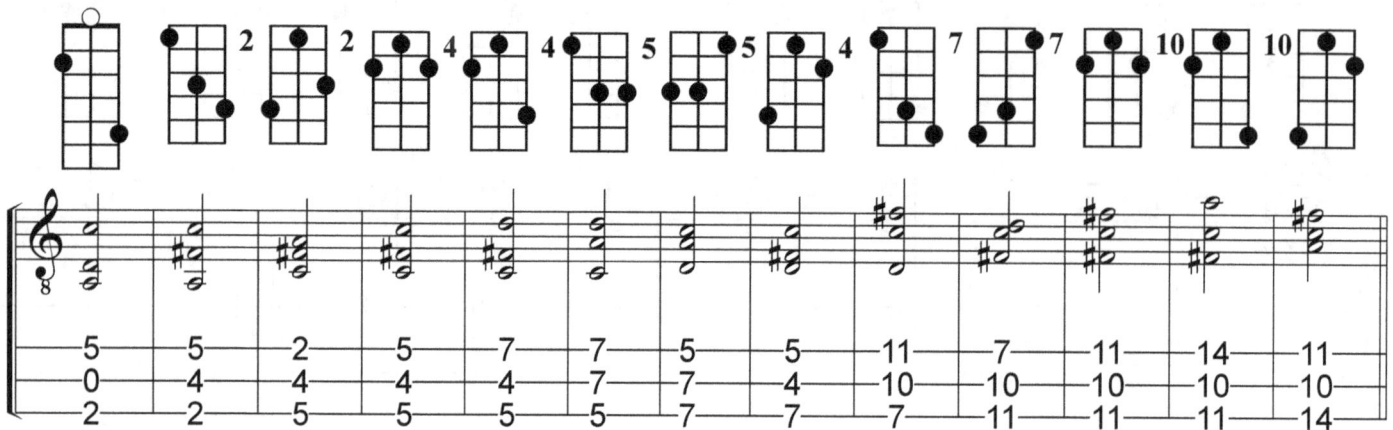

D9 (D F# A C E)

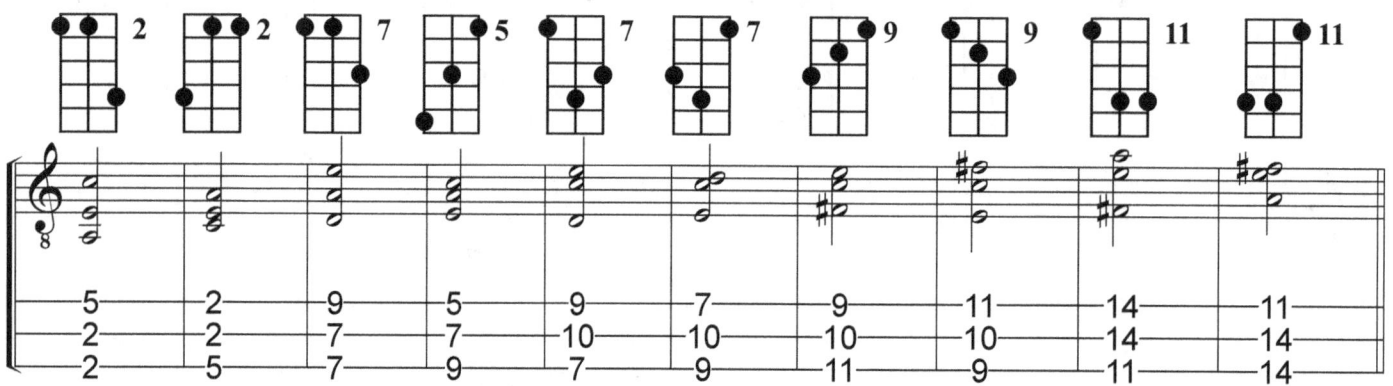

D13 (D F# A C E G B)

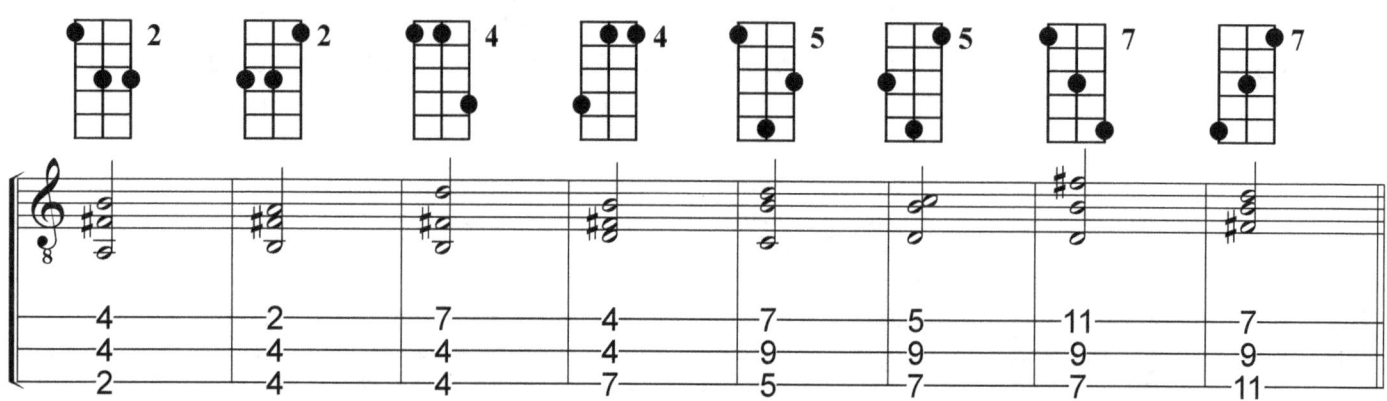

D7♭5 - D7♯5 - D7♯9

D7♭5 (D F♯ A♭ C)

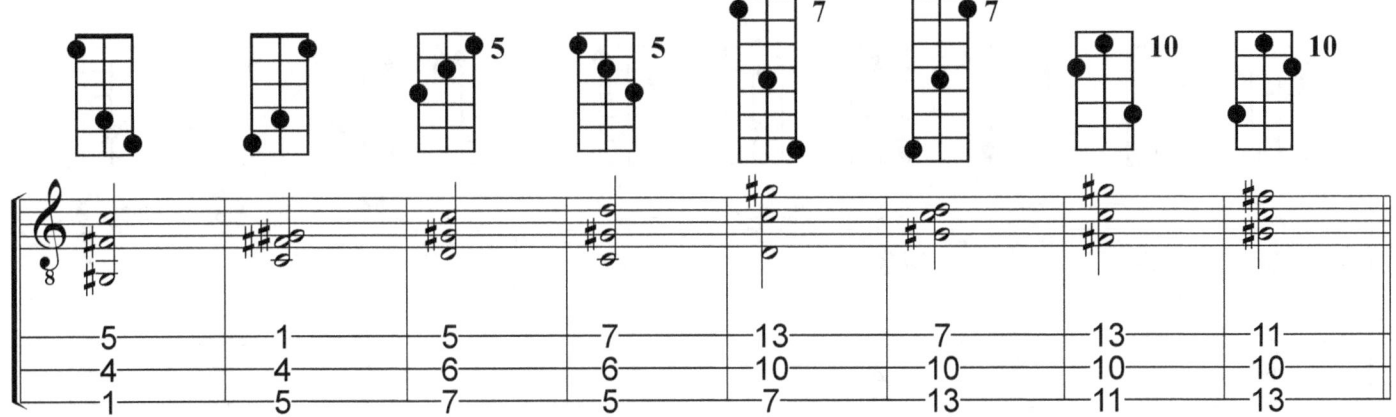

D7♯5 (D F♯ A♯ C)

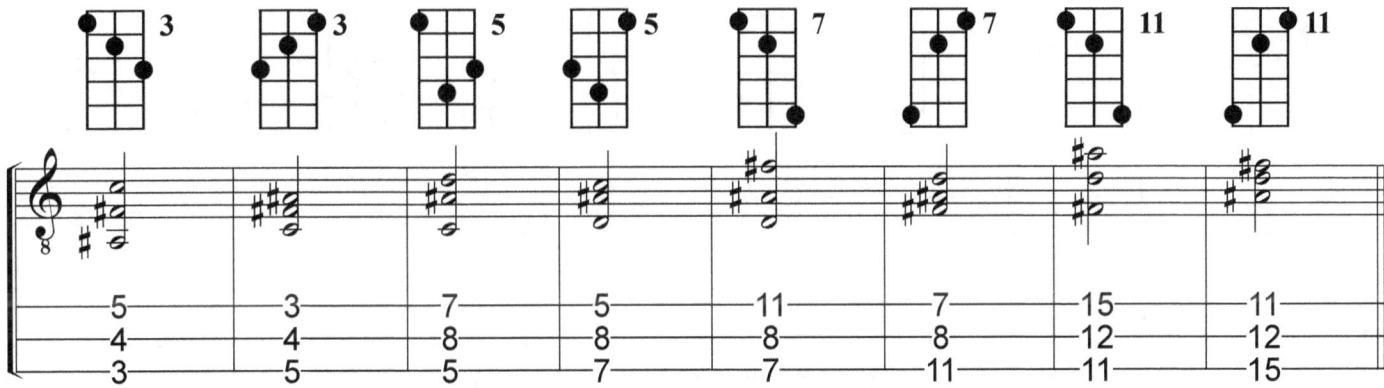

D7♯9 (D F♯ A C E♯)

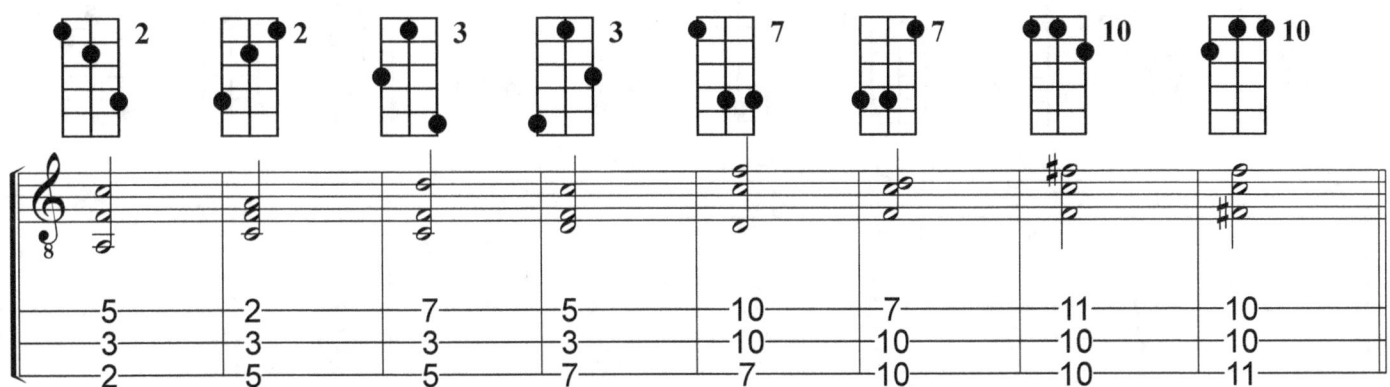

D7♭9 - D diminished - D°7

D7♭9 (D F# A C E♭)

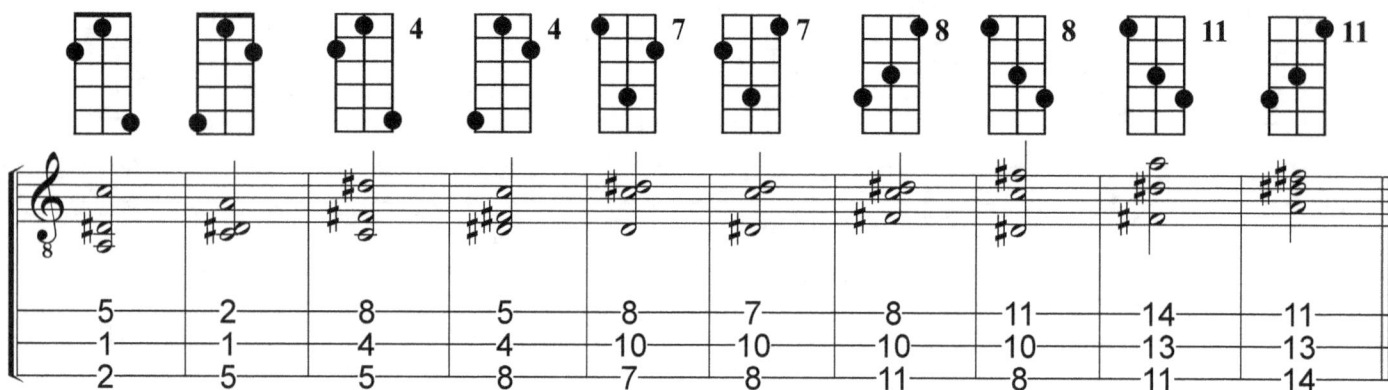

D diminished (D F A♭) **D°7** (D F A♭ C♭)

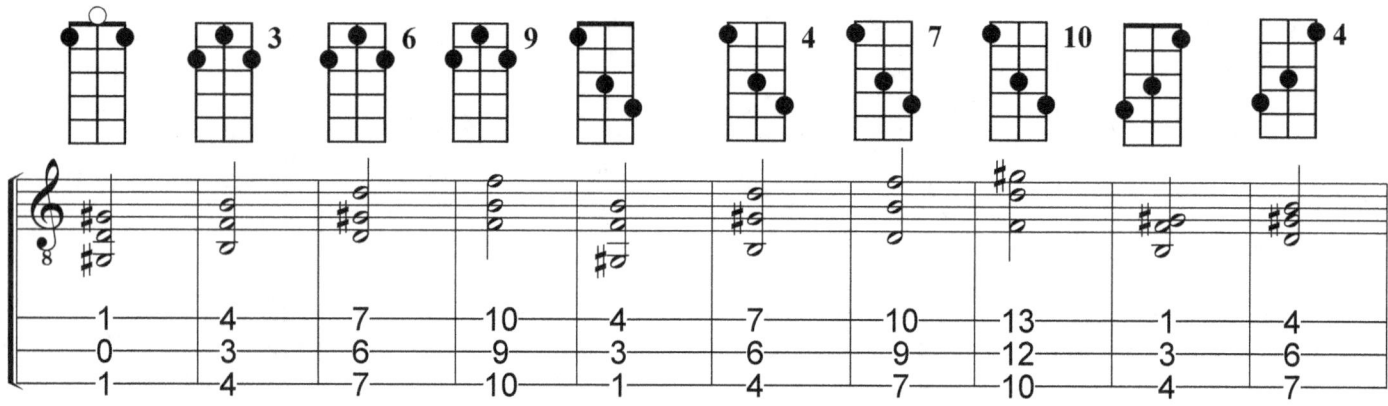

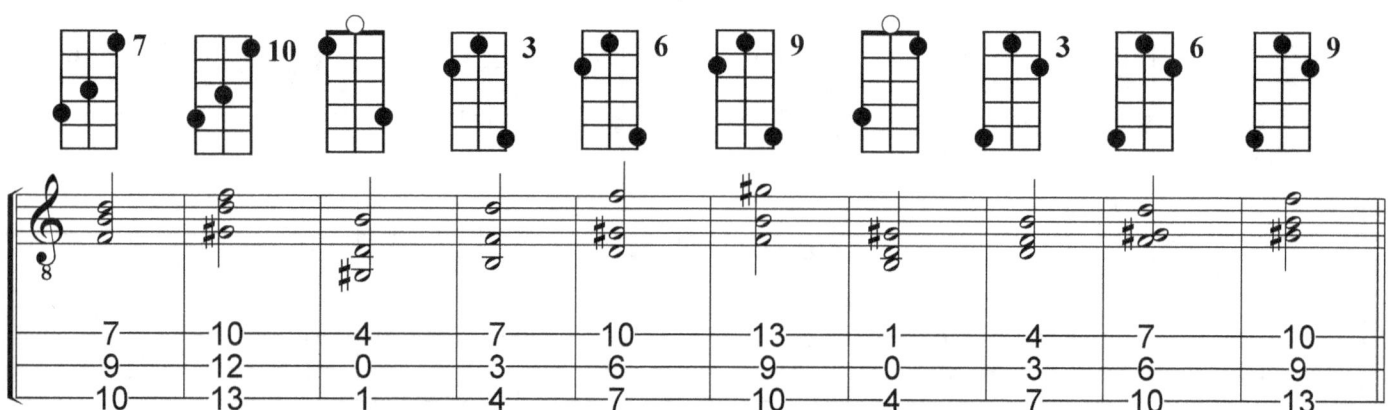

Dsus4 - Dsus2 - Dadd9 - D7sus - Power Chords D5

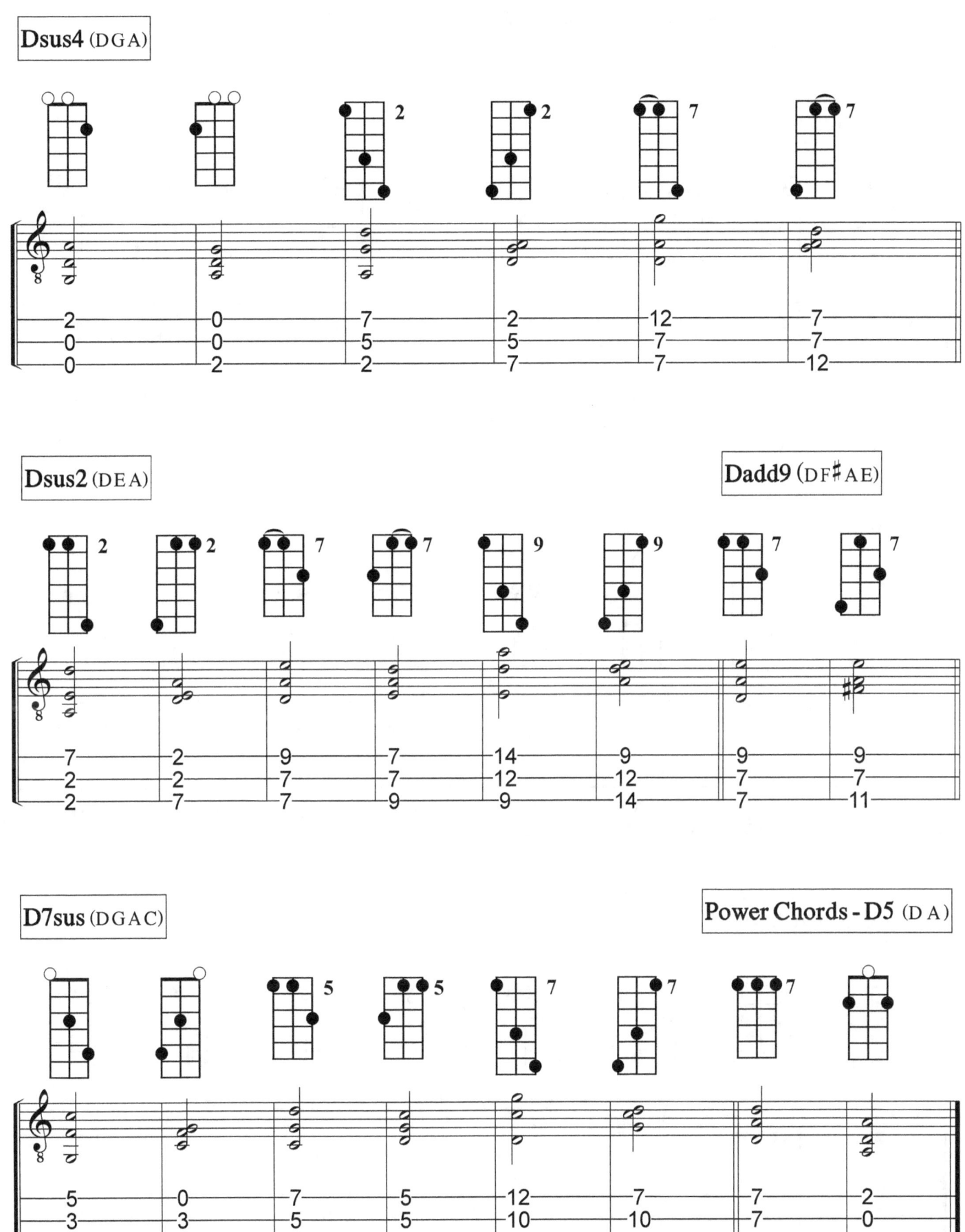

E♭ - E♭6 - E♭maj7

Some notes have been omitted from the chords to facilitate playability.
Notes in the chord are in brackets.

E♭ Major (E♭ G B♭)

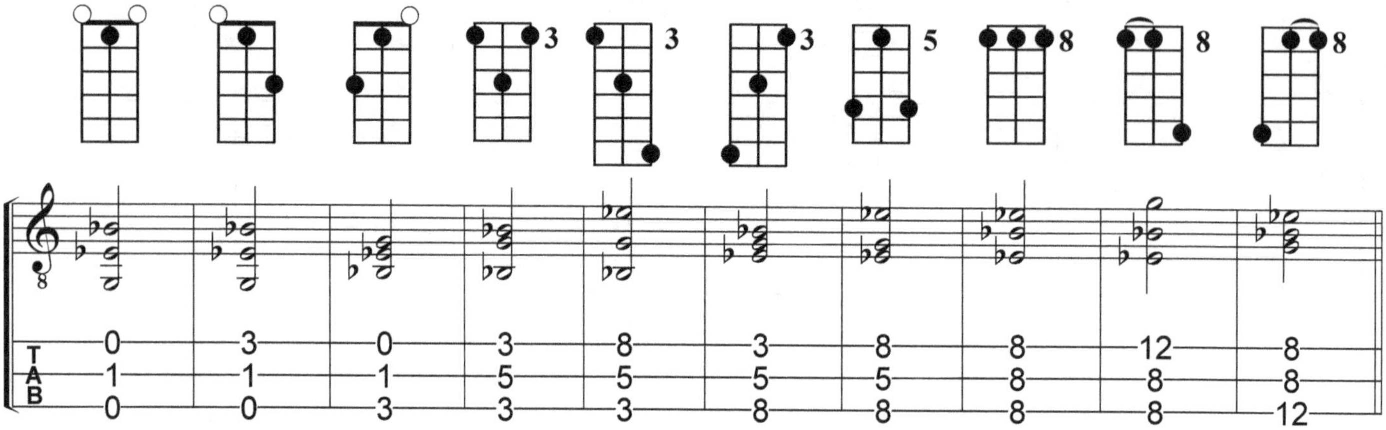

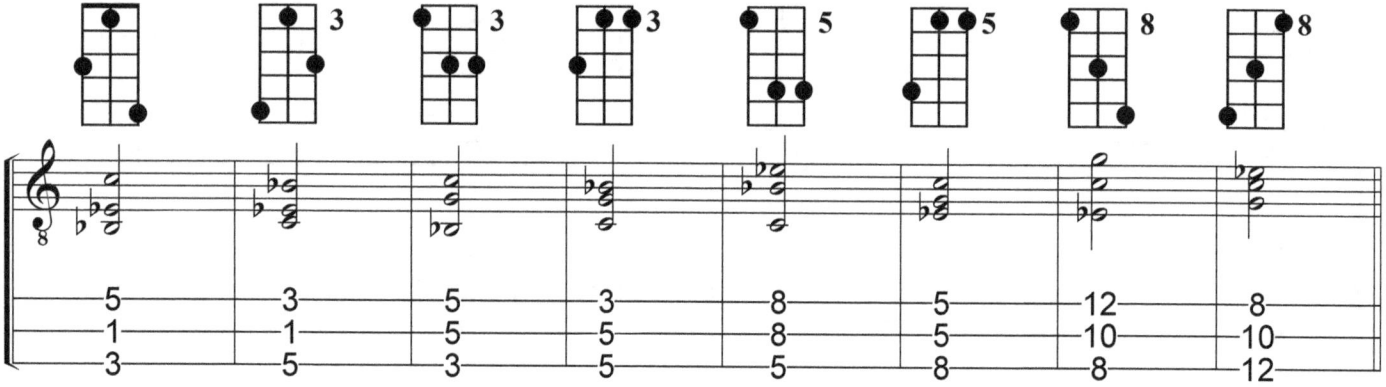

E♭6 (E♭ G B♭ C)

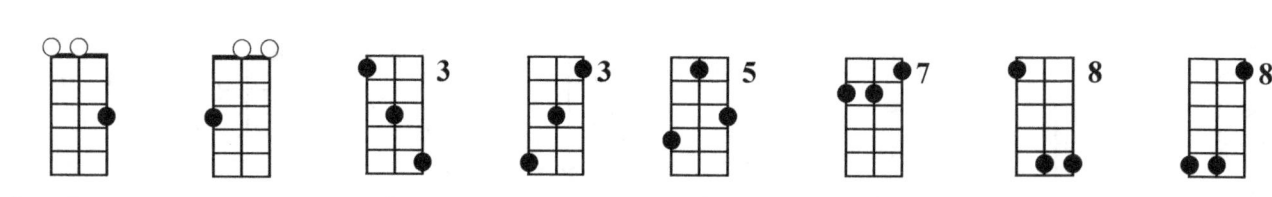

E♭maj7 (E♭ G B♭ D)

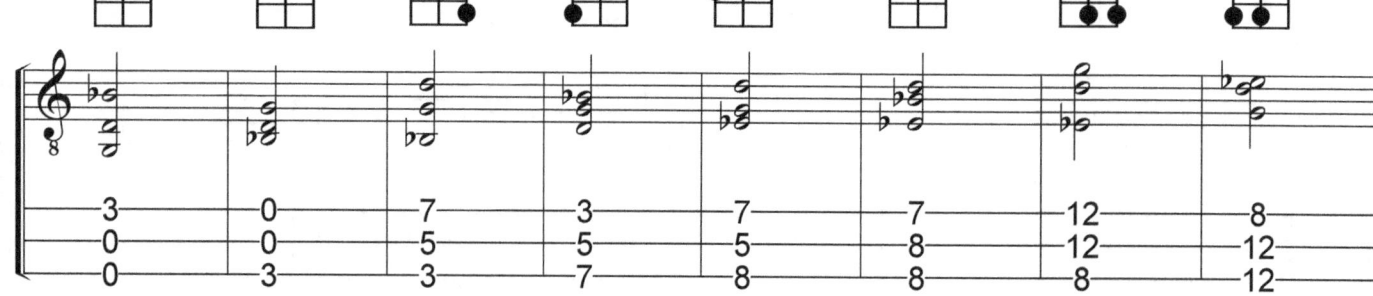

E♭maj9 - E♭6/9 - E♭+

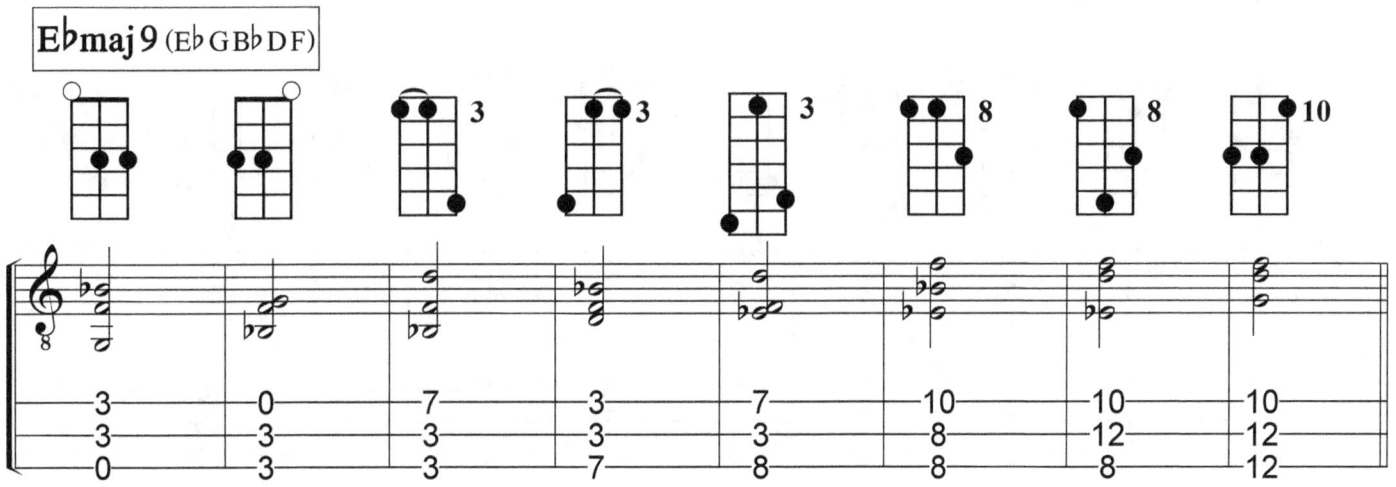

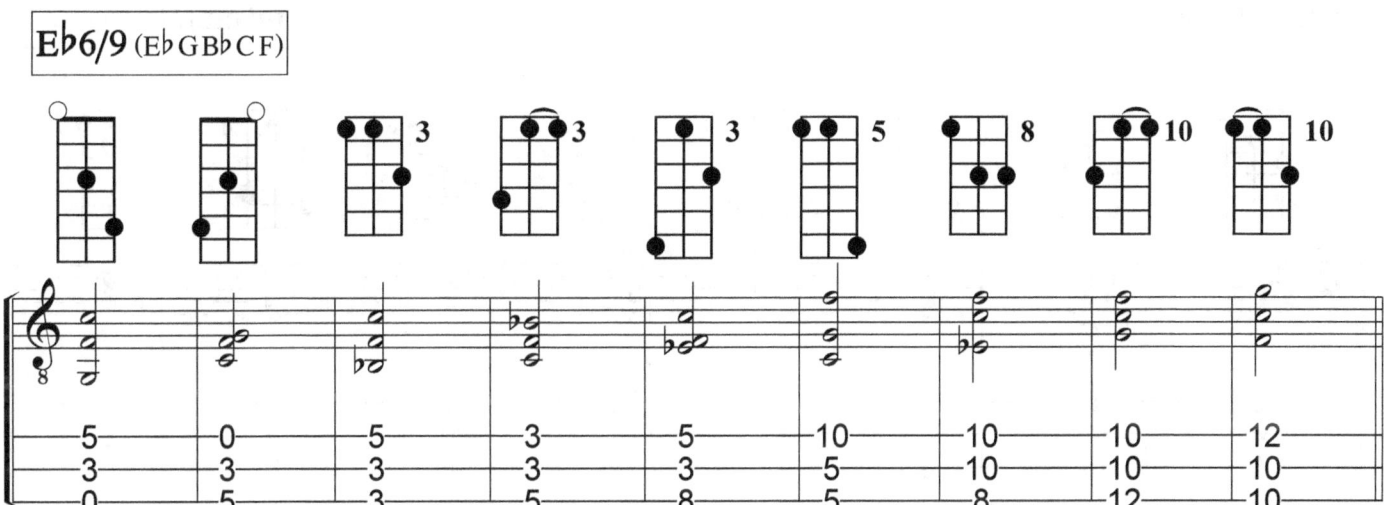

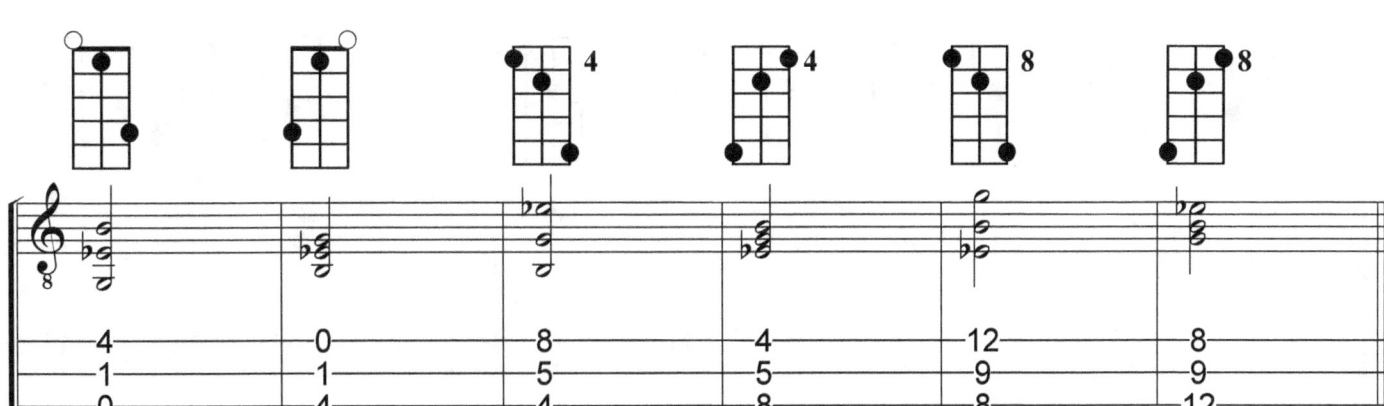

E♭m - E♭m6 - E♭m(maj7) - E♭m7

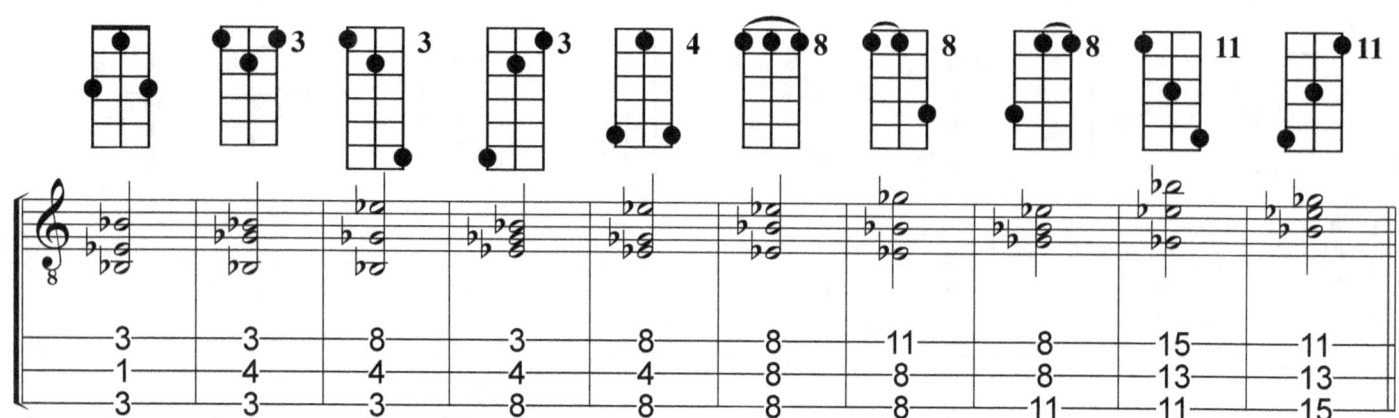

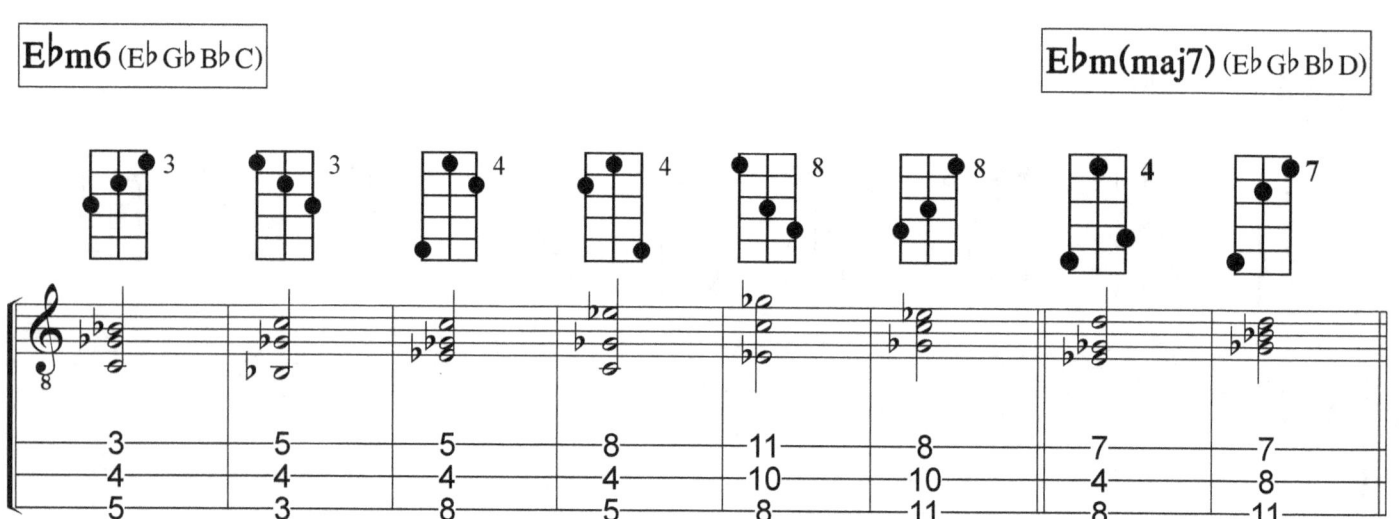

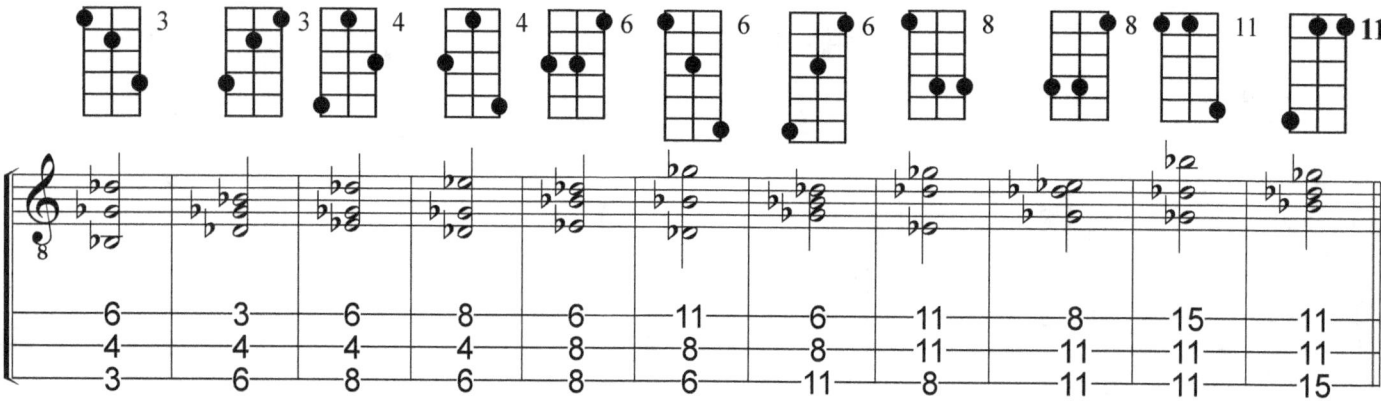

Ebm7b5 - Ebm9 - Ebm11

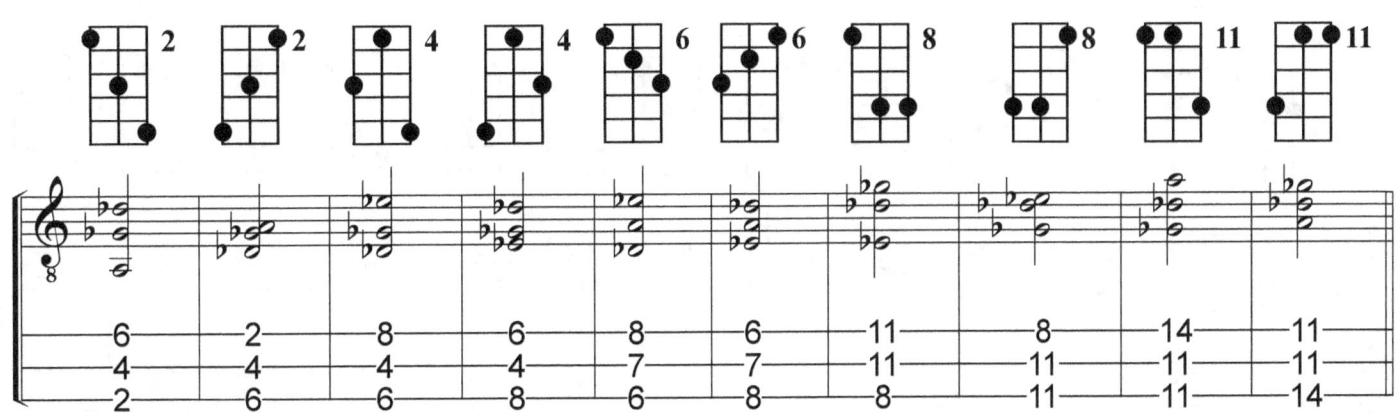

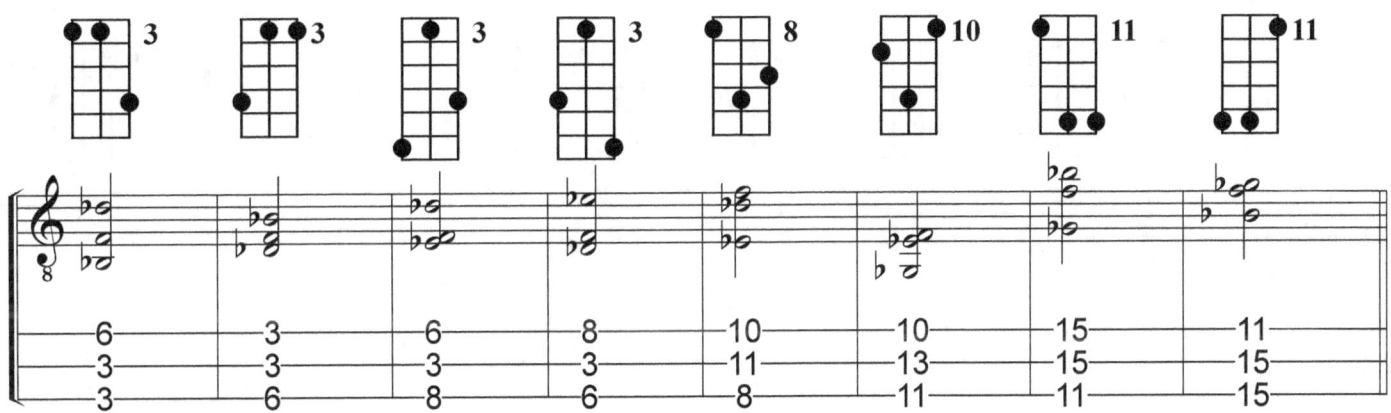

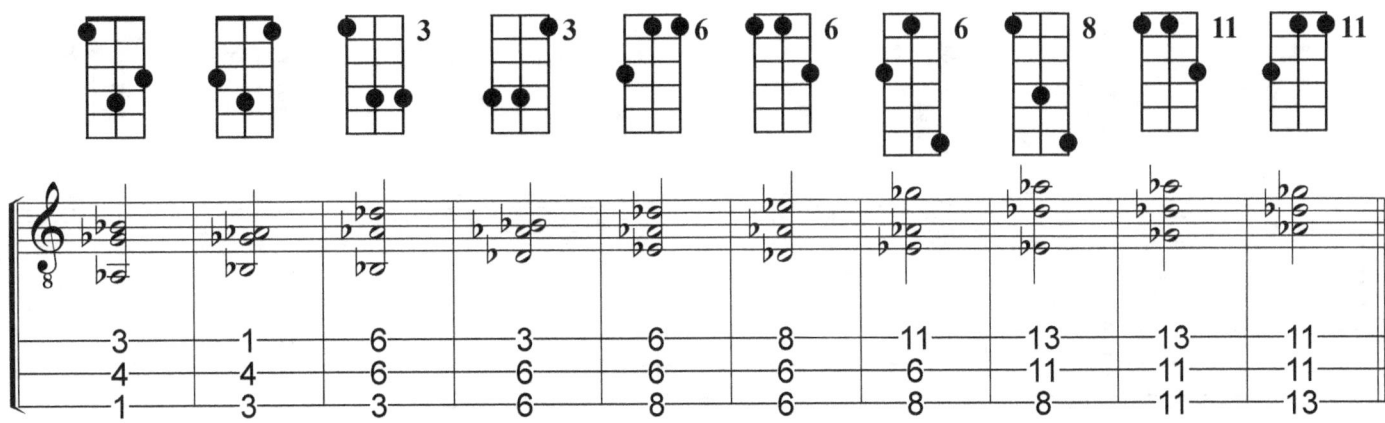

Eb7 - Eb9 - Eb13

Eb7 (Eb G Bb Db)

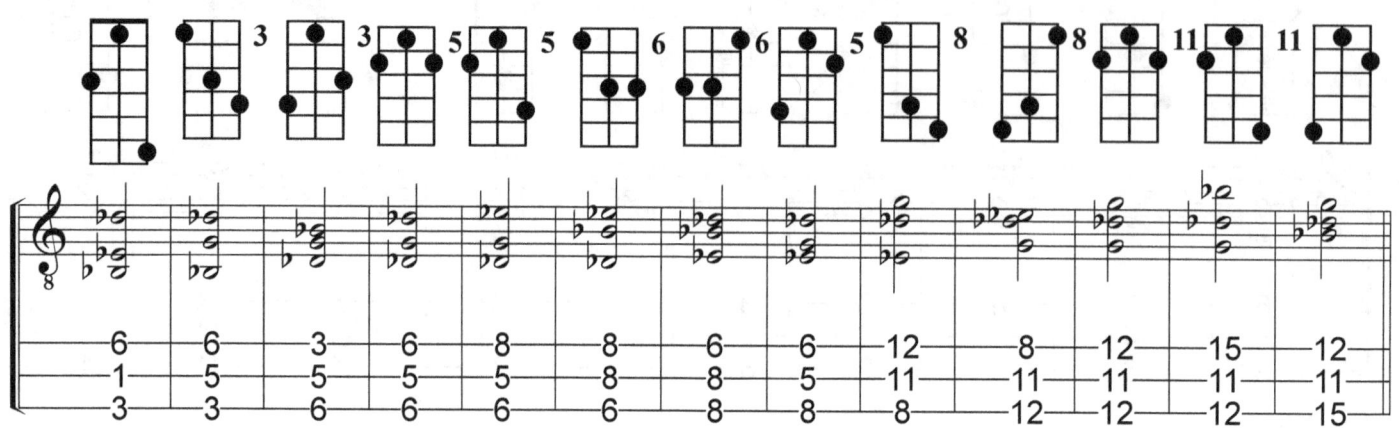

Eb9 (Eb G Bb Db F)

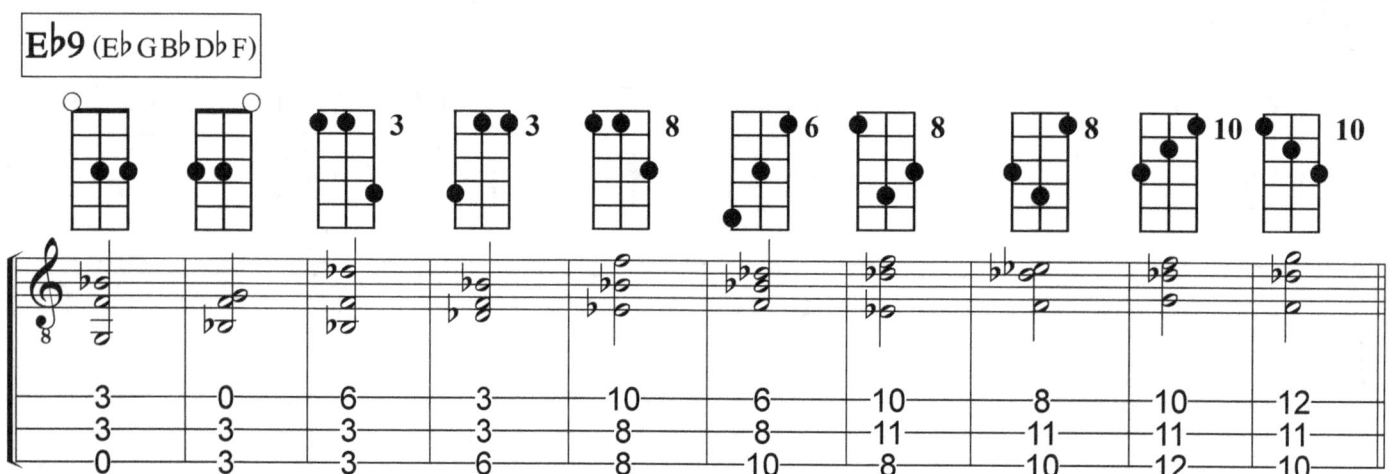

Eb13 (Eb G Bb Db F Ab C)

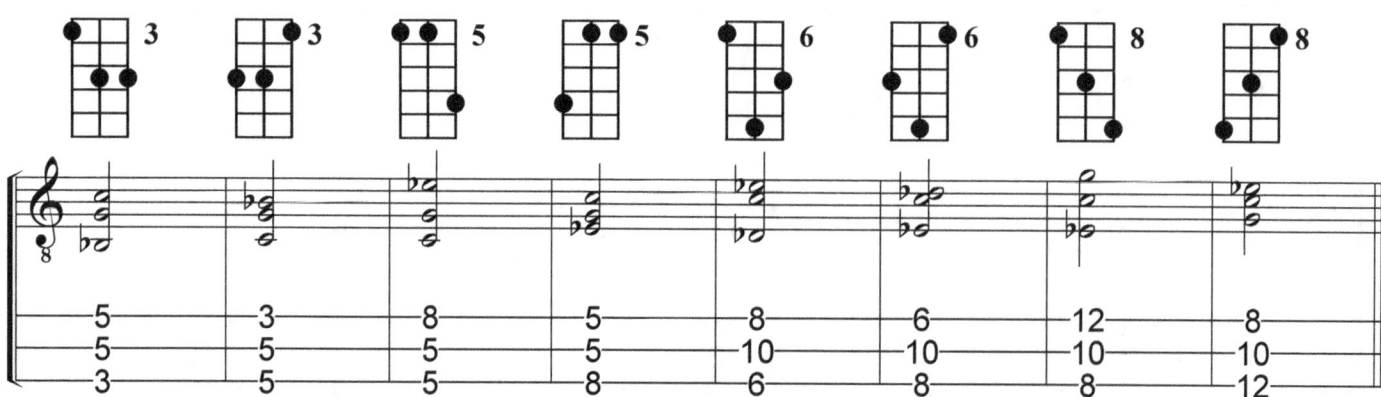

Eb7b5 - Eb7#5 - Eb7#9

Eb7b5 (Eb G Bbb Db)

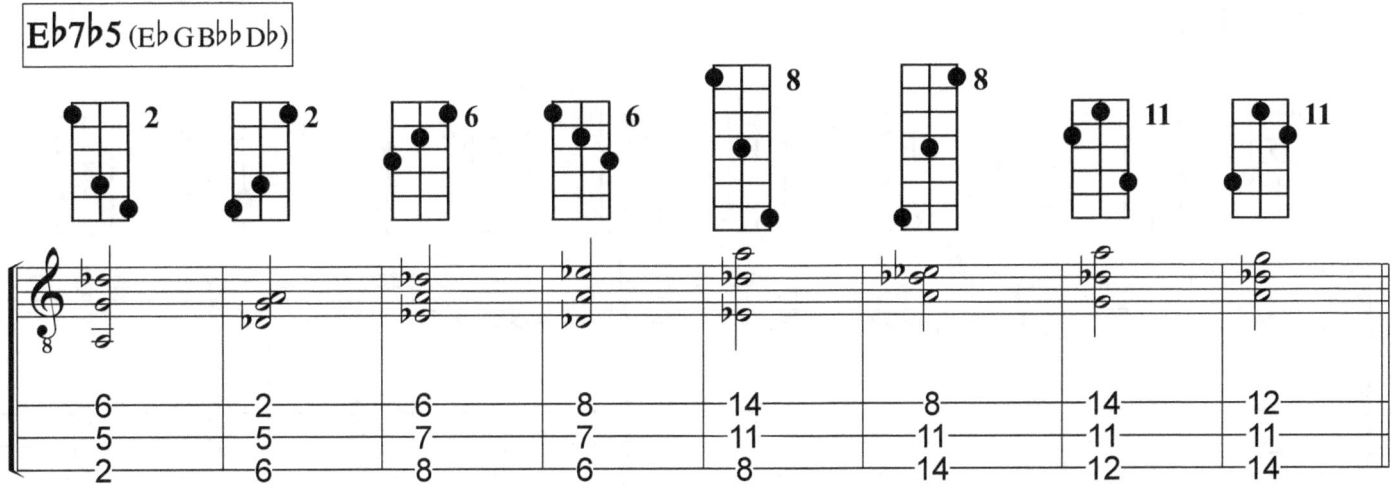

Eb7#5 (Eb G B Db)

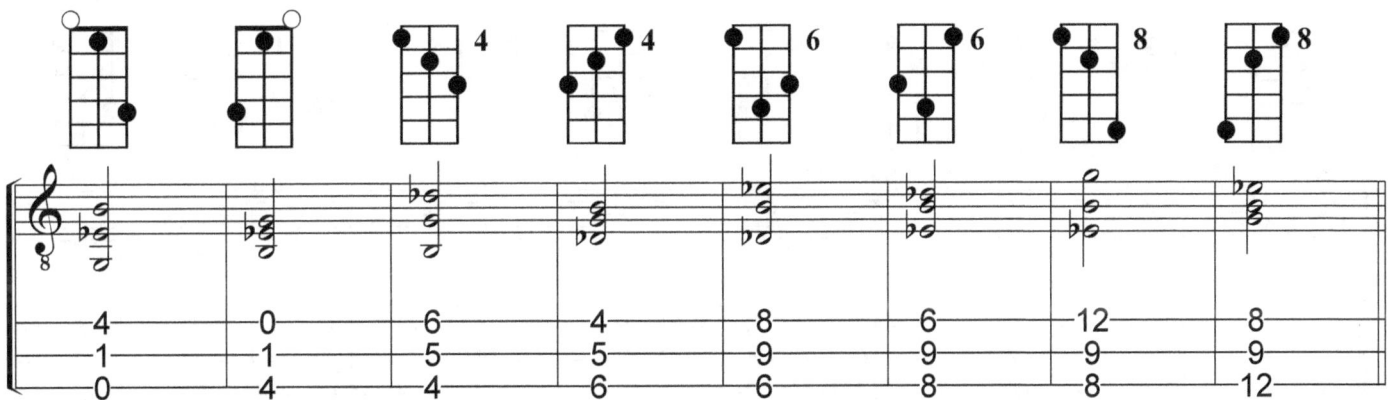

Eb7#9 (Eb G Bb Db F#)

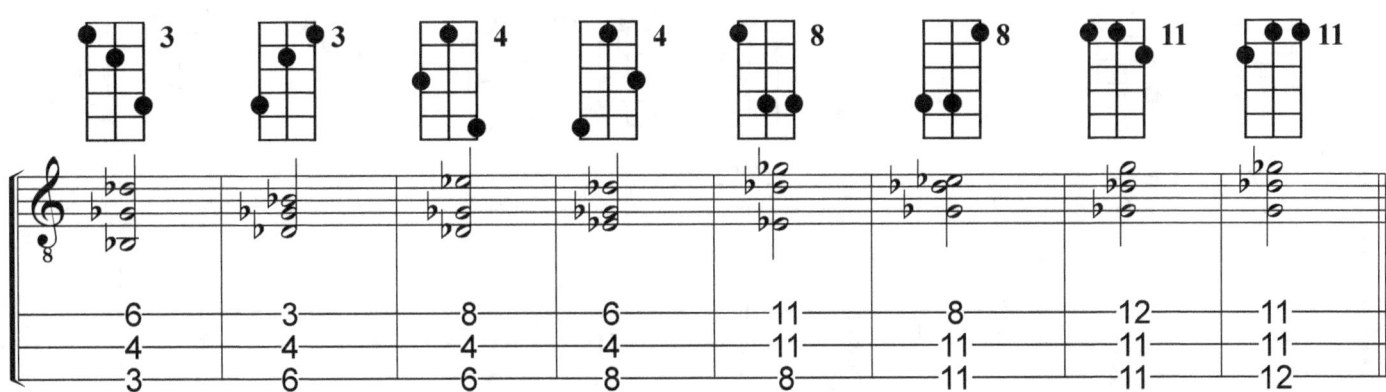

E♭7♭9 - E♭ diminished - E♭°7

E♭7♭9 (E♭ G B♭ D♭ F♭)

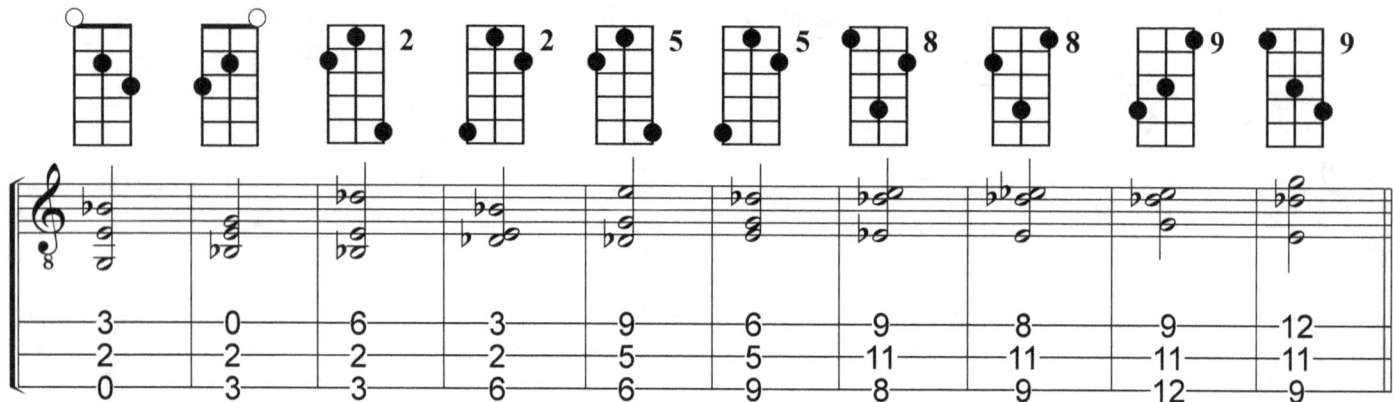

E♭ diminished (E♭ G♭ B♭♭) **E♭°7** (E♭ G♭ B♭♭ D♭♭)

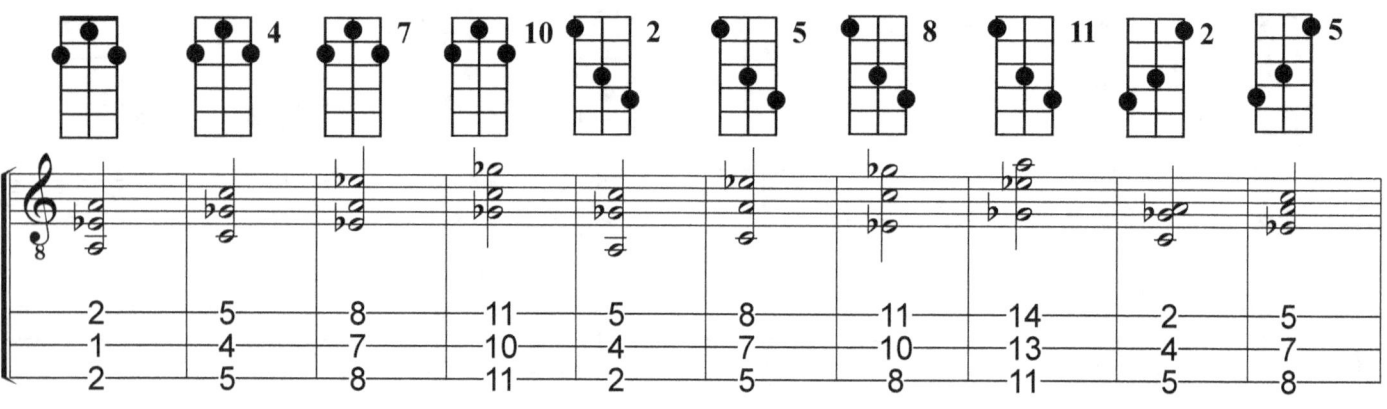

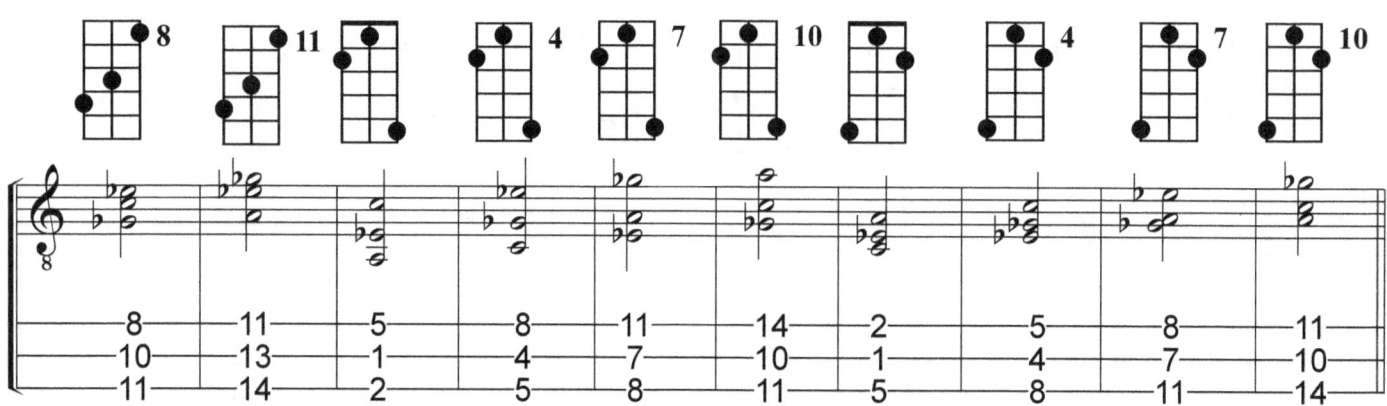

Ebsus4 - Ebsus2 - Ebadd9 - Eb7sus - Power Chords Eb5

E - E6 - Emaj7

Some notes have been omitted from the chords to facilitate playability.
Notes in the chord are in brackets.

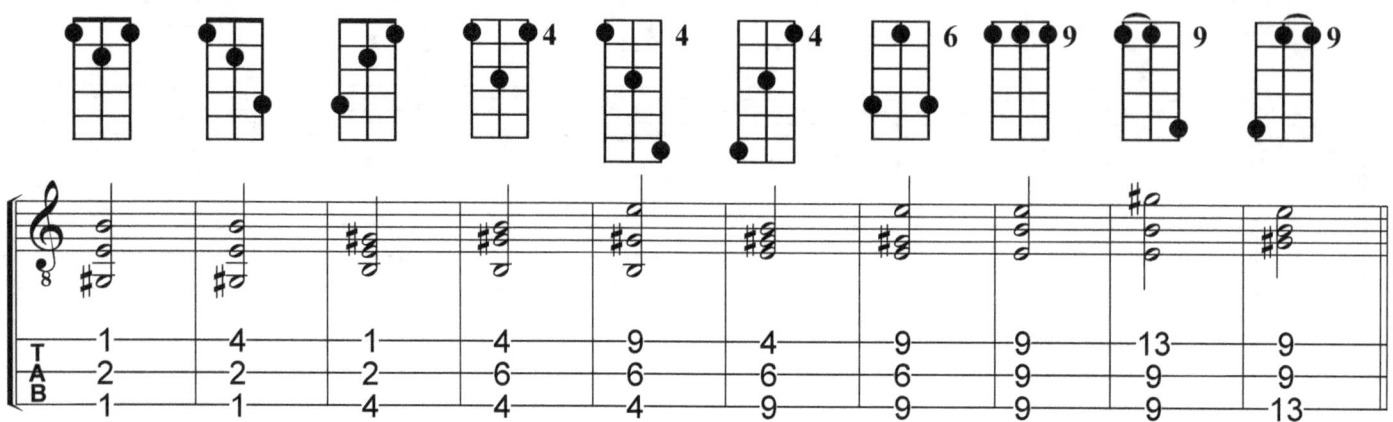

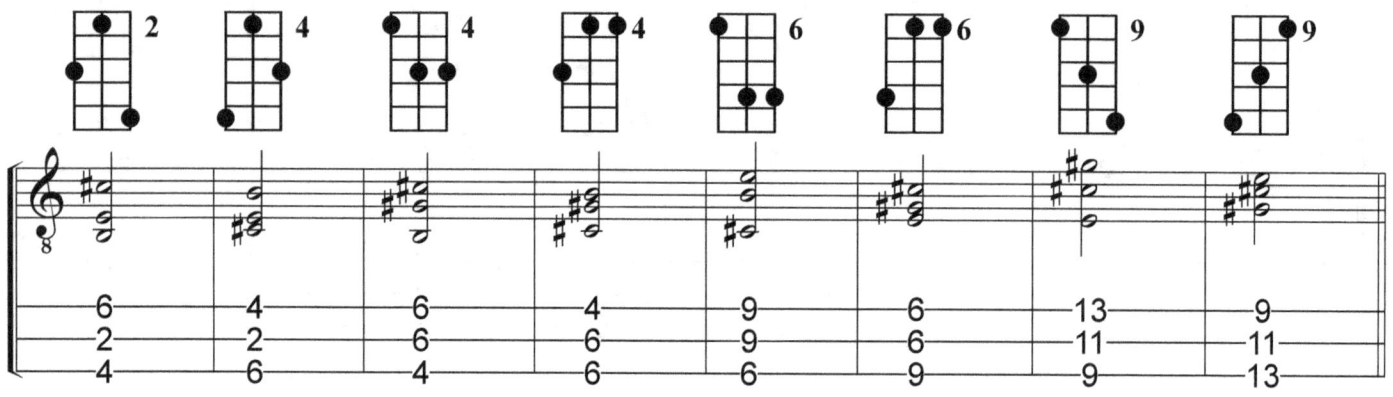

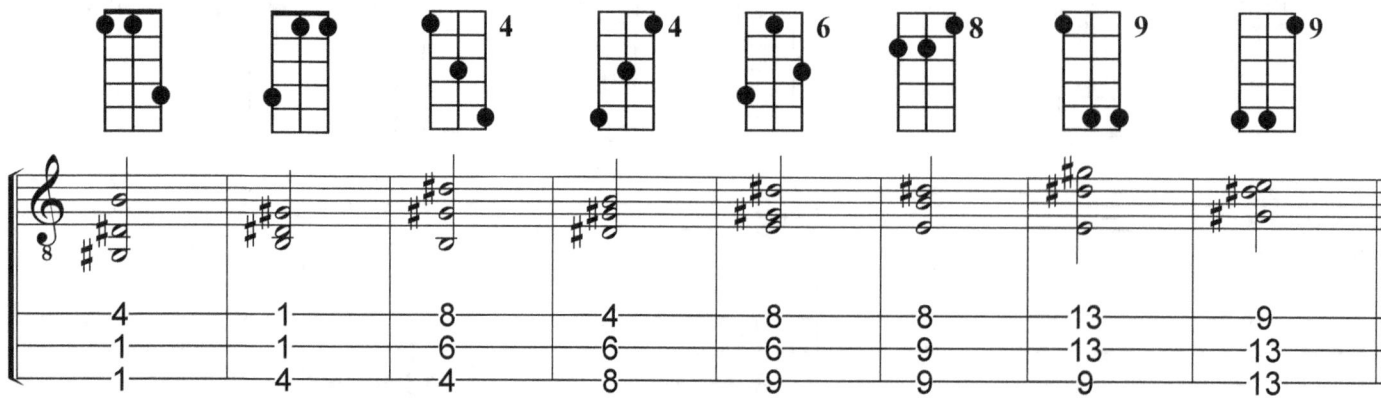

Emaj9 - E6/9 - E+

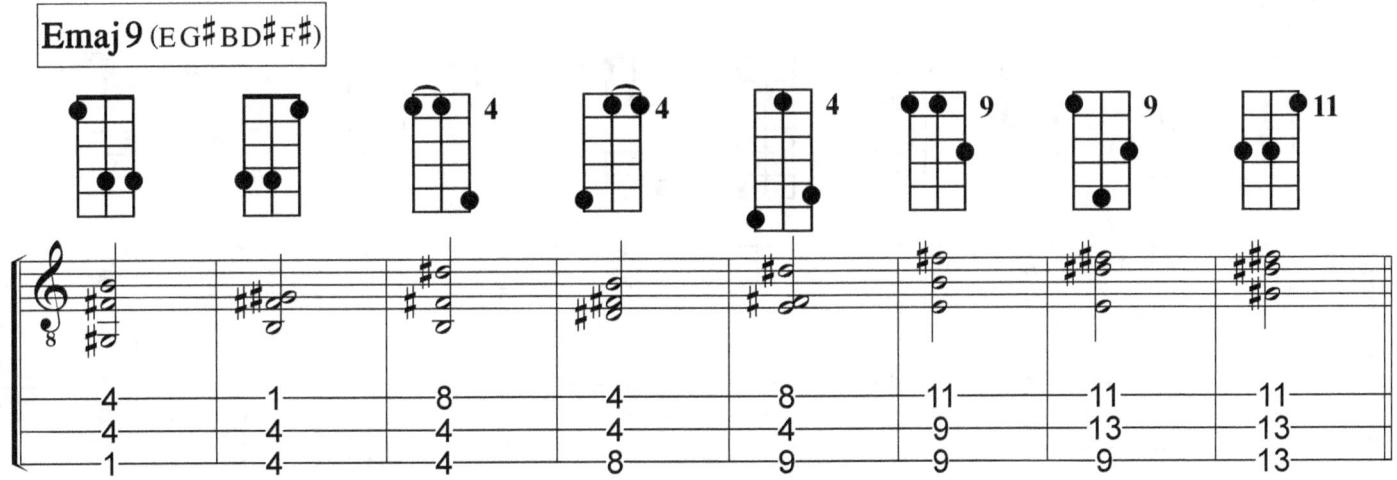

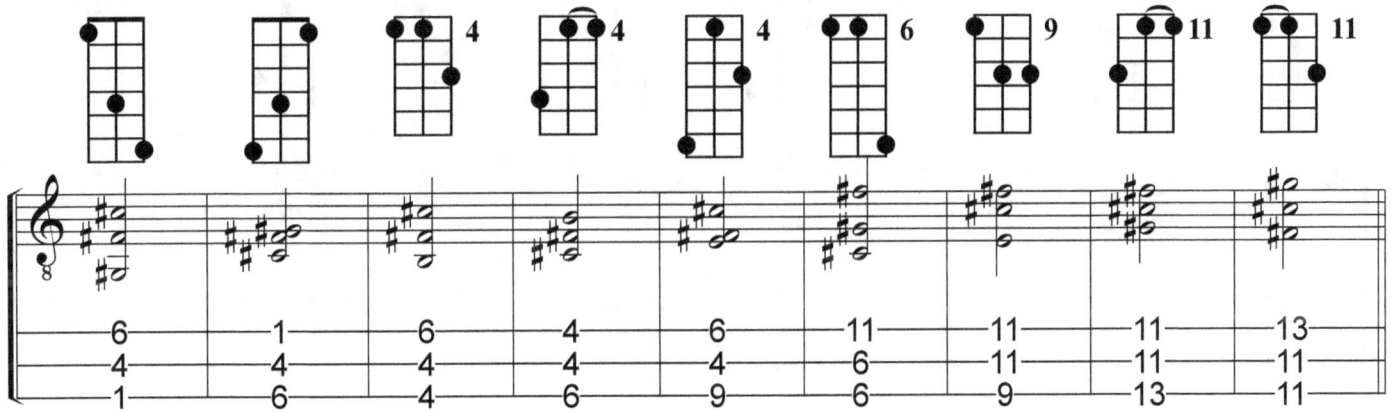

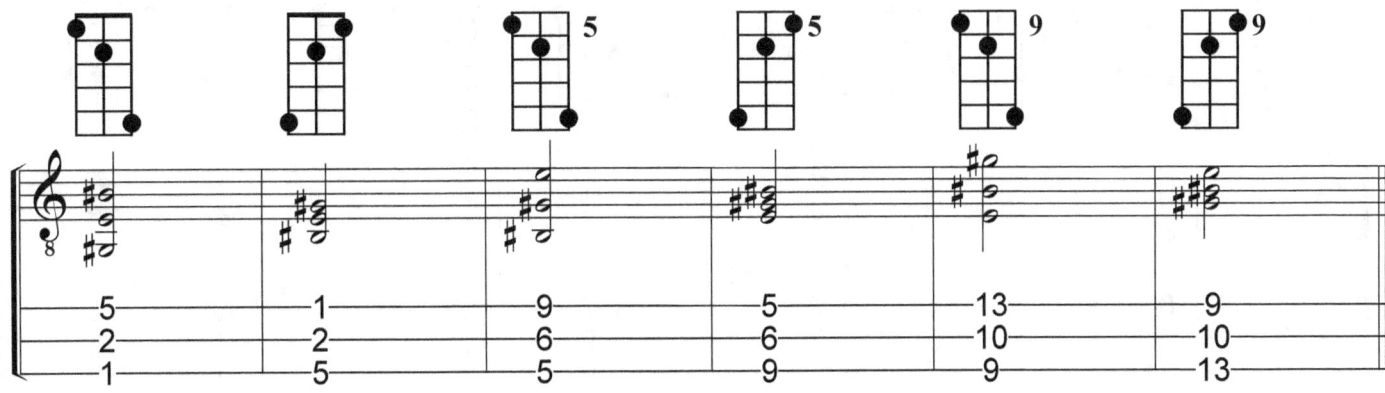

Em - Em6 - Em(maj7) - Em7

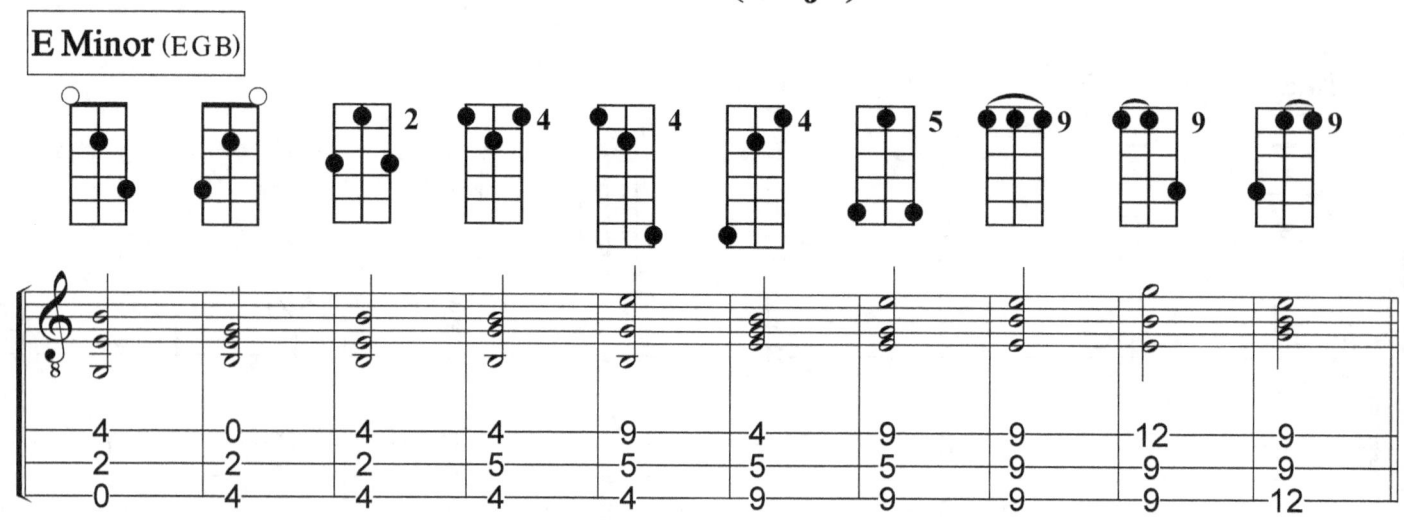

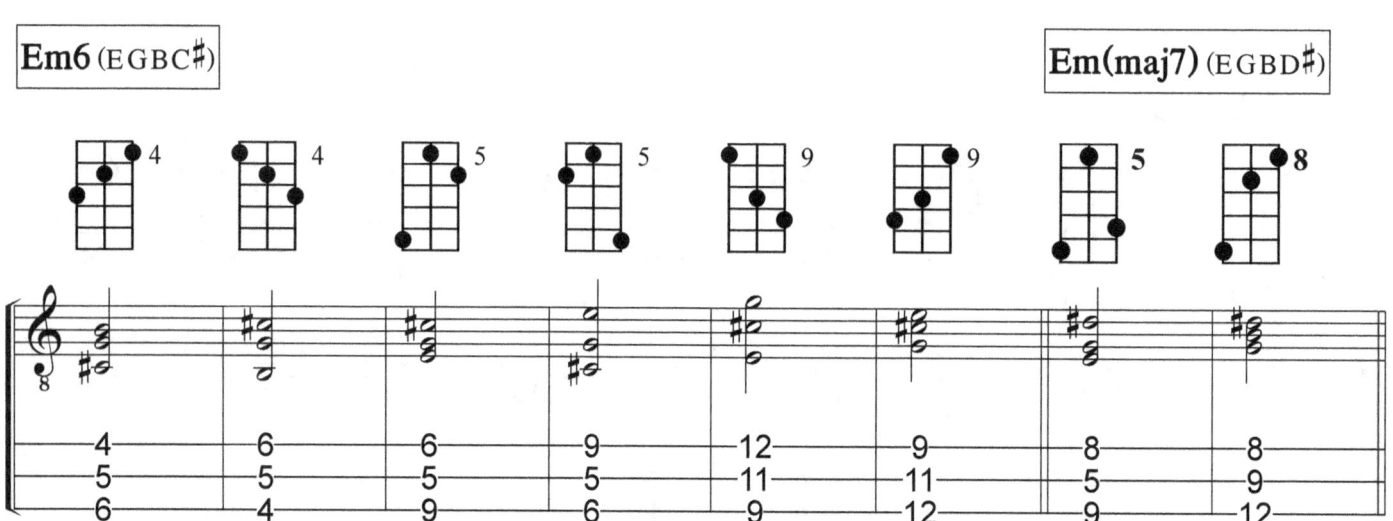

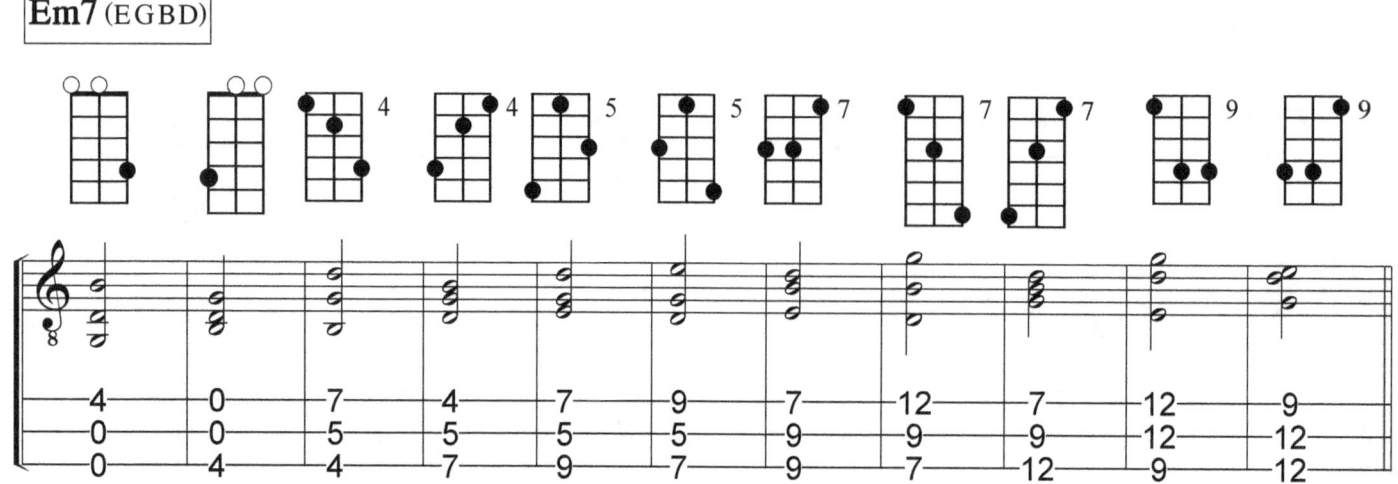

Em7♭5 - Em9 - Em11

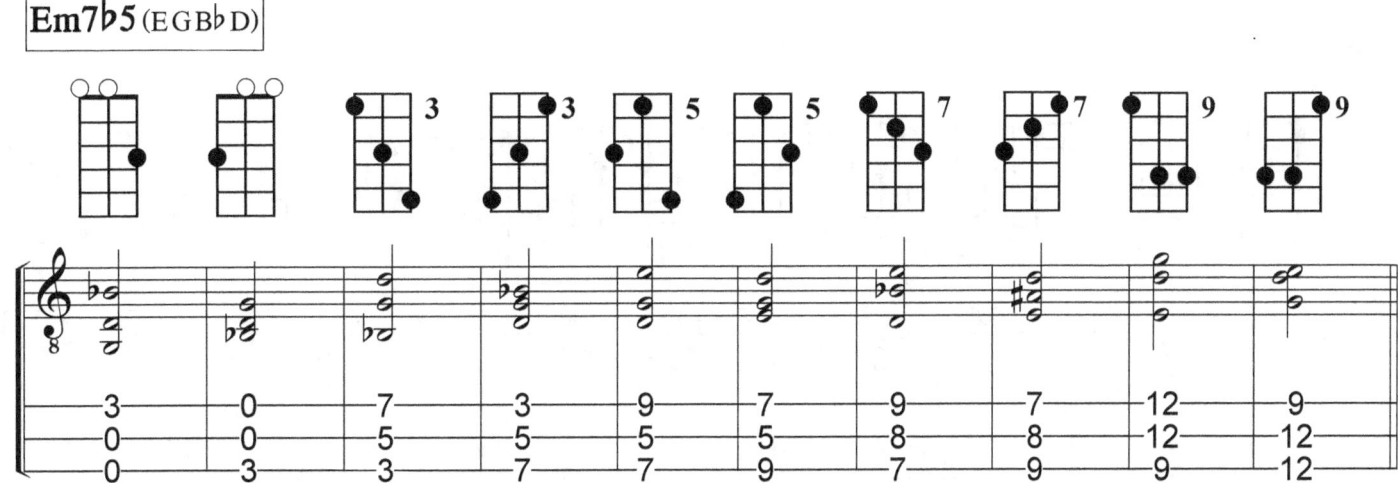

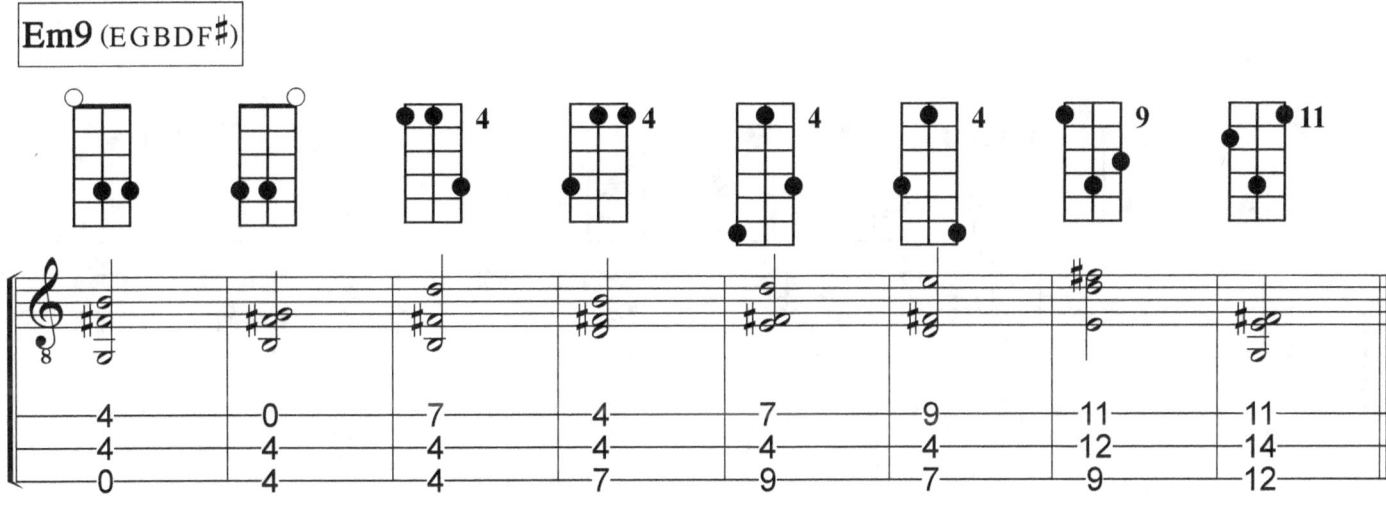

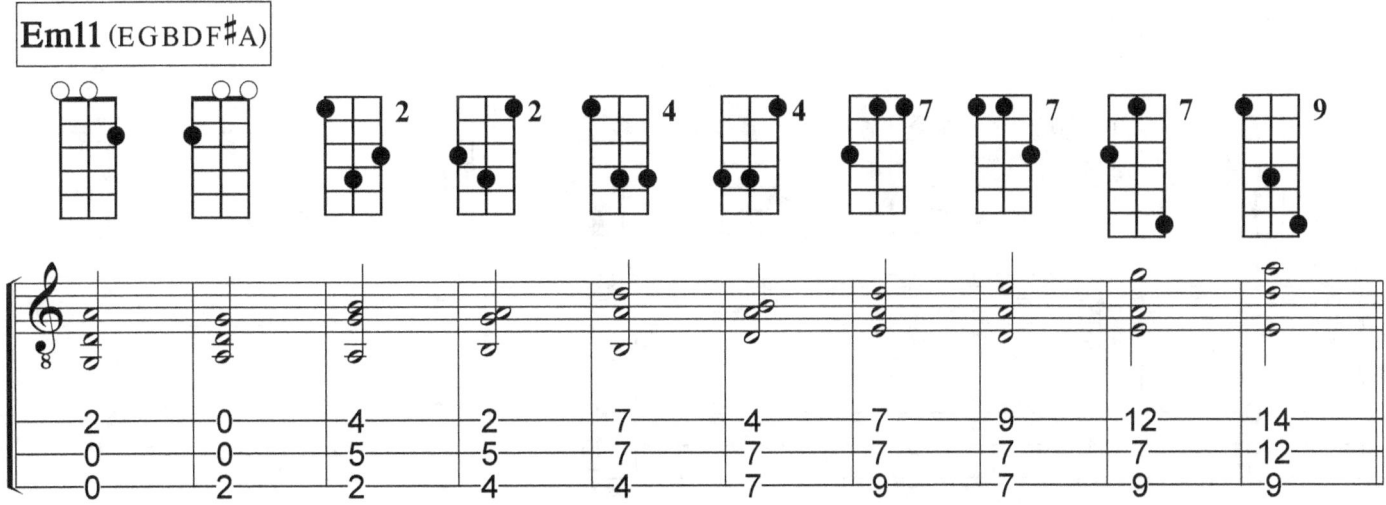

E7 - E9 - E13

E7 (E G# B D)

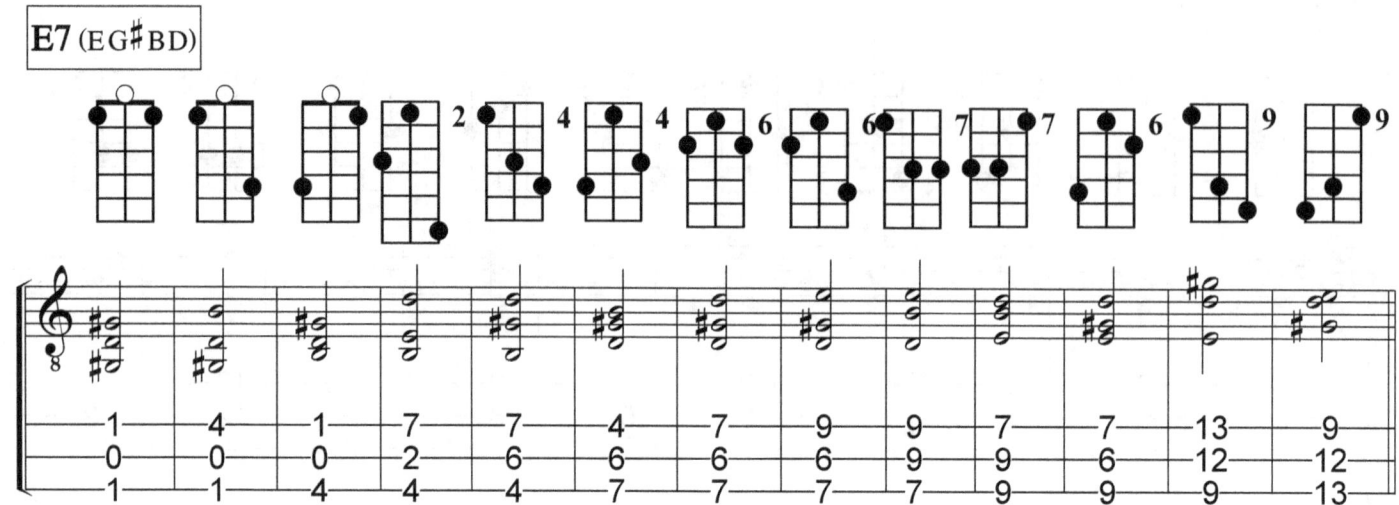

E9 (E G# B D F#)

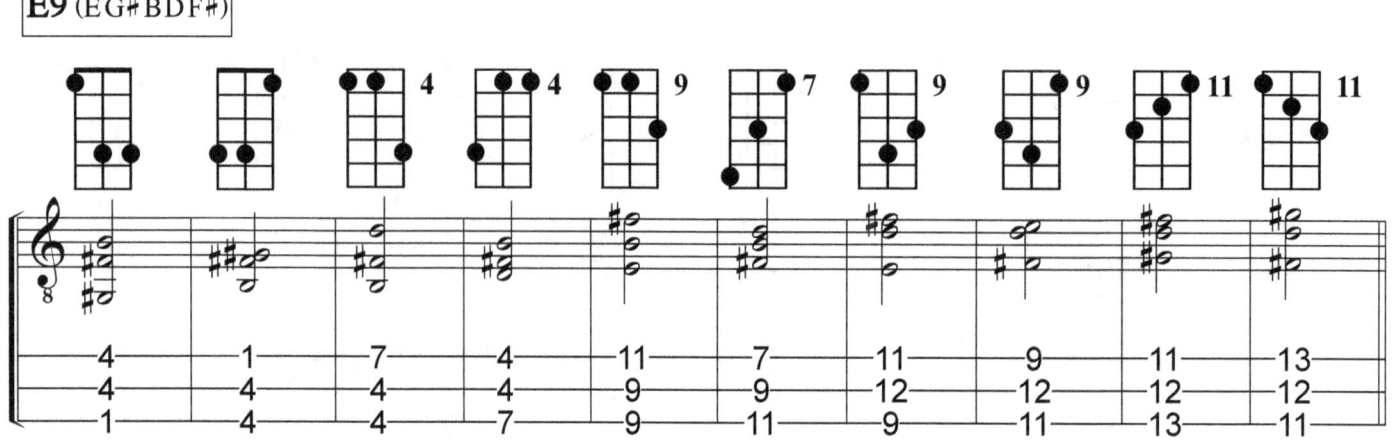

E13 (E G# B D F# A C#)

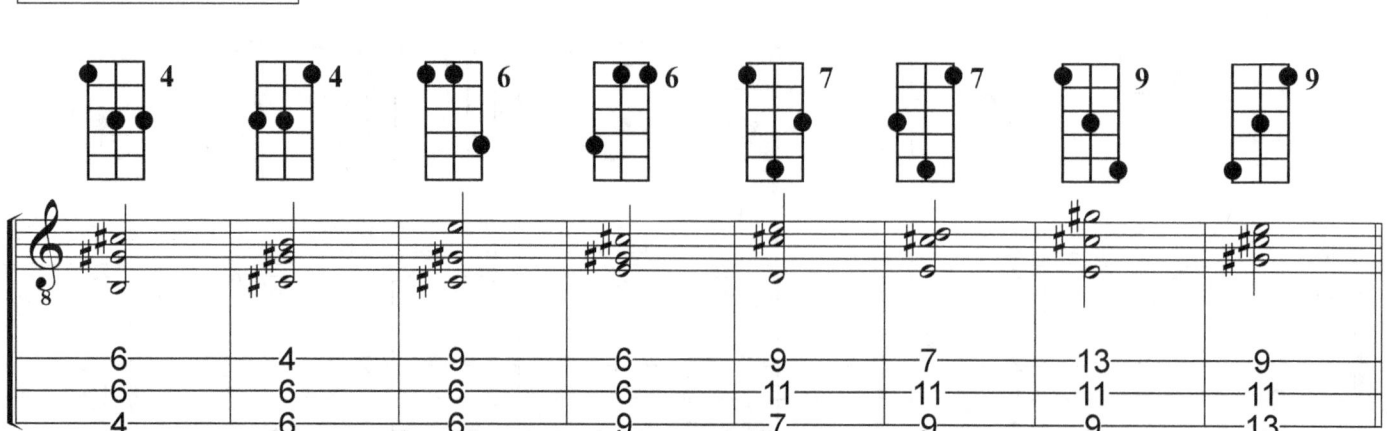

E7♭5 - E7♯5 - E7♯9

E7♭5 (E G♯ B♭ D)

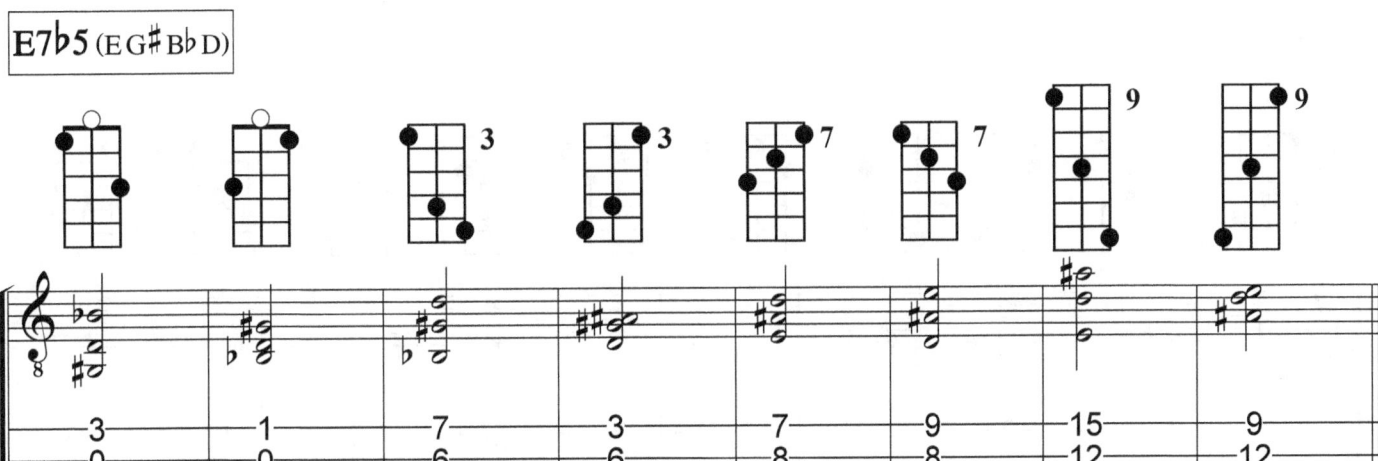

E7♯5 (E G♯ B♯ D)

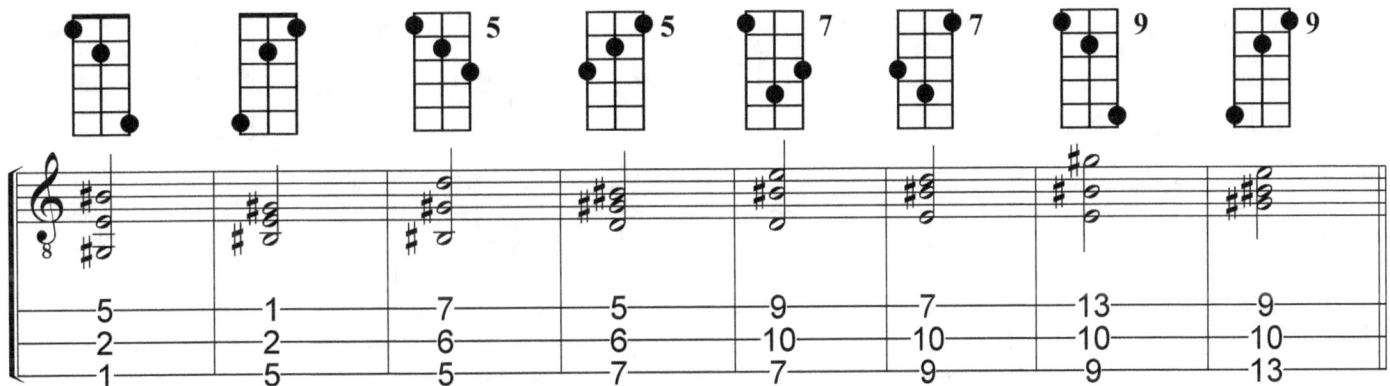

E7♯9 (E G♯ B D F𝆪)

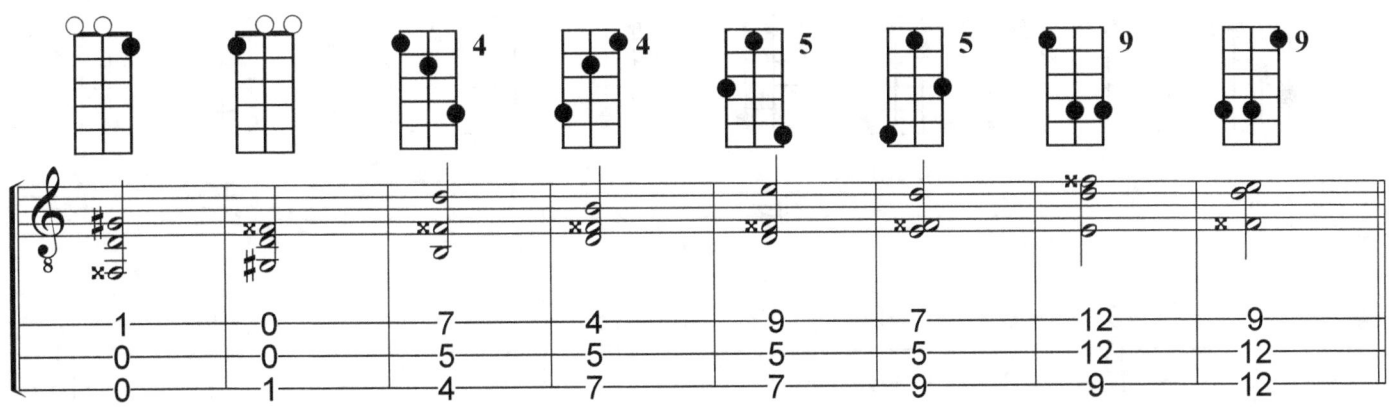

E7♭9 - E diminished - E°7

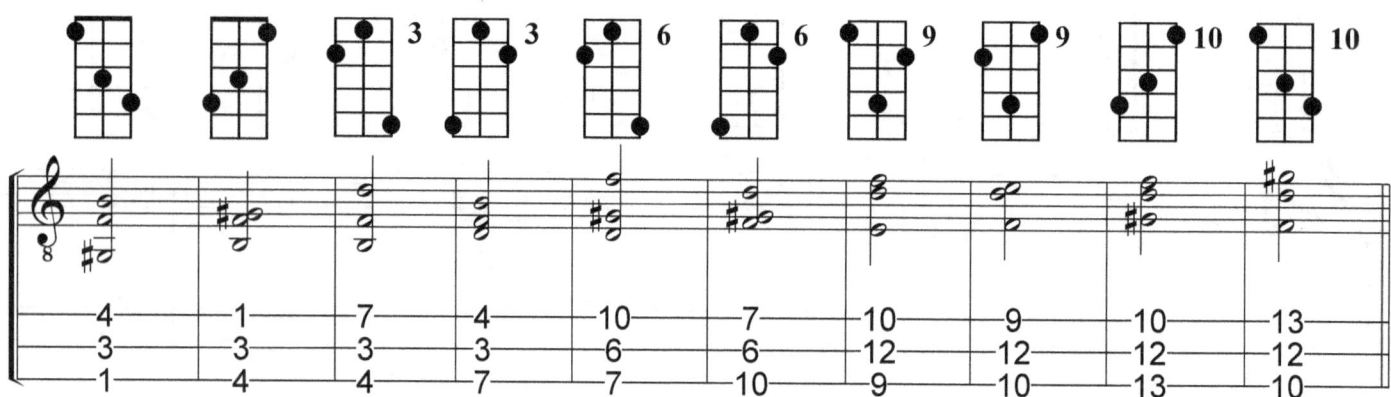

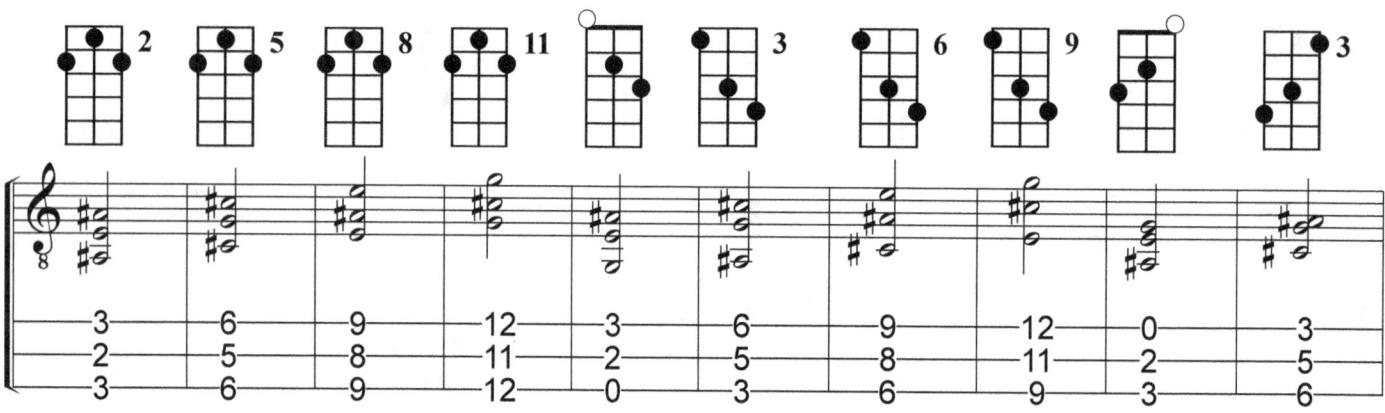

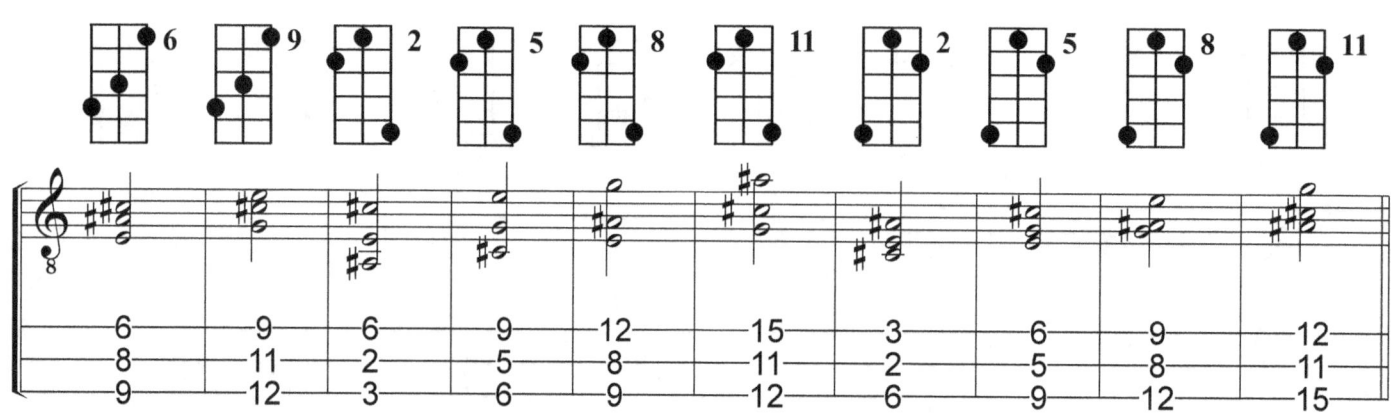

Esus4 - Esus2 - Eadd9 - E7sus - Power Chords E5

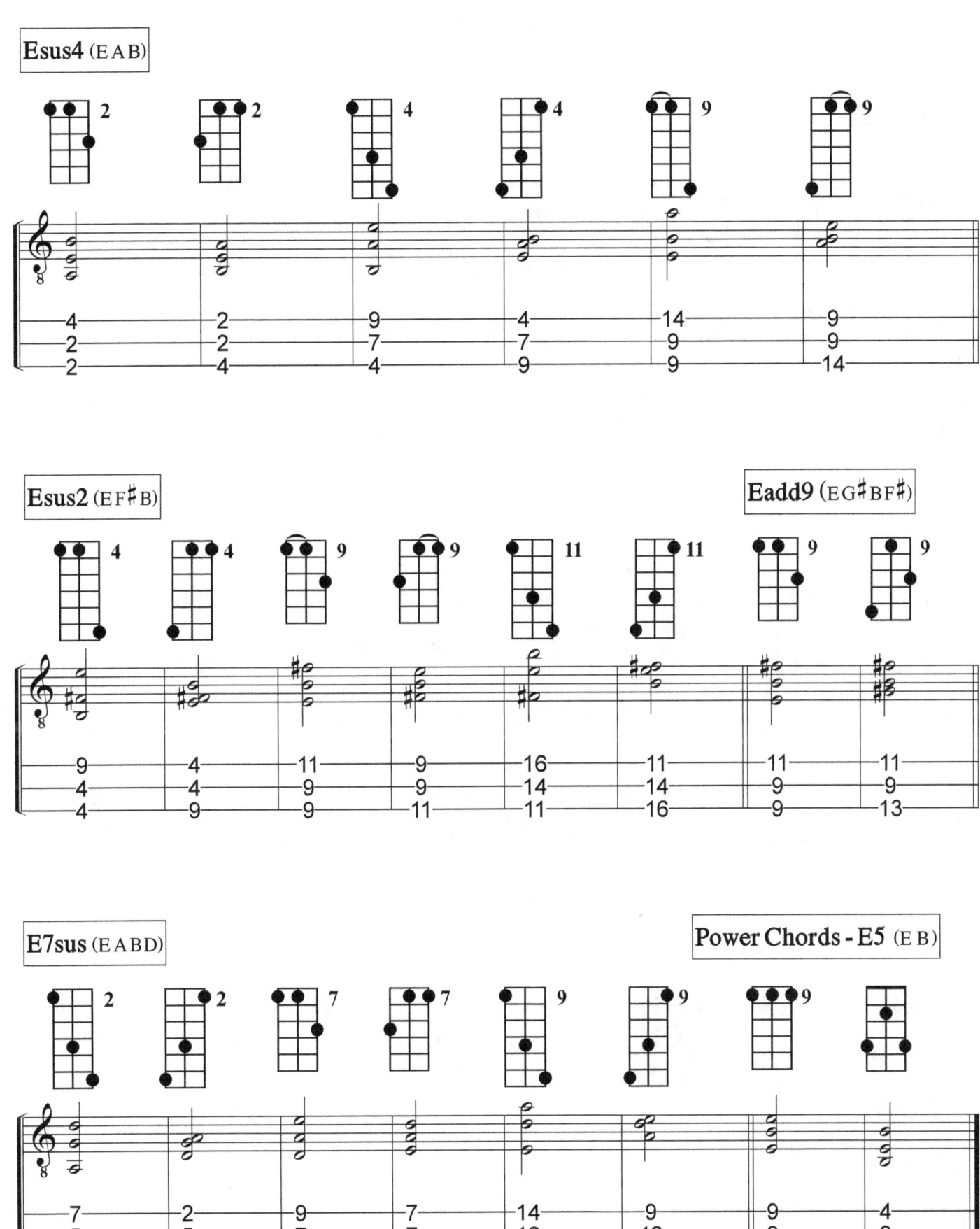

F - F6 - Fmaj7

Some notes have been omitted from the chords to facilitate playability.
Notes in the chord are in brackets.

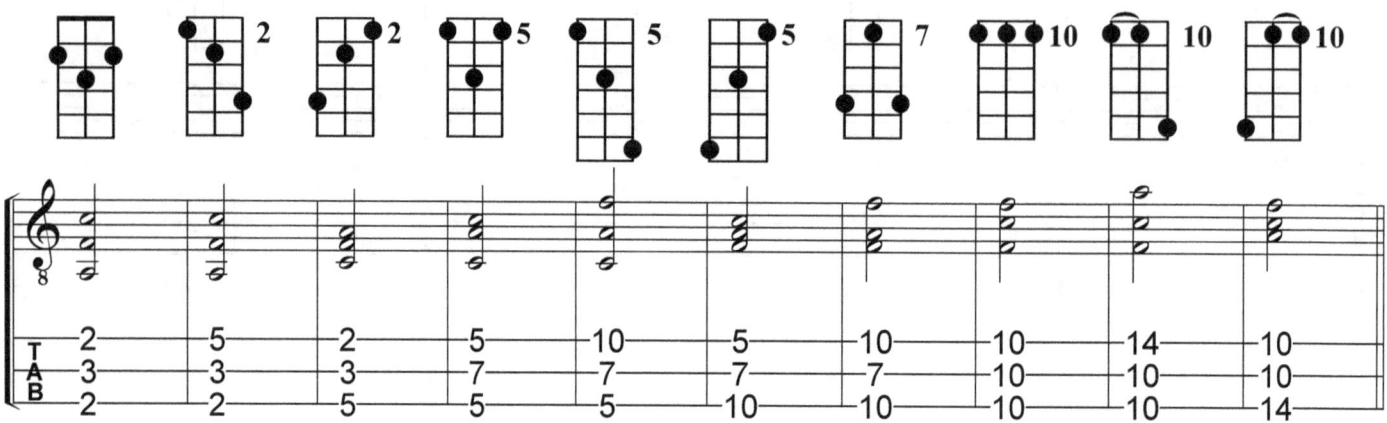

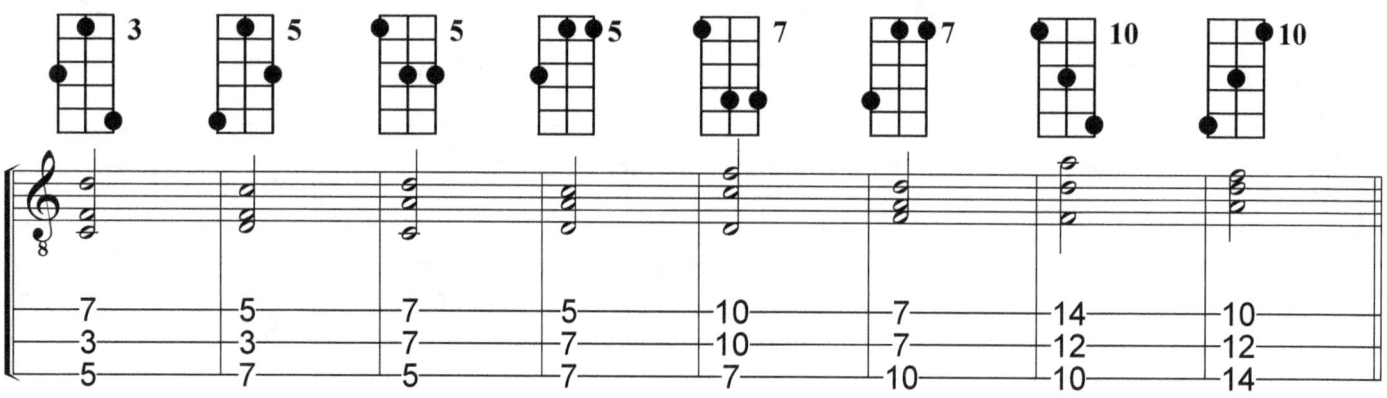

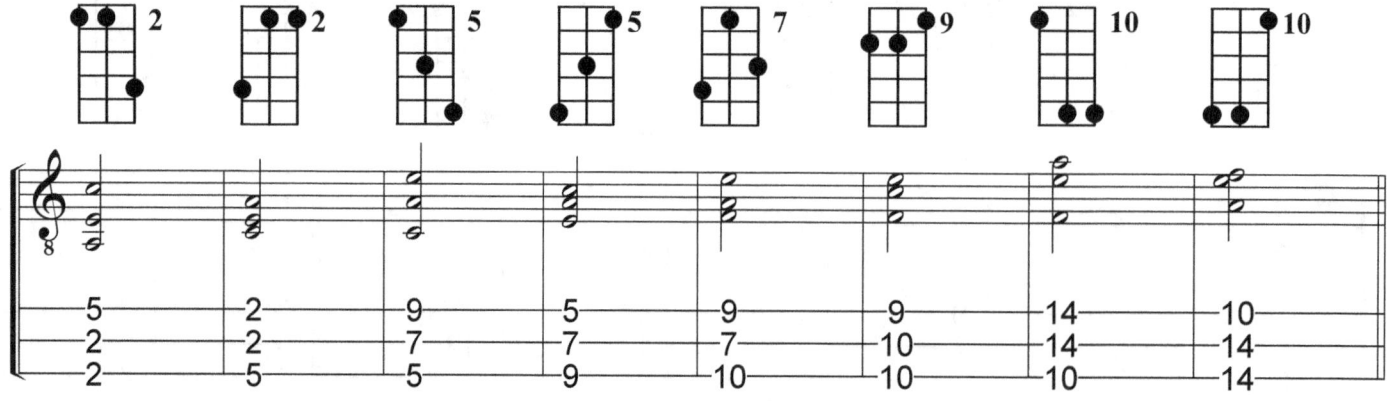

Fmaj9 - F6/9 - F+

Fmaj9 (F A C E G)

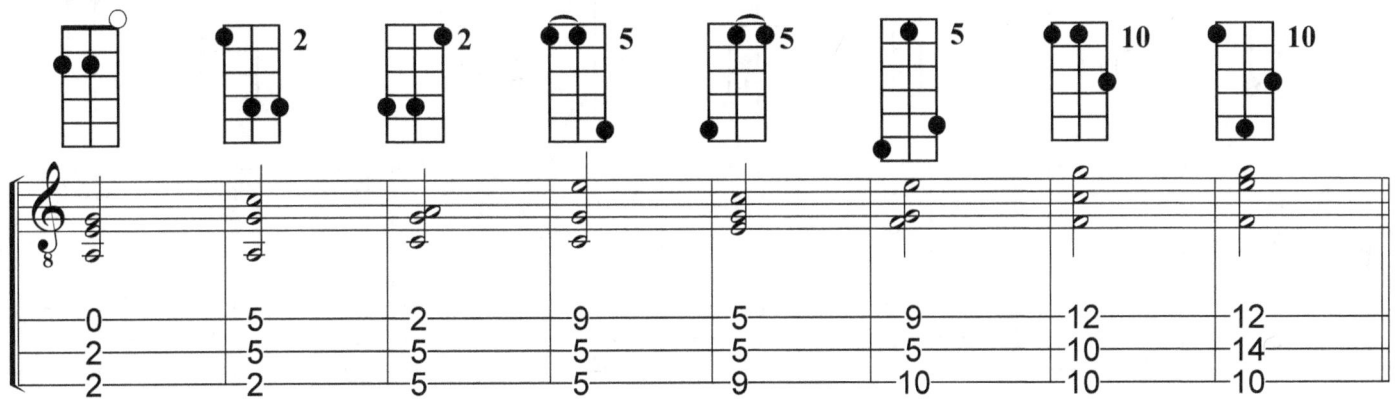

F6/9 (F A C D G)

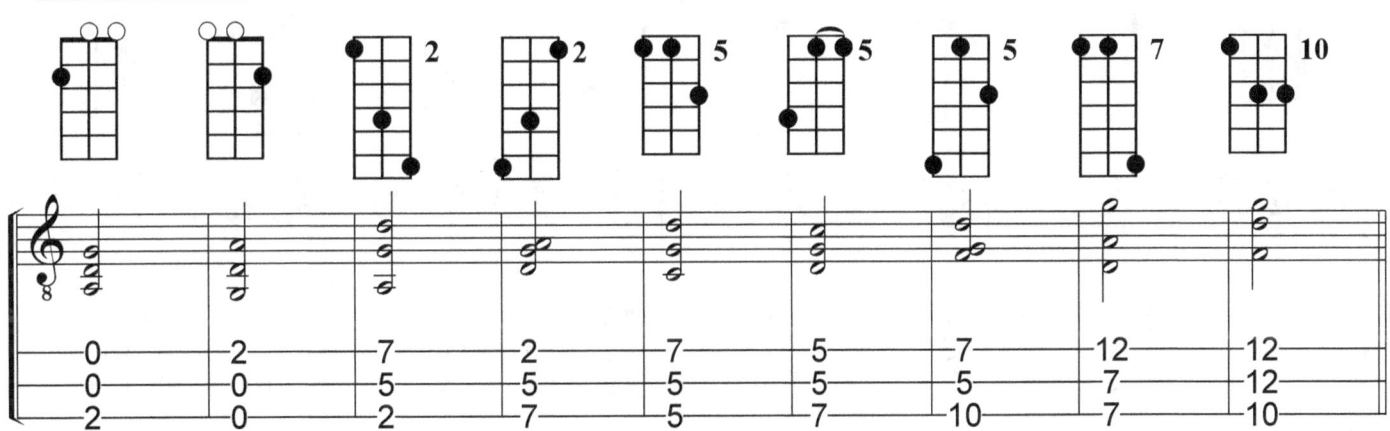

F Augmented - F+ (F A C#)

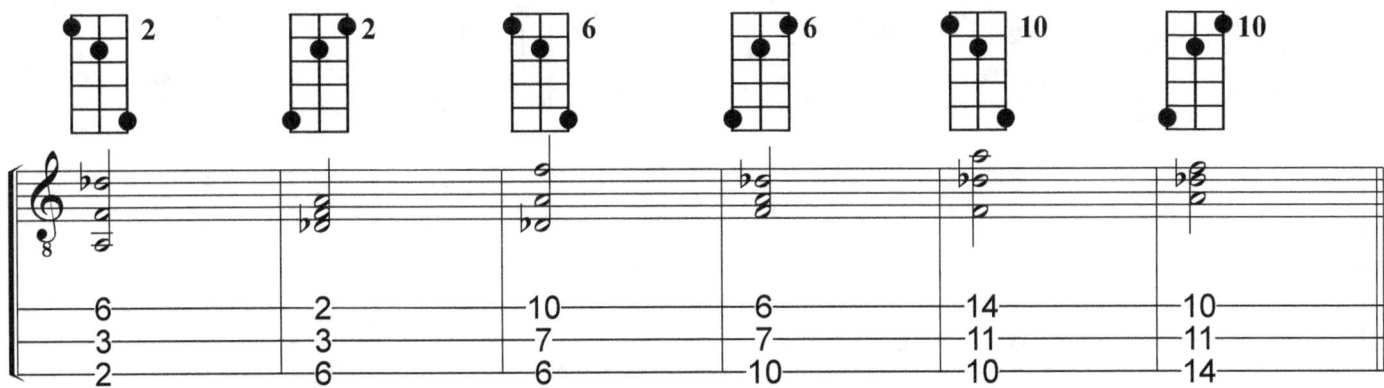

Fm - Fm6 - Fm(maj7) - Fm7

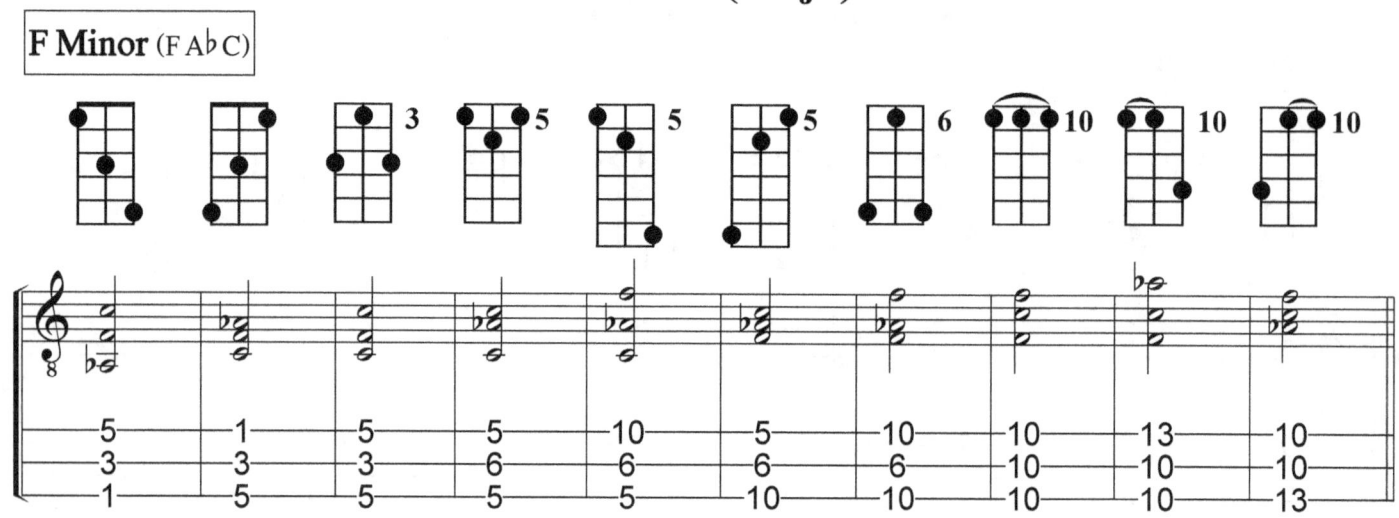

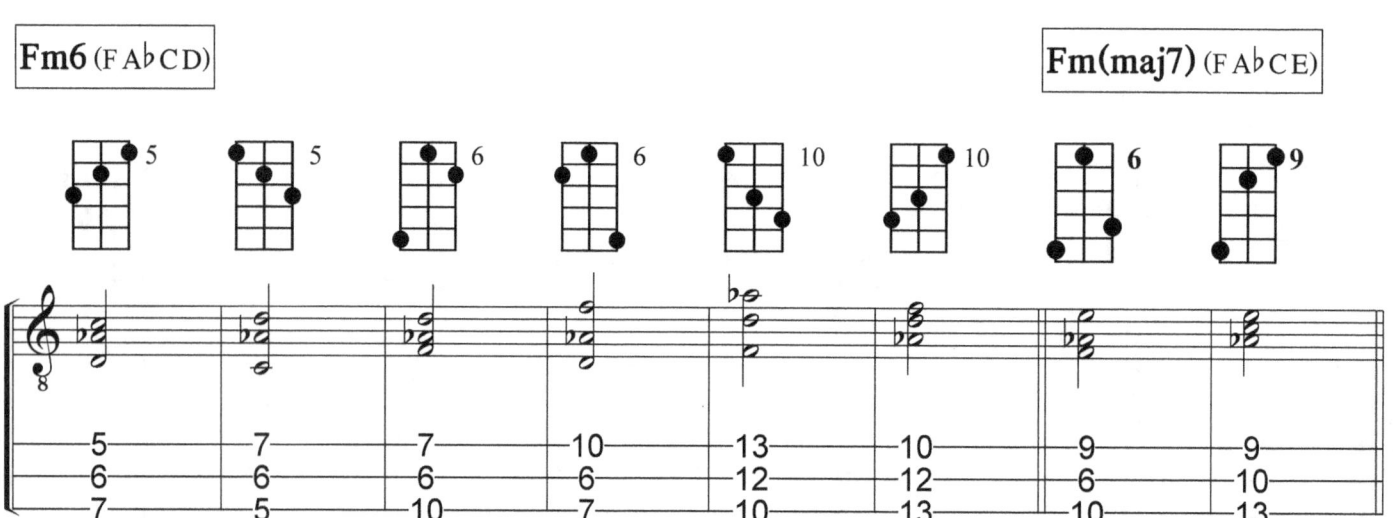

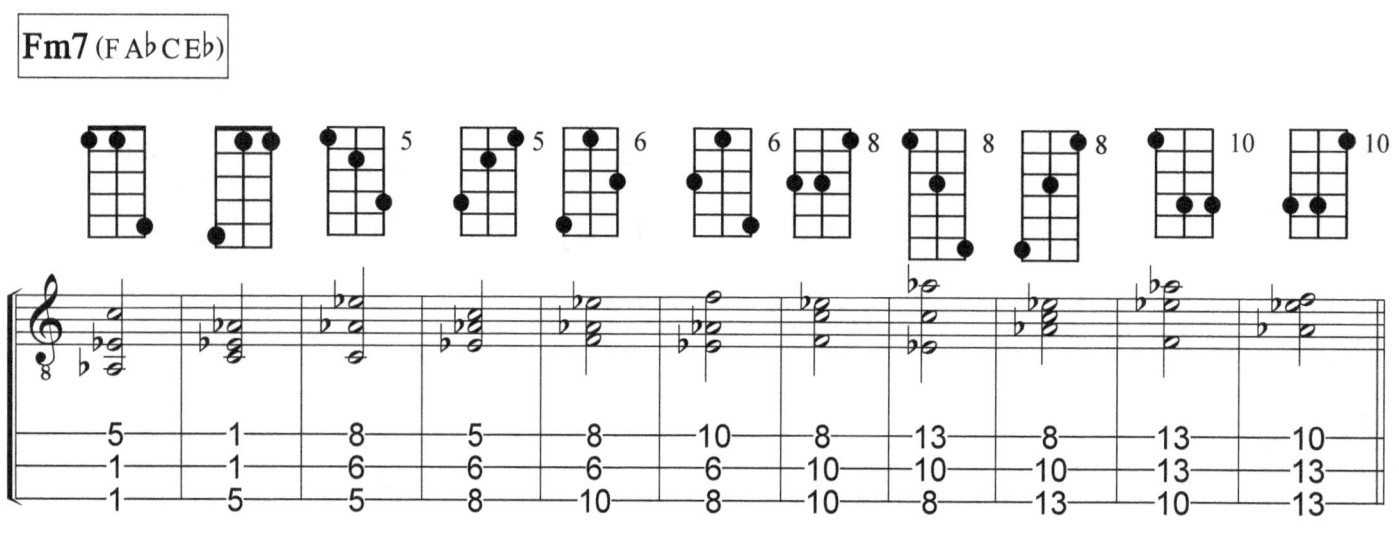

Fm7♭5 - Fm9 - Fm11

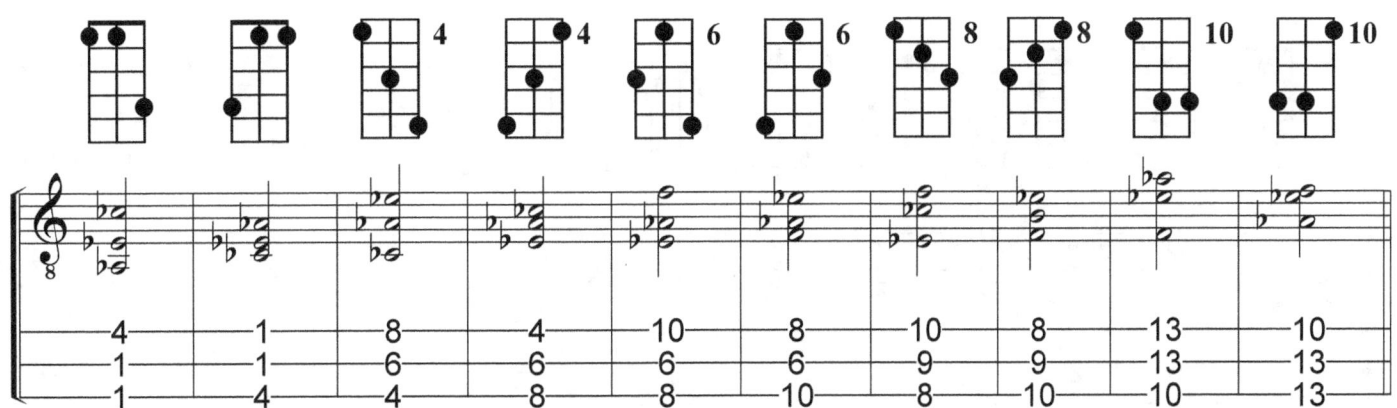

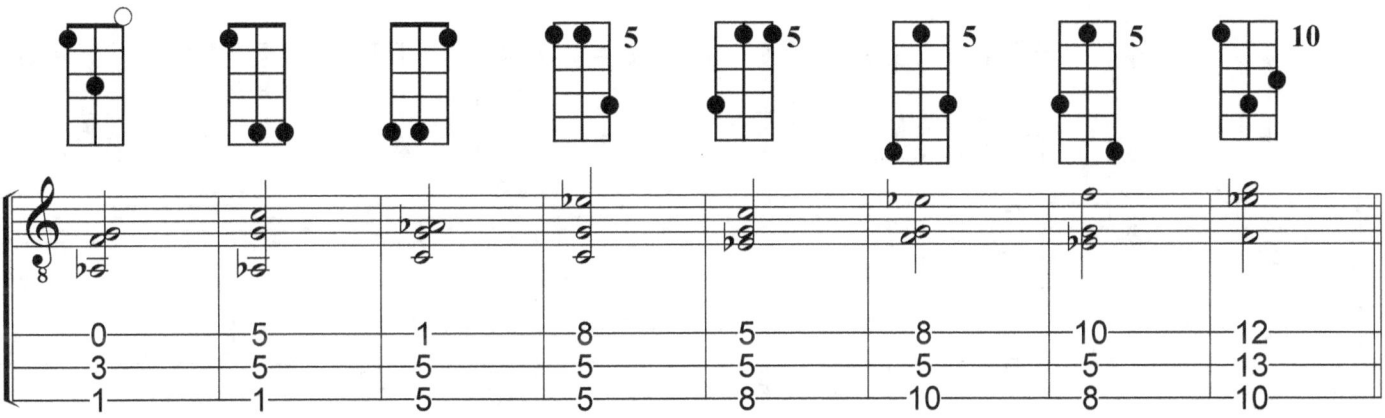

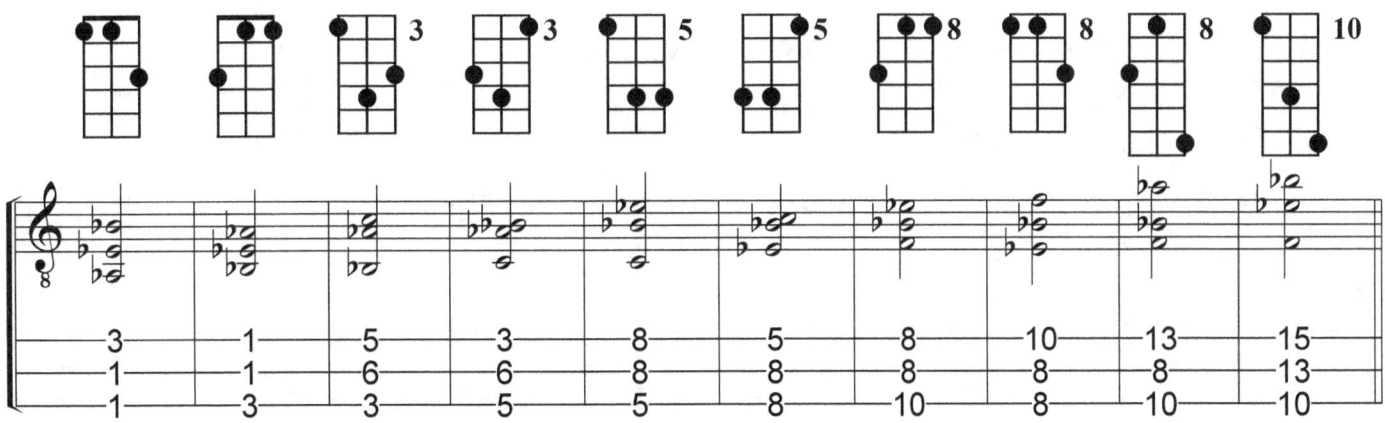

F7 - F9 - F13

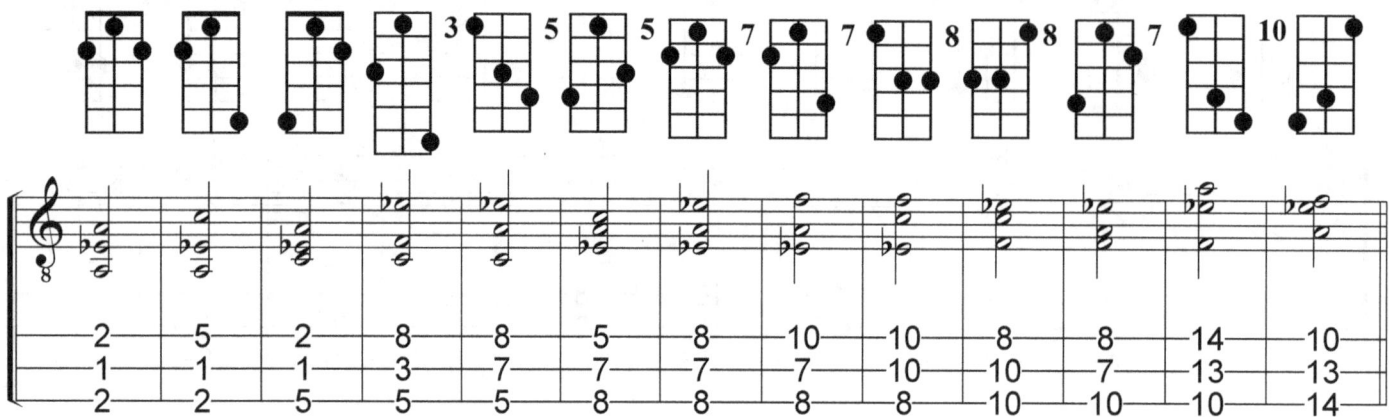

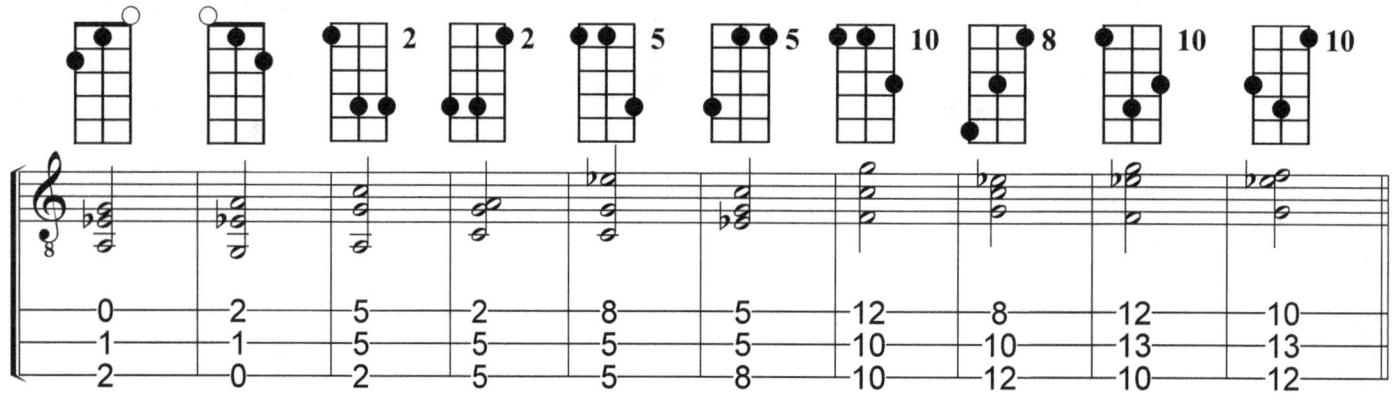

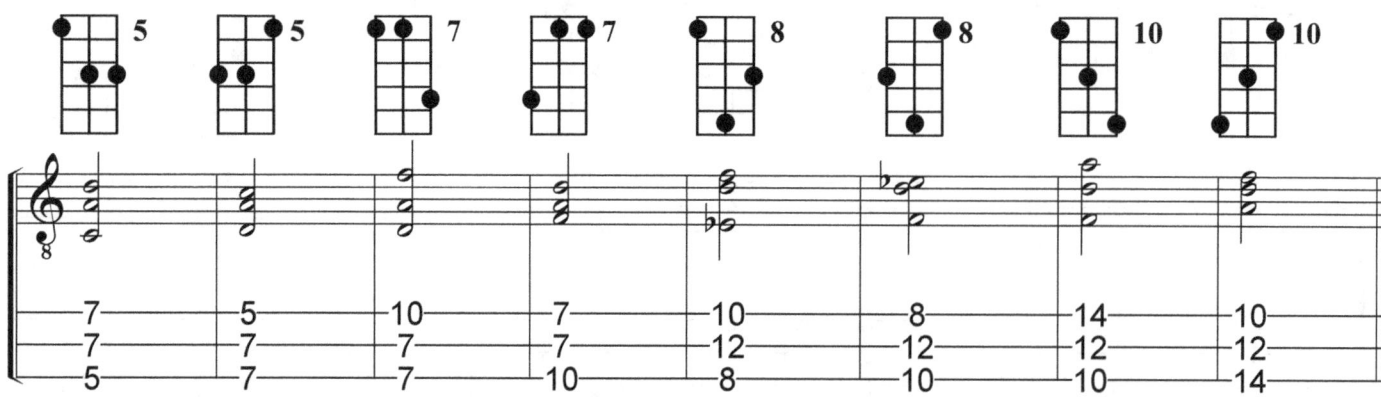

F7♭5 - F7♯5 - F7♯9

F7♭5 (F A C♭ E♭)

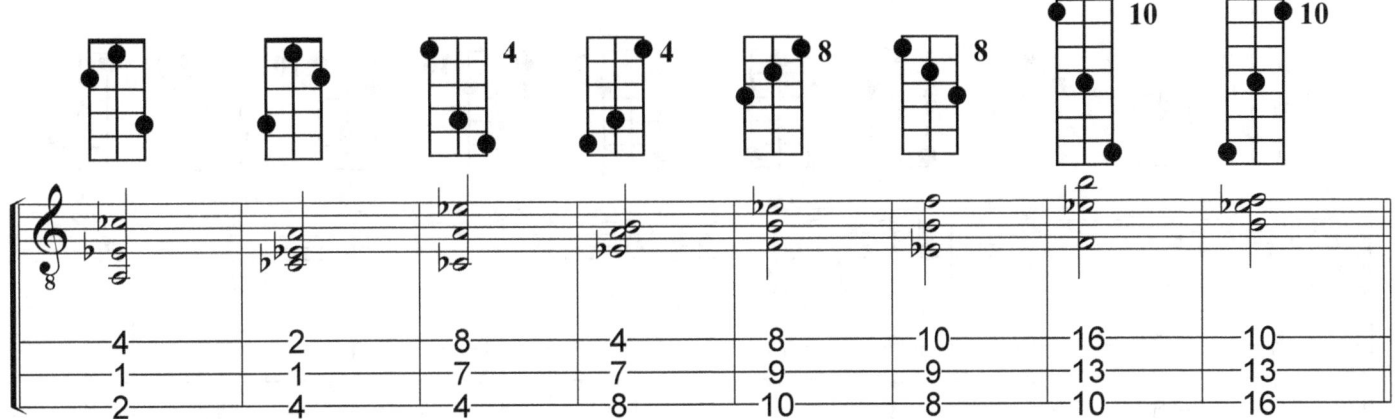

F7♯5 (F A C♯ E♭)

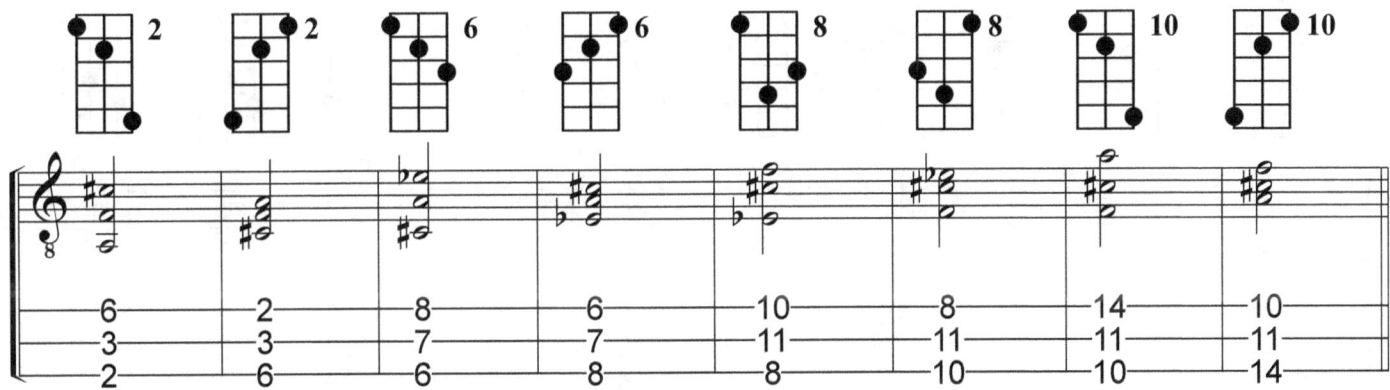

F7♯9 (F A C E♭ G♯)

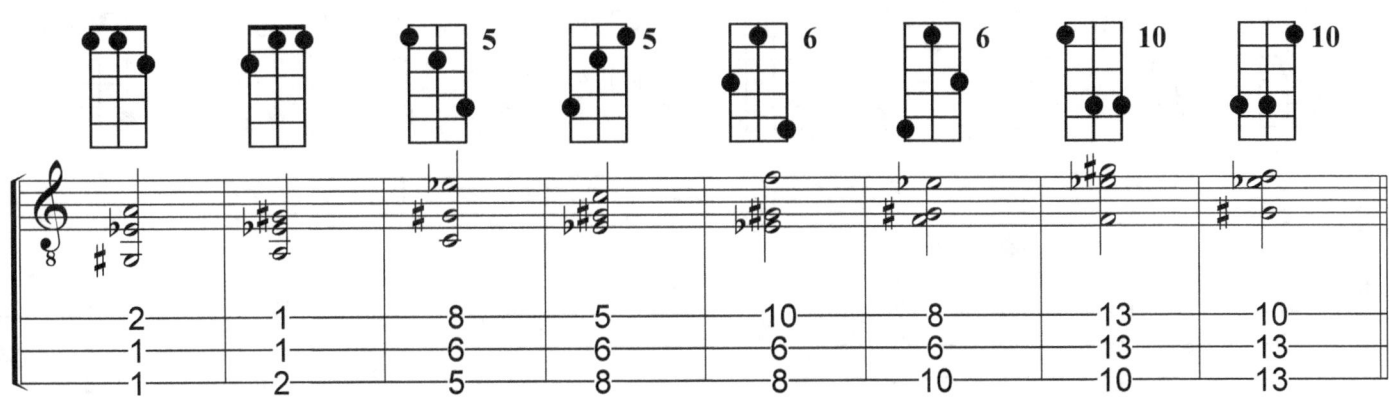

F7♭9 - F diminished - F°7

F7♭9 (F A C E♭ G♭)

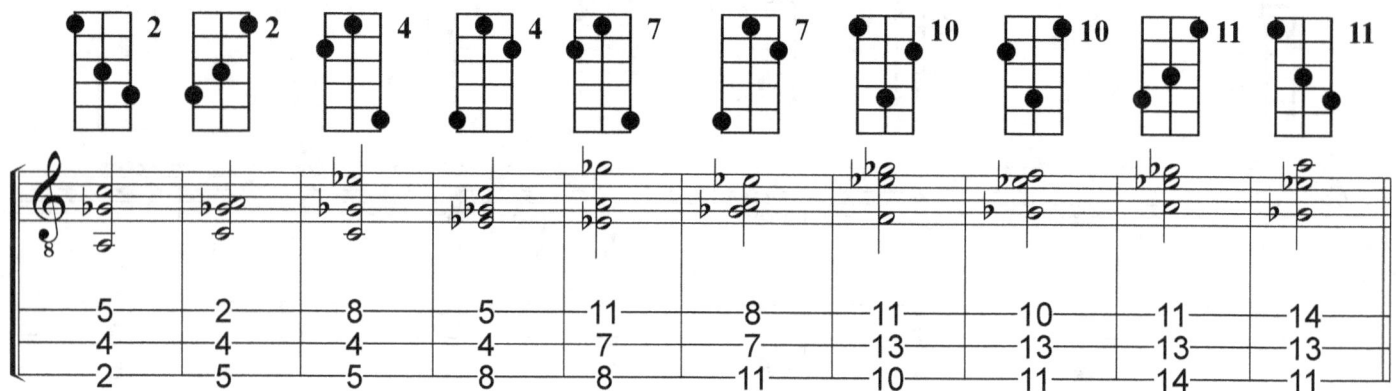

F diminished (F A♭ C♭) **F°7** (F A♭ C♭ E♭♭)

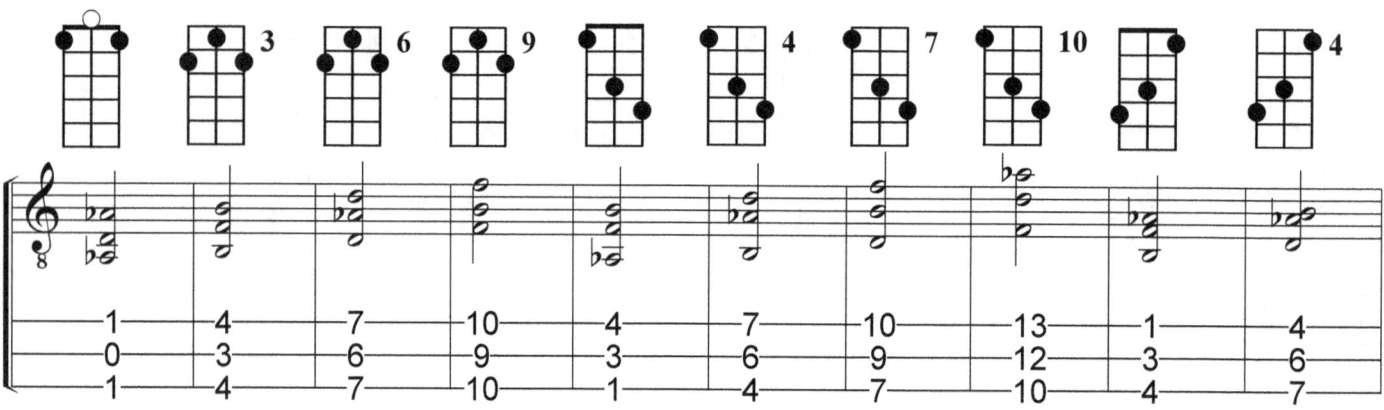

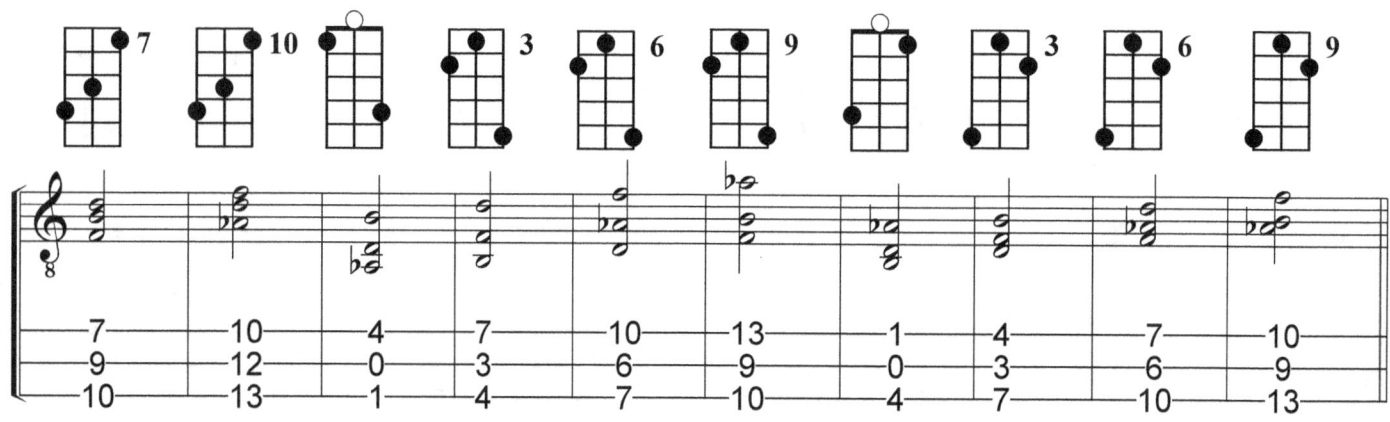

Fsus4 - Fsus2 - Fadd9 - F7sus - Power Chords F5

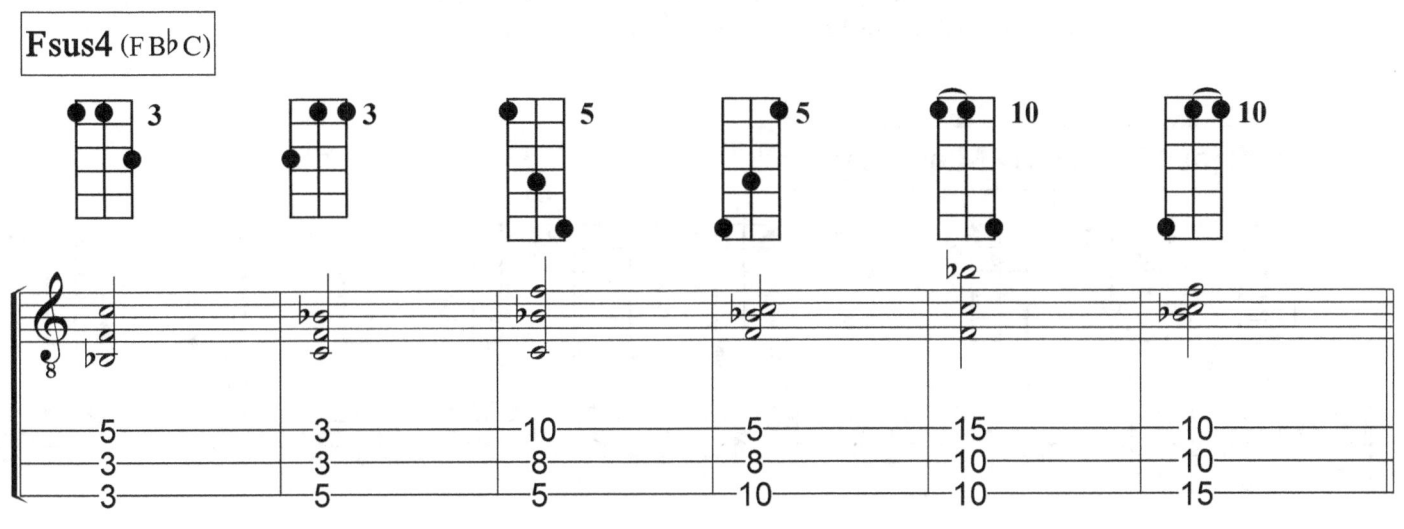

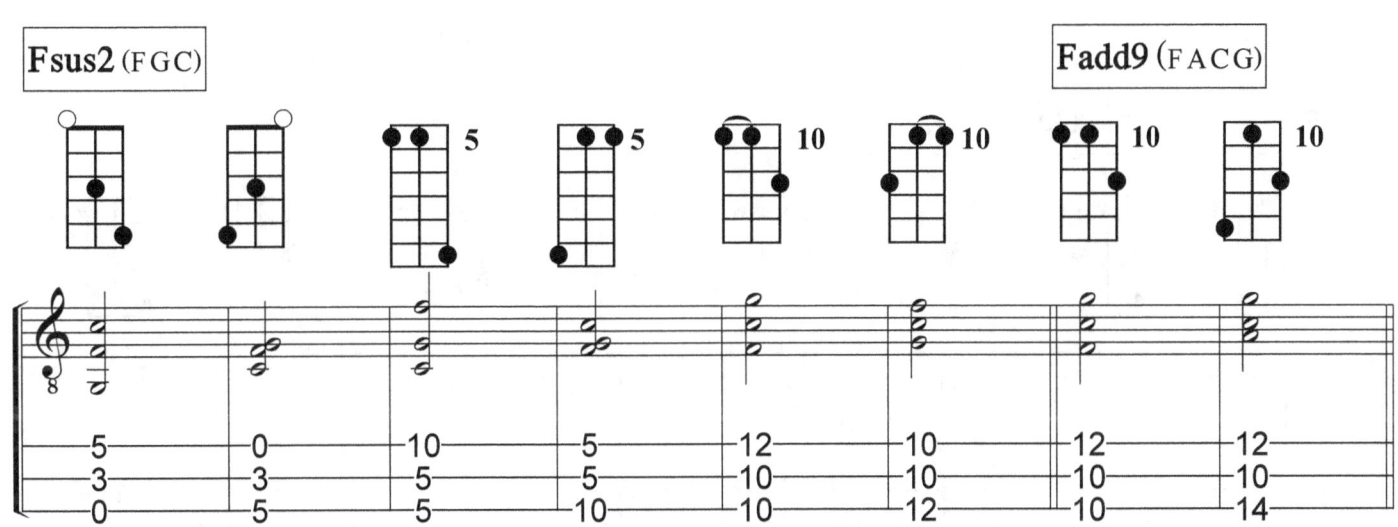

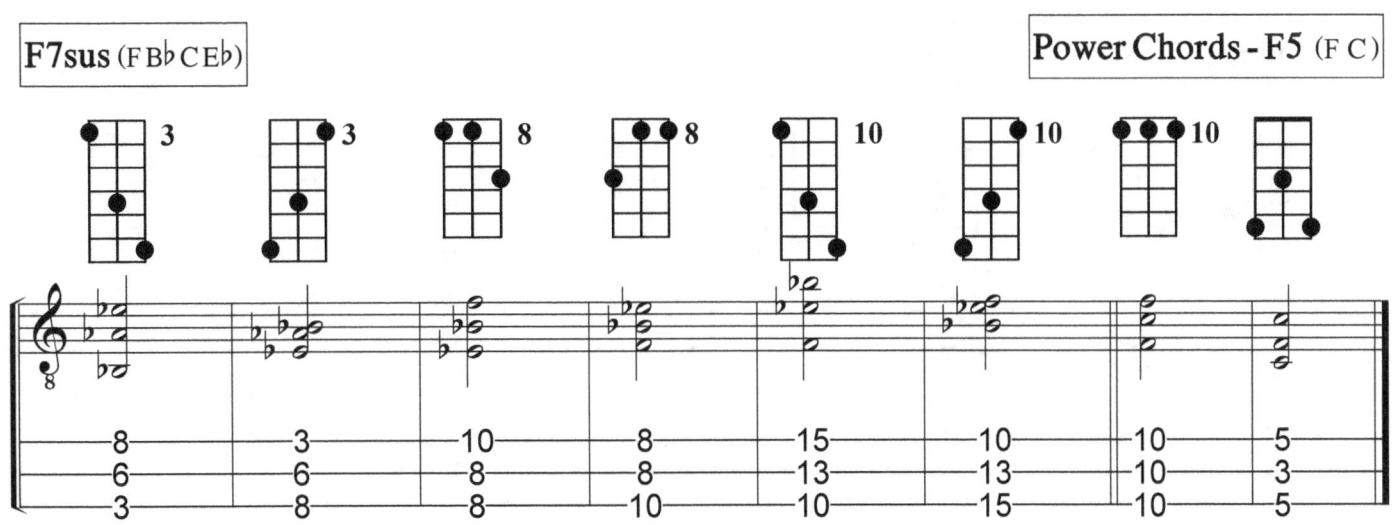

F# - F#6 - F#maj7 / G♭ - G♭6 - G♭maj7

Some notes have been omitted from the chords to facilitate playability.
F# and G♭ are the same note. F# notes are showing in notation.

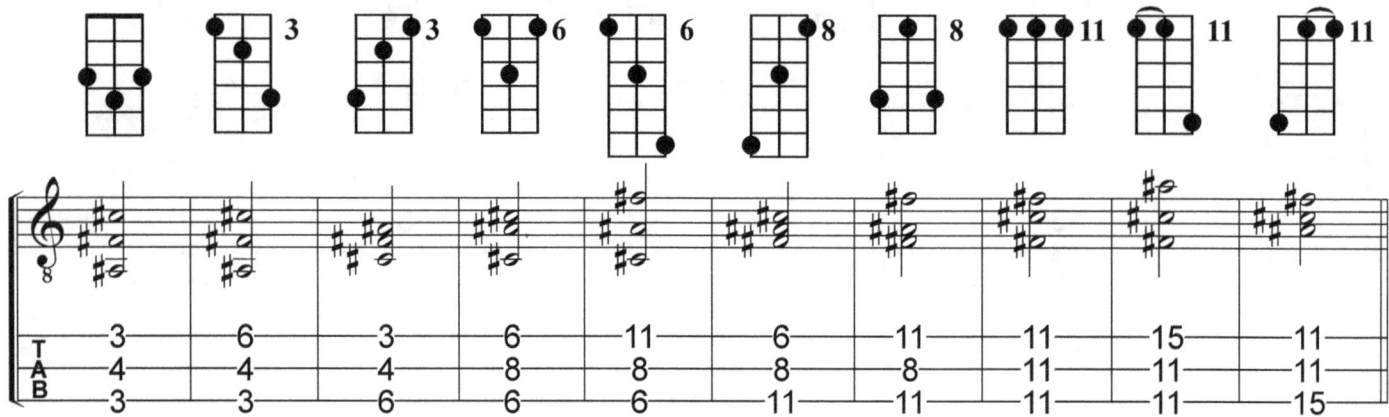

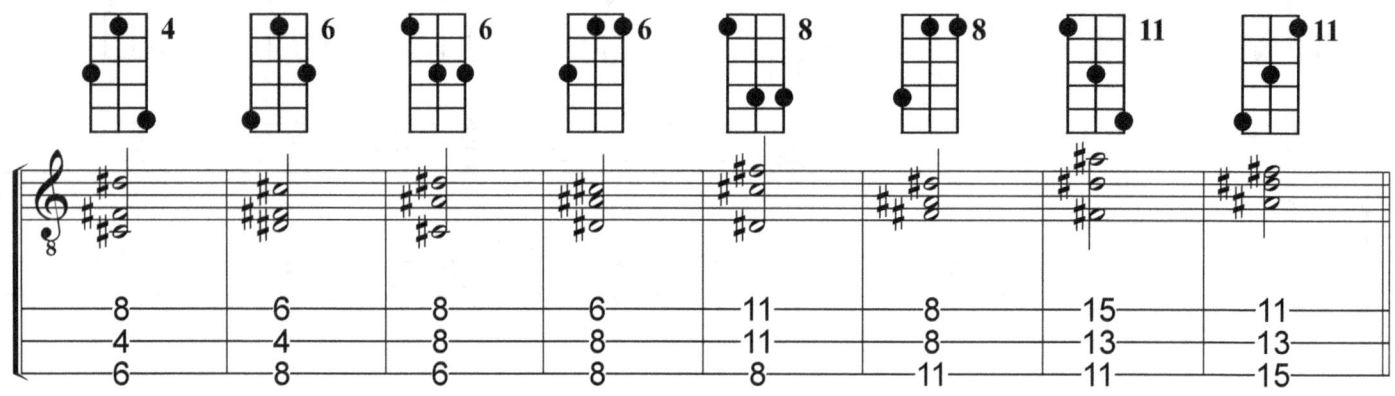

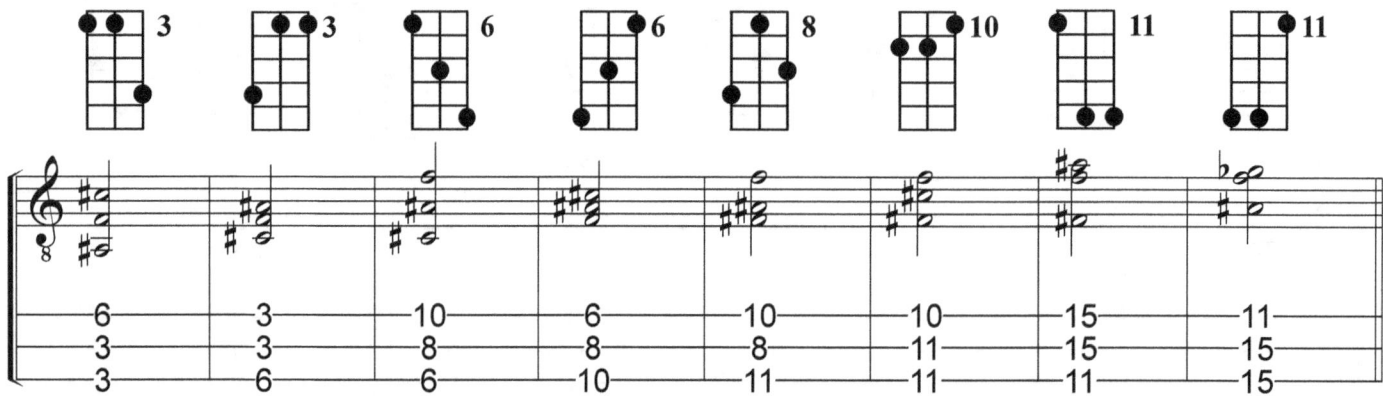

F#maj9 - F#6/9 - F#+ / Gbmaj9 - Gb6/9 - Gb+

F#maj 9 (F-A-C-E-G) **Gbmaj 9** (Gb-Bb-Db-F-Ab)

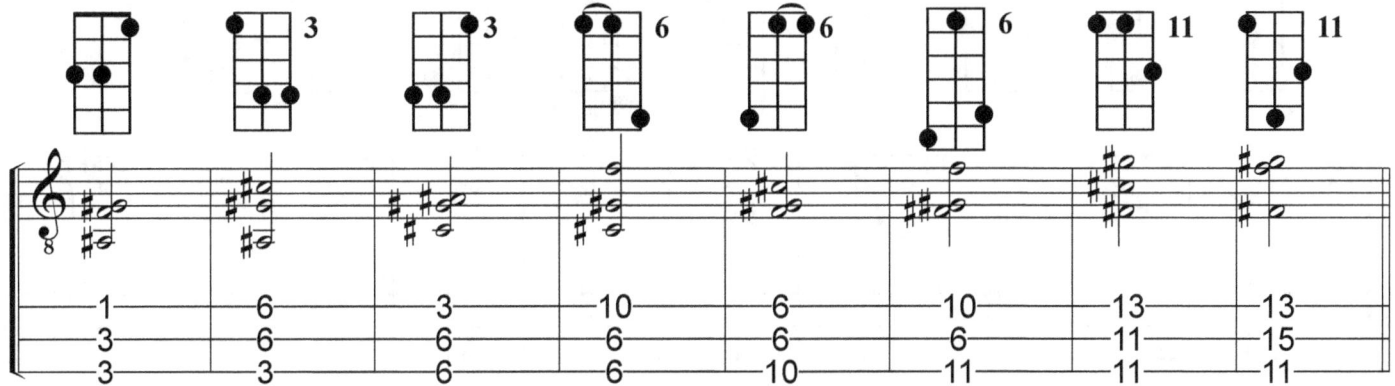

F#6/9 (F# A# C# D# G#) **Gb6/9** (Gb Bb Db Eb Ab)

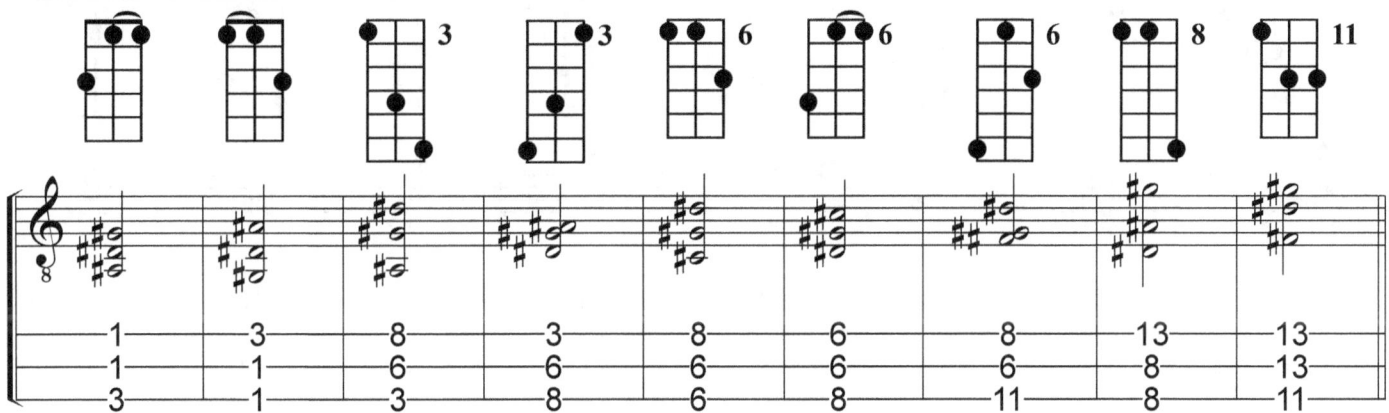

F# Augmented - F#+ (F# A# C𝄪) **Gb Augmented - Gb+** (Gb Bb D)

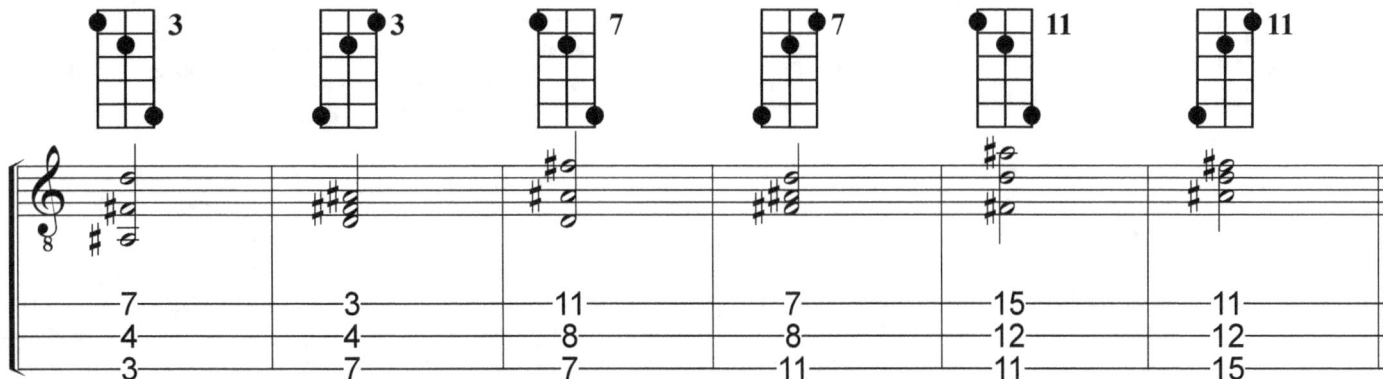

F#m-F#m6-F#m(maj7)-F#m7 / Gbm-Gbm6-Gbm(maj7)-Gbm7

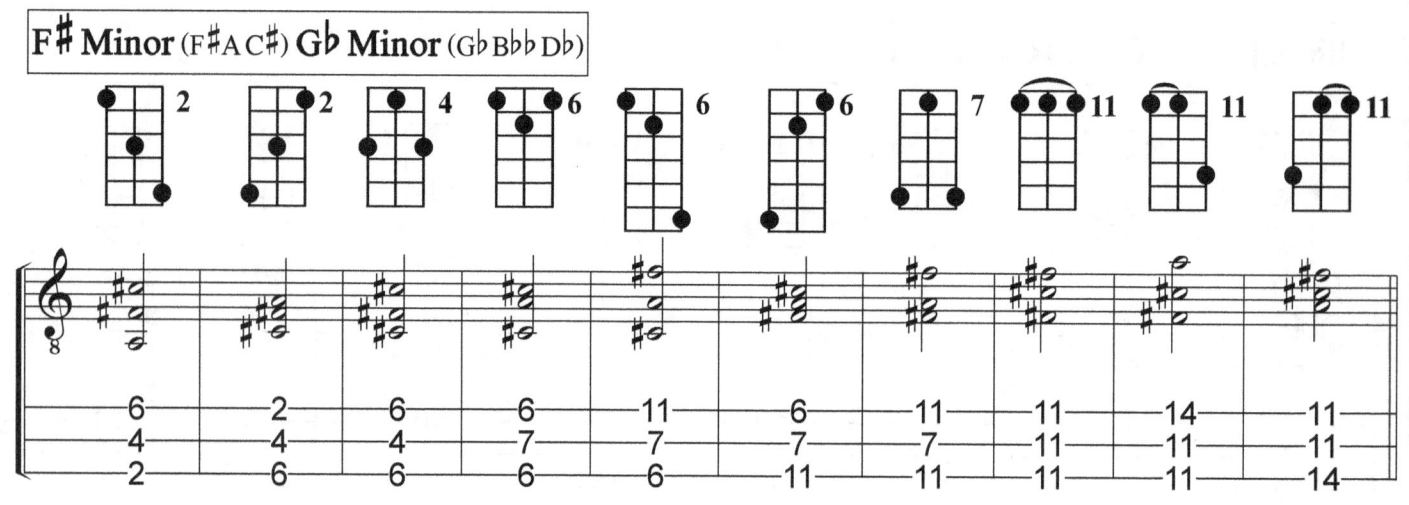

F# Minor (F# A C#) Gb Minor (Gb Bbb Db)

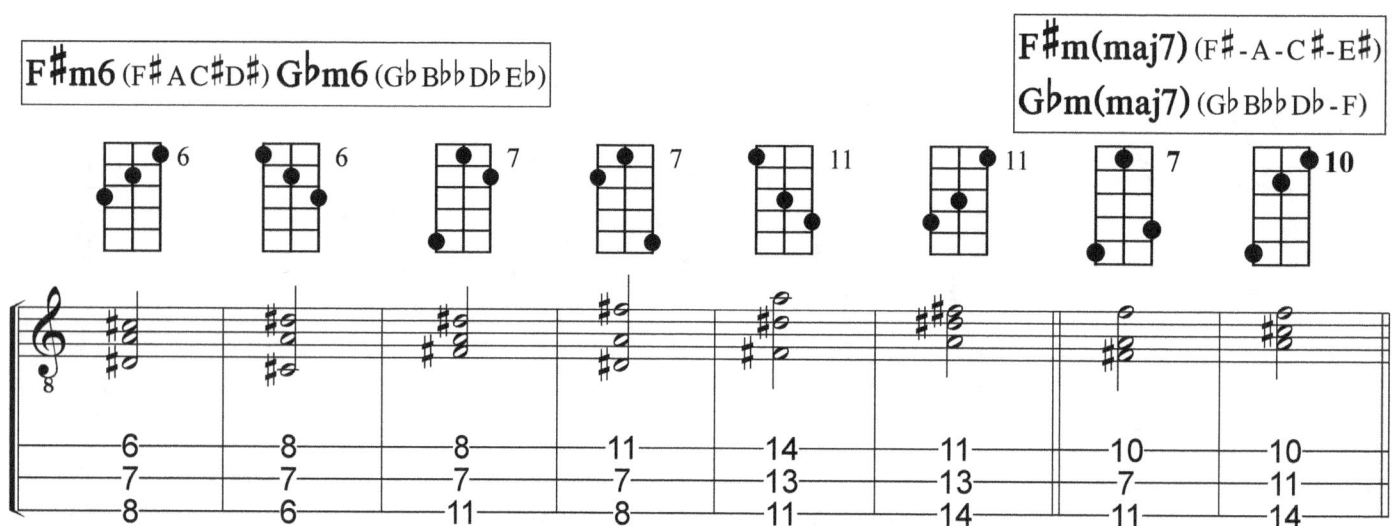

F#m6 (F# A C# D#) Gbm6 (Gb Bbb Db Eb)

F#m(maj7) (F#-A-C#-E#)
Gbm(maj7) (Gb Bbb Db - F)

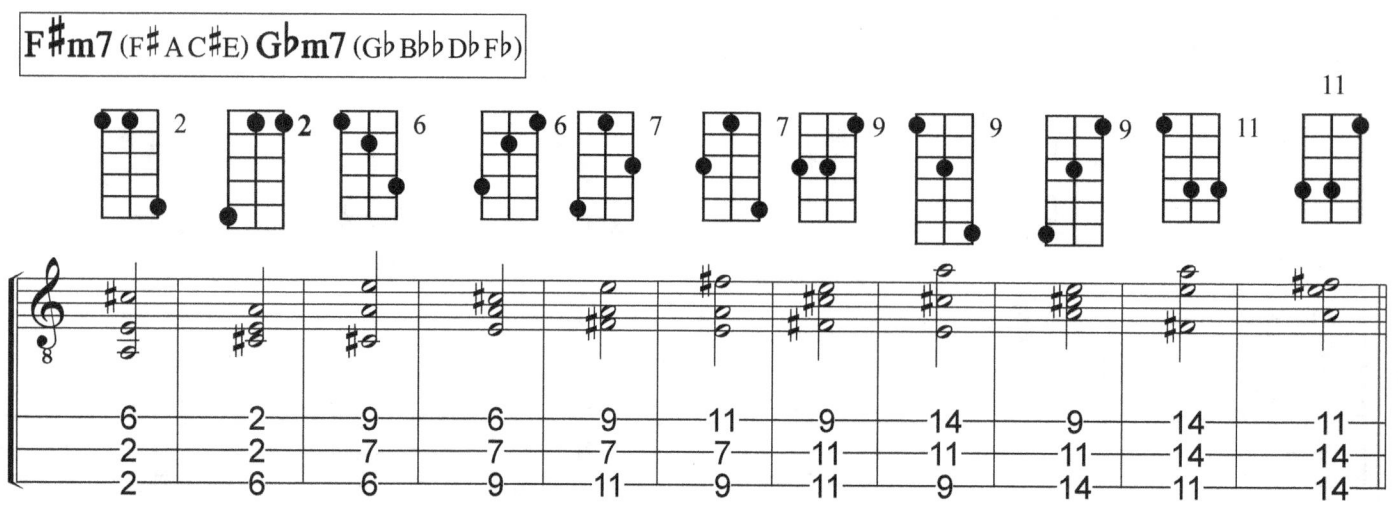

F#m7 (F# A C# E) Gbm7 (Gb Bbb Db Fb)

F#m7b5 - F#m9 - F#m11 / Gbm7b5 - Gbm9 - Gbm11

F#m7b5 (F# A C E) **Gbm7b5** (Gb Bbb Dbb Fb)

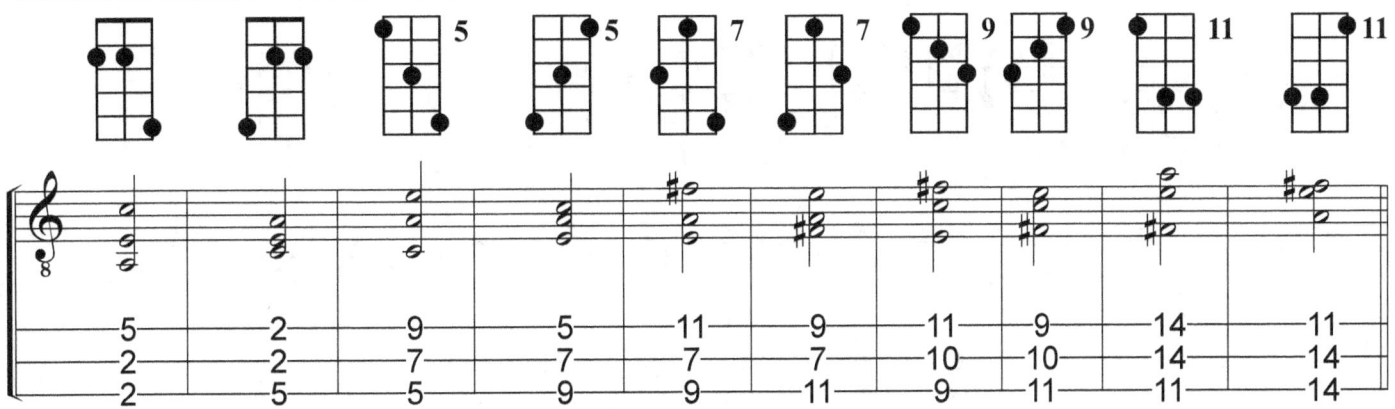

F#m9 (F# A C# E G#) **Gbm9** (Gb - Bbb - Db - Fb - Ab)

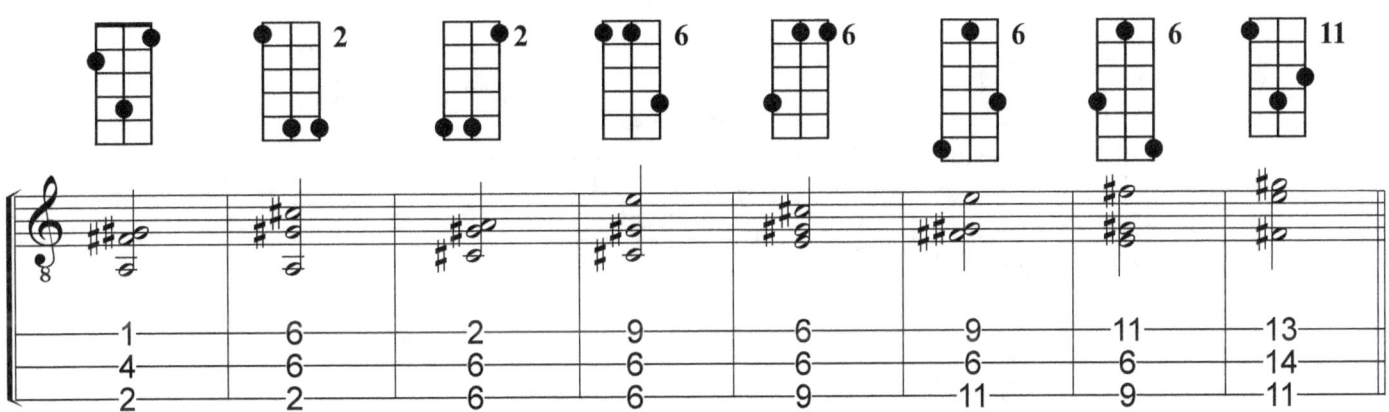

F#m11 (F# A C# E G# B) **Gbm11** (Gb Bbb Db Fb Gb Cb)

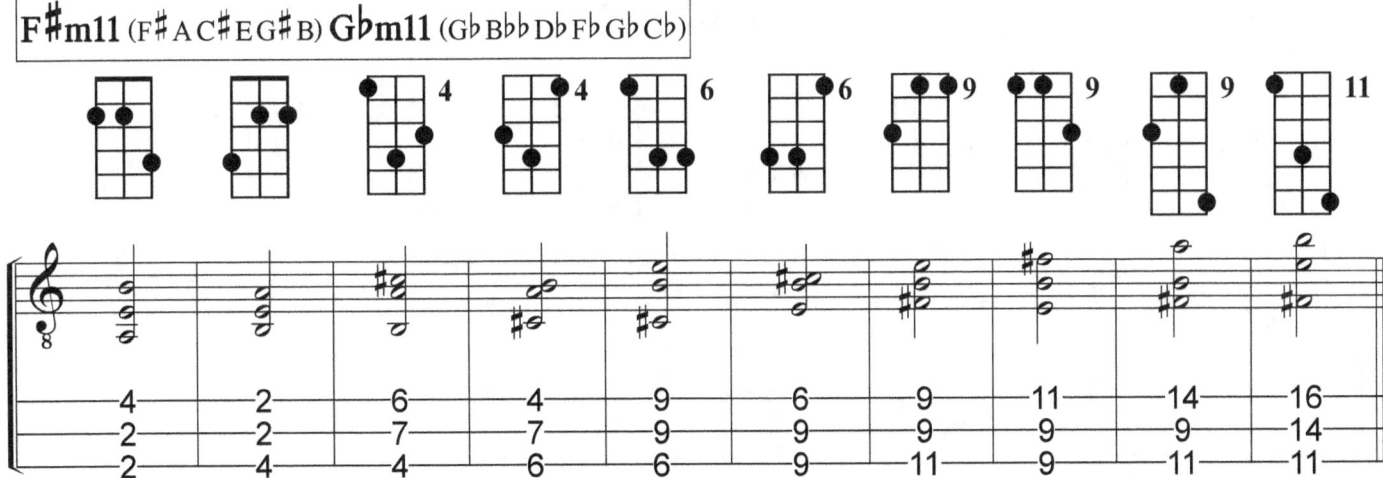

F#7 - F#9 - F#13 / Gb7 - Gb9 - Gb13

F#7 (F# A# C# E) **Gb7** (Gb Bb Db Fb)

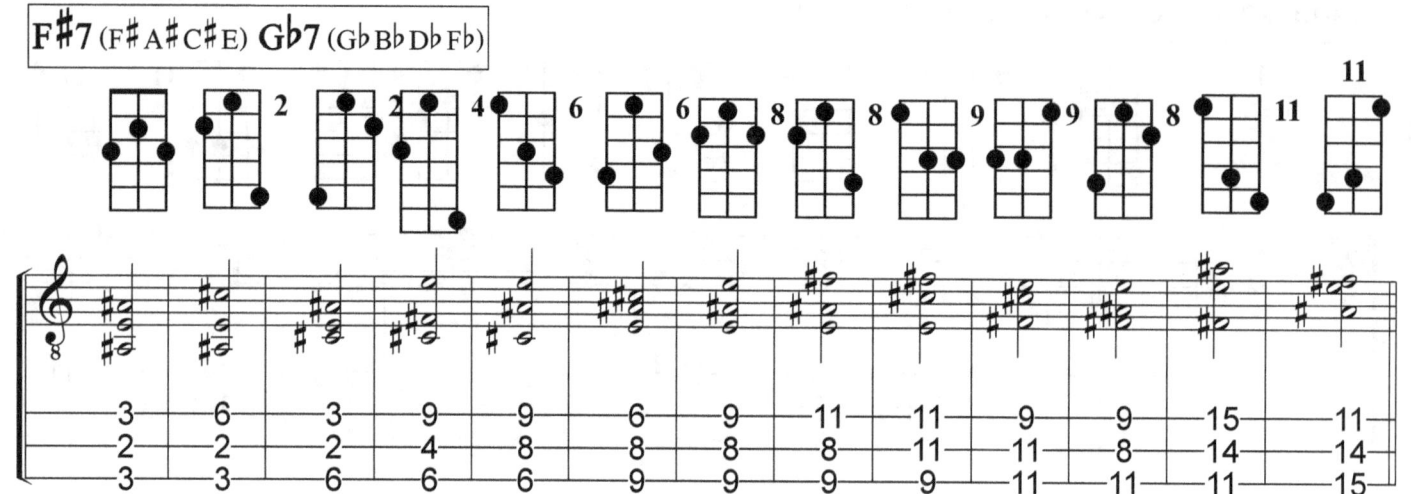

F#9 (F# A# C# E G#) **Gb9** (Gb Bb Db Fb Ab)

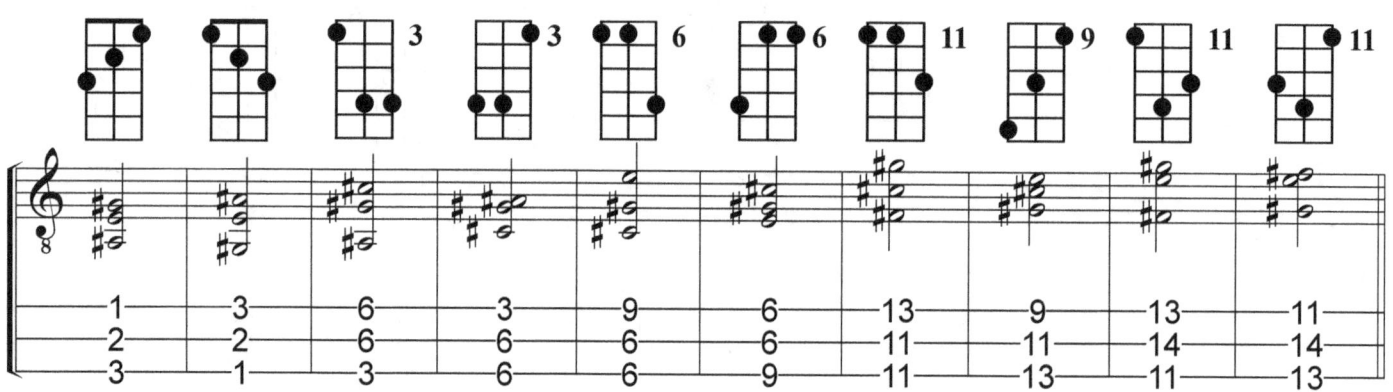

F#13 (F# A# C# E G# B D#) **Gb13** (Gb Bb Db Fb Ab Cb Eb)

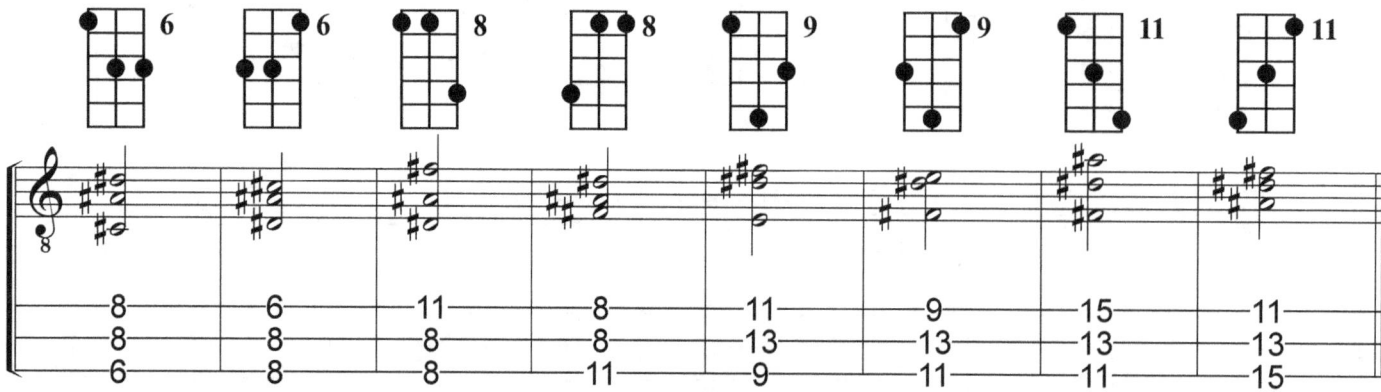

F#7b5 - F#7#5 - F#7#9 / Gb7b5 - Gb7#5 - Gb7#9

F#7b5 (F# A# C E) **Gb7b5** (Gb Bb Dbb Fb)

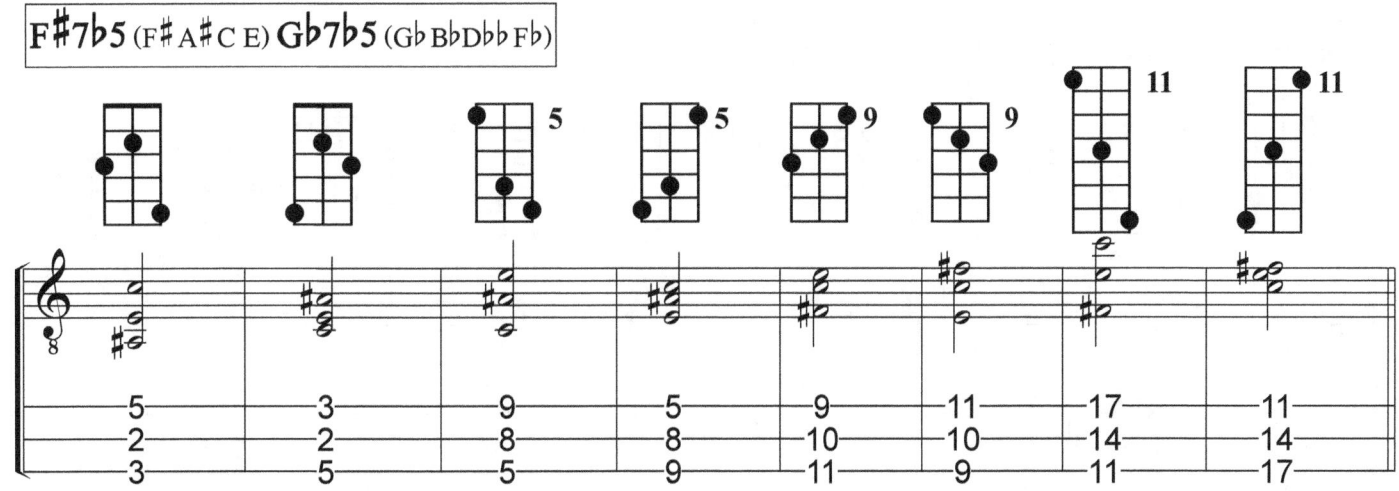

F#7#5 (F# A# C× E) **Gb7#5** (Gb Bb D Fb)

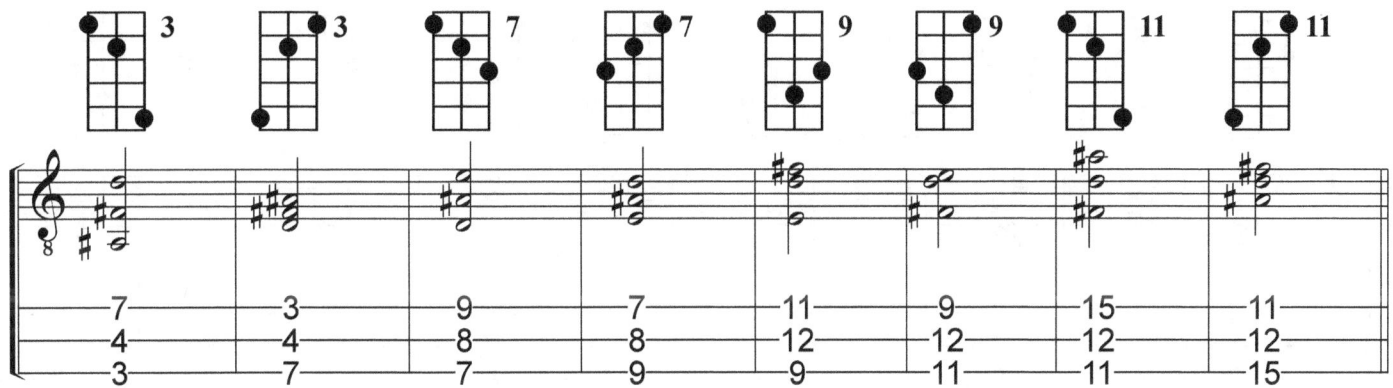

F#7#9 (F# A# C# E G×) **Gb7#9** (Gb Bb Db Fb A)

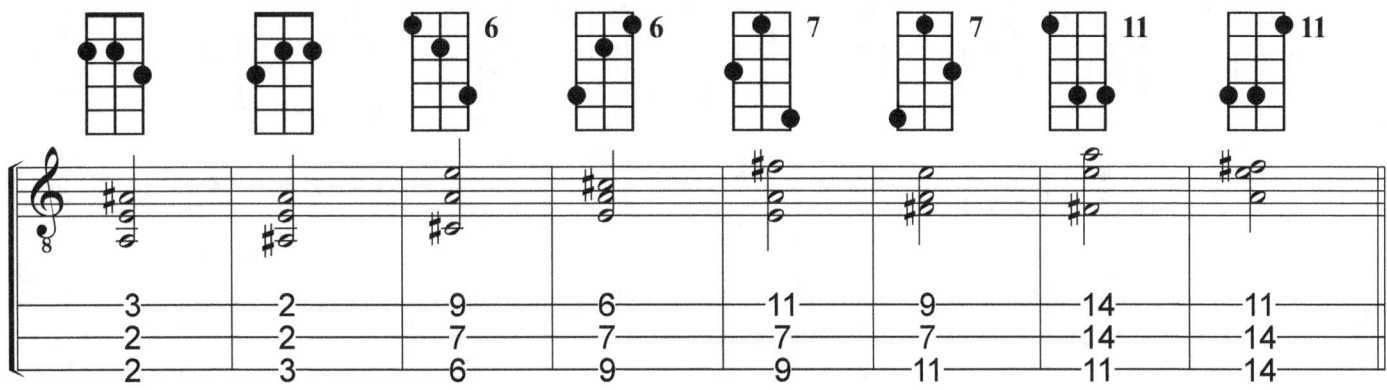

F#7b9 - F#diminished - F#°7 / Gb7b9 - Gb diminished - Gb°7

F#7b9 (F# A# C# E G) **Gb7b9** (Gb Bb Db Fb Abb)

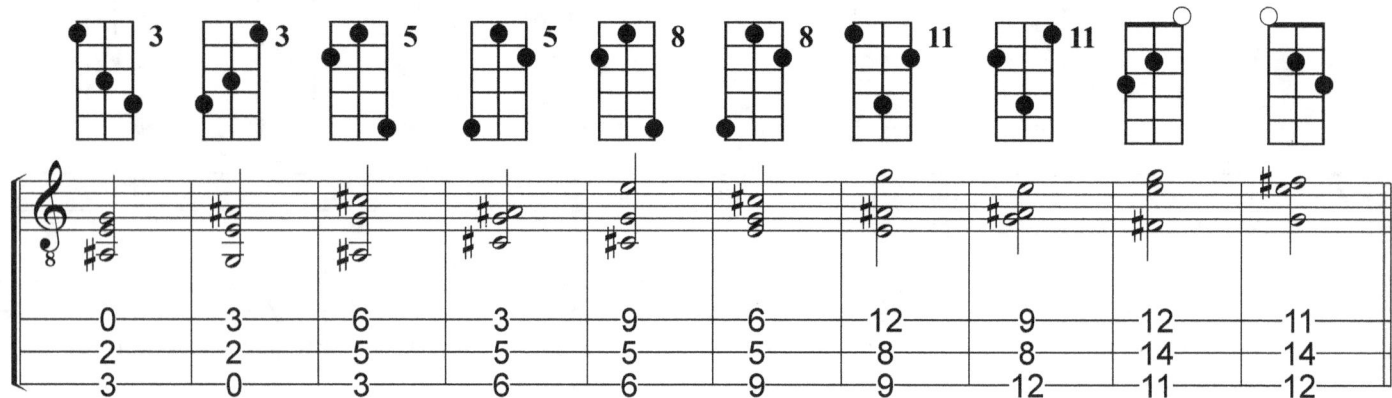

F# diminished - F#°7 (F# A C Eb) **Gb diminished - F#°7** (Gb Bbb Dbb Fbb)

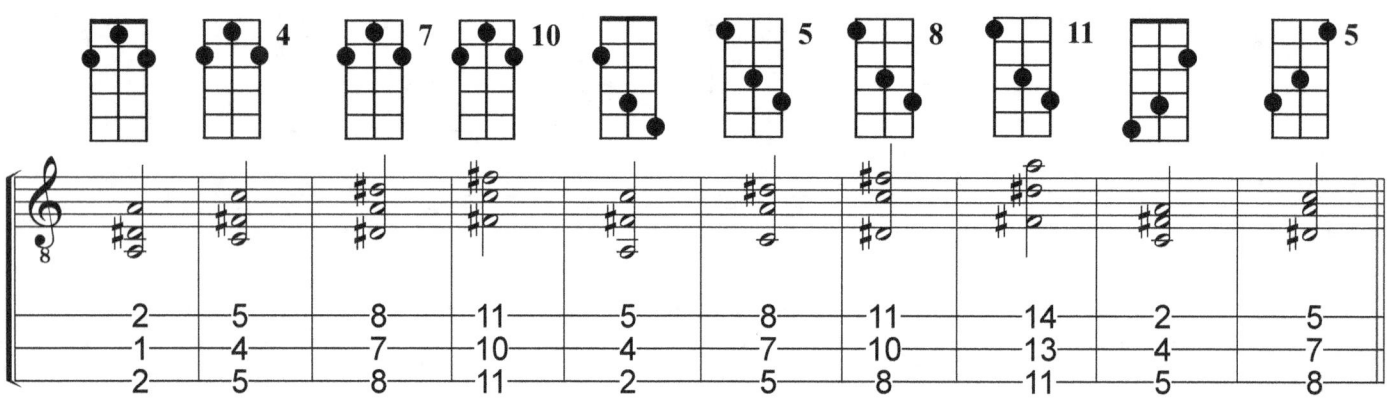

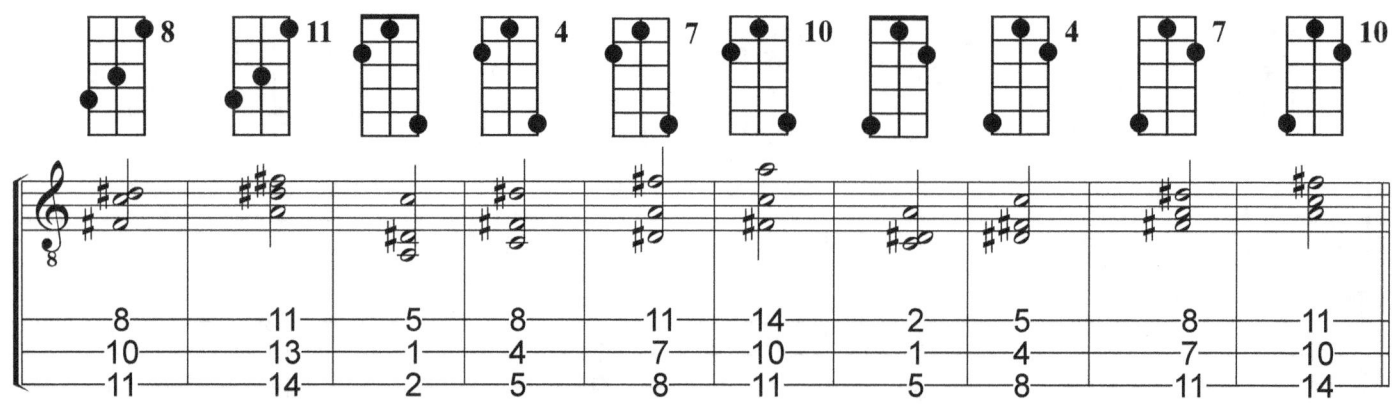

F#sus4 - F#sus2 - F#7sus - F#add9 - F#5 / Gbsus4 - Gbsus2 - Gb7sus - Gbadd9 - Gb5

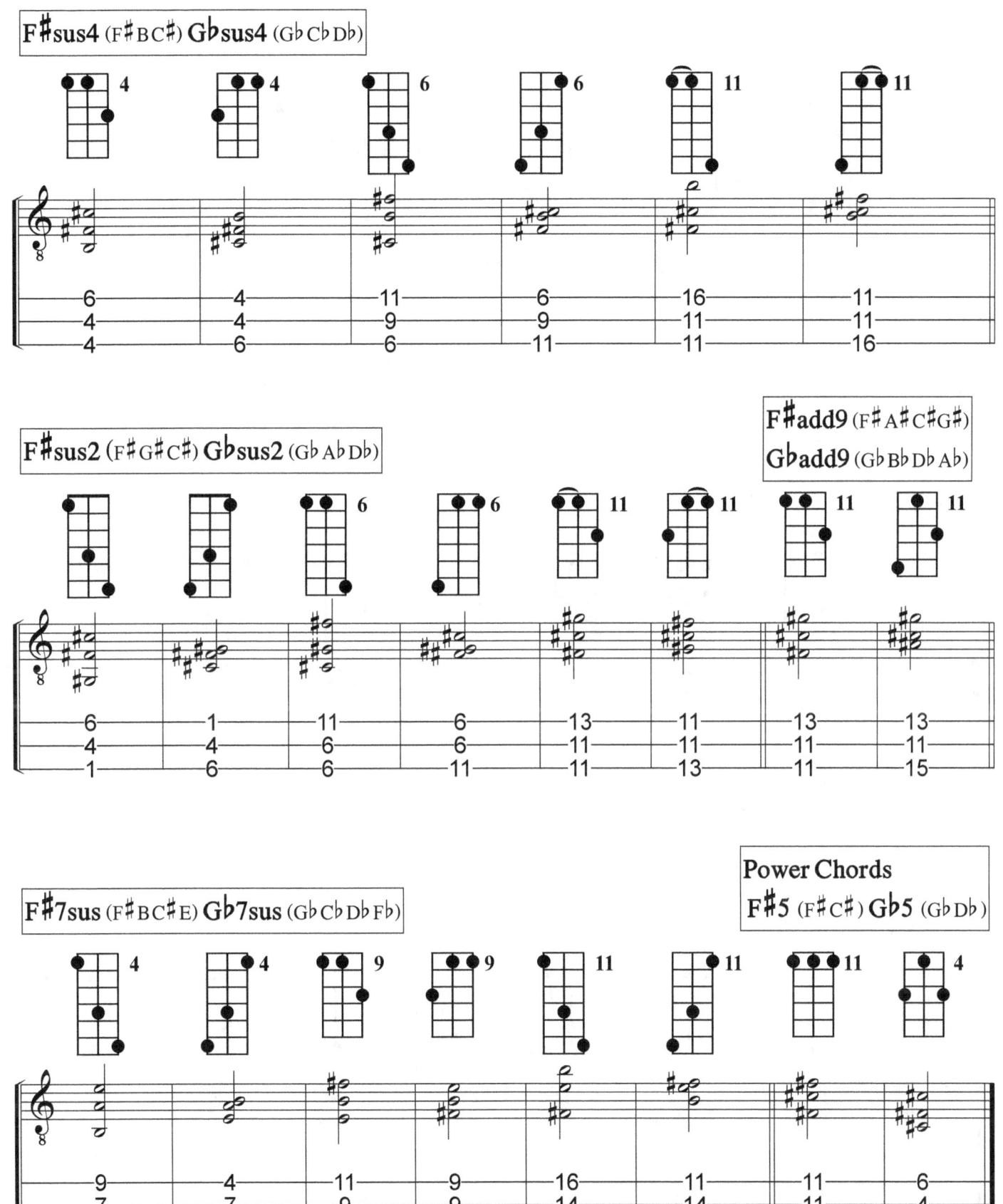

G - G - Gmaj7

Some notes have been omitted from the chords to facilitate playability.
The notes that form the chord are in brackets.

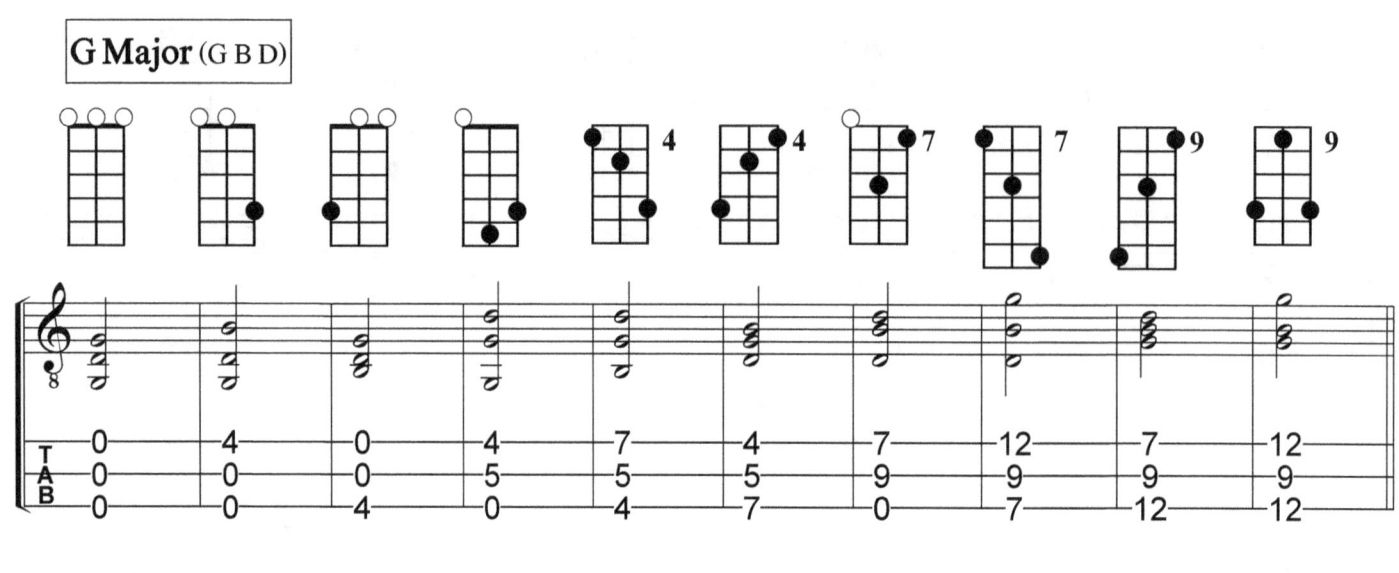

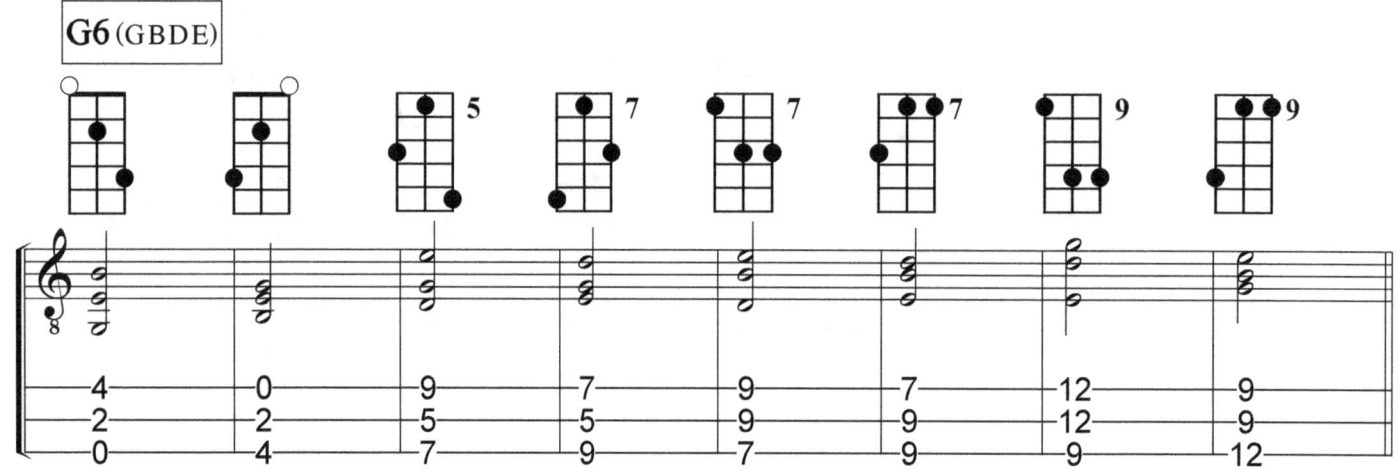

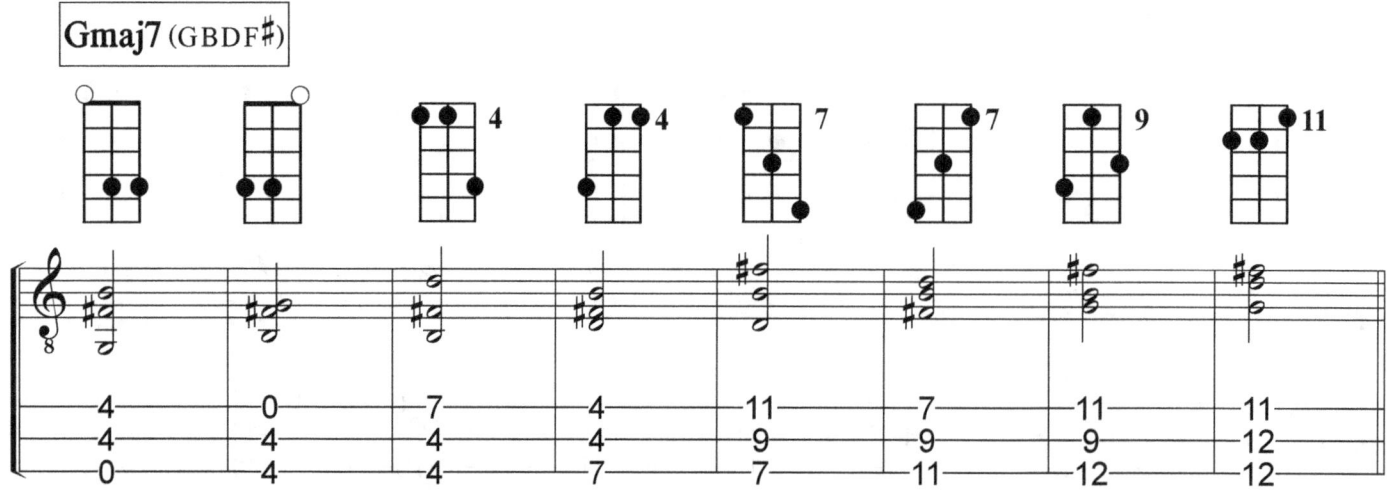

Gmaj9 - G6/9 - G+

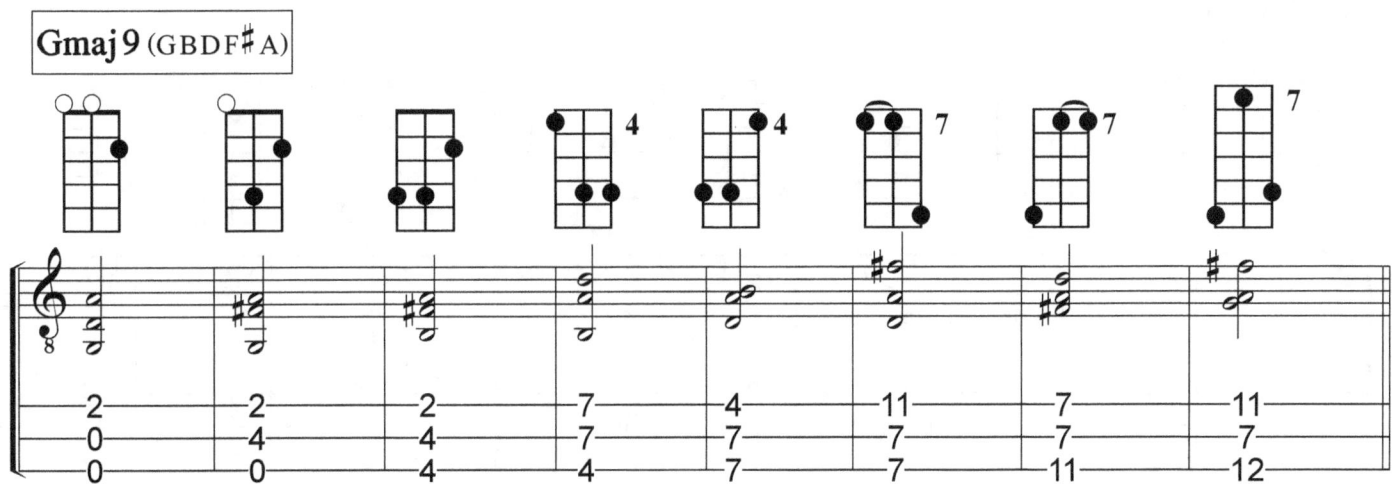

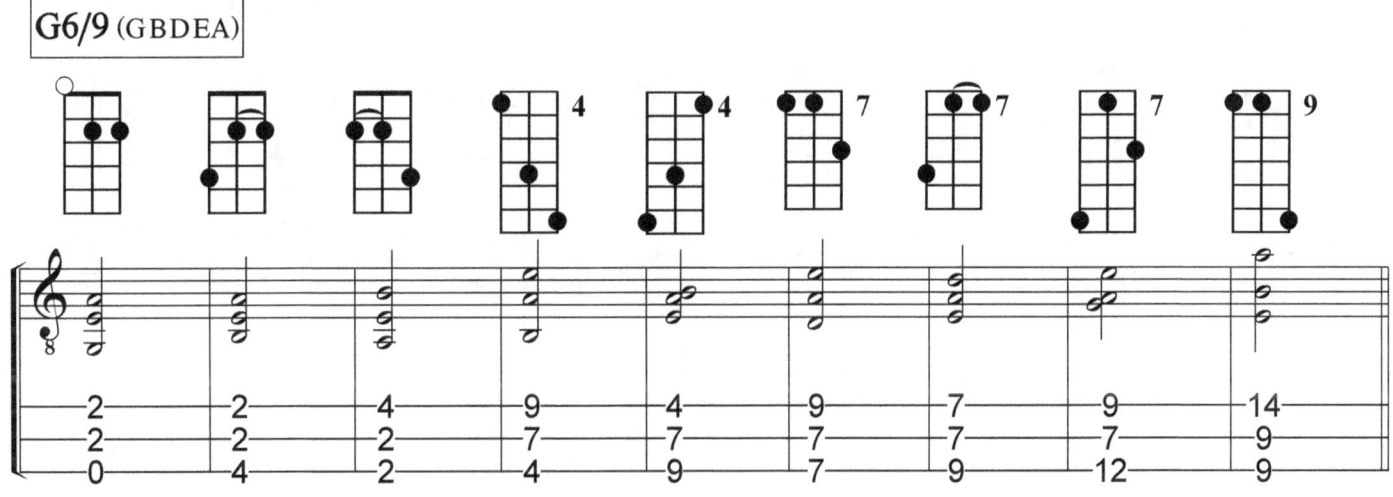

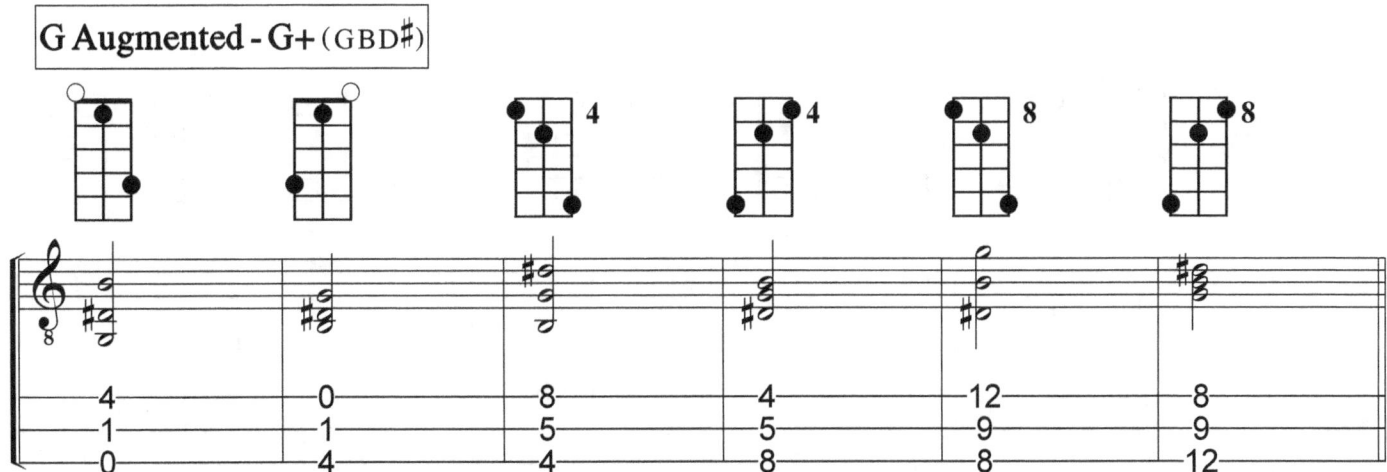

Gm - Gm6 - Gm(maj7) - Gm7

G Minor (G B♭ D)

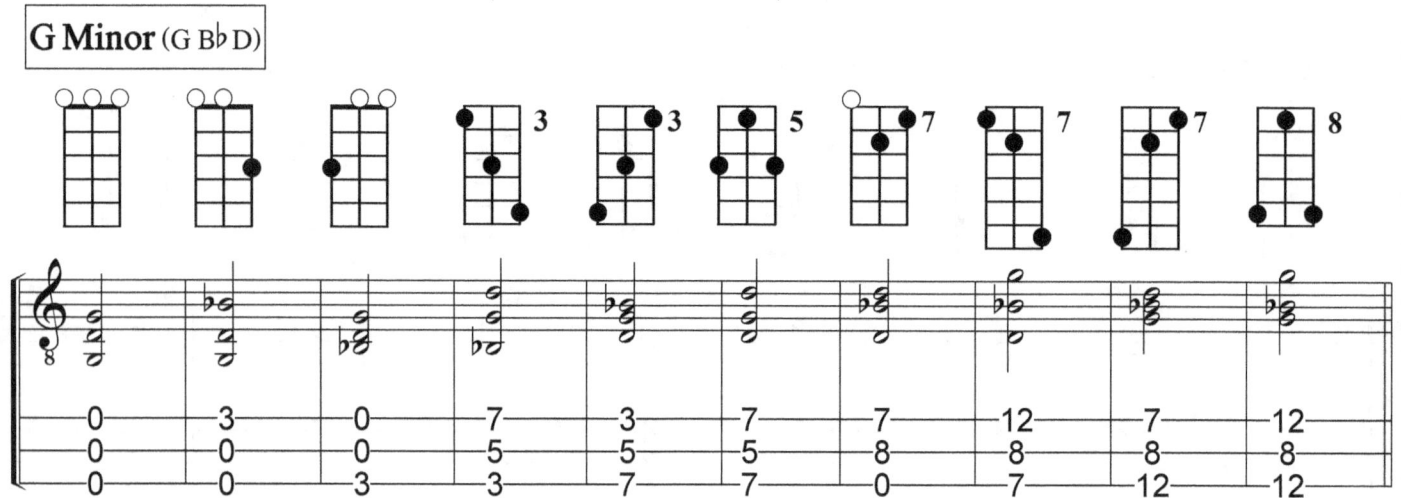

Gm6 (G B♭ D E)   **Gm(maj7)** (G B♭ D F♯)

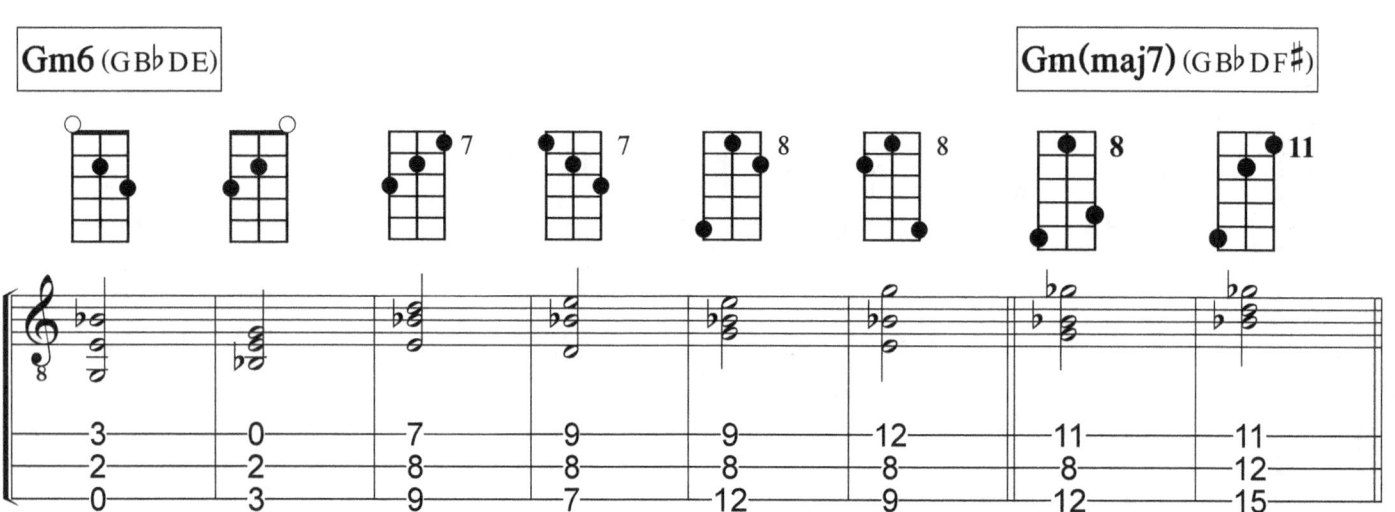

Gm7 (G B♭ D F)

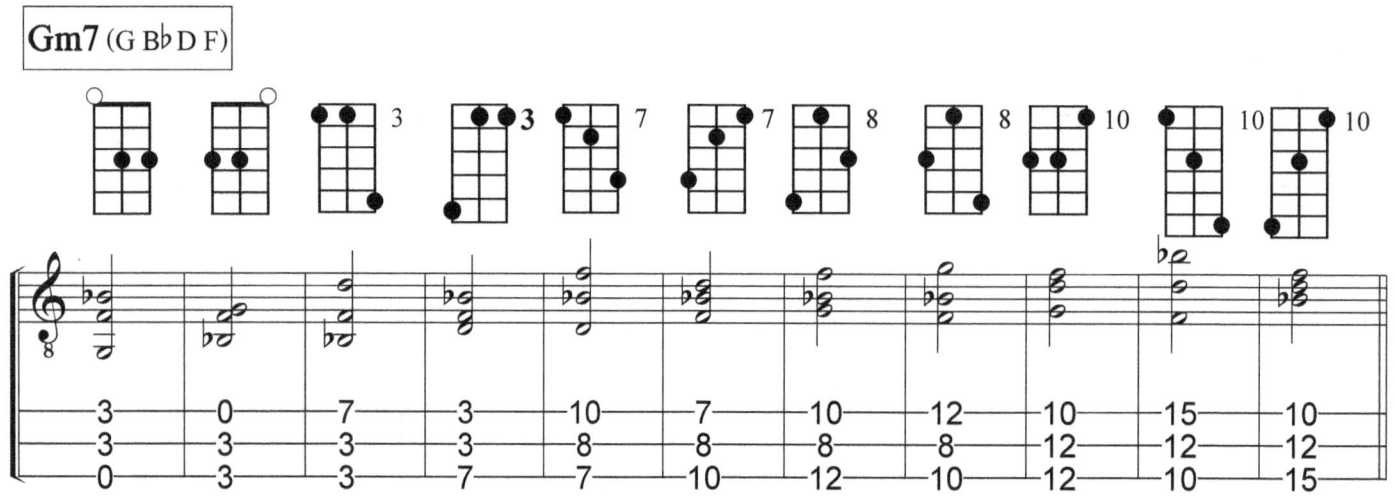

Gm7♭5 - Gm9 - Gm11

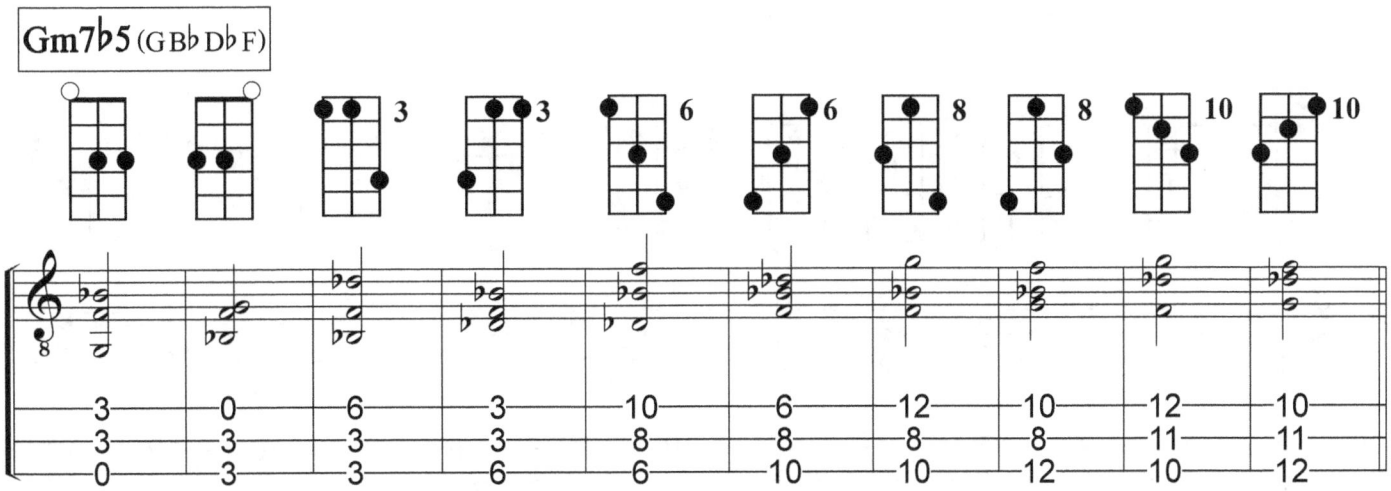

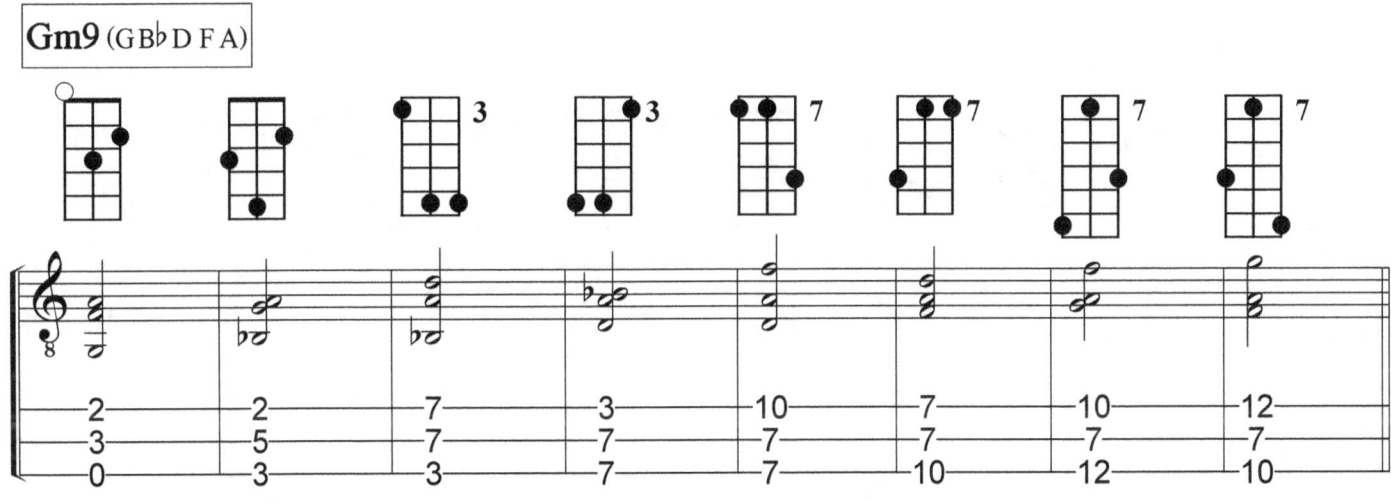

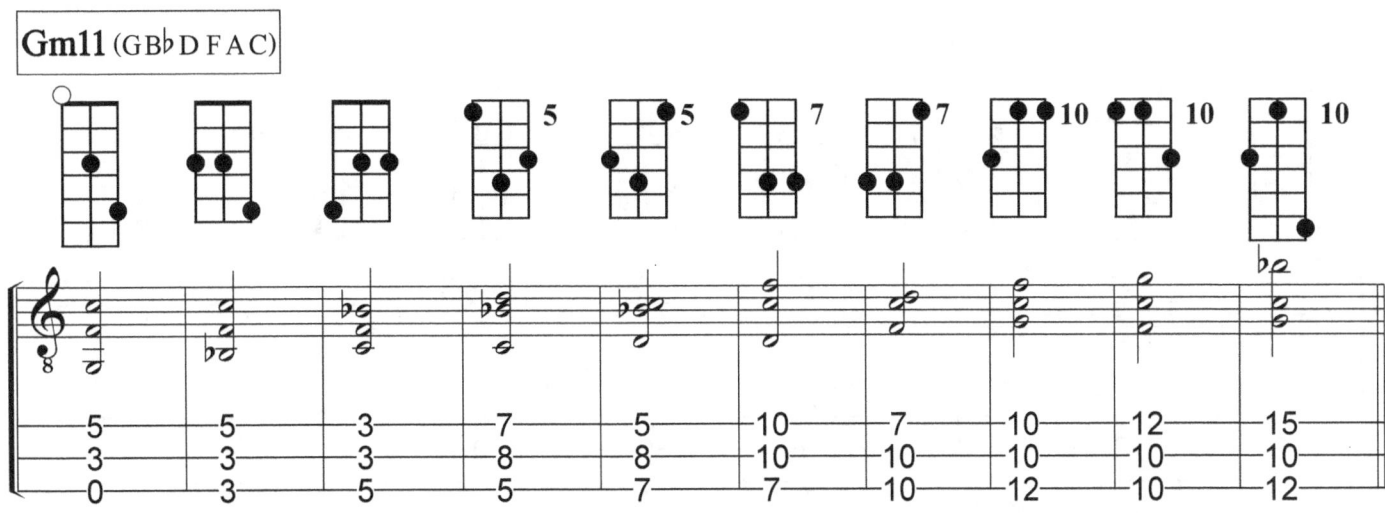

G7 - G9 - G13

G7 (GBDF)

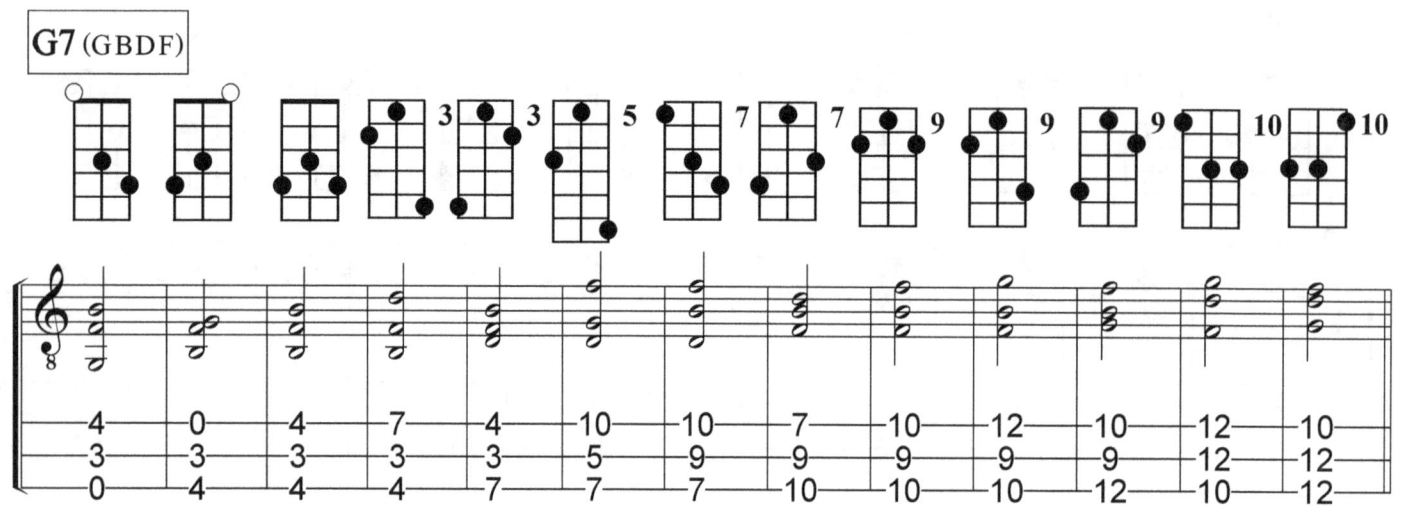

G9 (GBDFA)

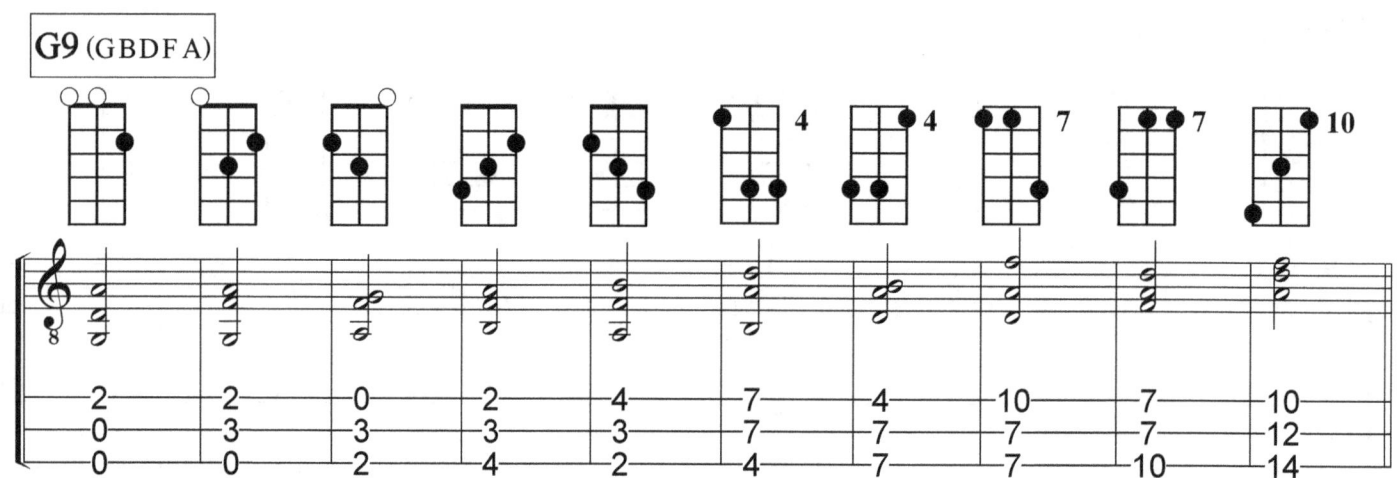

G13 (GBDFACE)

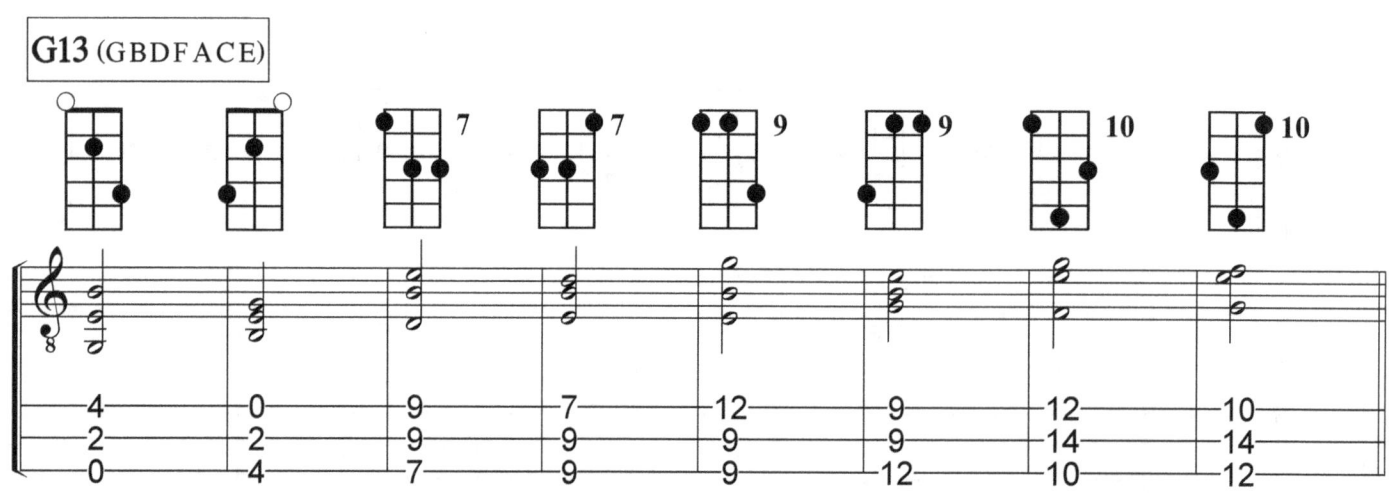

G7♭5 - G7#5 - G7#9

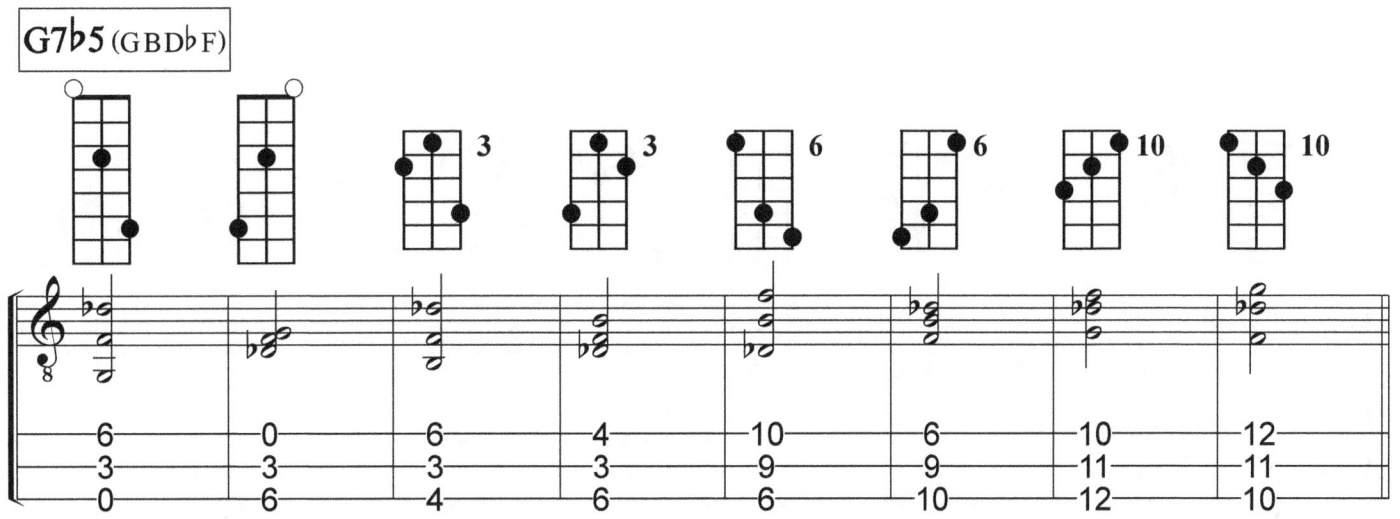

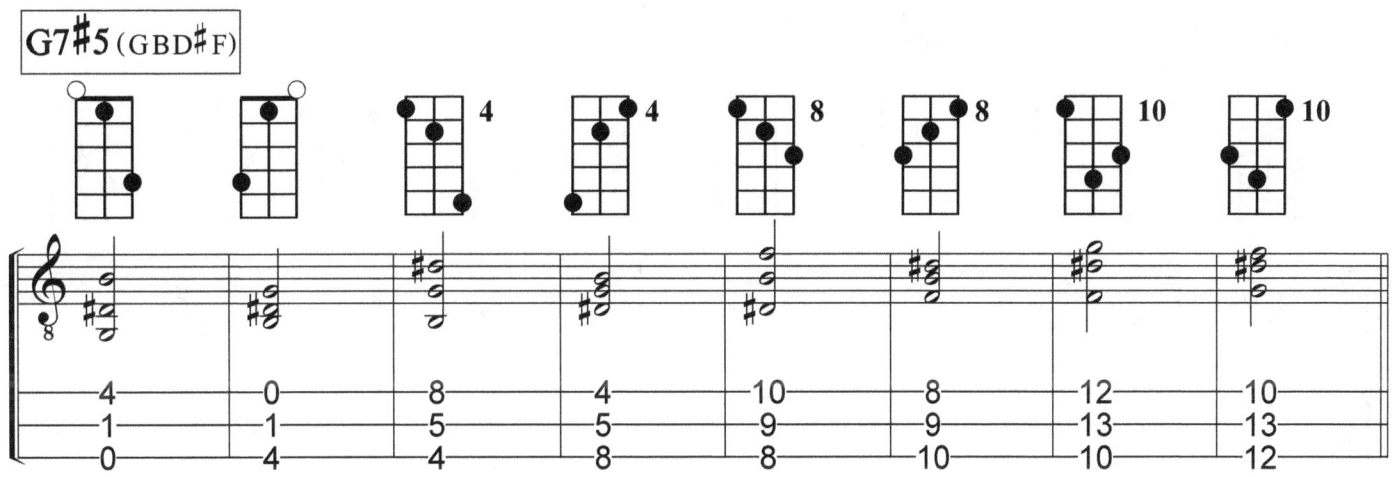

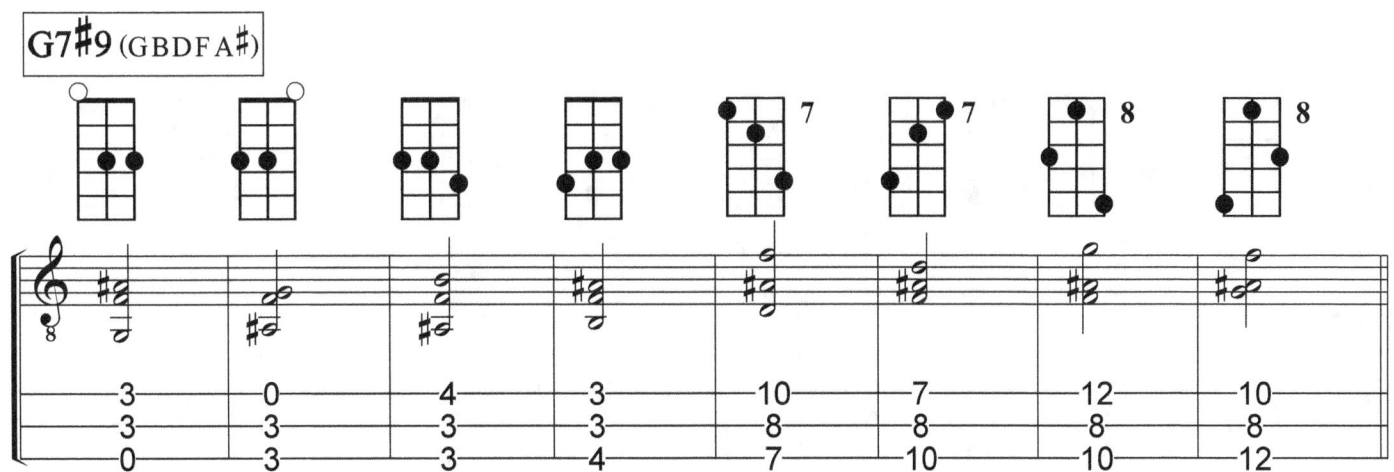

G7♭9 - G diminished - G°7

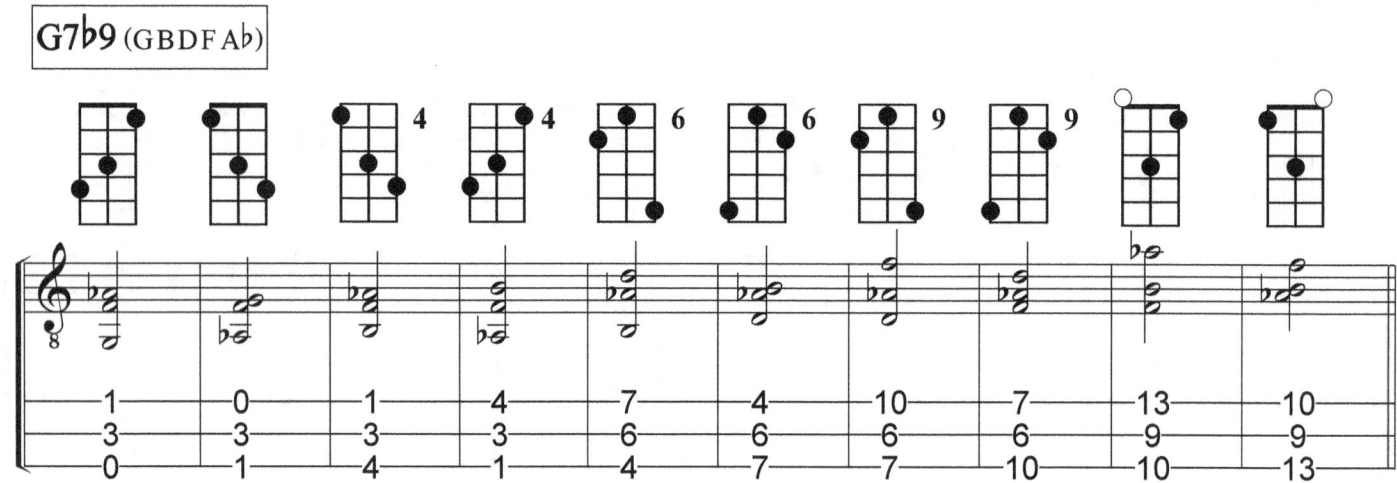

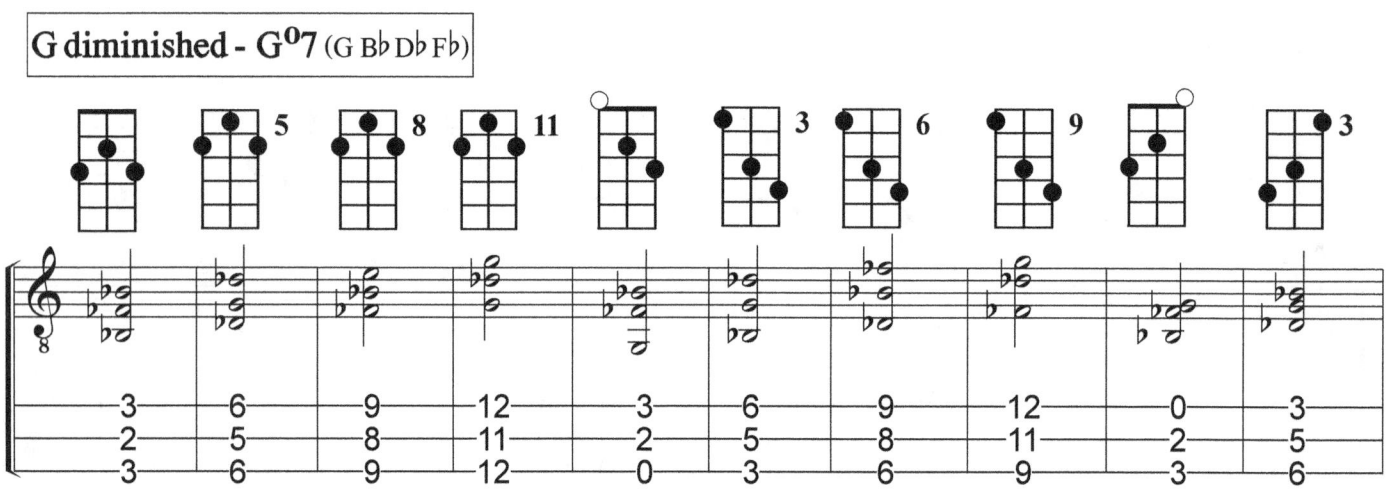

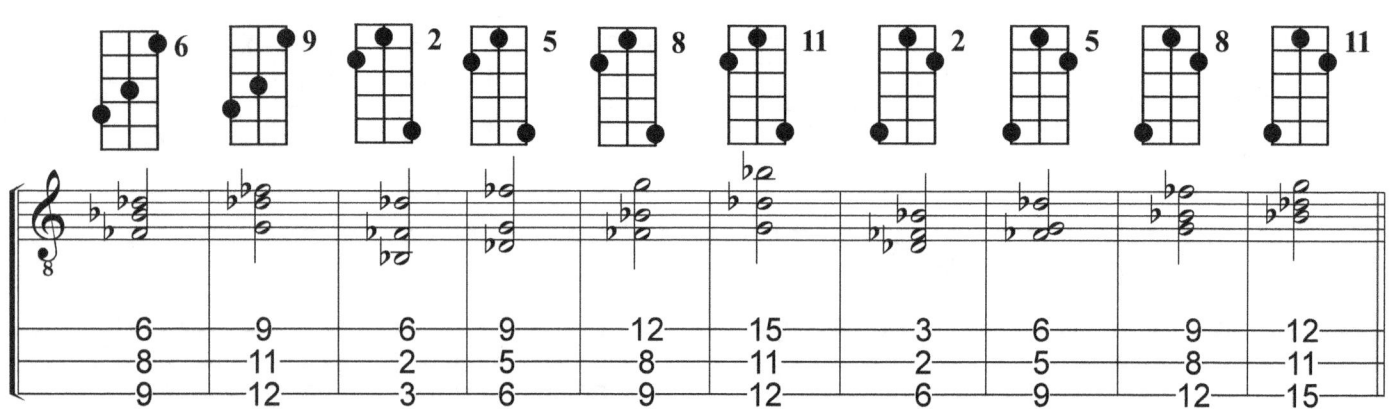

Gsus4 - Gsus2 - G7sus - Gadd9 - G5

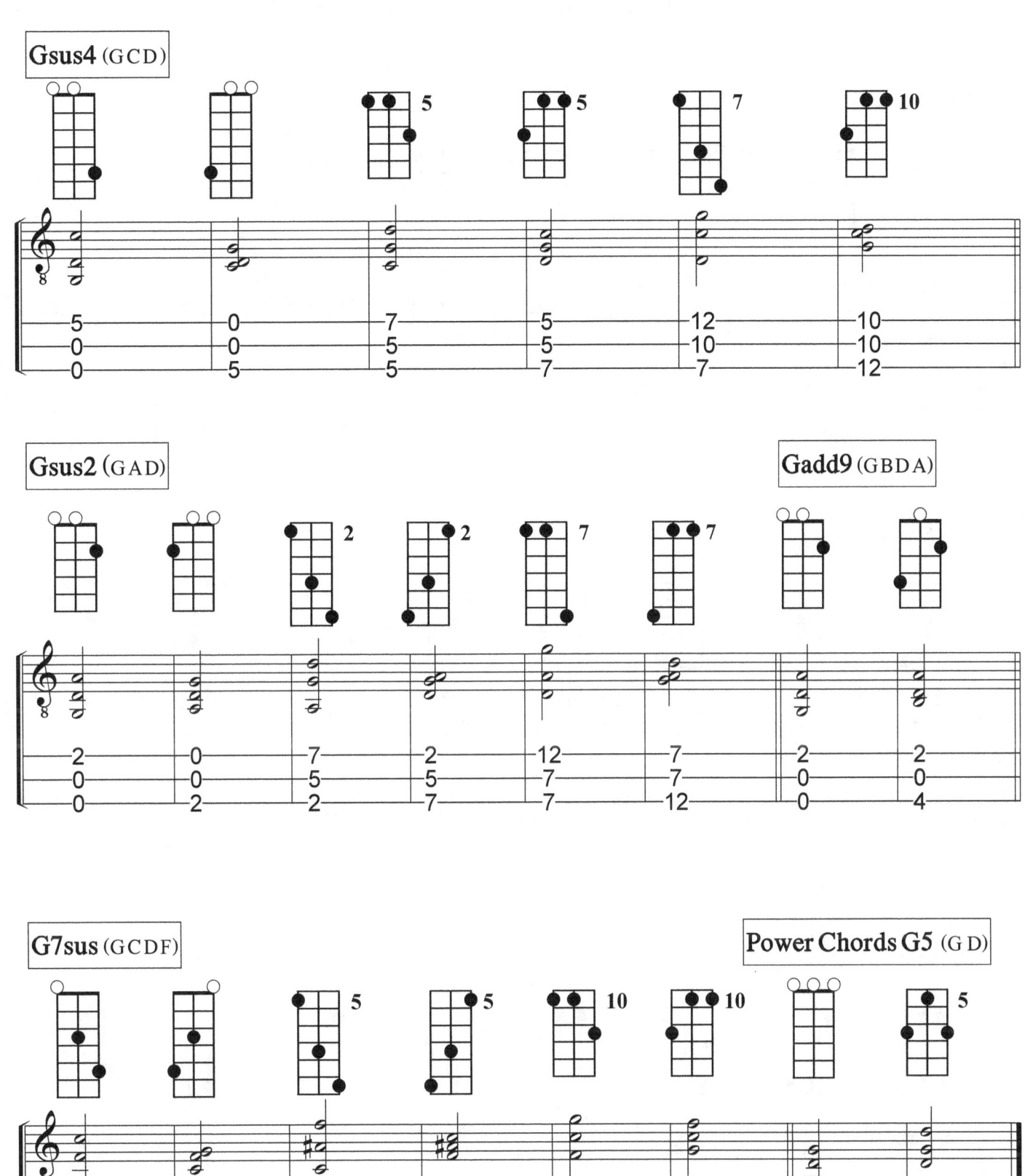

Ab - Ab6 - Abmaj7

Some notes have been omitted from the chords to facilitate playability.
Ab and G# are the same notes. The notes that form the chord are in brackets.

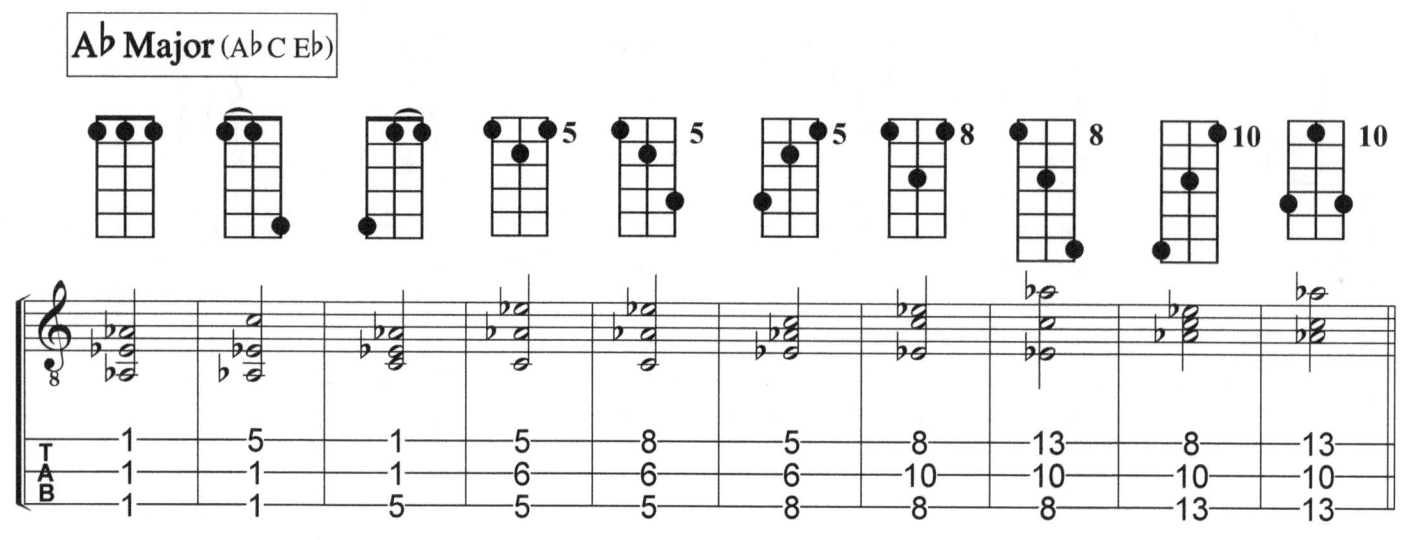

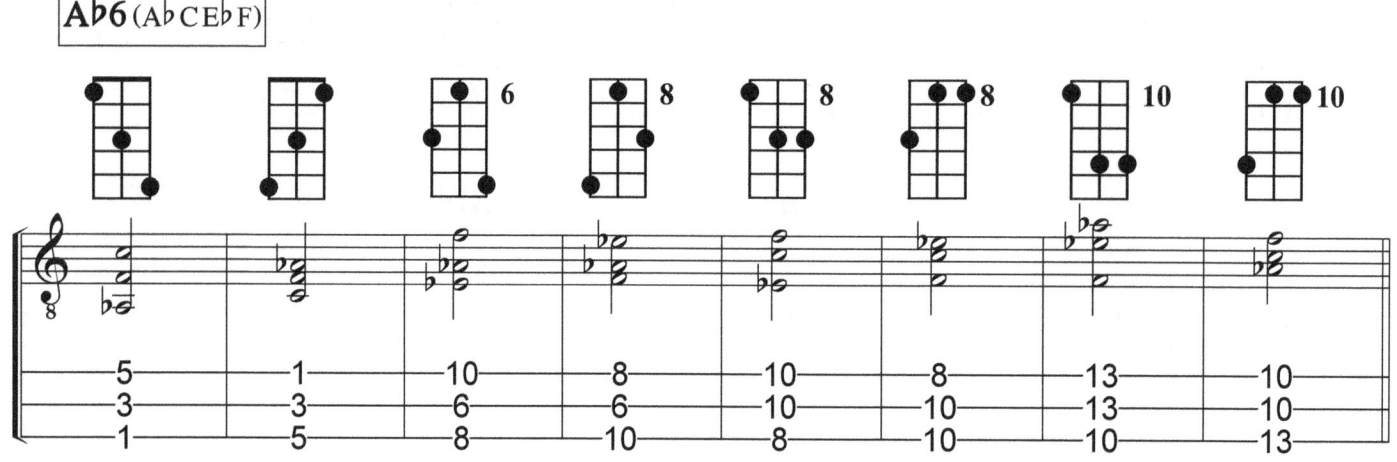

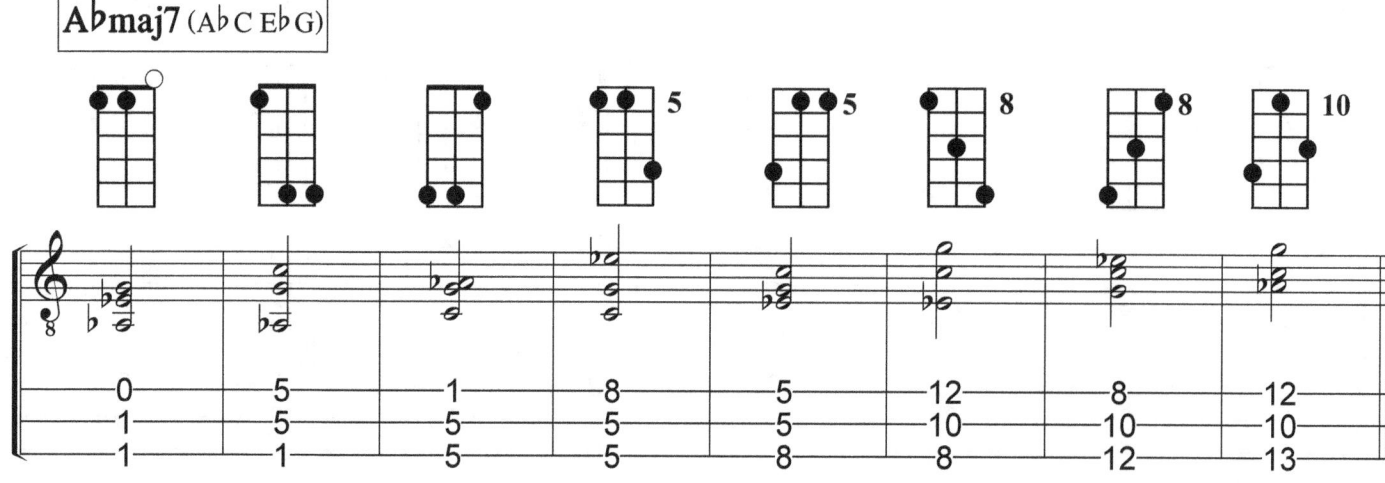

A♭maj9 - A♭6/9 - A♭+

A♭maj 9 (A♭ C E♭ G B♭)

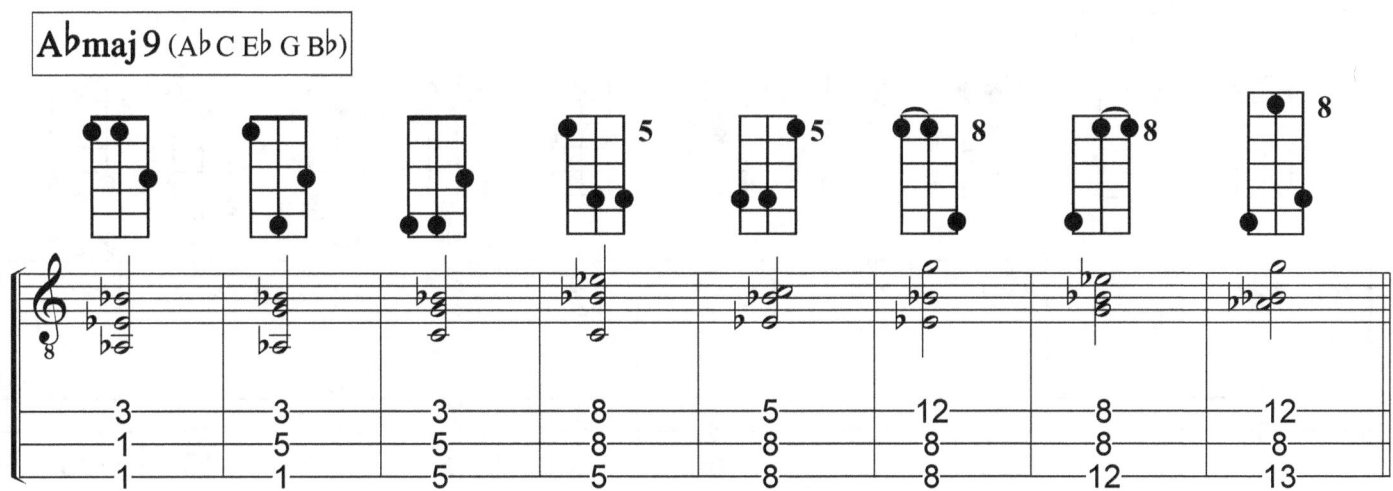

A♭6/9 (A♭ C E♭ F B♭)

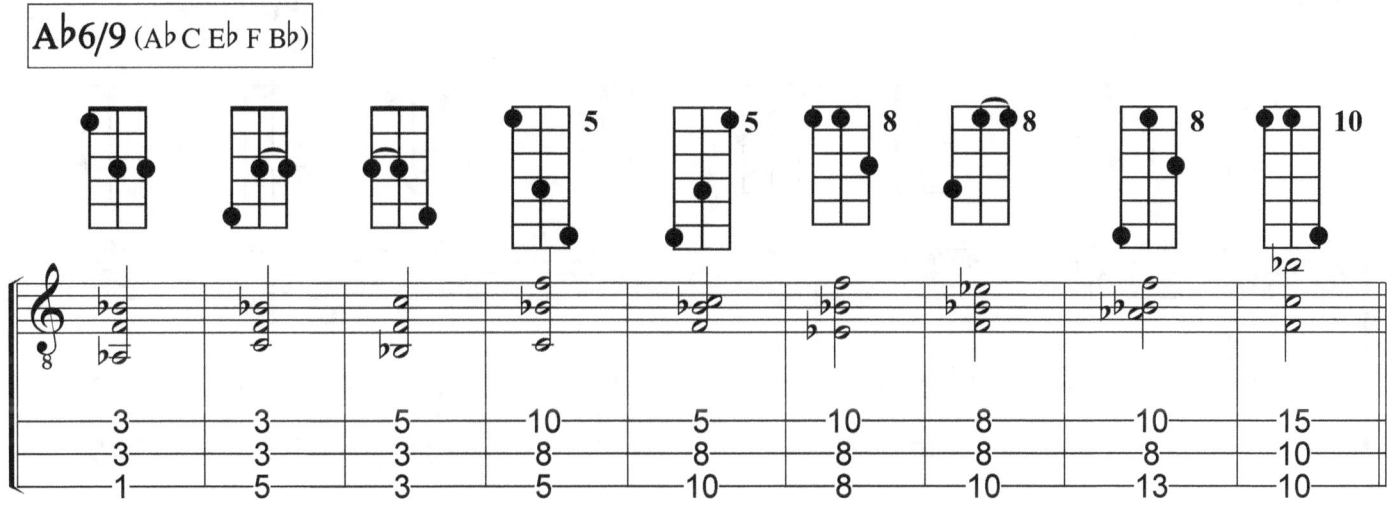

A♭ Augmented - A♭+ (A♭ C E)

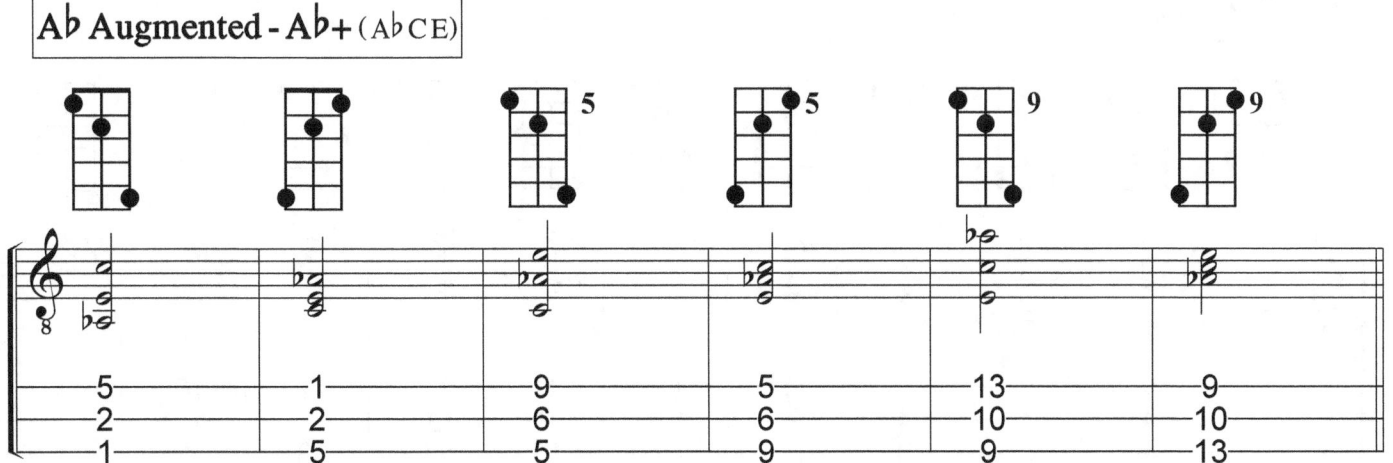

A♭m - A♭m6 - A♭m(maj7) - A♭m7

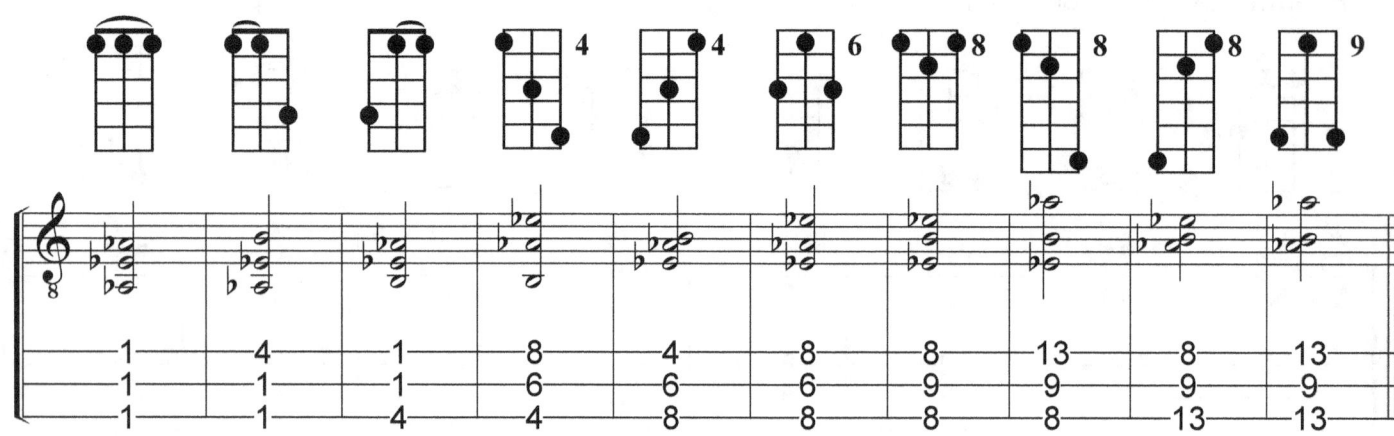

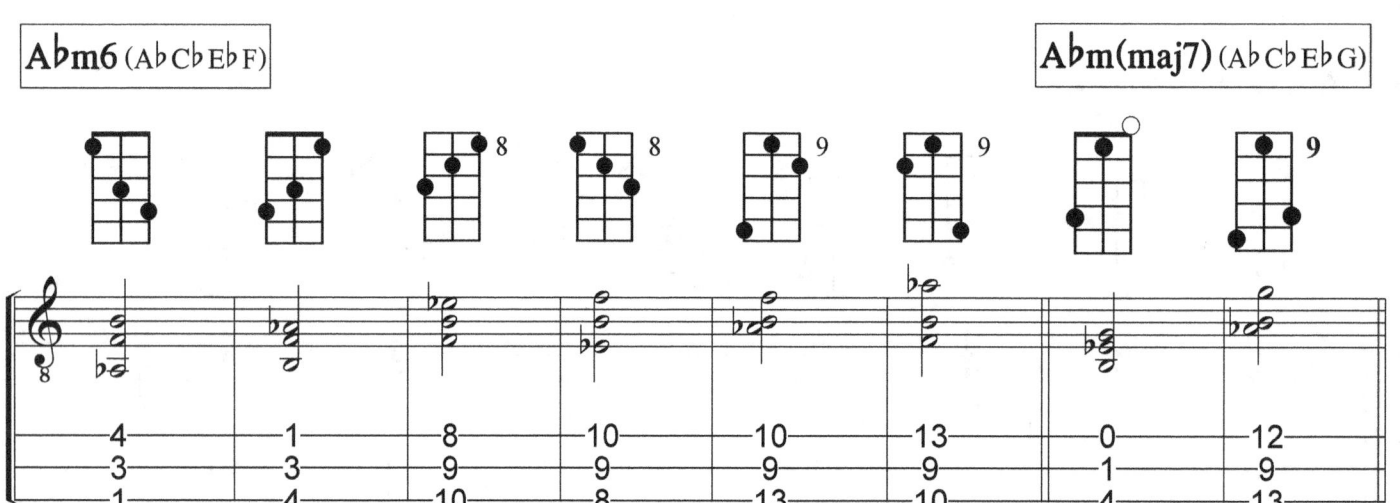

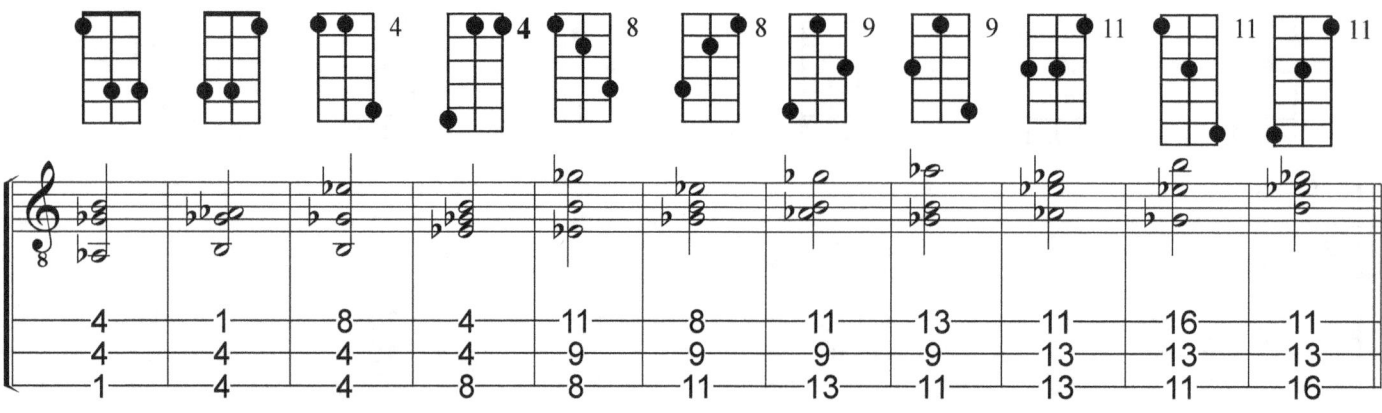

Abm7b5 - Abm9 - Abm11

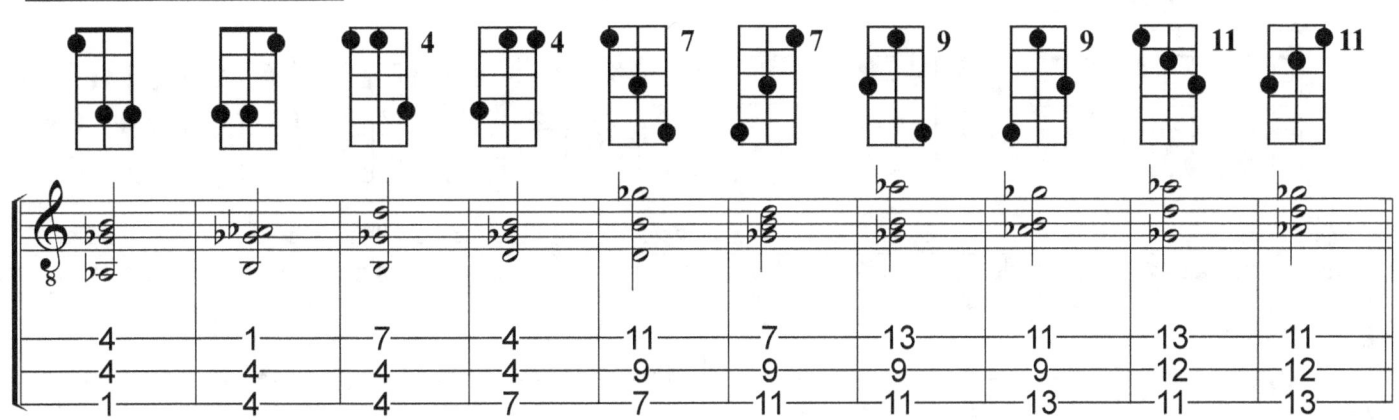

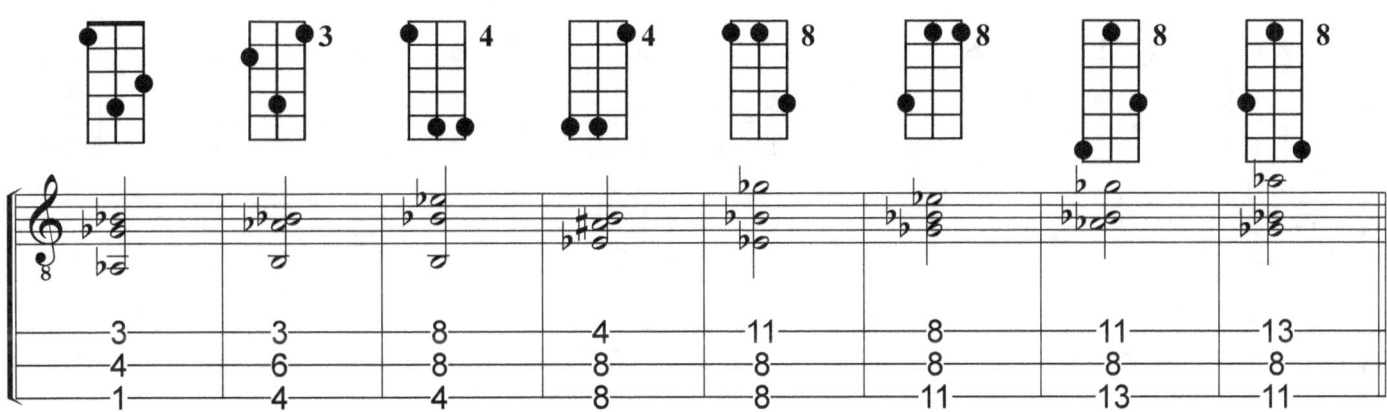

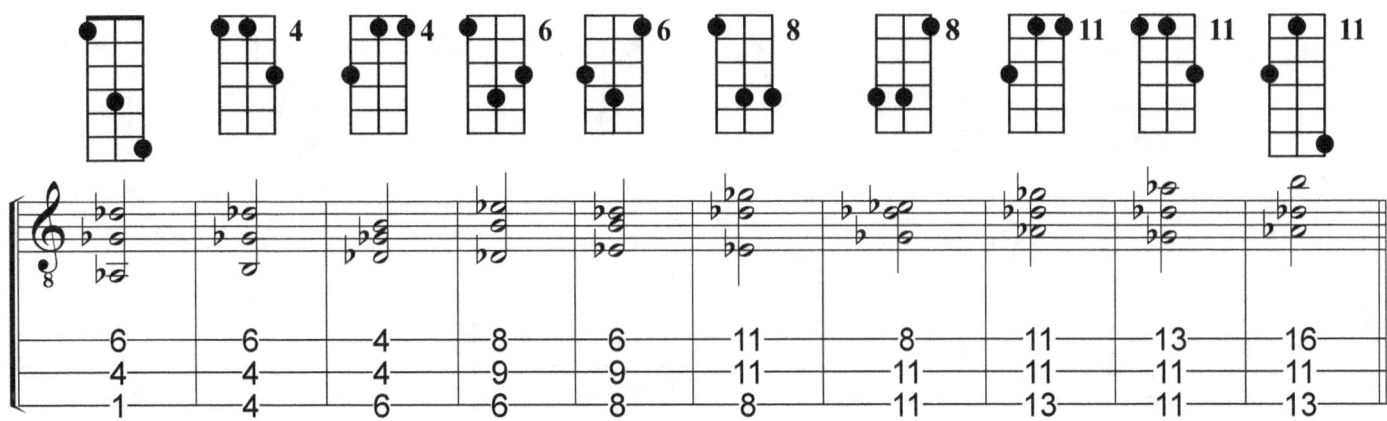

Ab7 - Ab9 - Ab13

Ab7 (Ab C Eb Gb)

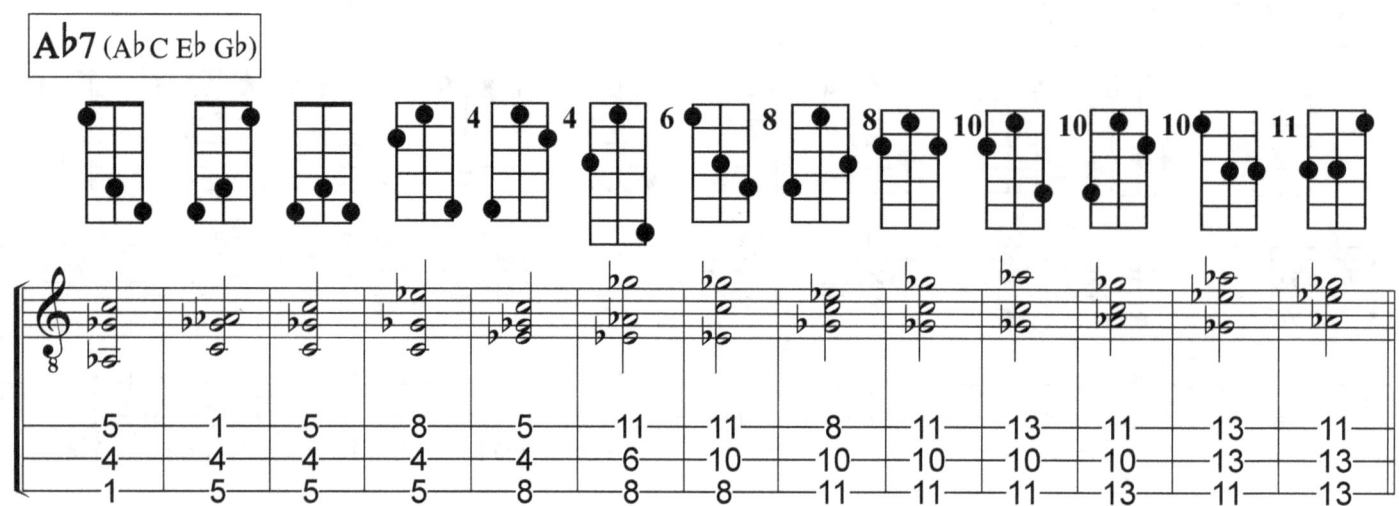

Ab9 (Ab C Eb Gb Bb)

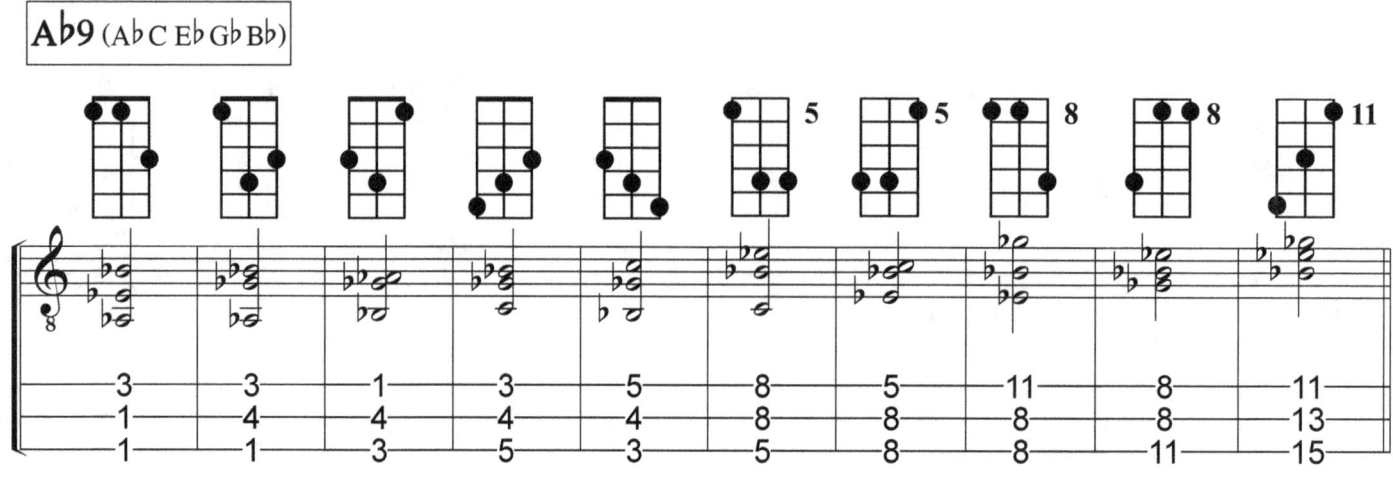

Ab13 (Ab C Eb Gb Bb Db F)

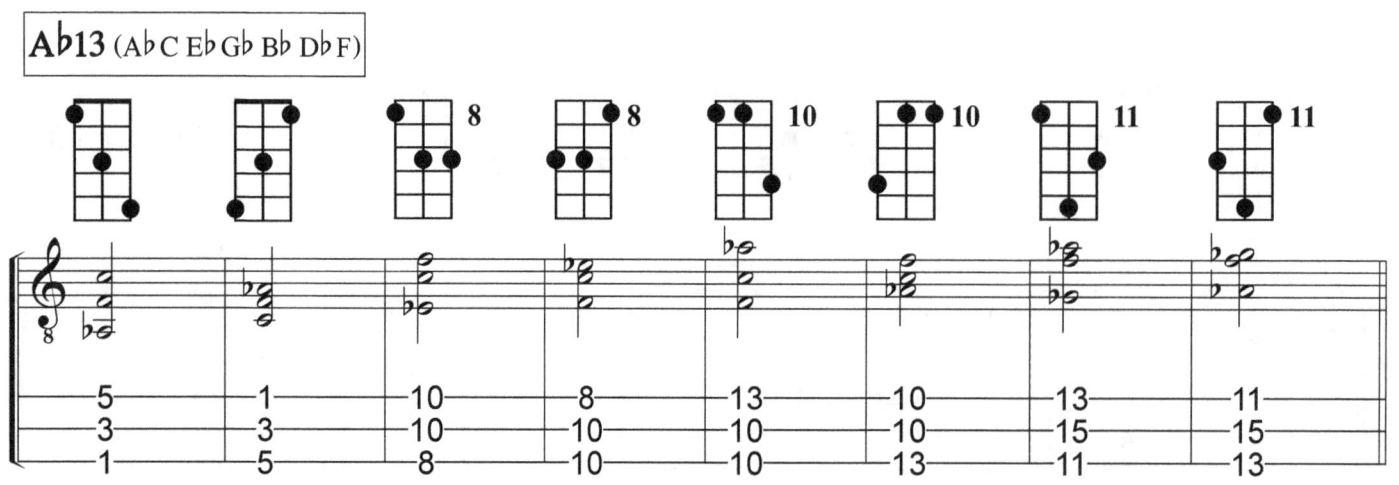

Ab7b5 - Ab7#5 - Ab7#9

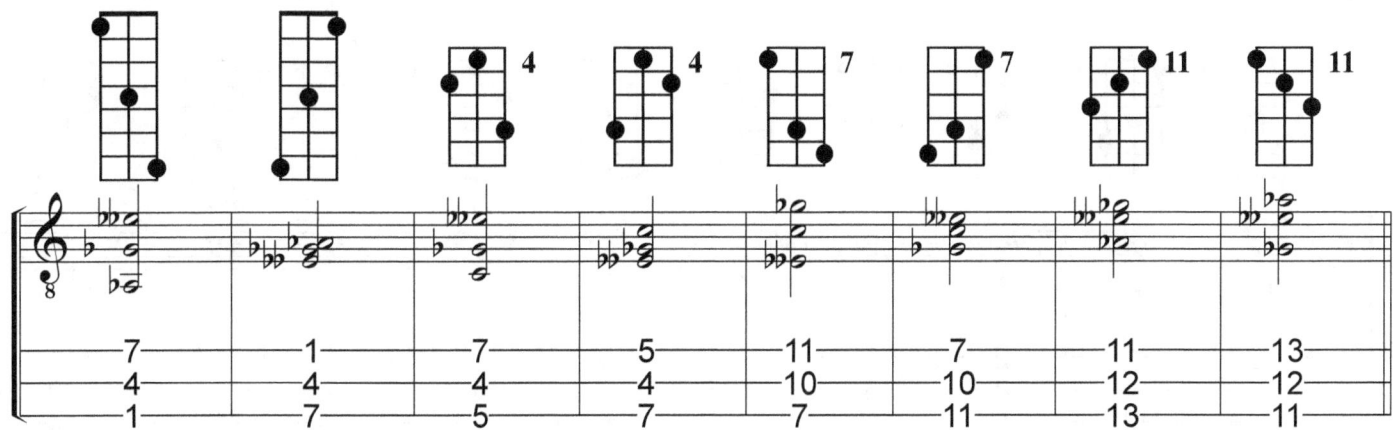

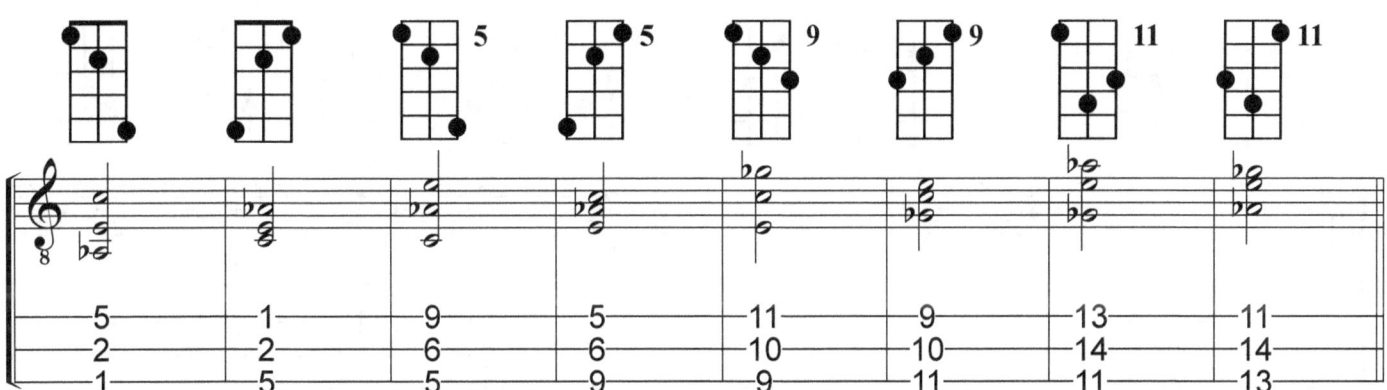

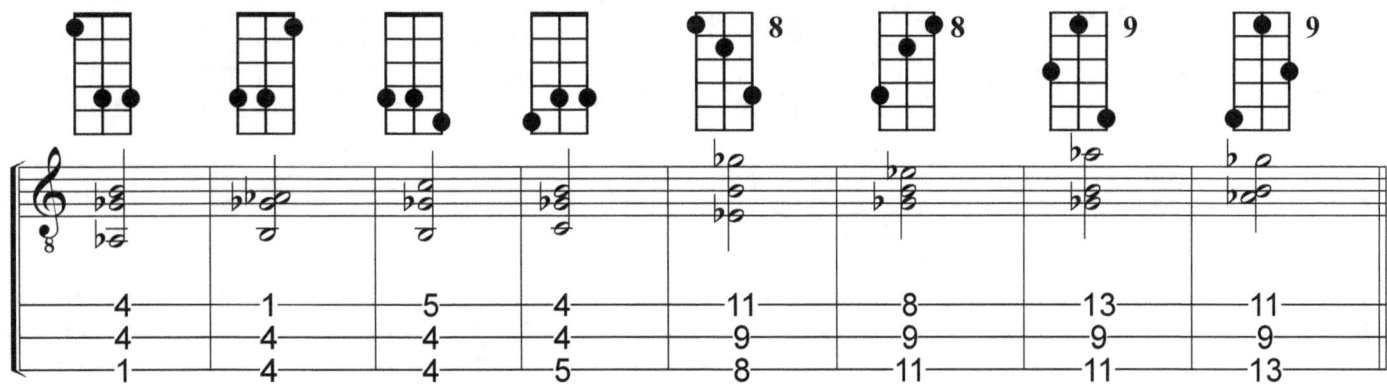

A♭7♭9 - A♭ diminished - A♭°7

A♭7♭9 (A♭ C E♭ G♭ B♭♭)

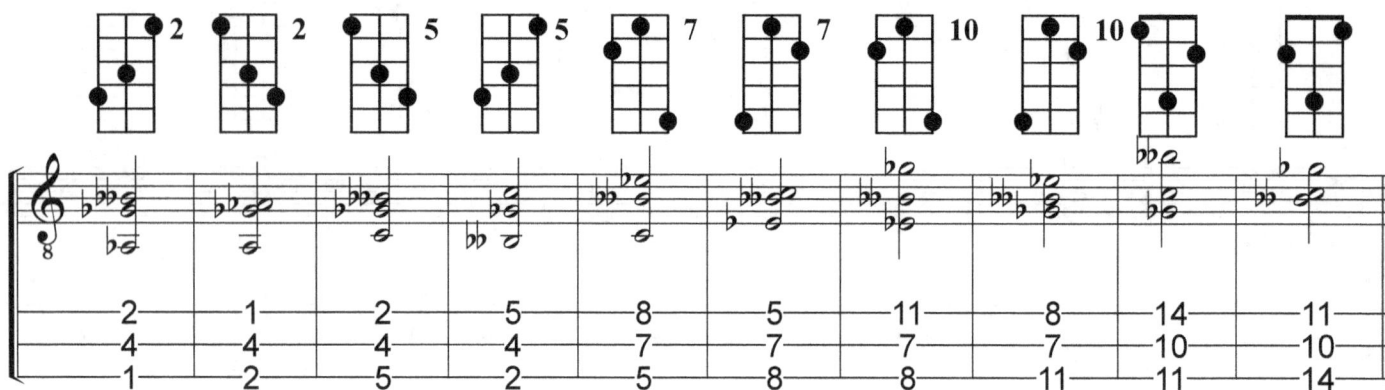

A♭ diminished - A°7 (A♭ C♭ E♭♭ G♭♭) / **G♯ diminished - G♯°7** (G♯ B D F)

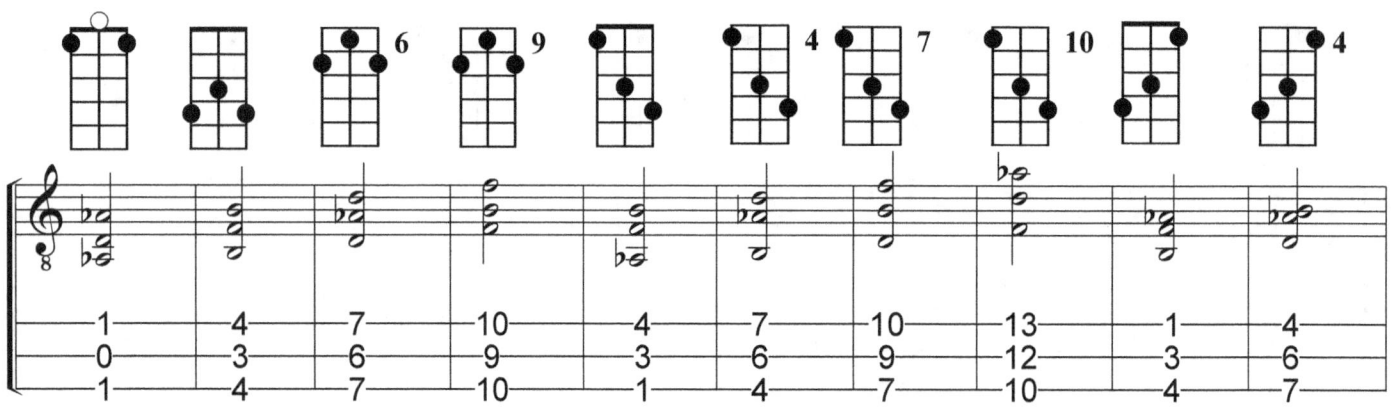

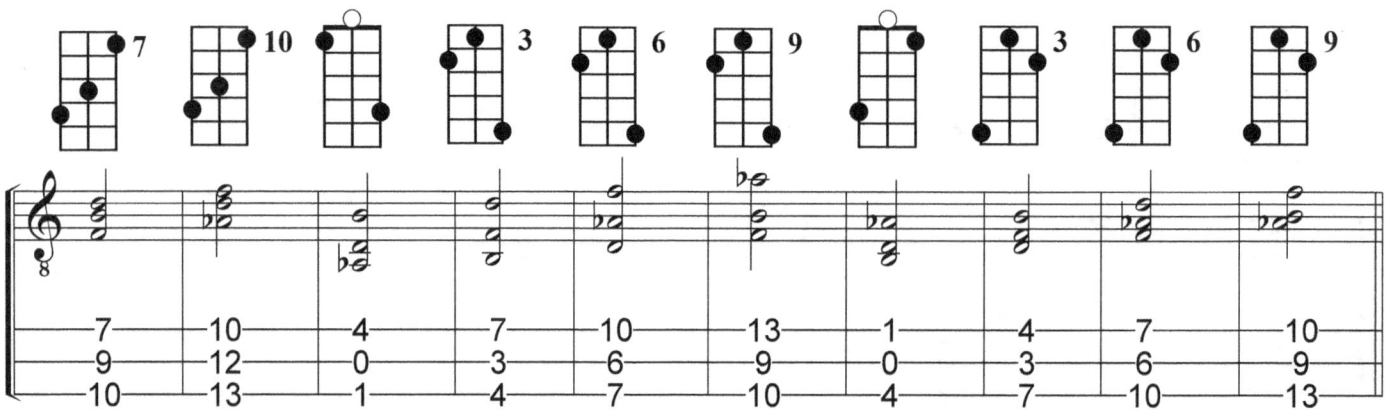

Absus4 - Absus2 - Ab7sus - Abadd9 - Ab5

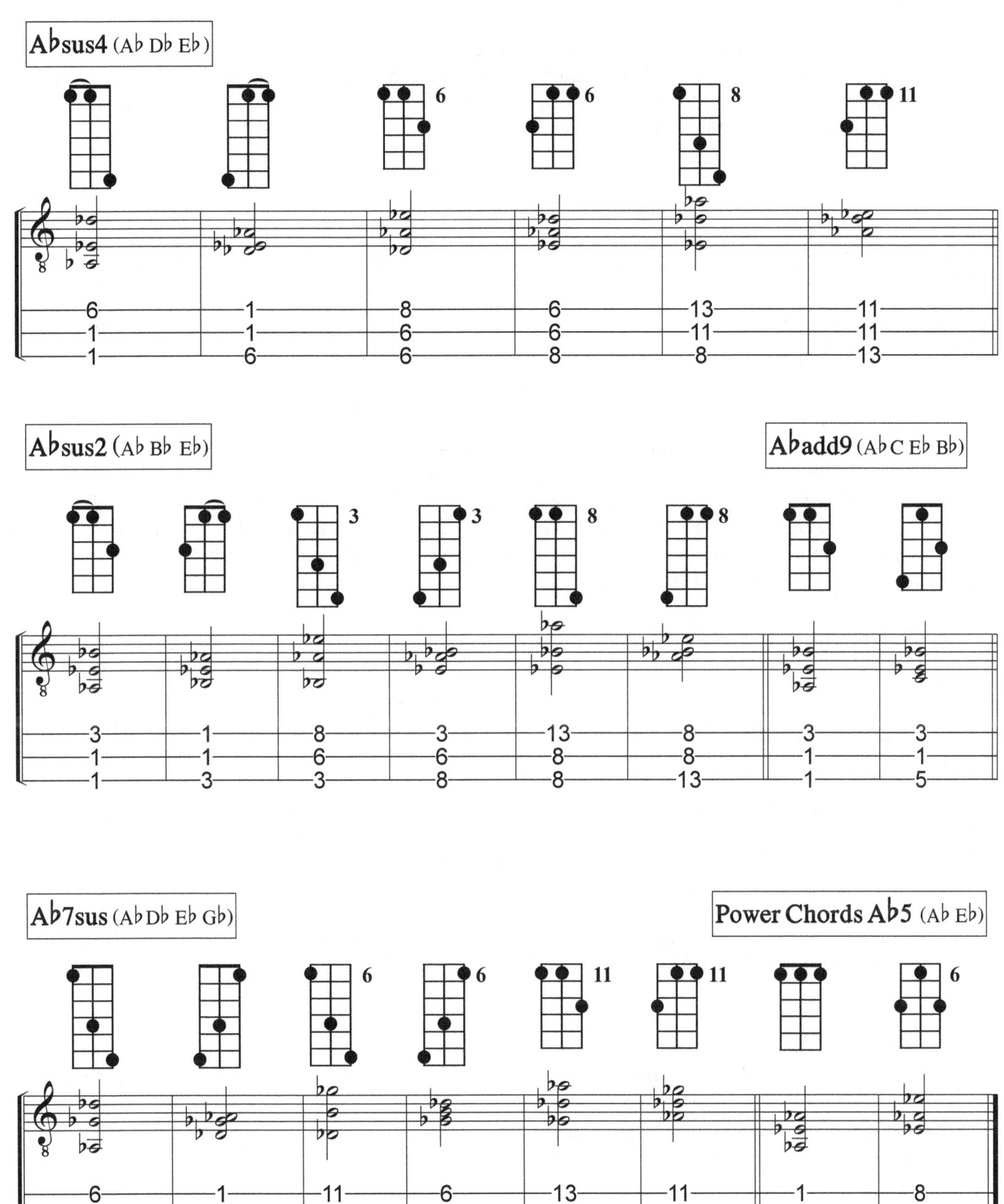

Chord Progressions and Theory

A chord progression is a set of chords played in a sequence. Each chord in a chord progression has a harmonic function that relates to a key in music. To fully understand chord progressions though, you first need to know how chords are formed. Let's start with writing out a major scale and numbering each note; in this example, we will use the C major scale:

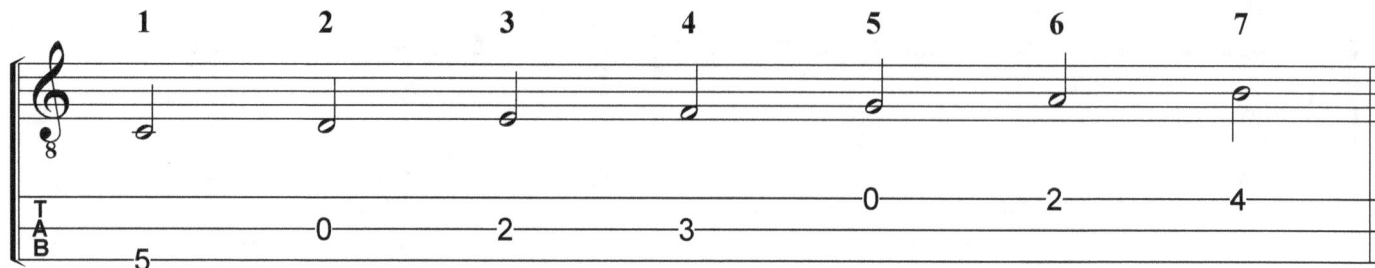

Next, let's stack two more notes on top of the original note in the scale to form a chord. When you stack the other two notes on top, make sure they are three letter names apart, or in intervals of "3rds." For example, if the note from the scale is an A, then stack a C and an E on top. These three note chords are called "triads," and when all the triads are taken from one scale, they are called "diatonic triads." Each triad in a key form a specific type of chord called either a major, minor or diminished triad depending on the distances or intervals between the notes:

TRIADS:

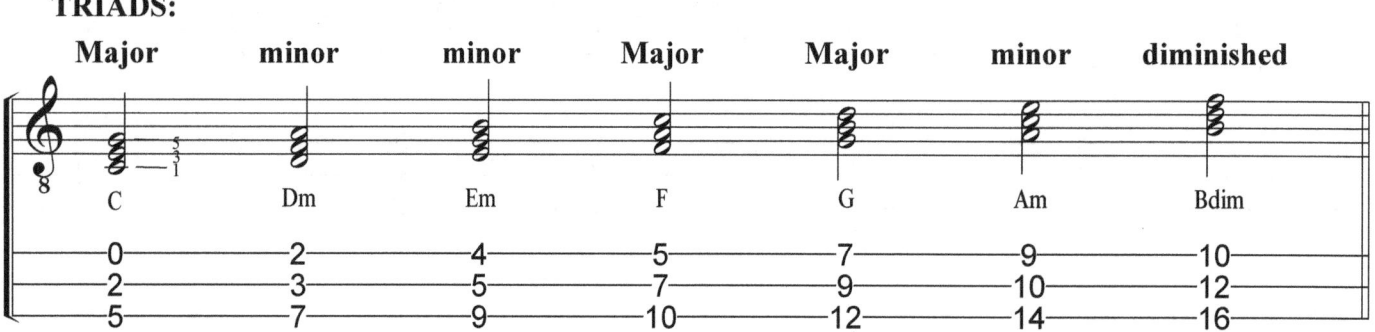

If you stack yet another note on top of the triad, you will create a four-note chord called "7th chords." So, the 7th chord has the root note on the bottom or the 1st, the 3rd, the 5th, and 7th note above the root note:

SEVENTH CHORDS:

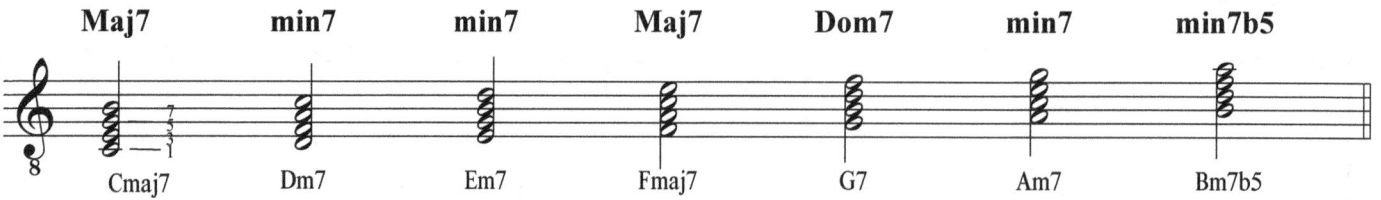

The initial scale used in this lesson was the C major scale, but chords can also be formed on other scales like the harmonic minor scale. The triads from the minor scale are different because they have different intervals between the notes. Here are the chords from the A harmonic minor scale, notice there is an augmented triad (+) when you build chords on this scale:

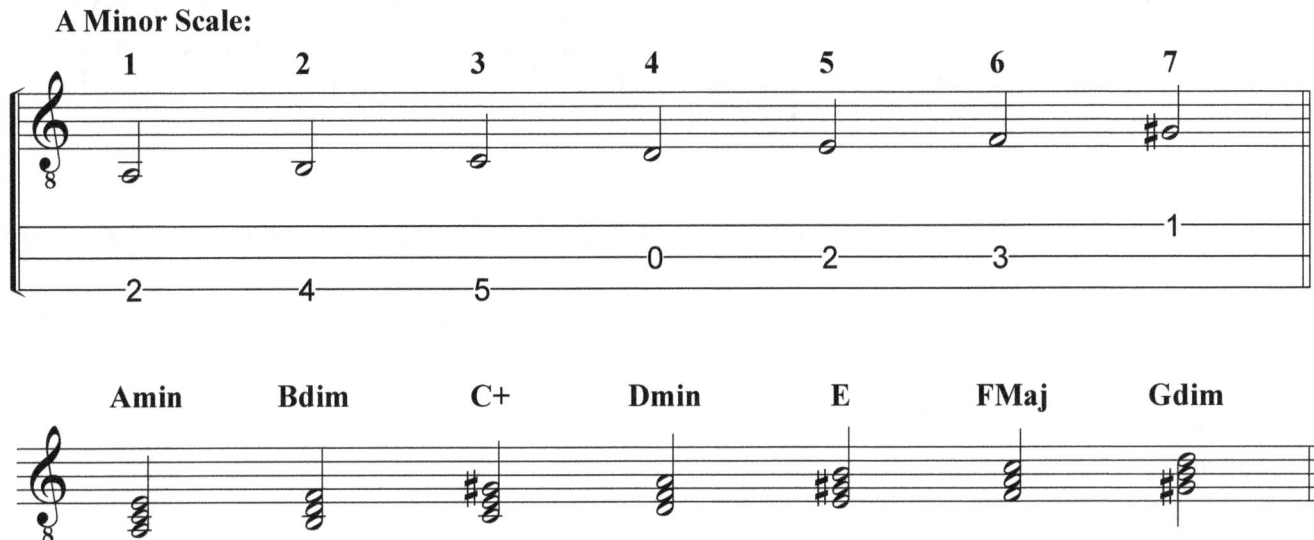

CHORD FUNCTIONS

When you play a chord and move to another chord, a certain harmonic function is created. So, some chords will want to move towards other chords, some will want to pull away, and some will remain relatively static. There is no right or wrong way to make a chord progression, though are "inner ears" have been conditioned to hear certain chords function in predictable ways. There are acoustical reasons to explain chord progressions, but that is beyond the scope of this book. Let's classify the chords into three main functions using a major key:

Tonic function - the 1st, 3rd and 6th chord of the major scale.
Sub-Dominant function - the 2nd and 4th chord of the major scale.
Dominant function - the 5th and 7th chord of the major scale.

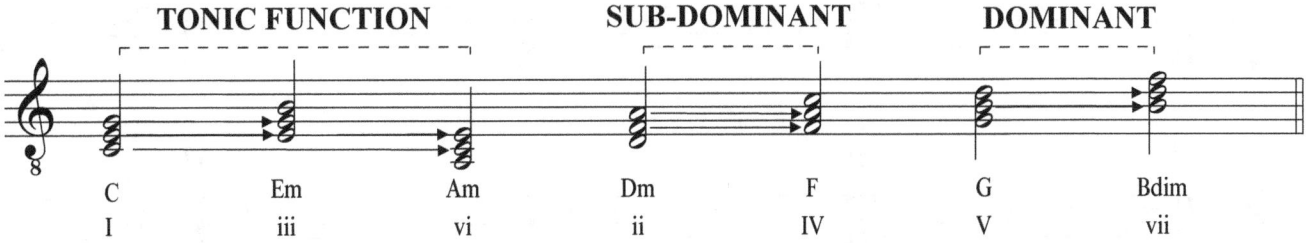

The tonic functioning chords are commonly referred to as being "stable" or like being at "home" because they share notes from the tonic "home" chord. For example, the notes in the tonic C chord are C E G, and the notes in the Em mediant chord are E G B, notice that both chords share the notes E and G. Likewise, The notes in the Am chord are A C E which share the notes C and E. So, the C, Em and Am generally share a tonic function in traditional chord progressions. Similarly, the sub-dominant and the dominant functions share notes with other chords in their group.

Chord Numbering Systems

Musicians often use a simplified system to write out chord progressions based on a number system. Each chord in a scale can be represented by a number 1 through 7. There are two systems to write the numbers down: the first and older system use "Roman Numerals" and more common in classical music, the other system is called "Nashville Numbers" and more common in blues, jazz, and popular music. Here are the chords in C major with both numbering systems:

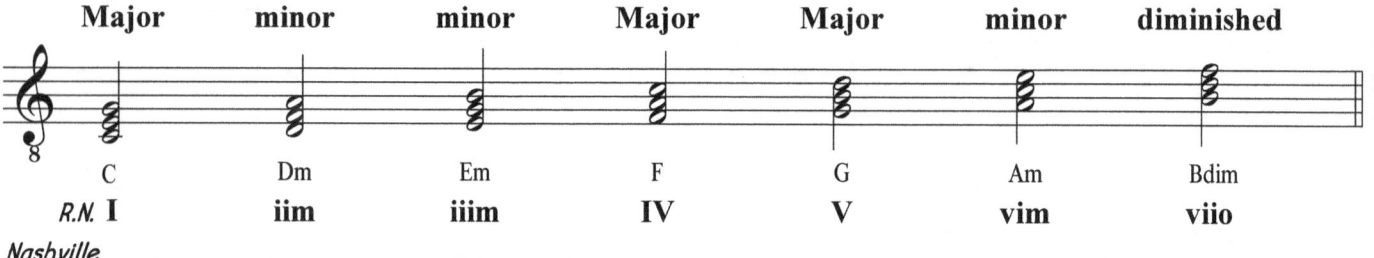

The Nashville numbering system can be used for all chord types including 7th chords:

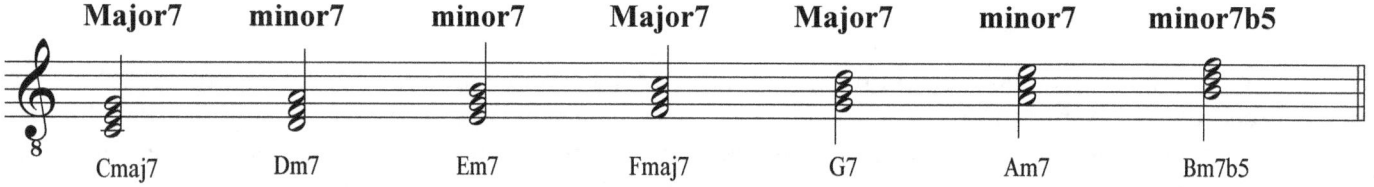

The number system helps to memorize chord progressions and to quickly change keys. Here is a standard 12 bar blues with both chord symbols and the Nashville numbering system:

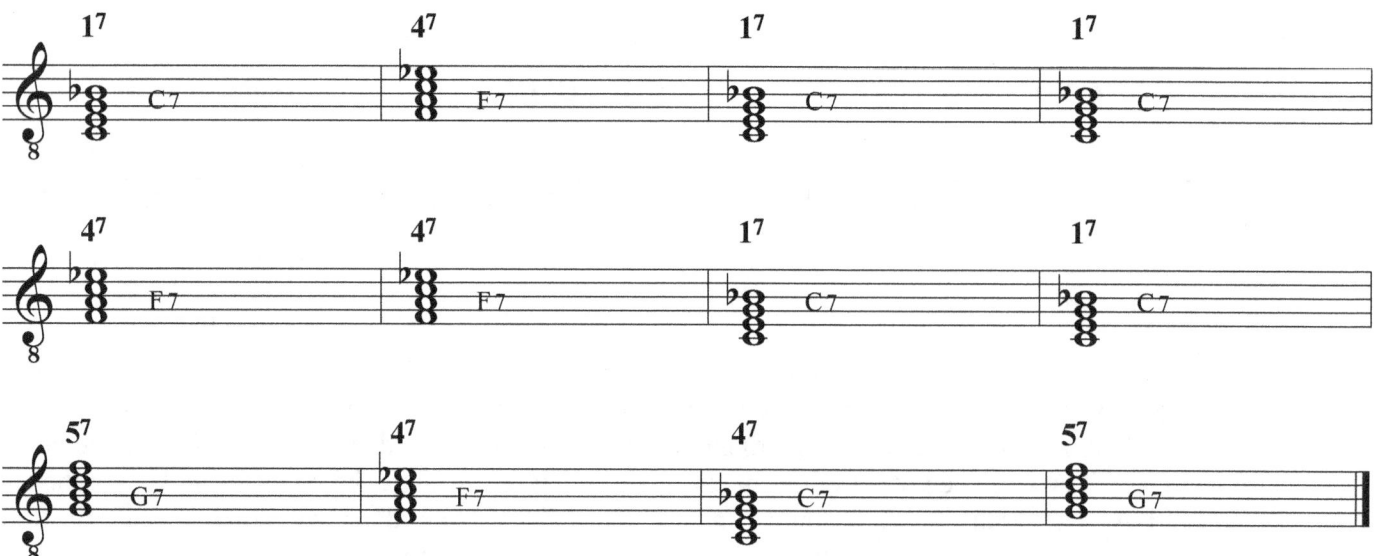

The most common jazz progression is the "2-5-1" (key of C):

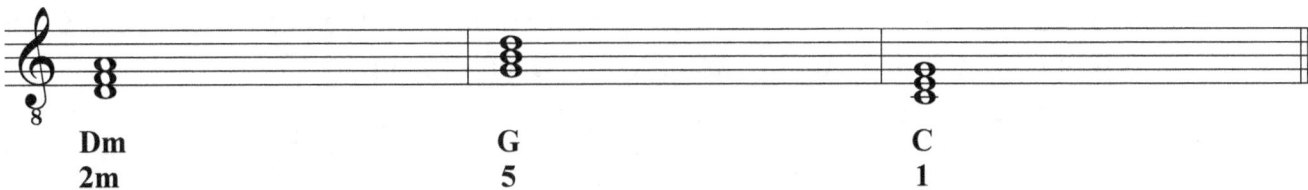

Here's the same progression using 7th chords:

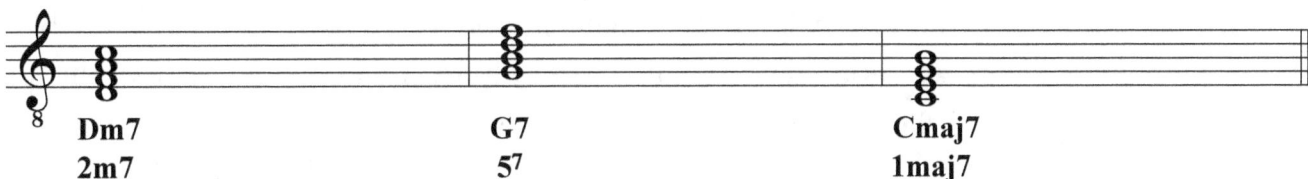

"Rhythm Changes" is a familar chord progression used in many jazz standards. Try to memorize the Nashville numbers and transpose to a different key.

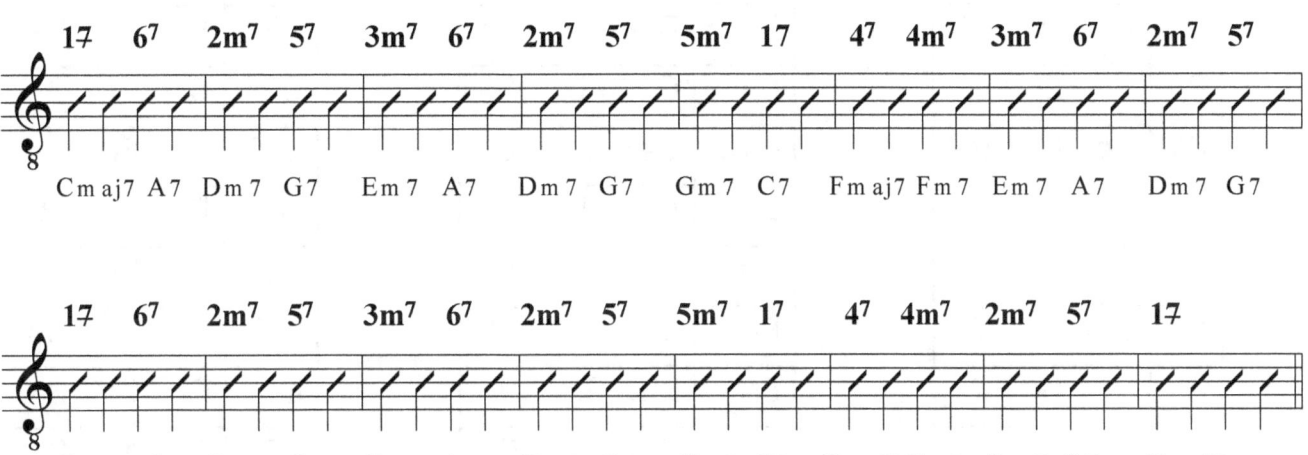

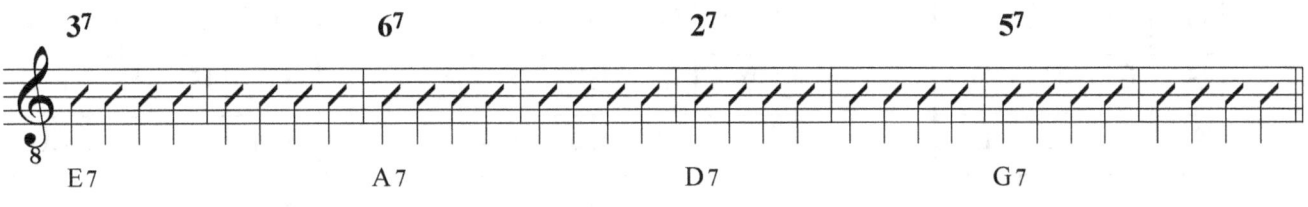

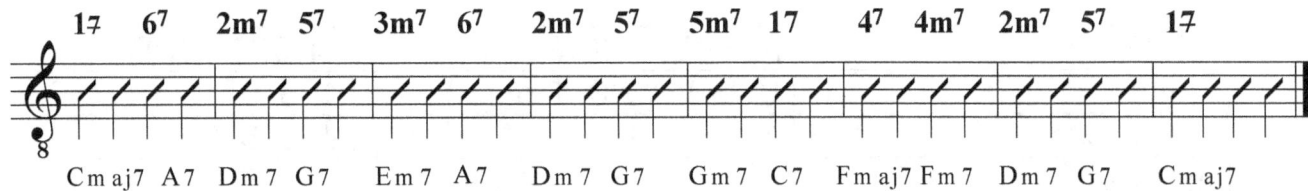

Understanding Chord Formulas

1) Each note in a scale can be represented by a number. In the chart below, the C major scale is written out with a number assigned for each note up to 13.

C	D	E	F	G	A	B	C	D	E	F	G	A
1	2	3	4	5	6	7	8	9	10	11	12	13

2) Each chord has a unique group of notes or "formula." For example, the major chord formula uses the 1st, 3rd and 5th notes of the major scale, so the notes in the **A** major chord are A, C# and E (see below). To make a minor chord, use the formula 1st, b3rd and 5th. Notice, the minor chord has a flat 3rd, so you must flatten the 3rd note of the major scale. That is, the A major chord has a C# whereas the A minor chord has been lowered to a C natural: A, C, and E. Here are the most frequently used chord formulas:

MAJOR (1-3-5)

A	A	C#	E
Bb	Bb	D	F
B	B	D#	F#
C	C	E	G
C#	C#	E#	G#
Db	Db	F	Ab
D	D	F#	A
Eb	Eb	G	Bb
E	E	G#	B
F	F	A	C
F#	F#	A#	C#
Gb	Gb	Bb	Db
G	G	B	D
Ab	Ab	C	Eb

MINOR (1-b3-5)

Am	A	C	E
Bbm	Bb	Db	F
Bm	B	D	F#
Cm	C	Eb	G
C#m	C#	E	G#
Dbm	Db	Fb	Ab
Dm	D	F	A
Ebm	Eb	Gb	Bb
Em	E	G	B
Fm	F	Ab	C
F#m	F#	A	C#
Gbm	Gb	Bbb	Db
Gm	G	Bb	D
Abm	Ab	Cb	Eb

DOMINANT 7th (1-3-5-b7)

A7	A	C#	E	G
Bb7	Bb	D	F	Ab
B7	B	D#	F#	A
C7	C	E	G	Bb
C#7	C#	E#	G#	B
Db7	Db	F	Ab	Cb
D7	D	F#	A	C
Eb7	Eb	G	Bb	Db
E7	E	G#	B	D
F7	F	A	C	Eb
F#7	F#	A#	C#	E
Gb7	Gb	Bb	Db	Fb
G7	G	B	D	F
Ab7	Ab	C	Eb	Gb

MAJOR CHORDS

NAME	ABBREVIATION	CHORD TONES
major	USUALLY NONE or (M)	1 3 5
major sixth	6	1 3 5 6
major seventh	maj7	1 3 5 7

major ninth	maj9	1 3 5 7 9
major sixth ninth	6/9	1 3 5 6 9
major seventh # eleven	Maj7#11	1 3 5 7 9 #11

MINOR CHORDS

NAME	ABBREVIATION	CHORD TONES
minor	m	1 b3 5
minor sixth	m6	1 b3 5 6
minor seventh	m7	1 b3 5 b7
minor major seventh	m/maj7	1 b3 5 7
minor seventh flat 5	m7b5 – (half diminished)	1 b3 b5 b7
minor Ninth	m9	1 b3 5 b7 9
minor eleventh	m11	1 b3 5 b7 9 11
minor thirteenth	m13	1 b3 5 b7 9 13

DOMINANT CHORDS

NAME	ABBREVIATION	CHORD TONES
dominant seventh	7, dom7	1 3 5 b7
dominant ninth	9	1 3 5 b7 9
dominant thirteenth	13	1 3 5 b7 9 13
dominant seventh flat 5	7b5	1 3 b5 b7
dominant seventh sharp 5	7#5	1 3 #5 b7
dominant seventh flat 9	7b9	1 3 5 b7 b9
dominant seventh sharp 9	7#9	1 3 5 b7 #9
dominant thirteenth flat 9	13b9	1 3 5 b7 b9 13

SUSPENDED CHORDS

NAME	ABBREVIATION	CHORD TONES
suspended 2nd	Sus2	1 2 5
suspended 4th	sus4	1 4 5
dominant 7suspended 4th	7sus4	1 4 5 b7
dominant 9 suspended 4th	9sus4	1 4 5 b7 9

DIMINISHED & AUGMENTED CHORDS & POWER CHORDS

NAME	ABBREVIATION	CHORD TONES
diminished	dim, 0	1 b3 b5
diminished seventh	dim7, 07	1 b3 b5 bb7
augmented	aug, +	1 3 #5
augmented seventh	aug7, +7	1 3 #5 7
power chord	5	1 5

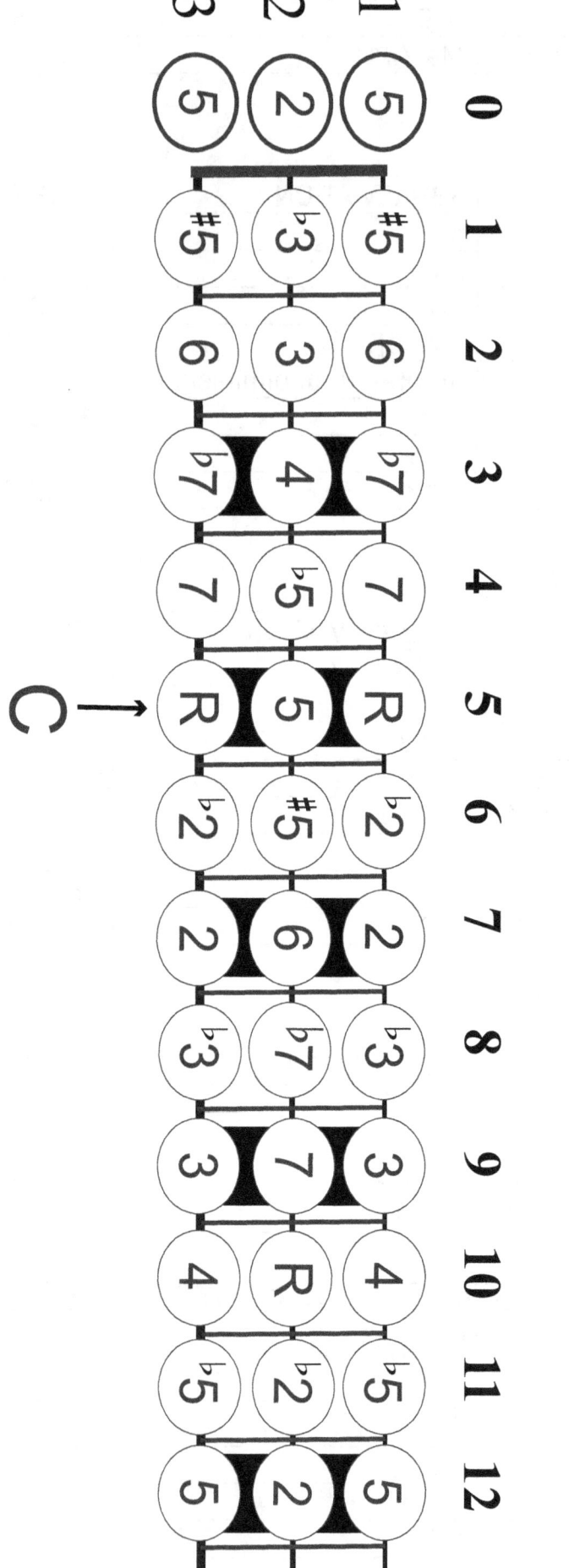

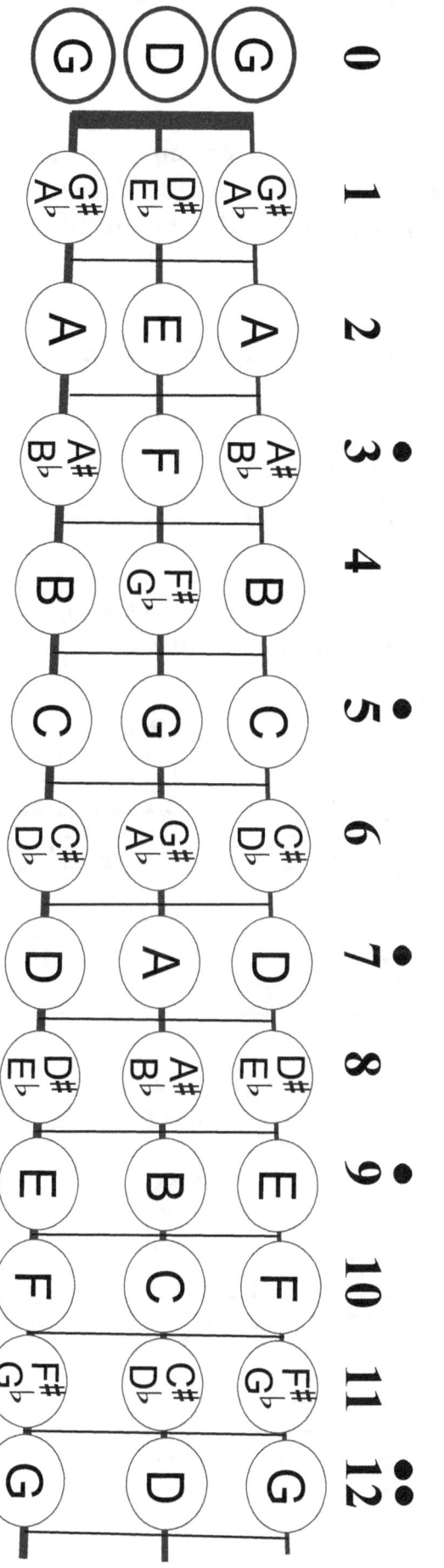

Strumming and Picking Techniques

Palm Muting - Place the left side of your (strumming hand) palm on the strings close to the bridge or on the bridge to produce a muted deadened sound. Experiment with different pressures on the string to produce different muted tones.

Let Ring - Hold a chord down while you strum and/or pick notes from the chord letting the notes ring freely. This is sometimes written as *l.r.*

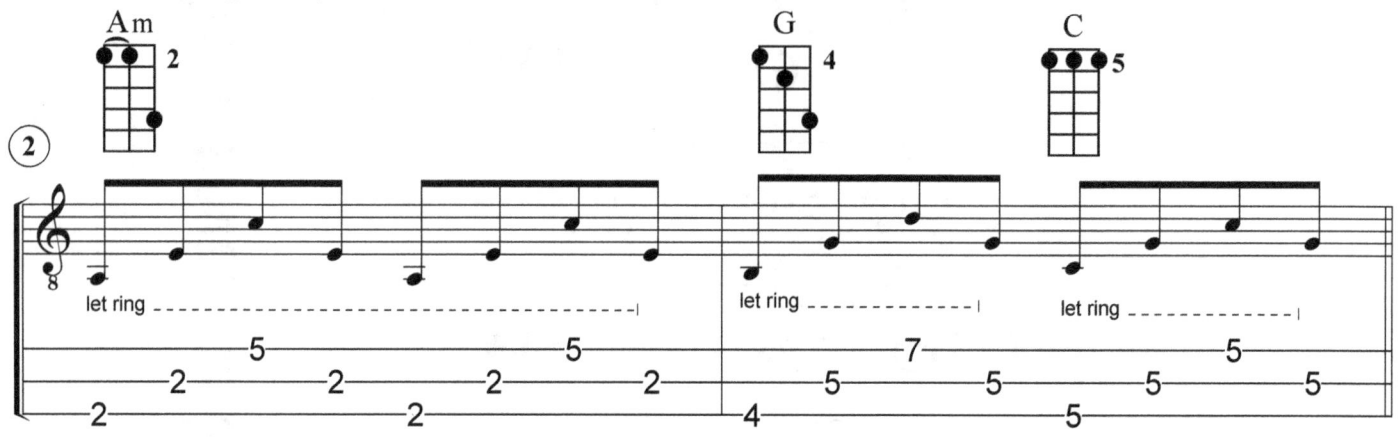

Bass Note Strum - Play a single low note then strum the chord.

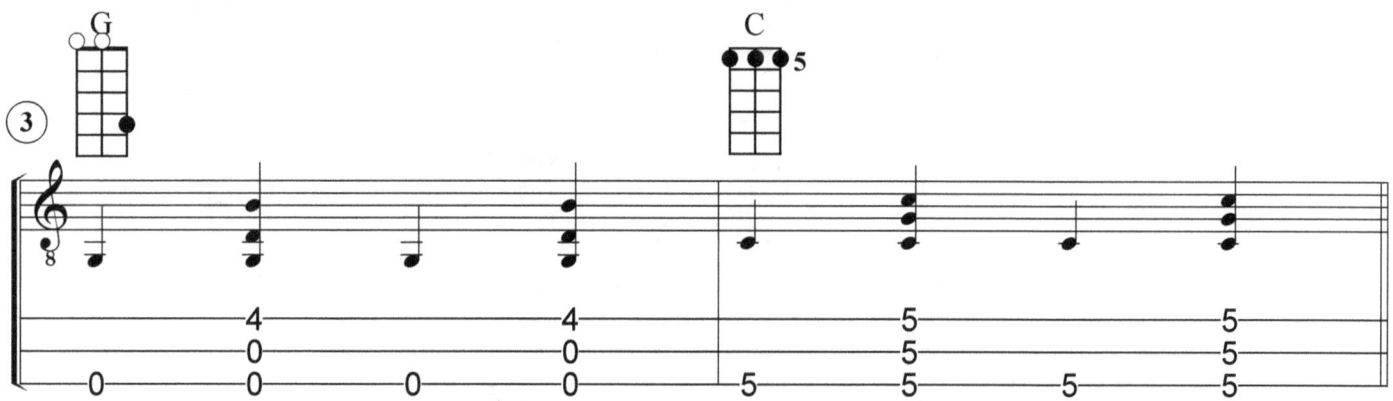

Alternating Bass Note Strum - Play a single low note, strum the chord, then play another single higher or lower note and strum the chord again.

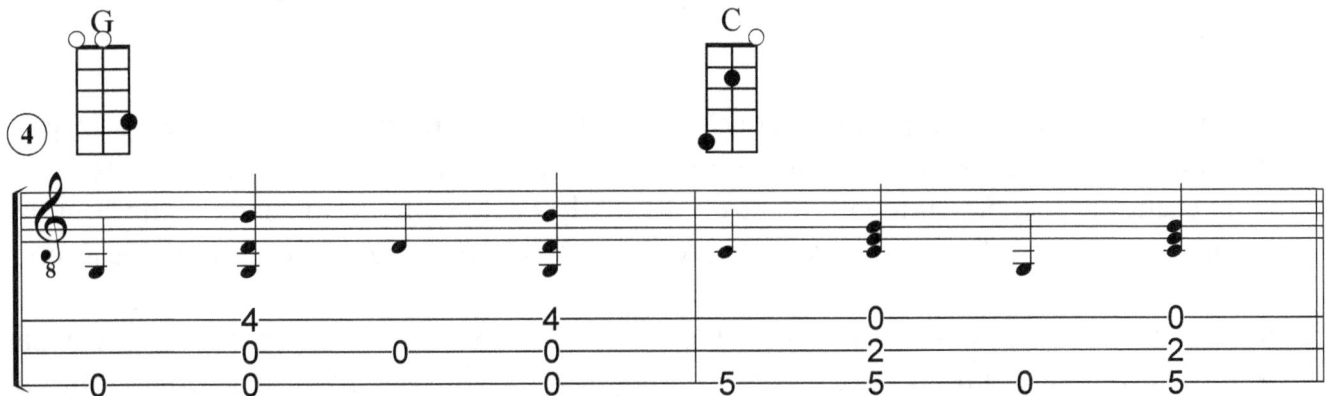

Hybrid Picking - Play with pick and fingers. In this example, play all the notes on the 3rd string with your pick and notes on the 1st and 2nd string with your fingers.

Left Hand Muting - Release the left hand string pressure stopping the notes ringing.

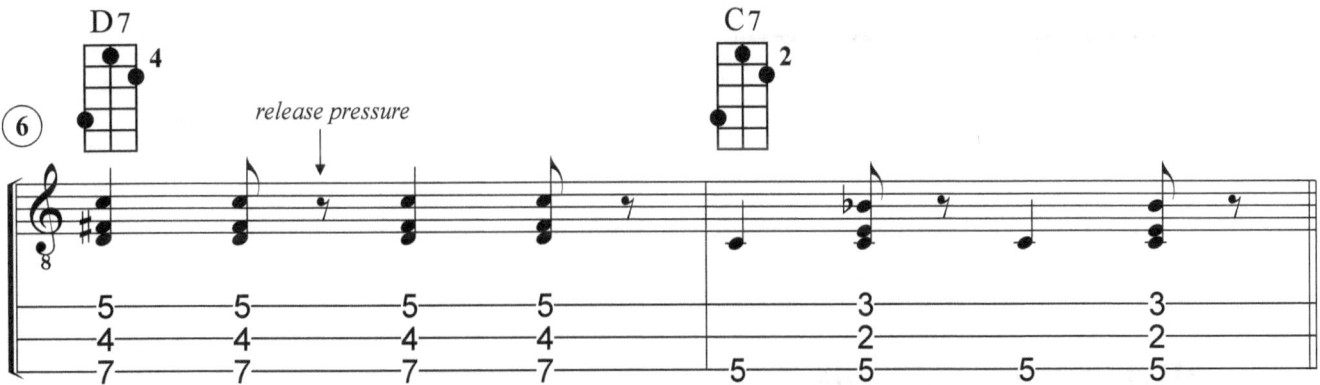

Pick Slap - Mute the strings with the left hand and stum the chord producing a rhythmic clicking sound. Pick slaps are notated with an x.

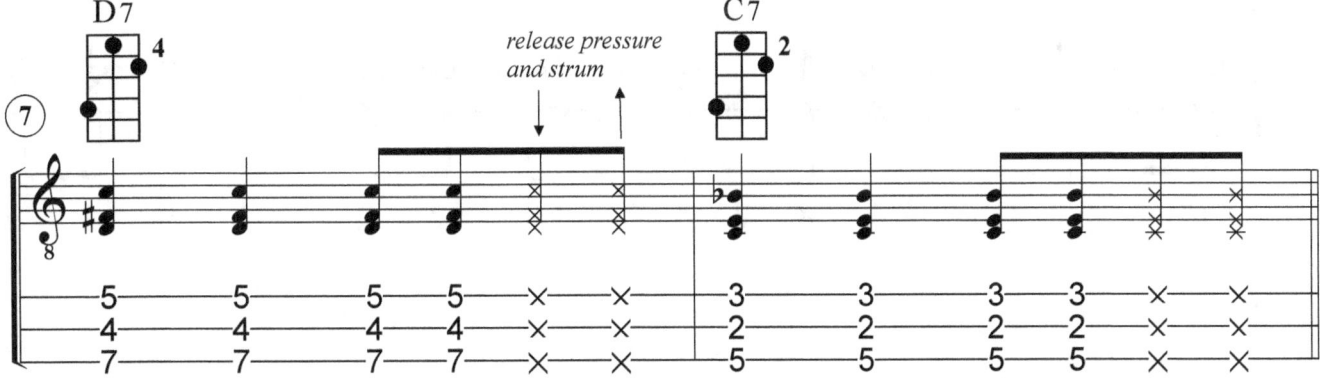

Strumming Pattern Practice

Here is an excellent exercise to practice up and down strumming. The following 15 patterns are all the variations possible using eighth notes in a measure of 2/4. The examples are using eighth notes, but sixteenth notes could easily be substituted instead. Count out loud or in your head: 1 & 2 &. If you prefer thinking with sixteenth notes, count out: 1 e & a.

Practice the strumming patterns with a single chord or with a chord progression. Repeat each pattern, make sure to keep the strumming arm moving evenly up and down, and play with a metronome if possible. If you don't have a metronome then tap your foot on the 1st beat of every bar.

Patterns with 4 strums

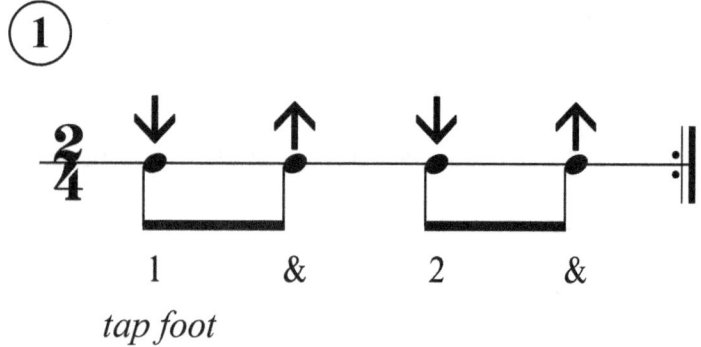

Patterns with 3 strums

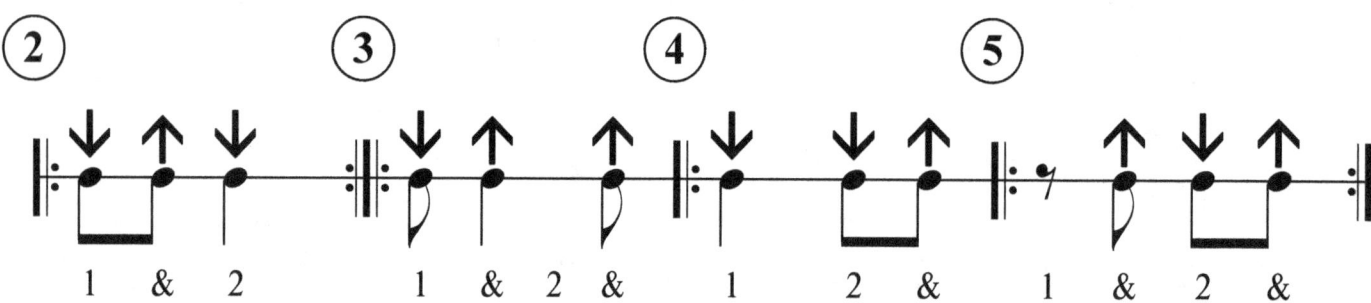

Patterns with 2 strums

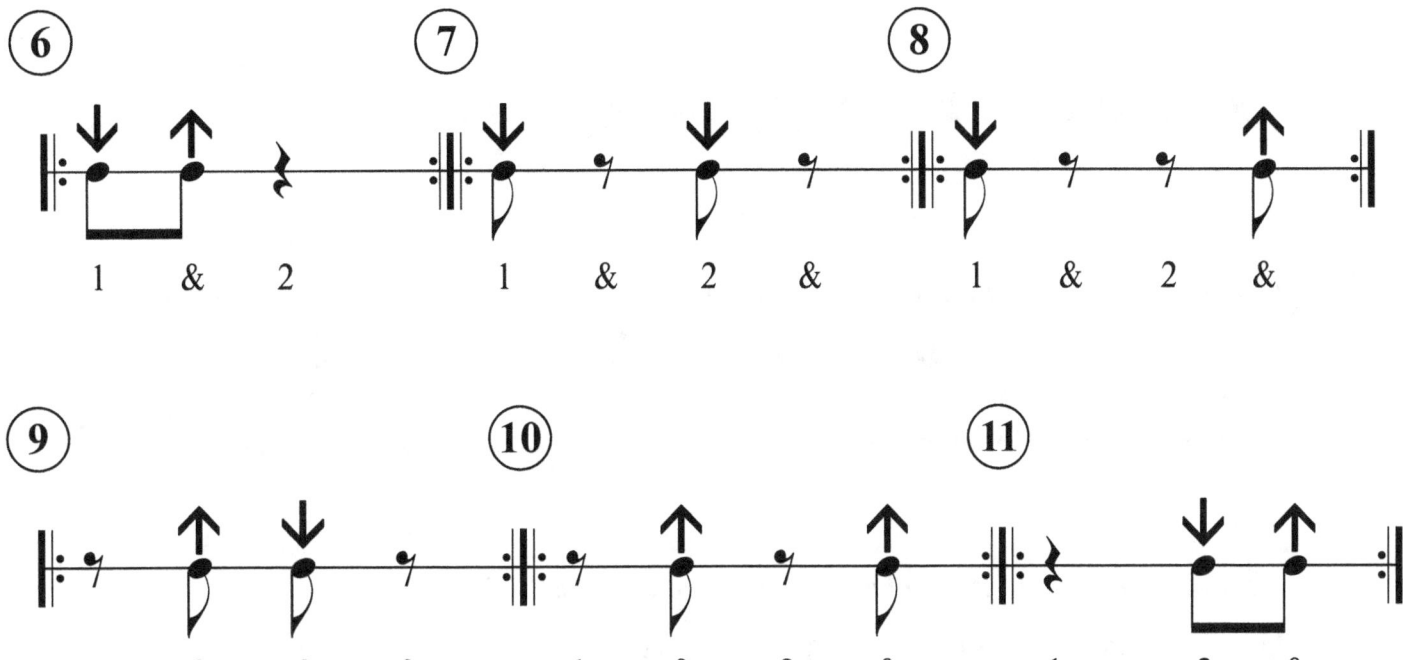

Patterns with 1 strum

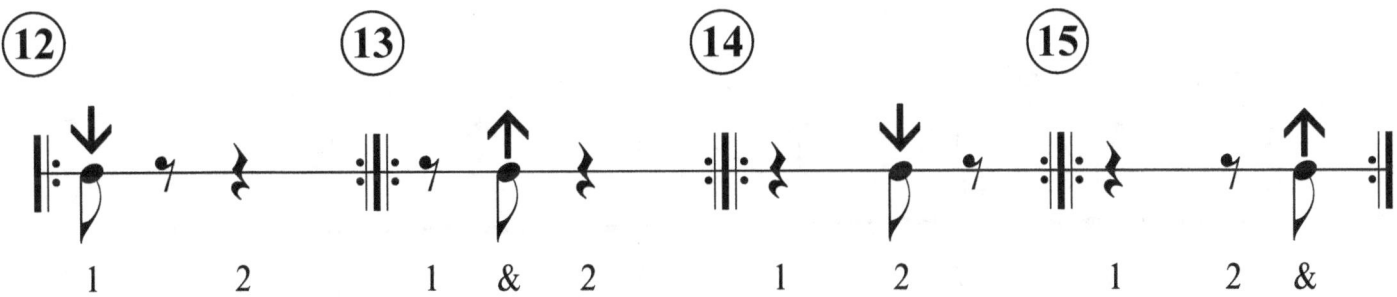

Strumming Patterns - Basic

Practice the following strumming patterns using any single chord or a chord progression. Use a metronome to help keep an even steady tempo or tap your foot.

DOWN STROKE ↓   UP STROKE ↑   ACCENT >   MUTE **X**

1. Down / Up Pattern. Play with even straight eighth notes or swing shuffle eighth notes.

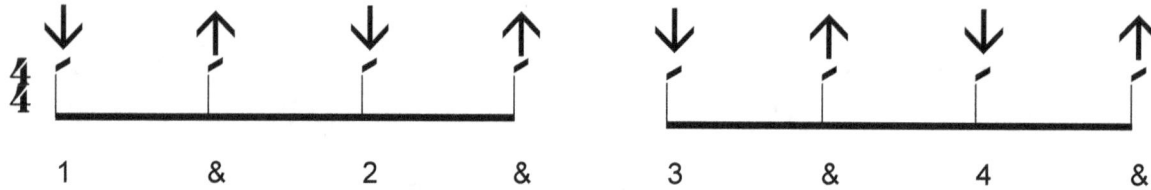

2. Down / Up Pattern with emphasis or accent on 2nd and 4th beat.

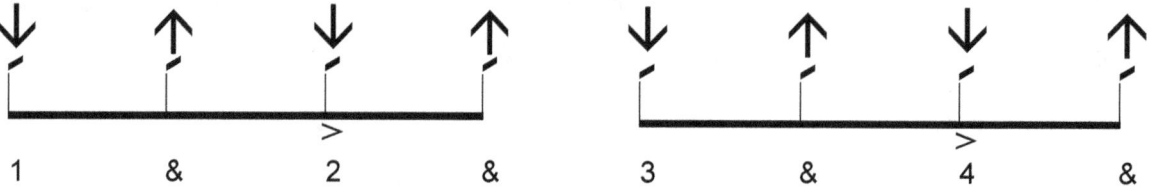

3. Left Hand Mute. Mute the strings (x) with the left hand while continuing strumming.

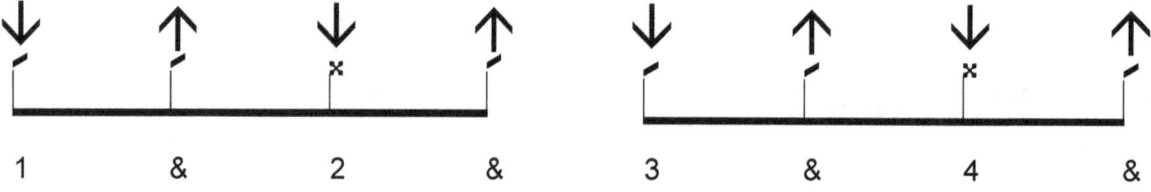

4. Accent the Up stroke.

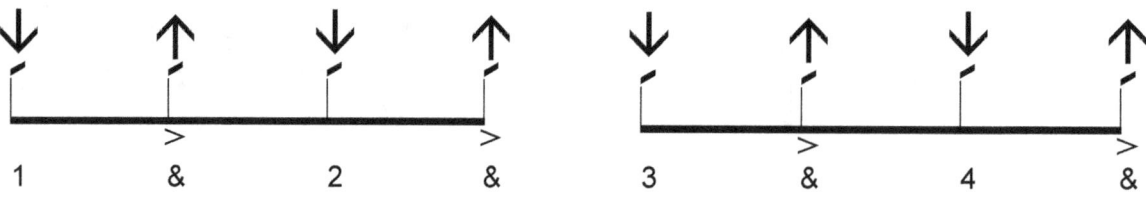

5. Tied Note. Let notes ring without playing the tied note. In this example, don't strum on beat 3.

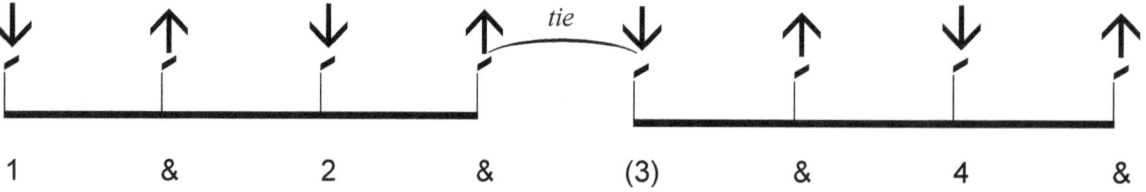

Strumming Patterns Styles

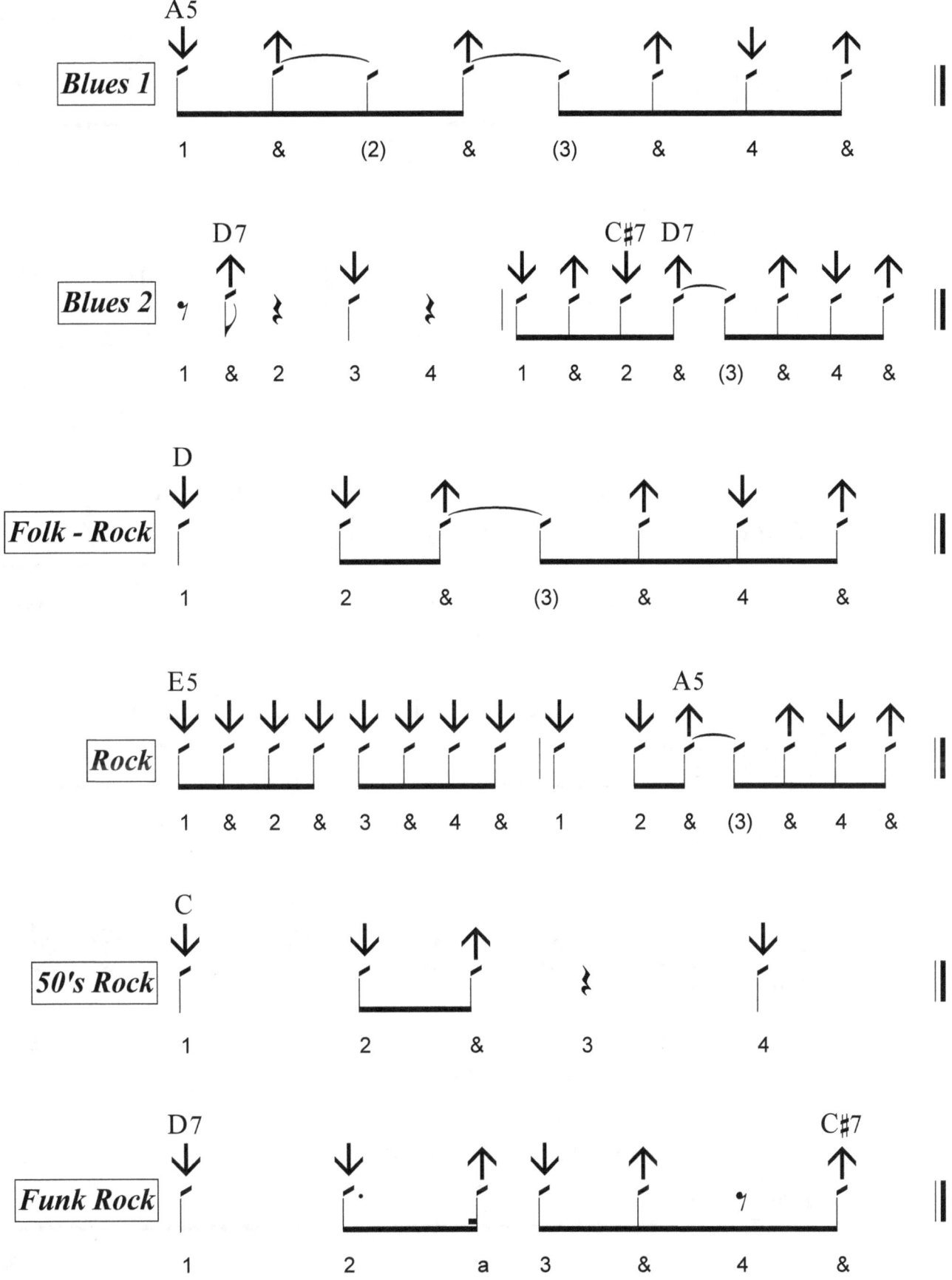

Strumming Patterns Styles

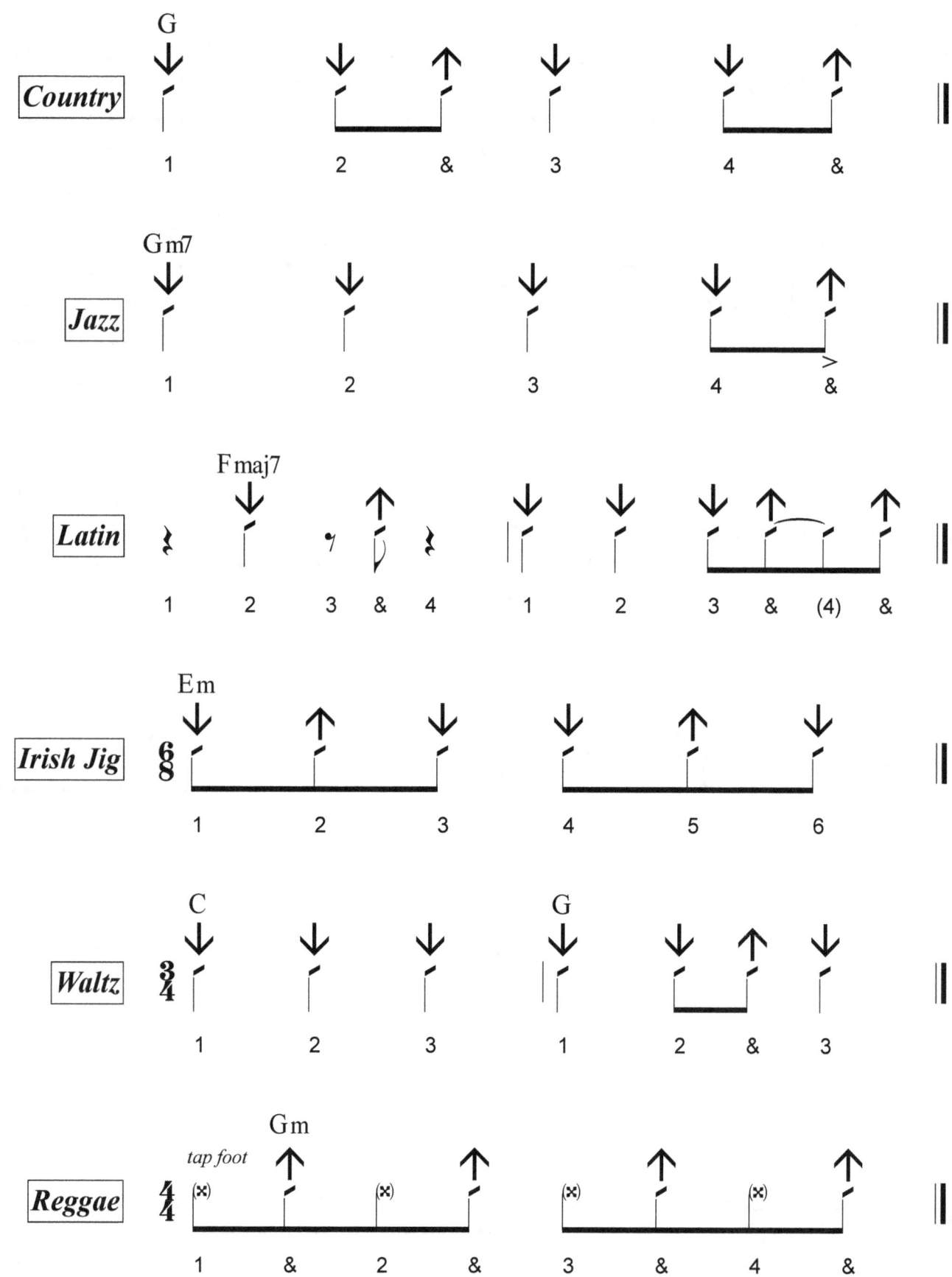

Tips for Accompanying on the Cigar Box Guitar

1. Before you start to play a song, it is a good idea to know how the rhythm is structured. In written music, "Time Signatures" are used to group the beats. The most common grouping is four beats per measure. This time signature is written as 4/4. Other standard time signatures are 3/4, where beats are grouped in three and 6/8 where beats are grouped in two groups of three. 6/8 is counted 1-2-3 4-5-6.

2. Once you have figured out the time signature you are playing in, try to keep a steady rhythm going that is in sync with the grouping of the beats, so if you are in 4/4 time, tap your foot or count to four. Pick one of the strumming or fingerstyle patterns and practice the chords with a focus on maintaining an even strumming or fingerpicking rhythm. Keep your right hand moving even as you change chords.

3. To keep a nice even flow, memorize all the chords in the song you are playing. If you already have the chords memorized, then think ahead and prepare your fingers for the proceeding chord. Most chords change at the start or middle of the measure, so prepare your fingers to land on the correct beat and keep fingers close to the frets to avoid fret buzz — practice changing chords with the chord progressions provided in this book.

4. Because the cigar box guitar only has 3 or 4 strings, you may have to simplify some chords to play songs. Substituting one chord for another helps get around this issue. A common substitution is to use the basic barre chord like a C5 in place of another chord. For example, if you have a C major or C minor chord, a simple C5 barre chord works for either chord. The C5 doesn't have a 3rd, which defines the major or minor quality of a chord. Therefore, the C5 functions as either a C major or C minor.

5. Learn several ways to play each chord in different positions. Knowing different chords positions gives the song variety and helps connect chords that are nearby. Learn the most common chords in all the regular keys you play in.

Blues Chord Progressions - Key of A and Am

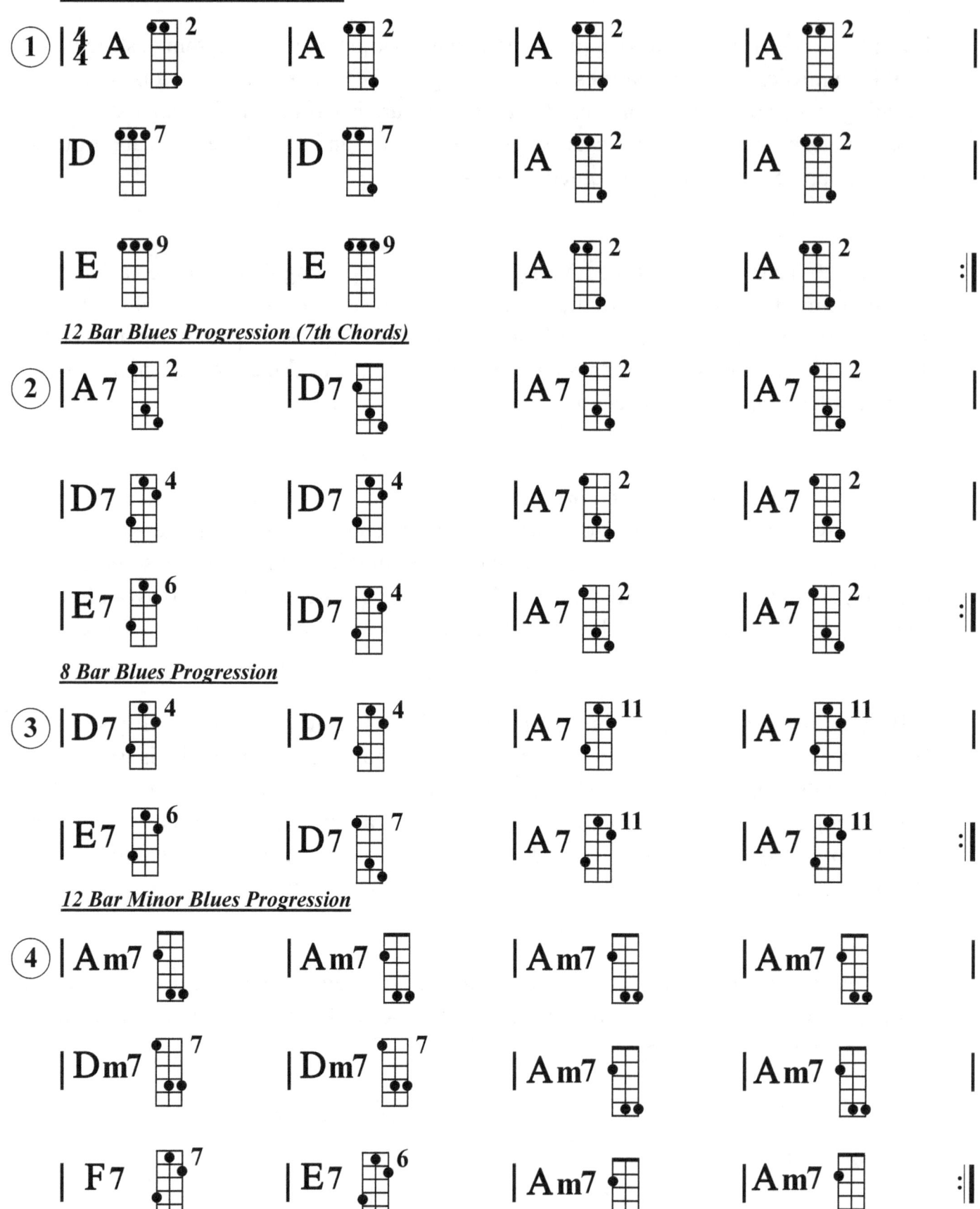

Blues Chord Progessions - Key of B♭ and B♭m

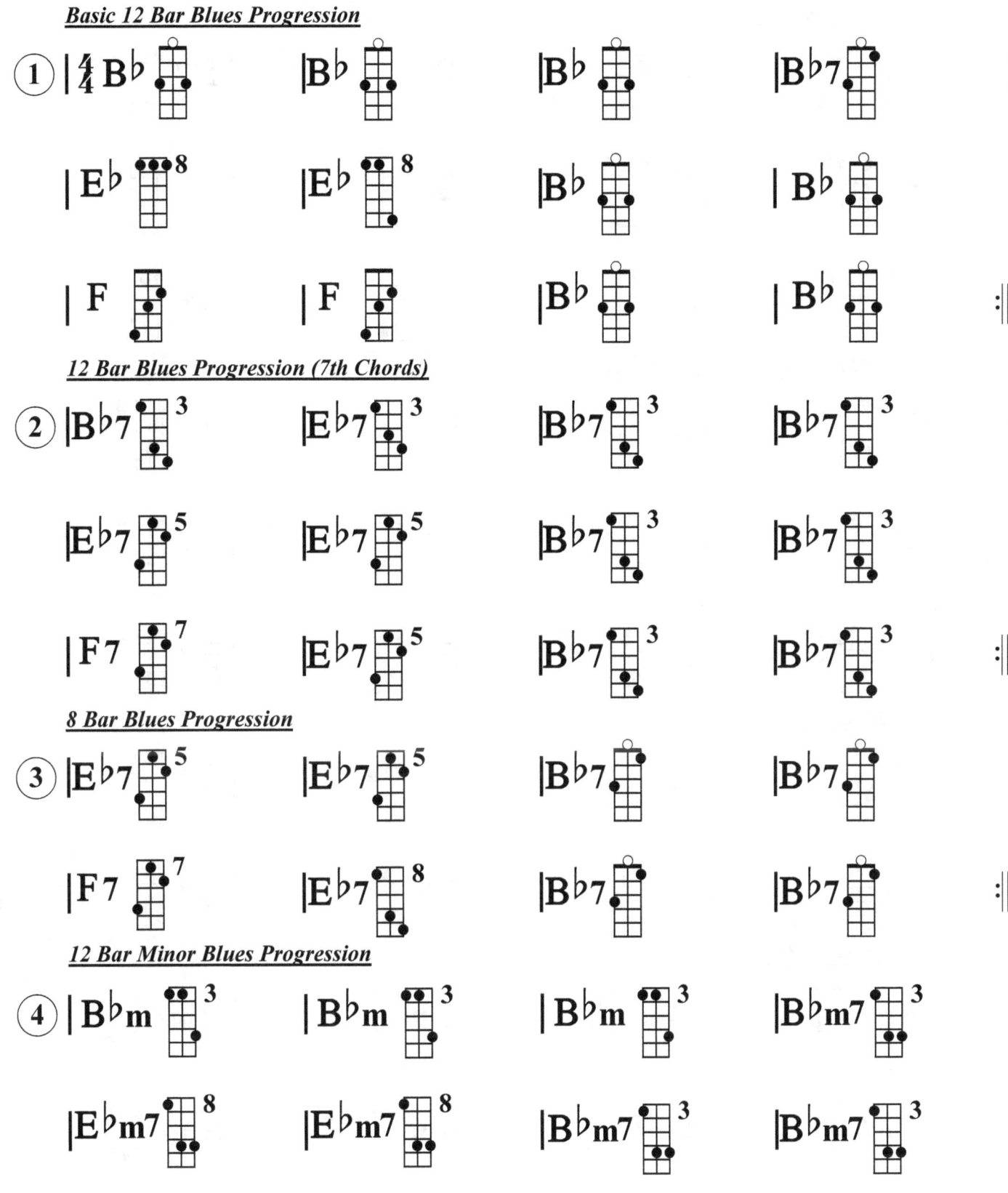

Blues Chord Progressions - Key of B and Bm

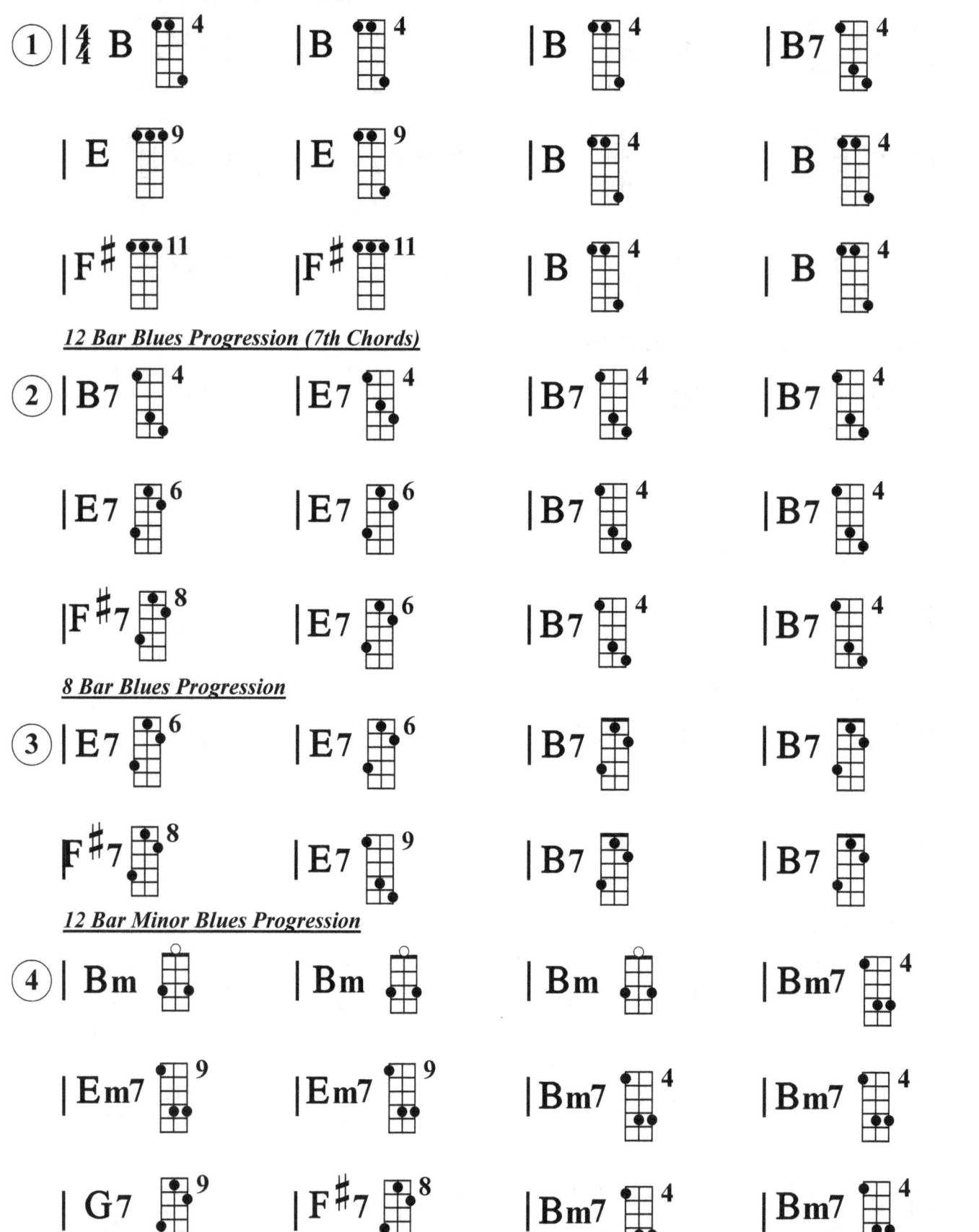

Blues Chord Progessions - Key of C and Cm

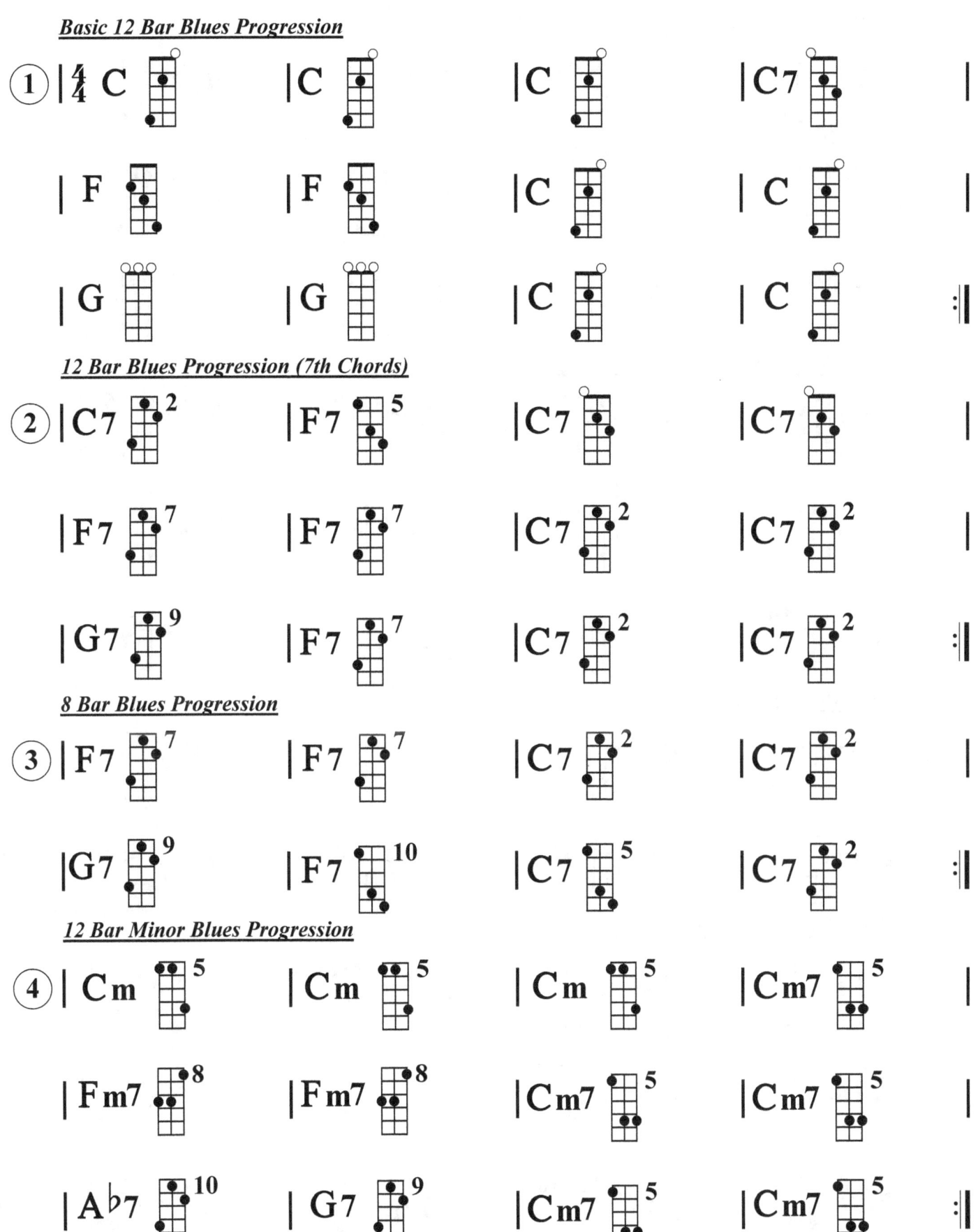

Blues Chord Progessions - Key of D♭/C♯ and D♭m/C♯m

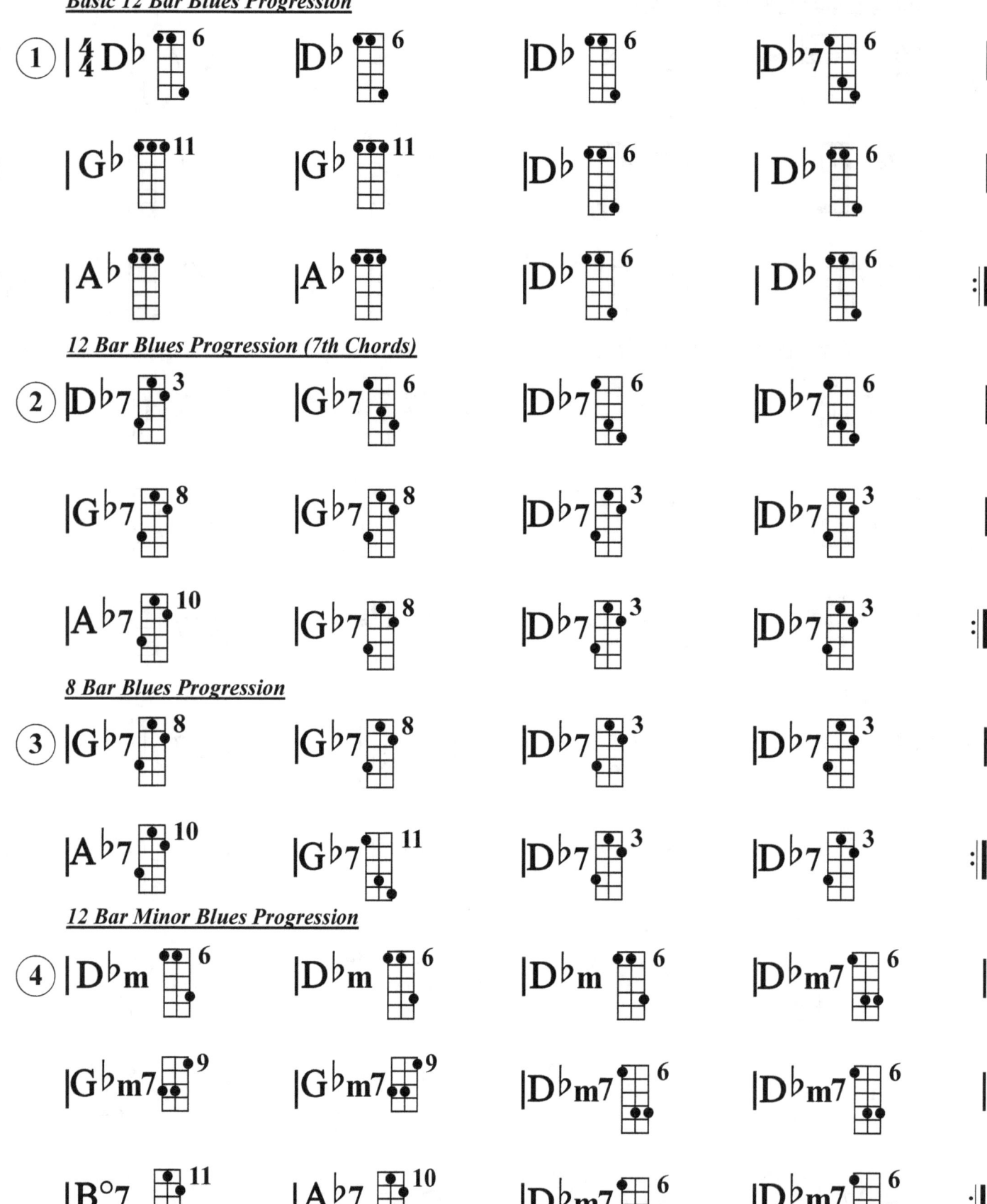

Blues Chord Progressions - Key of D and Dm

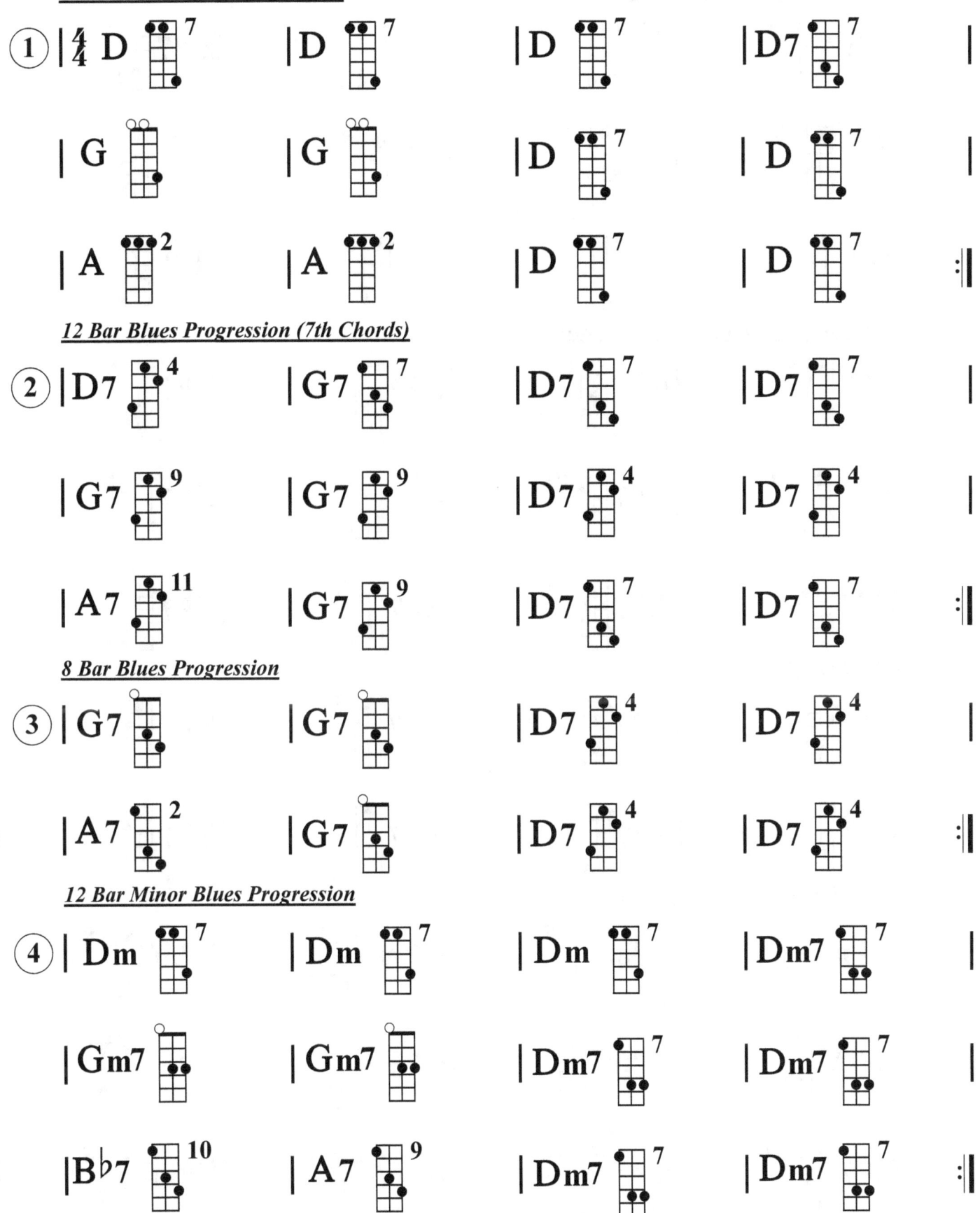

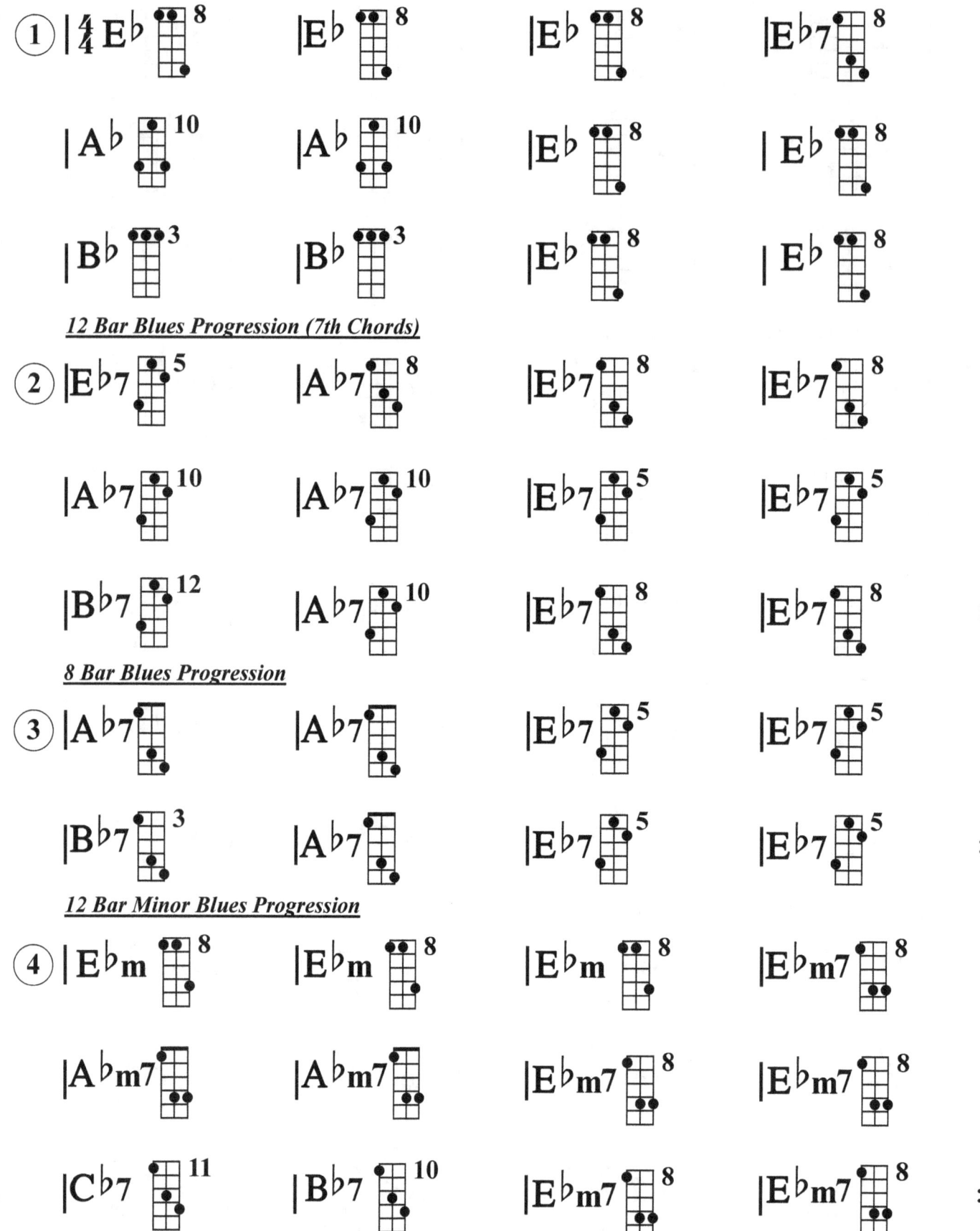

Blues Chord Progressions - Key of E and Em

Basic 12 Bar Blues Progression

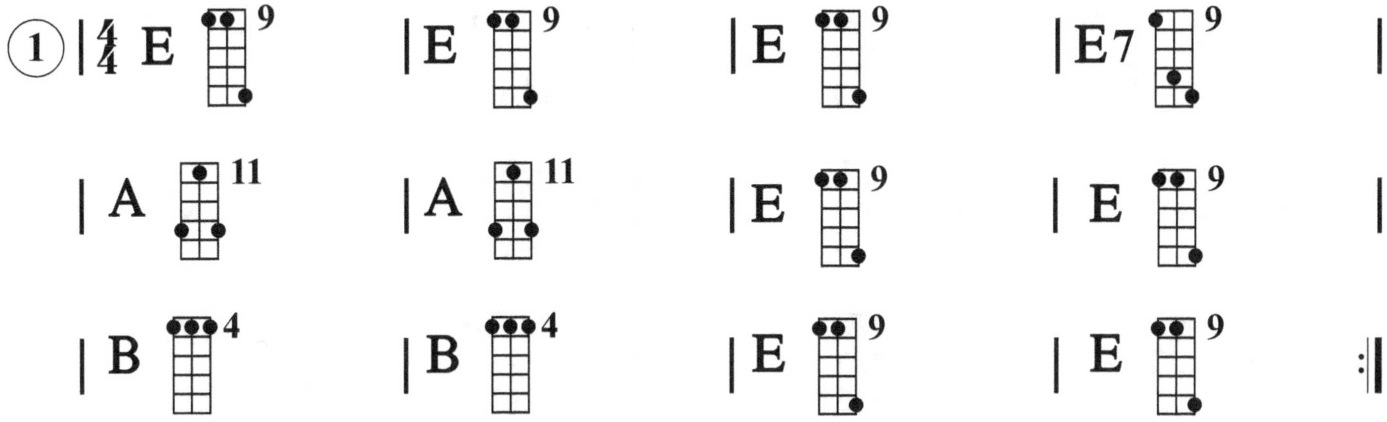

① | 4/4 E⁹ | E⁹ | E⁹ | E7⁹ |
| A¹¹ | A¹¹ | E⁹ | E⁹ |
| B⁴ | B⁴ | E⁹ | E⁹ :||

12 Bar Blues Progression (7th Chords)

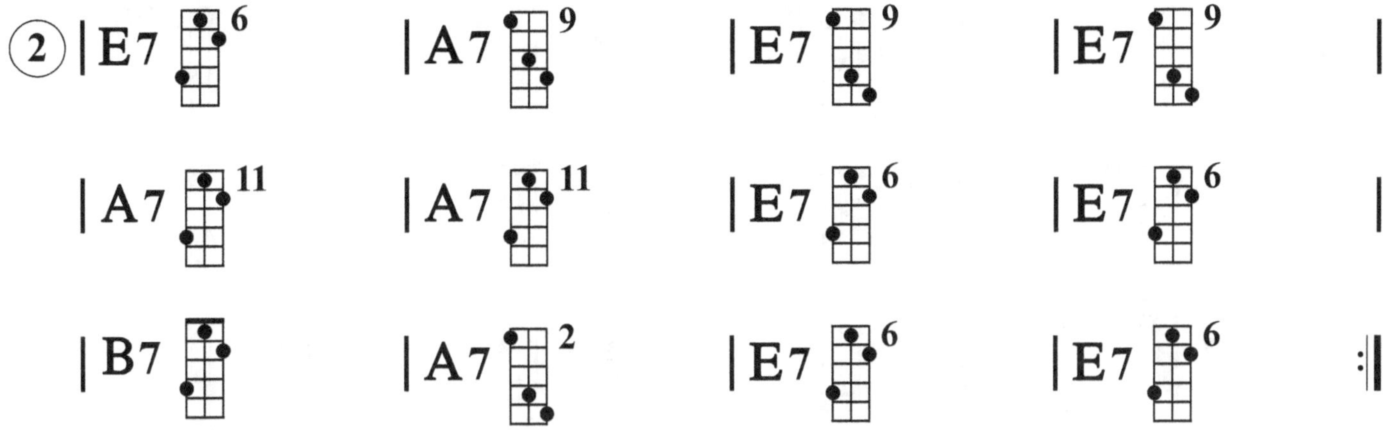

② | E7⁶ | A7⁹ | E7⁹ | E7⁹ |
| A7¹¹ | A7¹¹ | E7⁶ | E7⁶ |
| B7 | A7² | E7⁶ | E7⁶ :||

8 Bar Blues Progression

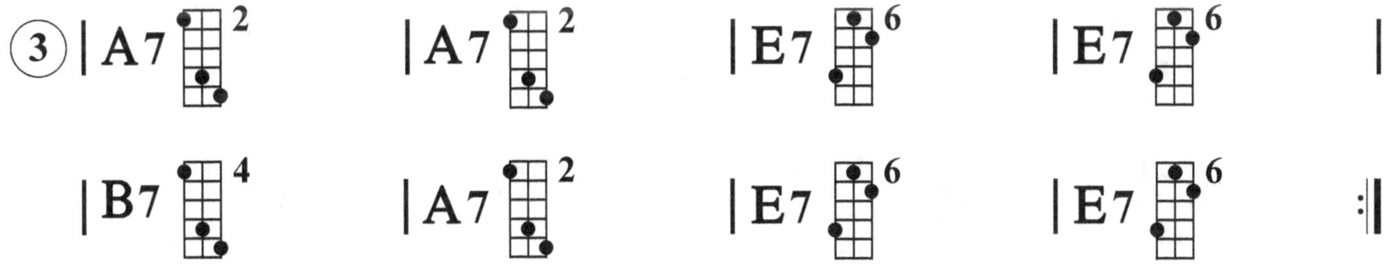

③ | A7² | A7² | E7⁶ | E7⁶ |
| B7⁴ | A7² | E7⁶ | E7⁶ :||

12 Bar Minor Blues Progression

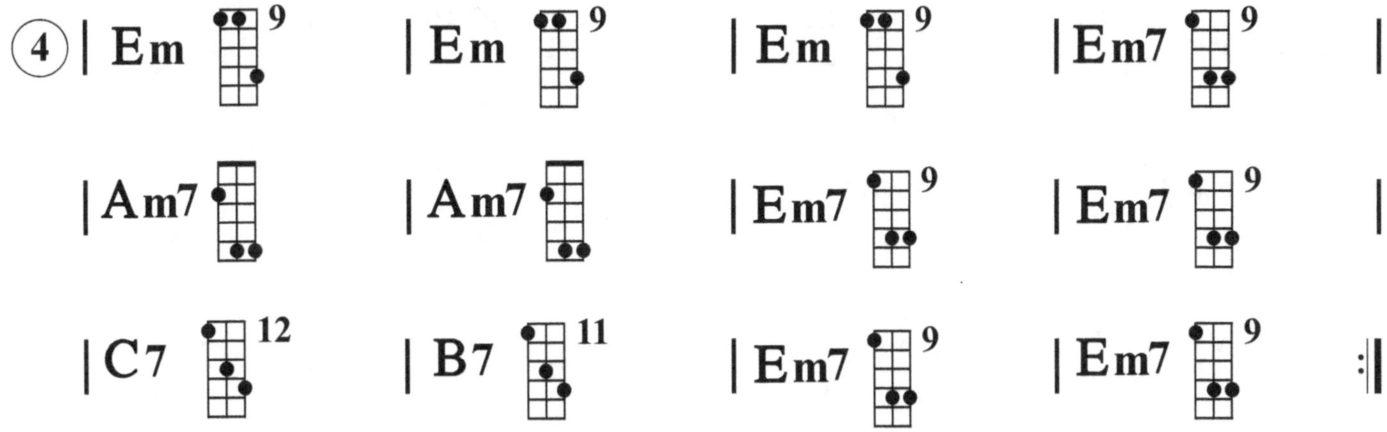

④ | Em⁹ | Em⁹ | Em⁹ | Em7⁹ |
| Am7 | Am7 | Em7⁹ | Em7⁹ |
| C7¹² | B7¹¹ | Em7⁹ | Em7⁹ :||

Blues Chord Progessions - Key of F and Fm

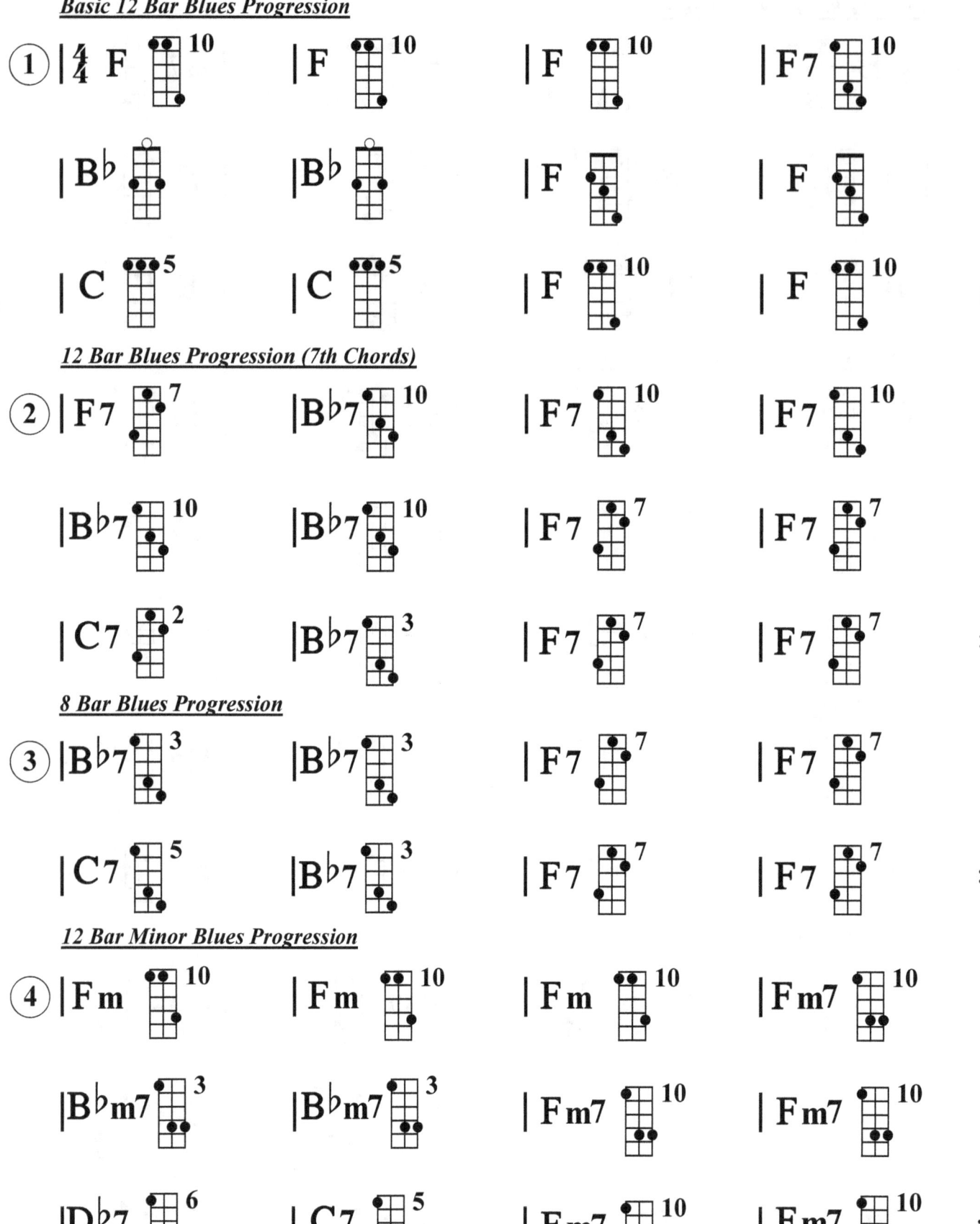

Blues Chord Progressions - Key of F# and F#m

Basic 12 Bar Blues Progression

① | 4/4 F# | F# | F# | F#7 |
| B | B | F# | F# |
| C# | C# | F# | F# :||

12 Bar Blues Progression (7th Chords)

② | F#7 | B7 | F#7 | F#7 |
| B7 | B7 | F#7 | F#7 |
| C#7 | B7 | F#7 | F#7 :||

8 Bar Blues Progression

③ | B7 | B7 | F#7 | F#7 |
| C#7 | B7 | F#7 | F#7 :||

12 Bar Minor Blues Progression

④ | F#m | F#m | F#m | F#m7 |
| Bm7 | Bm7 | F#m7 | F#m7 |
| D7 | C#7 | F#m7 | F#m7 :||

Blues Chord Progressions - Key of G and Gm

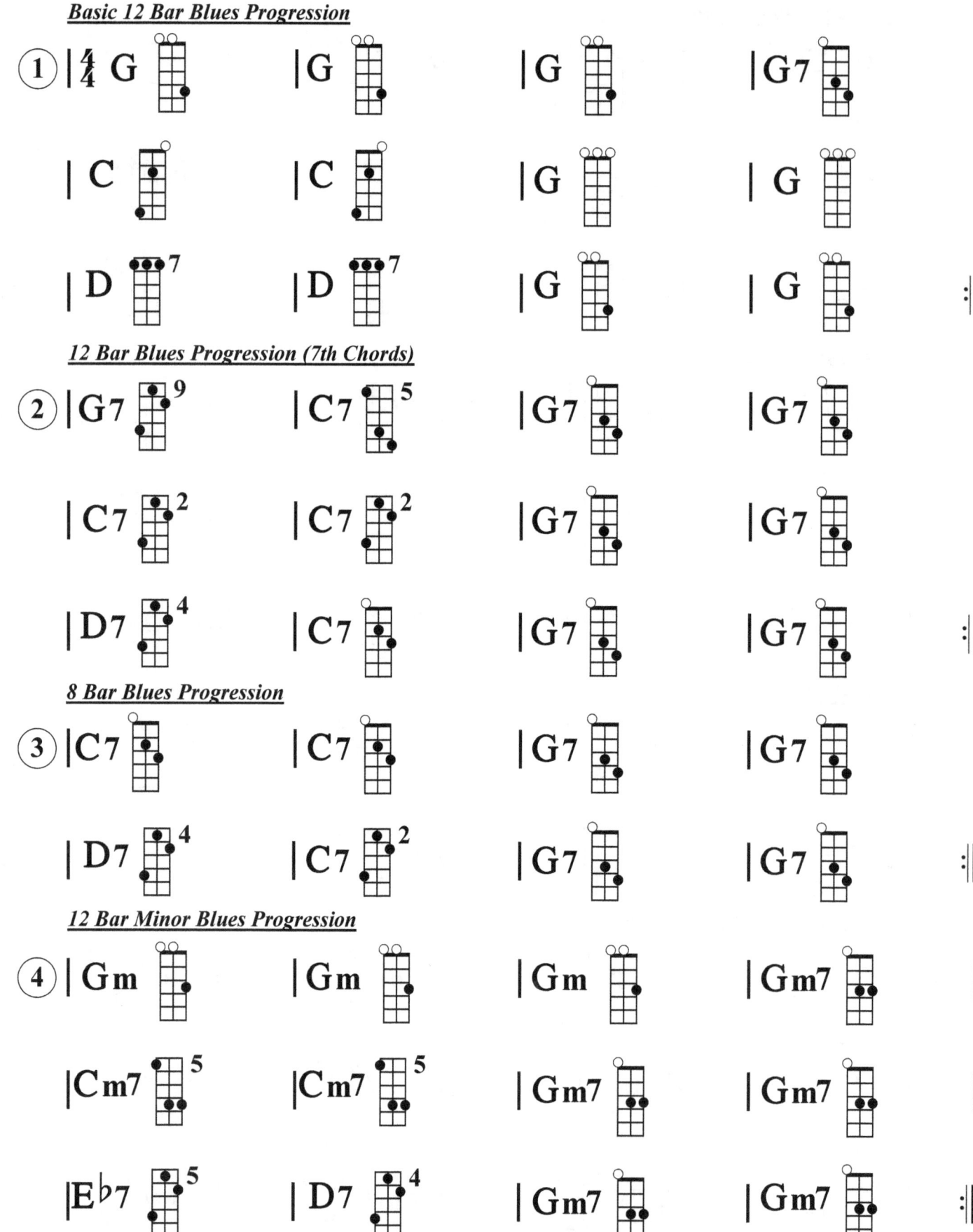

Blues Chord Progessions - Key of A♭ and A♭m

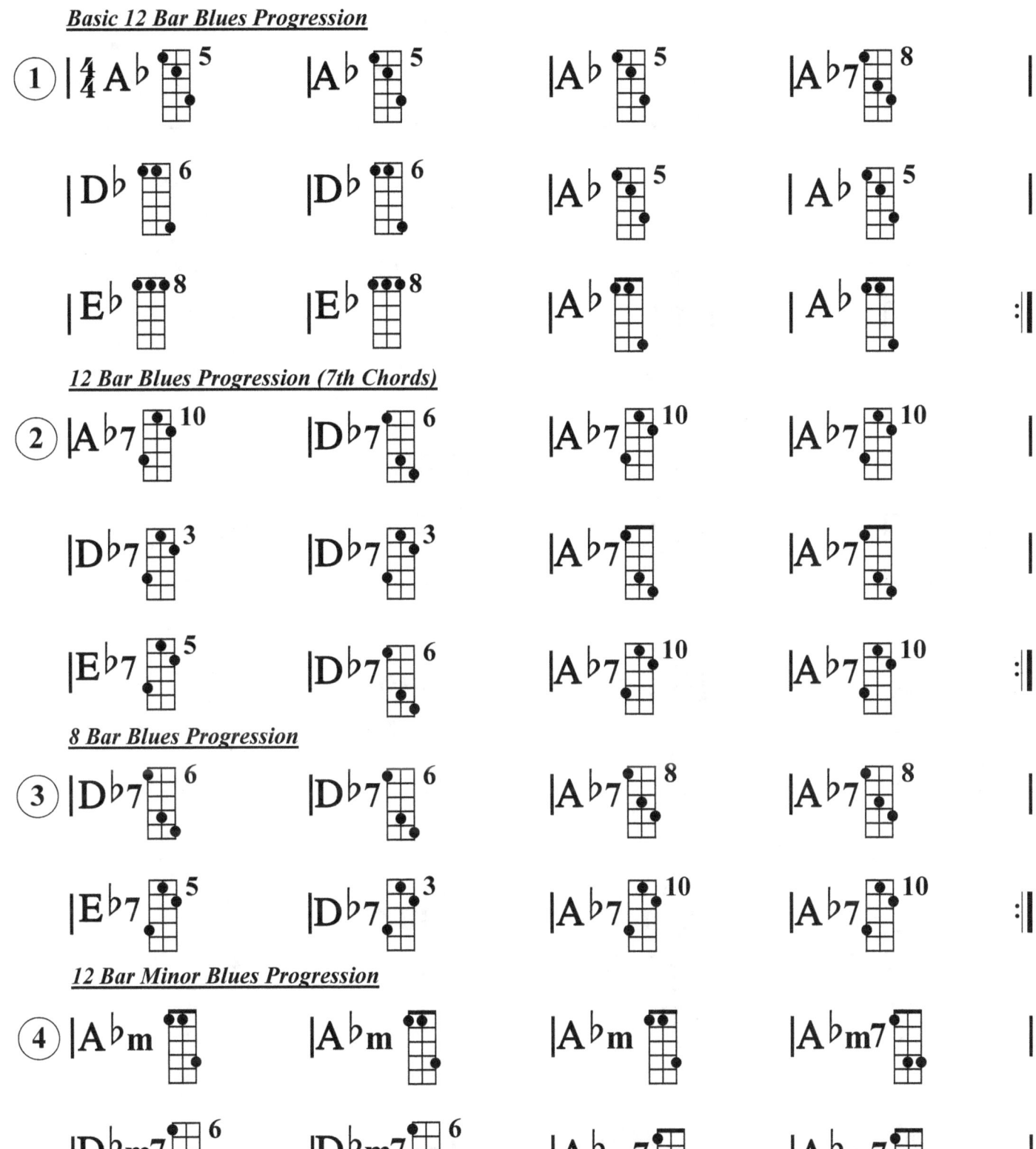

POP CHORD PROGRESSIONS - KEY OF A

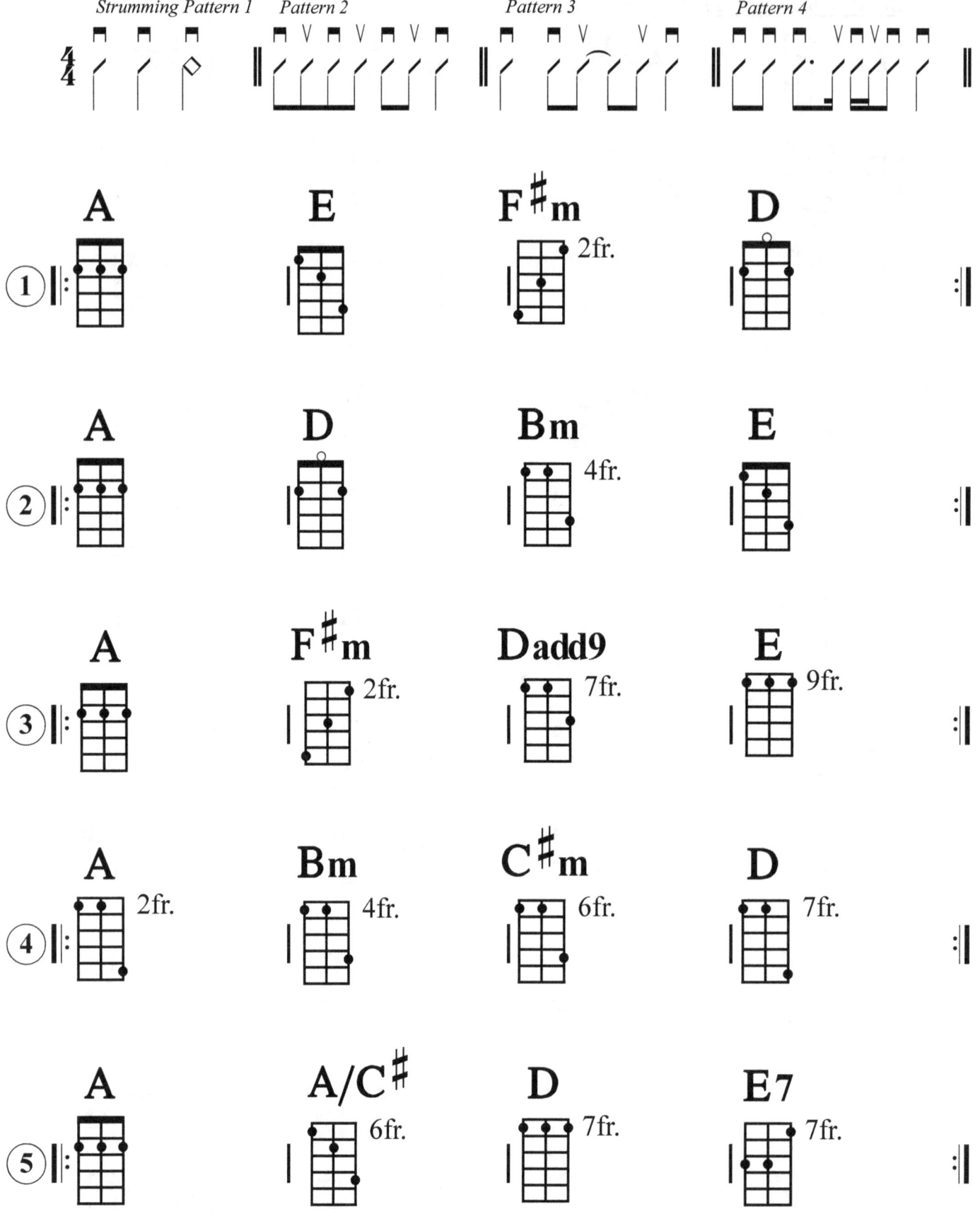

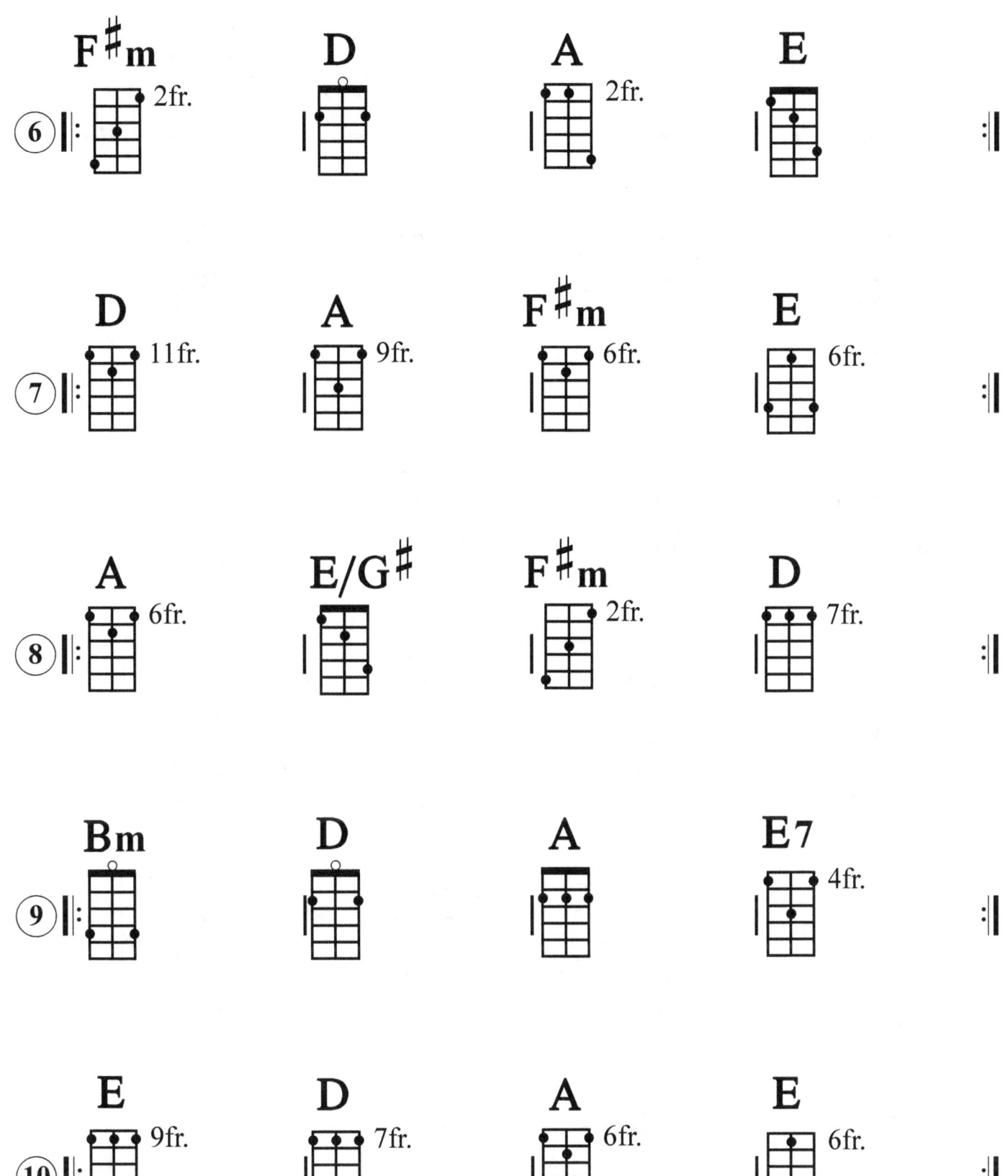

POP CHORD PROGRESSIONS - KEY OF B♭

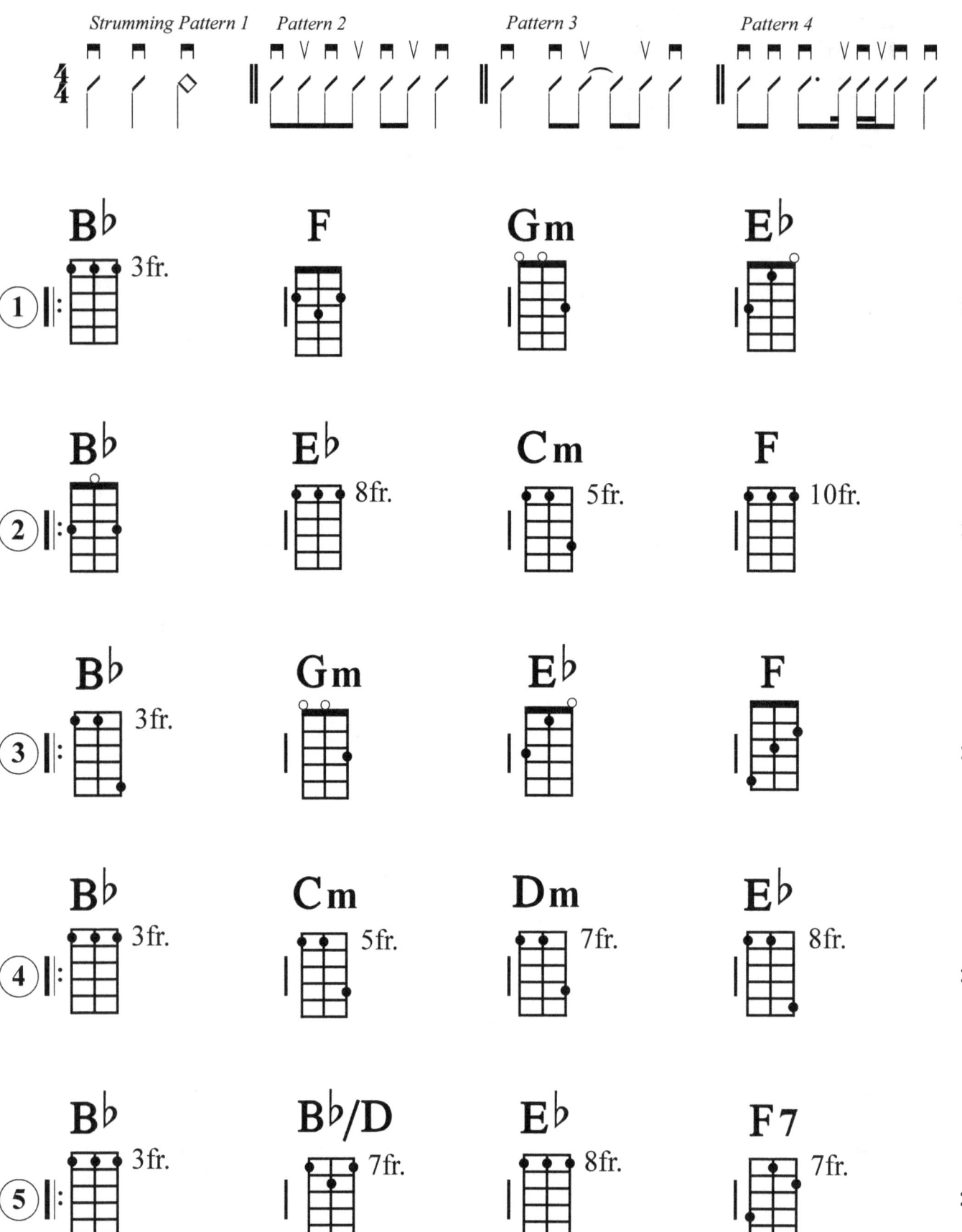

151

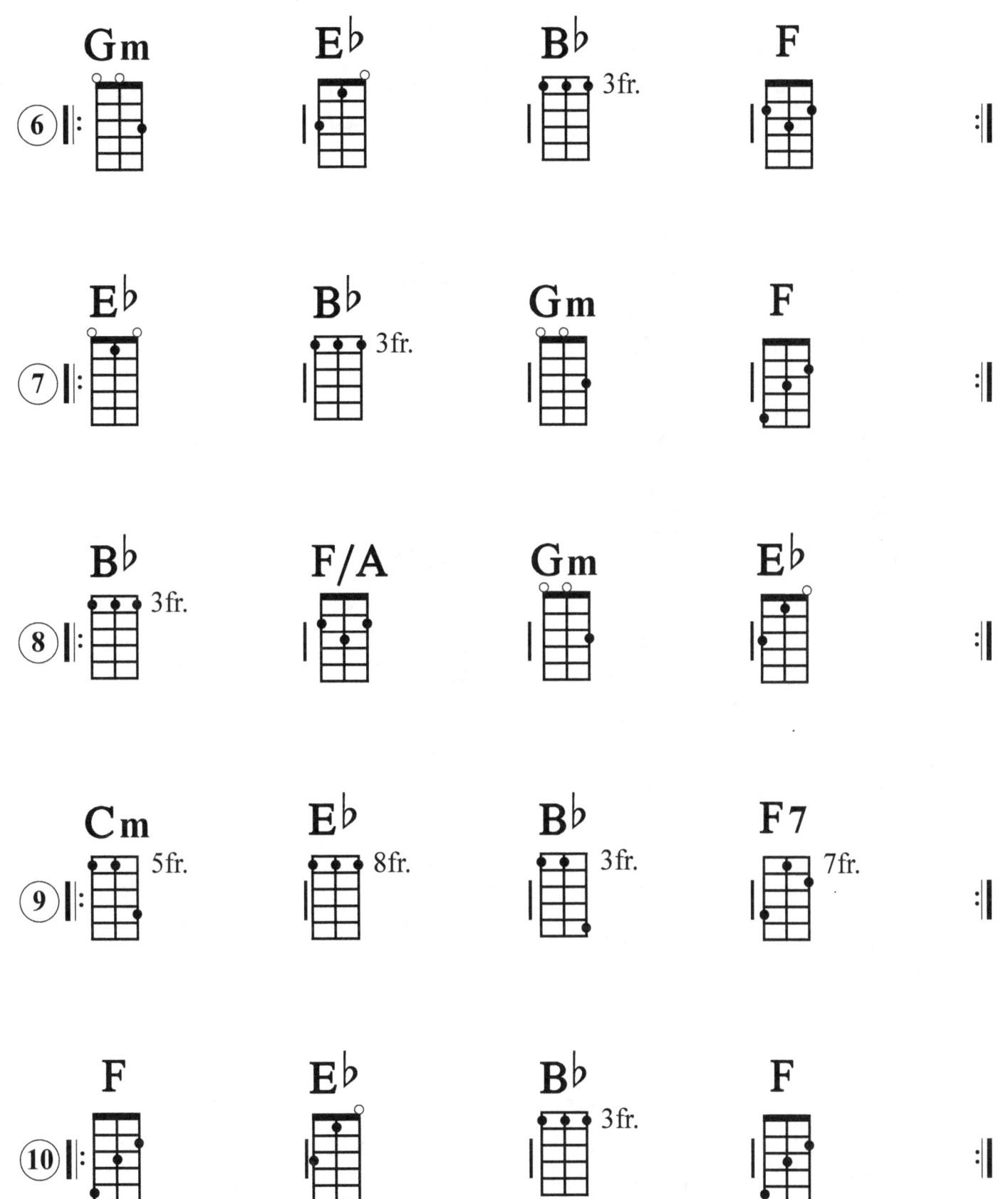

POP CHORD PROGRESSIONS - KEY OF B

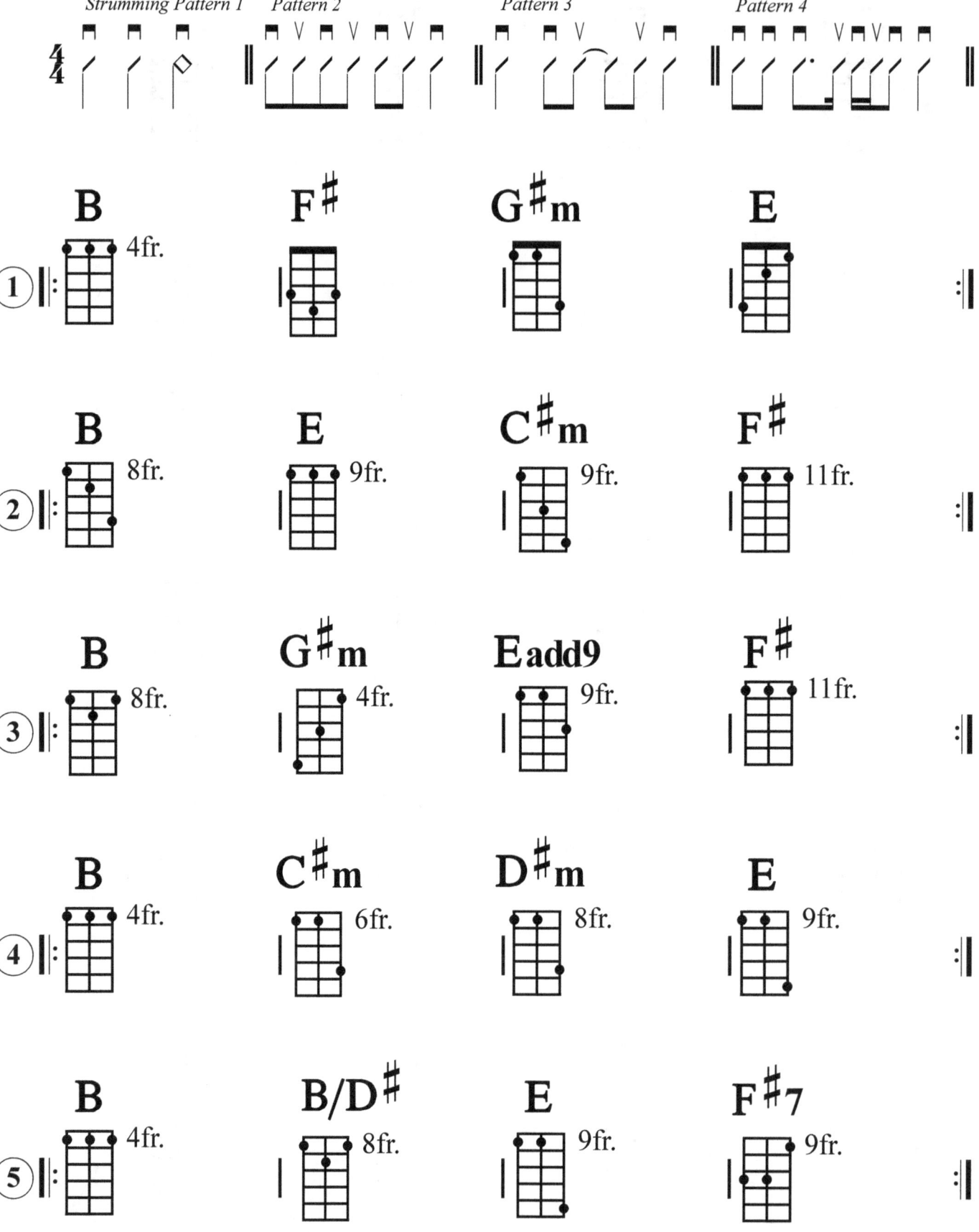

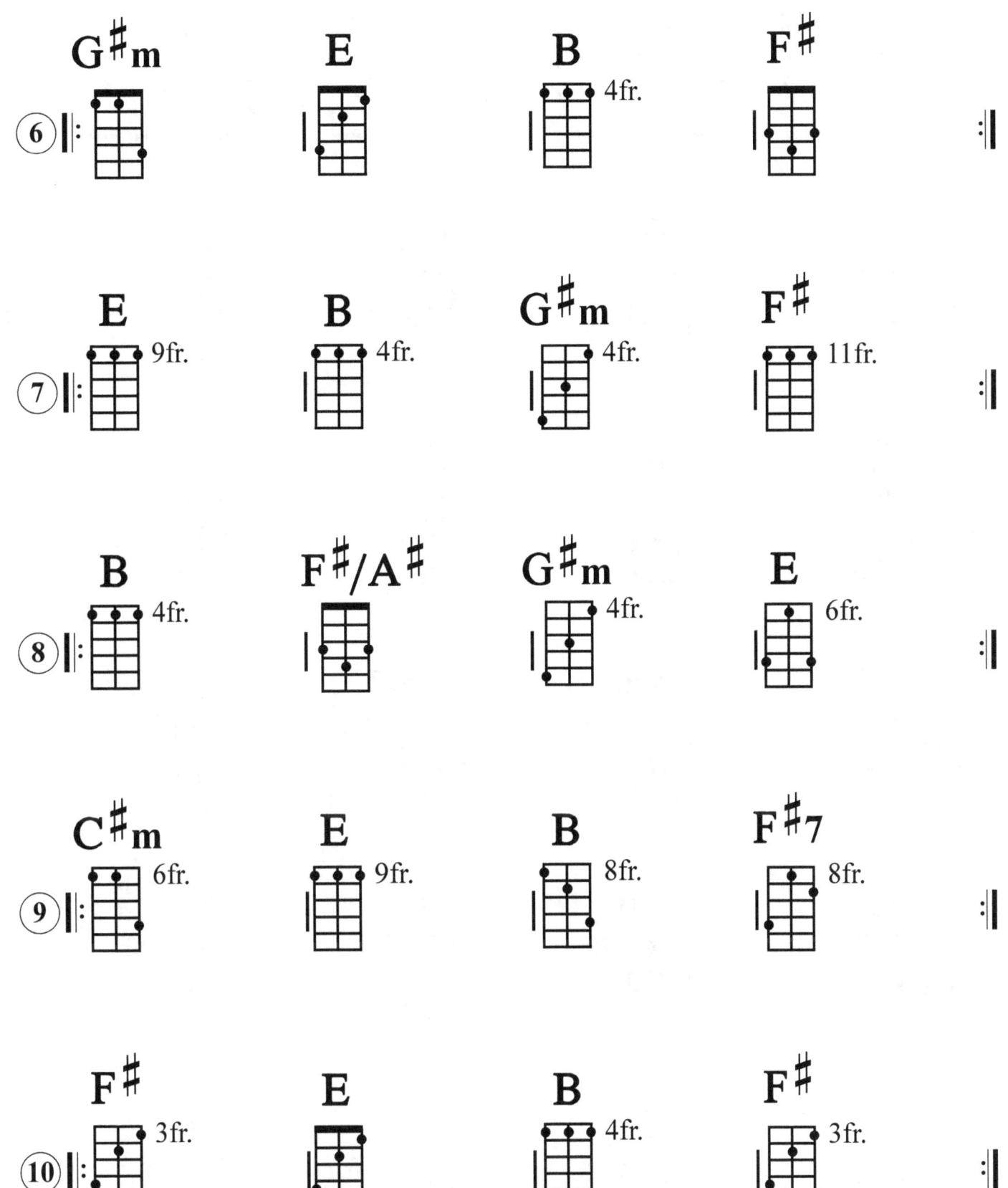

POP CHORD PROGRESSIONS - KEY OF C

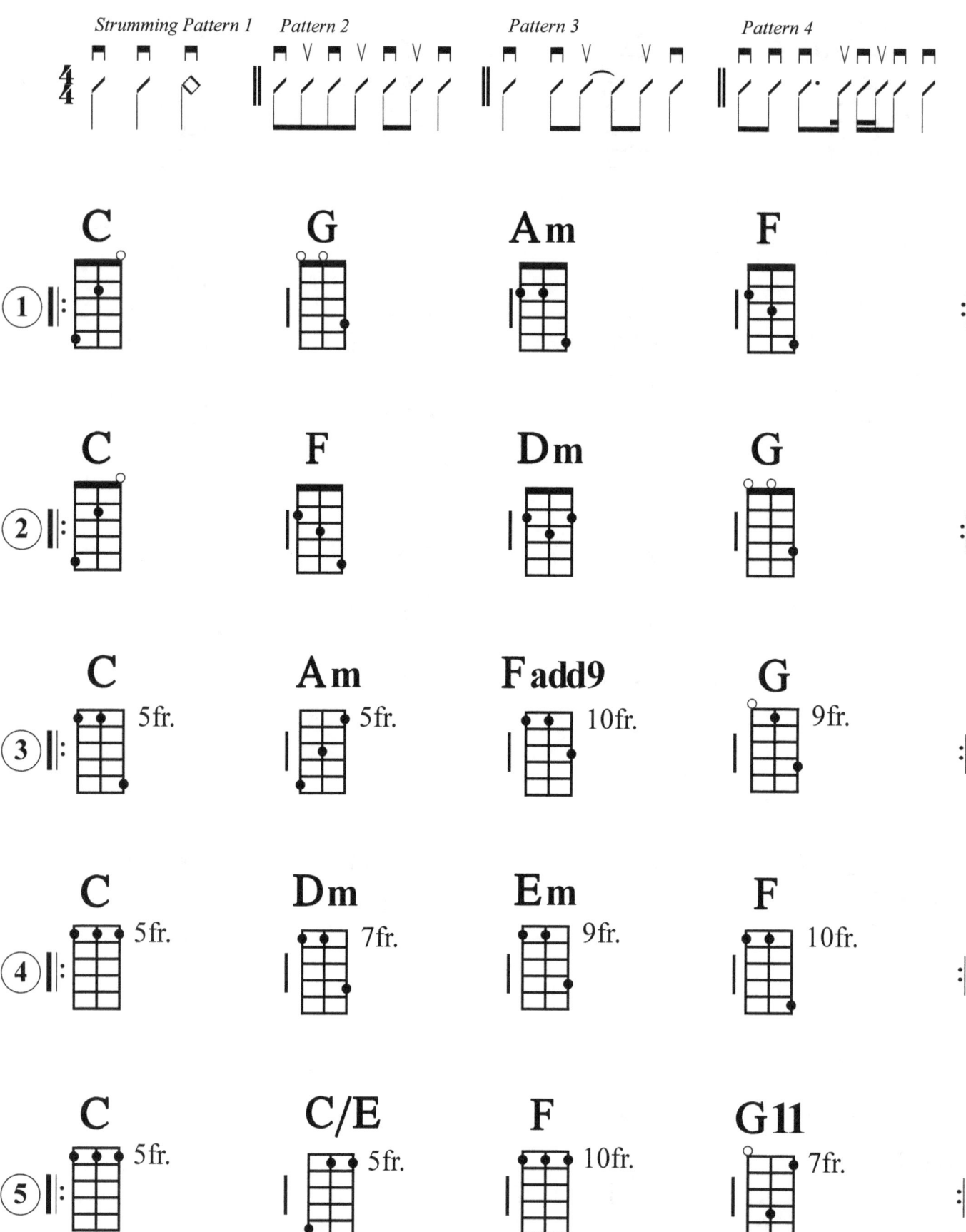

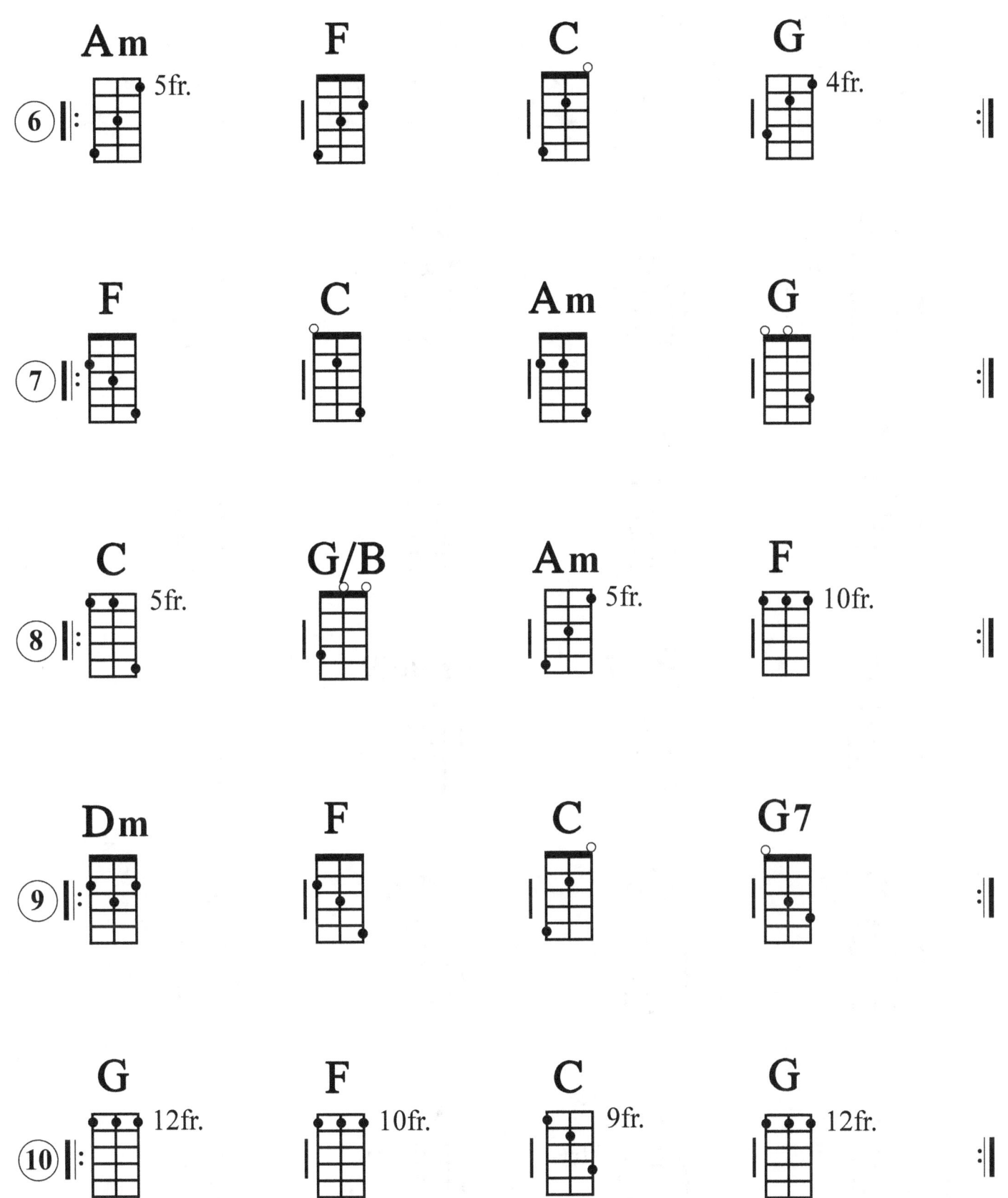

POP CHORD PROGRESSIONS - KEY OF D

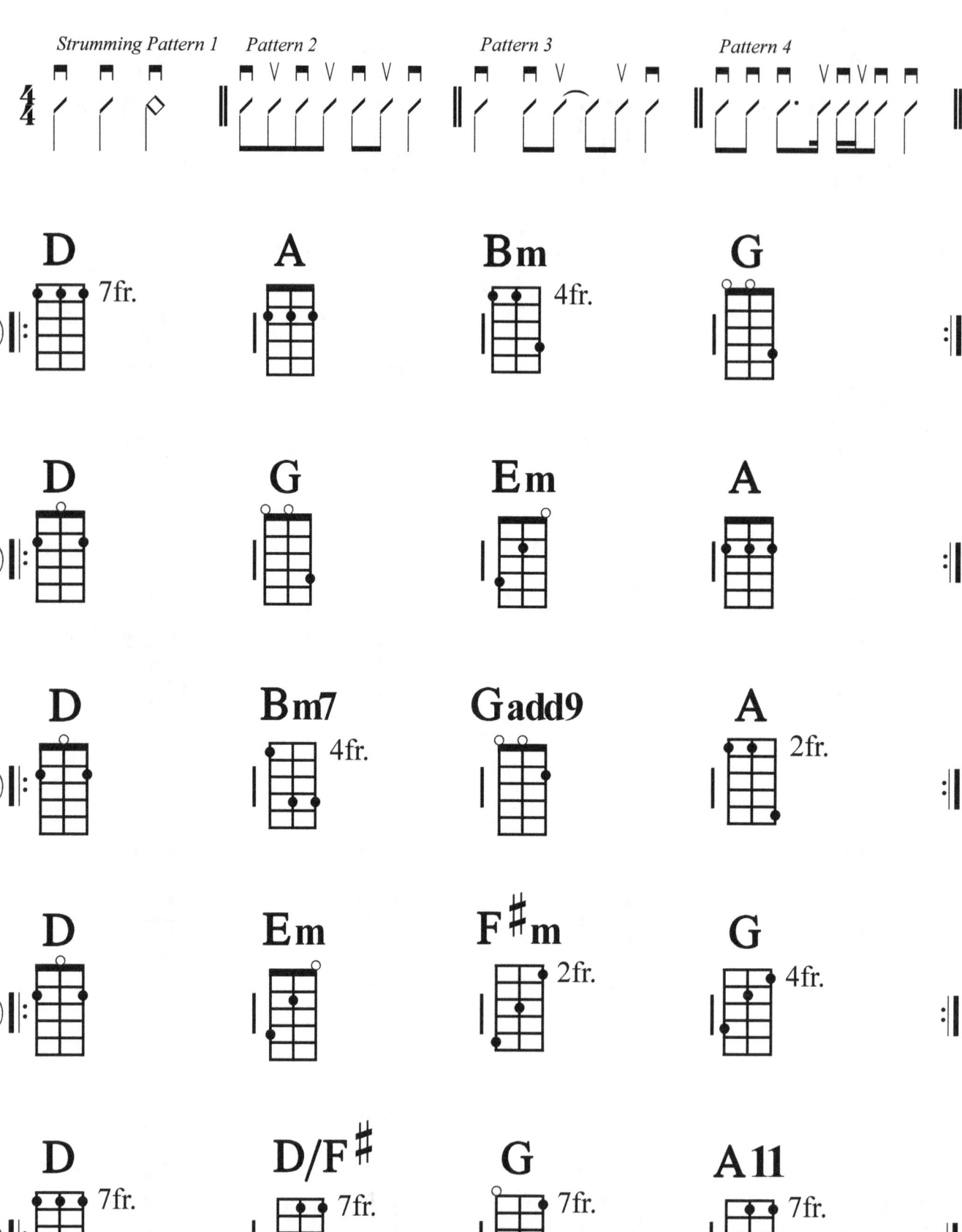

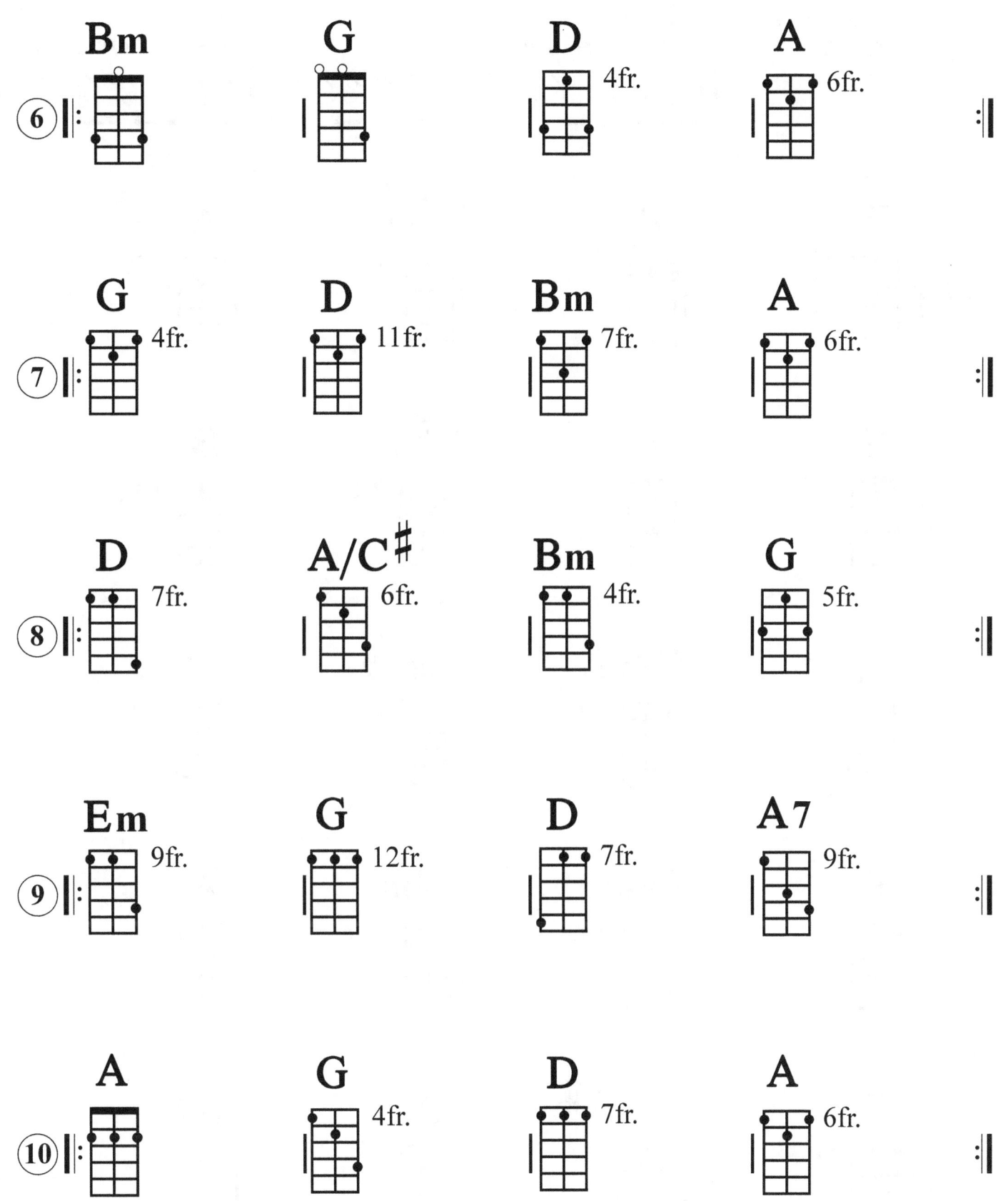

POP CHORD PROGRESSIONS - KEY OF E

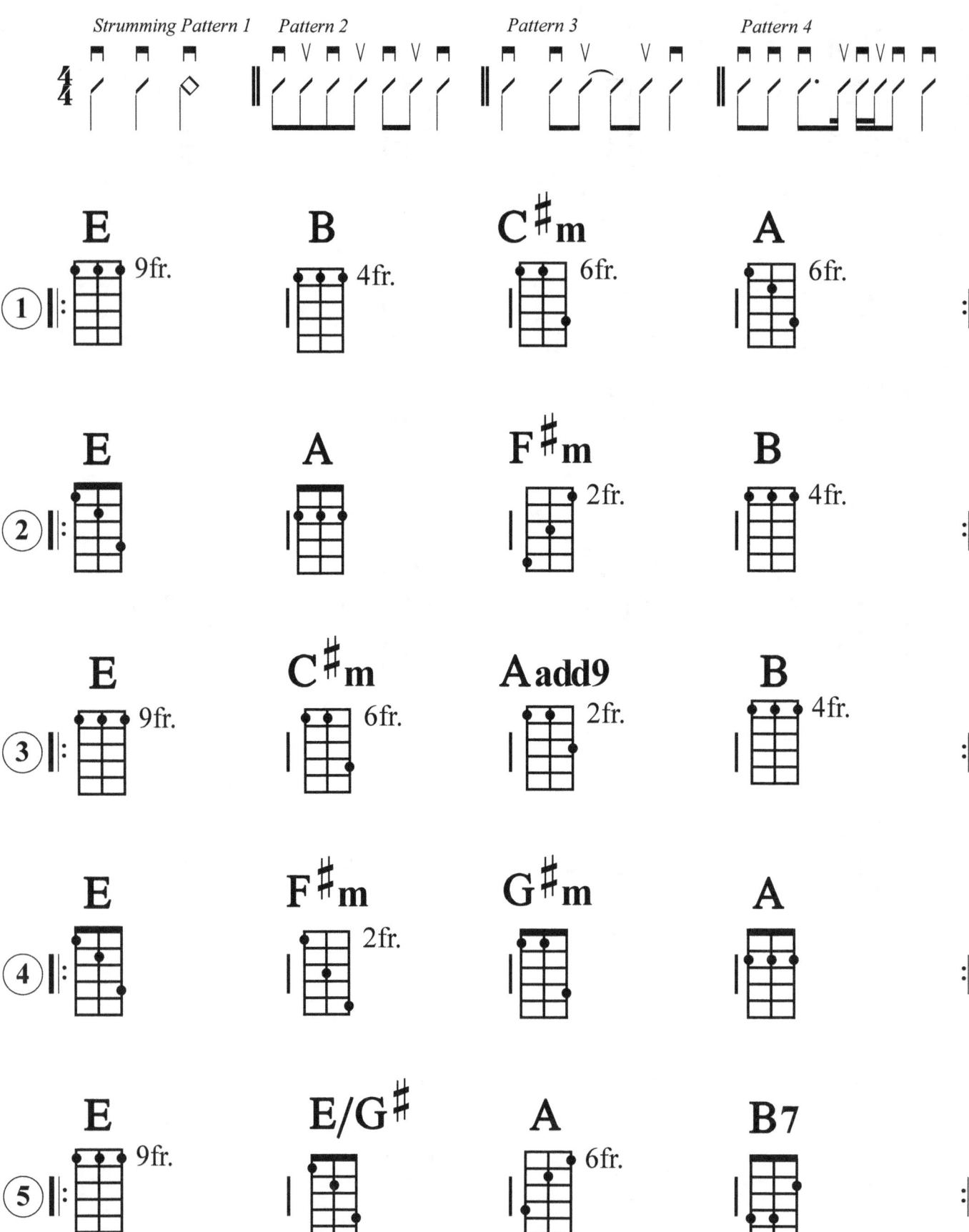

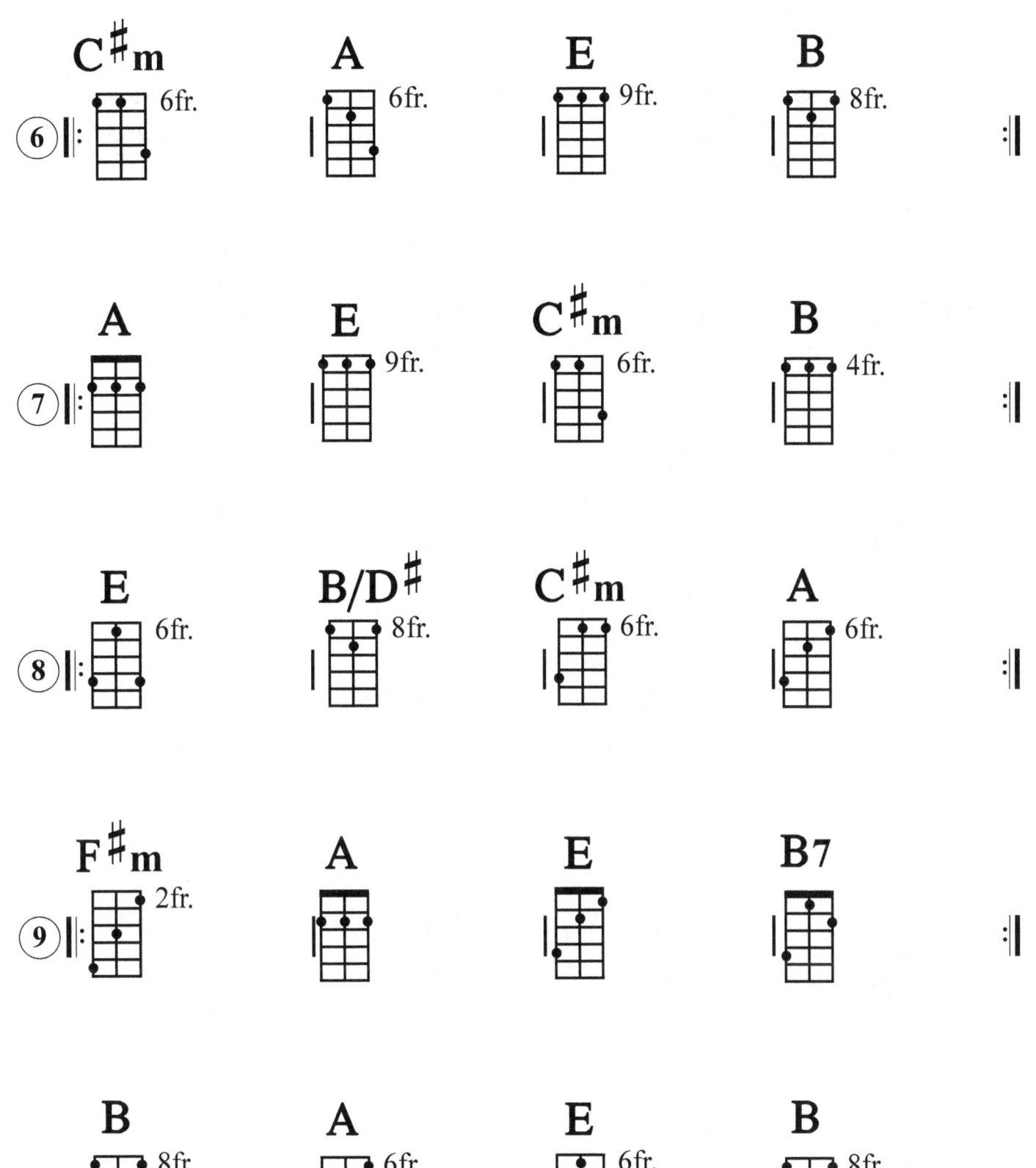

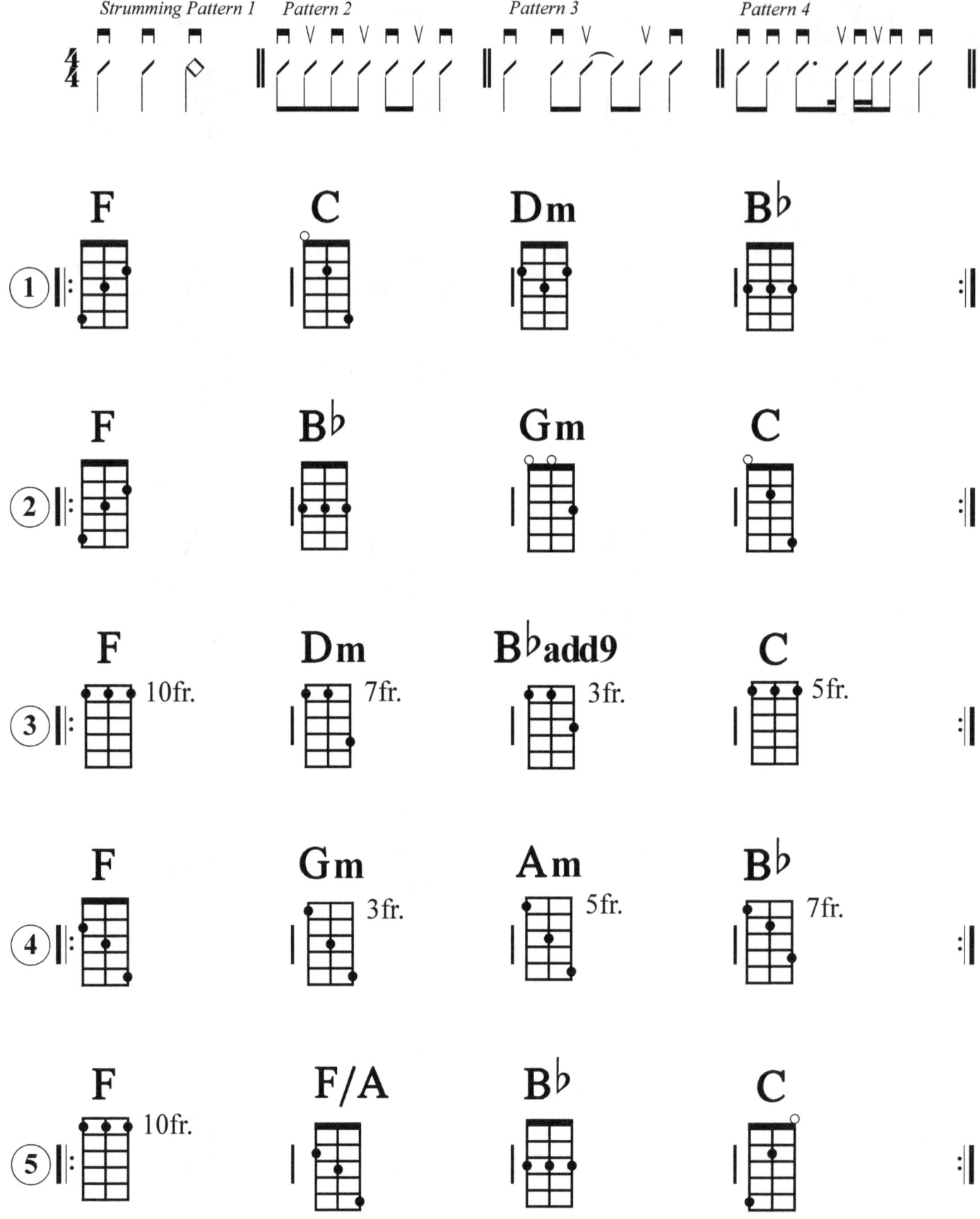

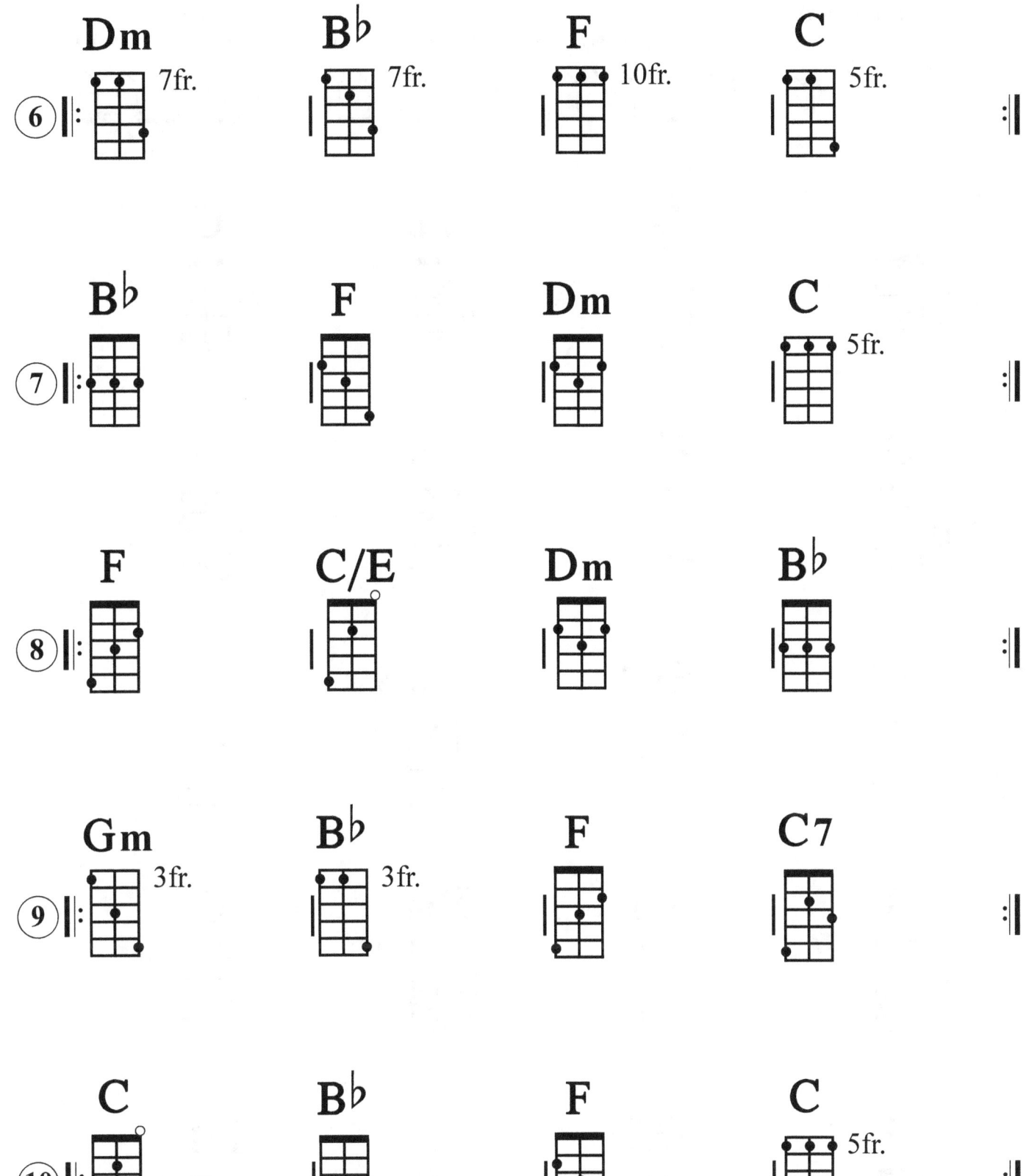

POP CHORD PROGRESSIONS - KEY OF G

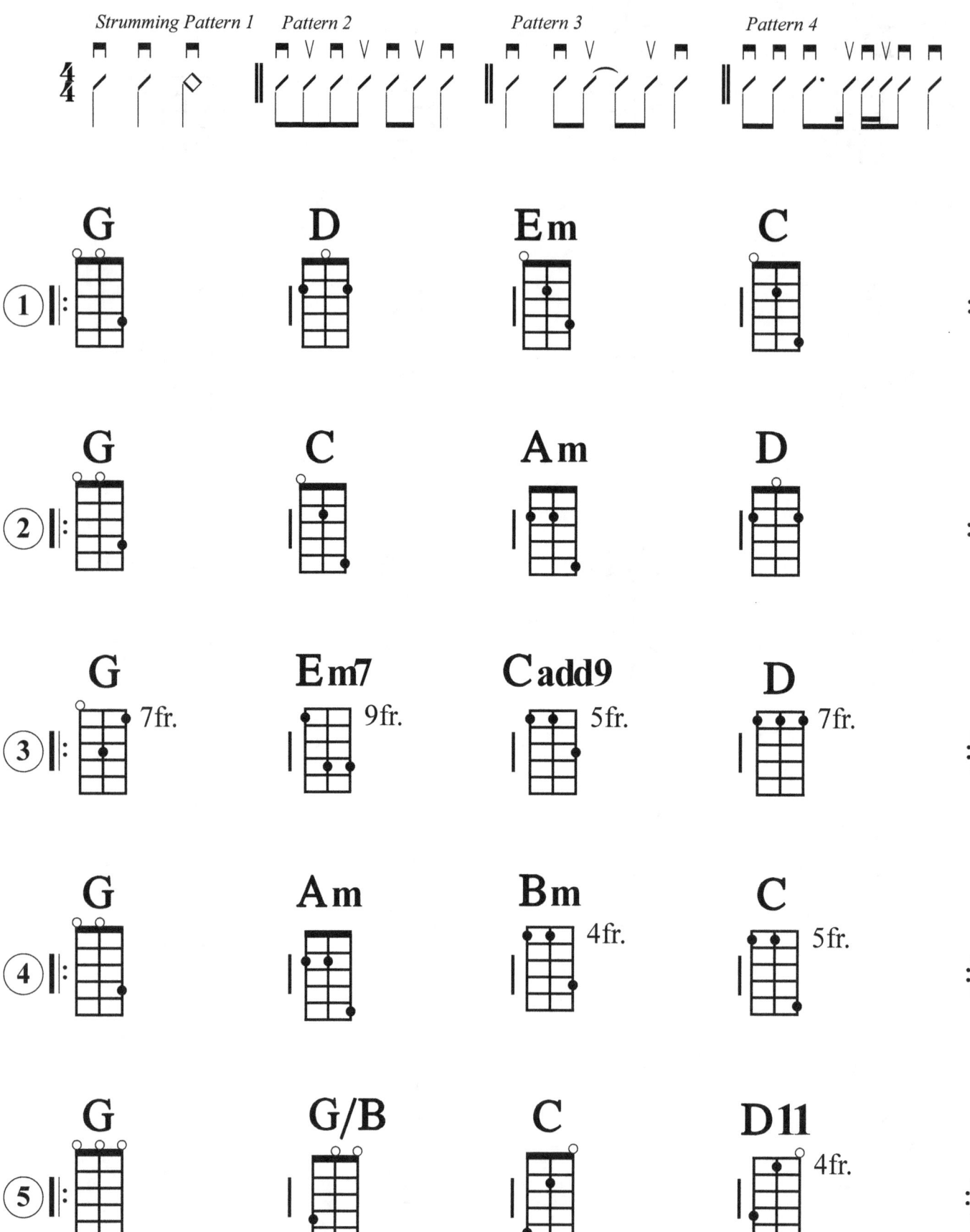

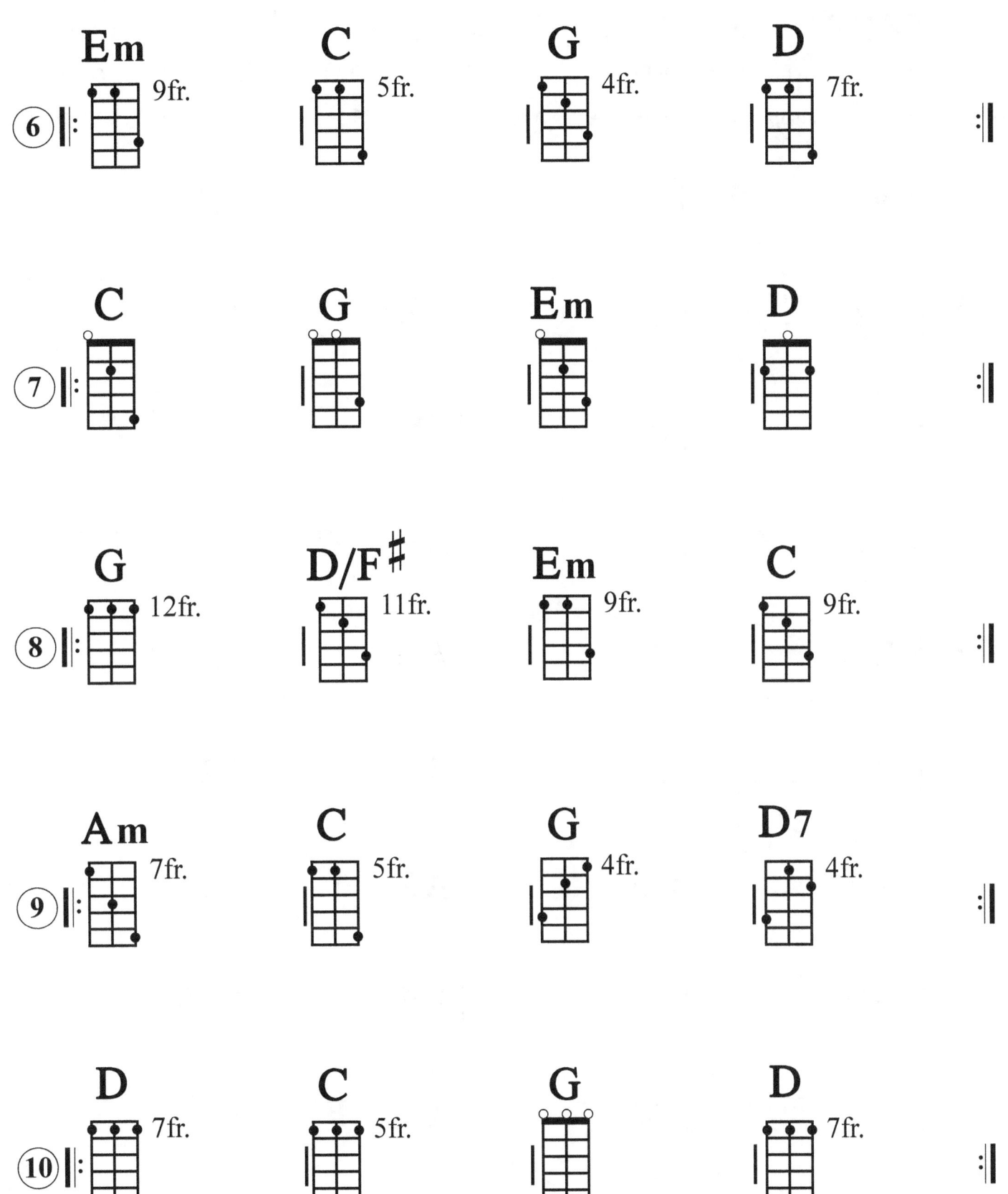

Rock Chord Progressions - A

Fingerboard Notes on 2nd and 3rd String:

FRET	0	1	2	3	4	5	6	7	8	9	10	11	12
2nd string	D	D#E♭	E		F	F#G♭	G	G#A♭	A	A#B♭	B	C	C#D♭	D
3rd string	G	G#A♭	A	A#B♭	B		C	C#D♭	D	D#E♭	E	F	F#G♭	G

① ‖: A   E |D |A   E |D   :‖

② ‖: A5 |D5 |C5 |F5   :‖

③ ‖: A |G |D |D   C5 :‖

④ ‖: A5   C5 |D5 |A5   C5 |E♭5   D5 :‖

⑤ ‖: Dm |B♭ |Am |C   :‖

⑥ ‖: Am |G | F |E   :‖

⑦ ‖: A5 |G5 |A5 |E   :‖

⑧ ‖: A5 | C5 |D5 | F5   G :‖

⑨ ‖: A5   F5 |D5 |A5   F5 |D5   E :‖

⑩ ‖: A5   C5 |A5   D5 |A5   C5 |A5 E♭5 D5 :‖

Rock Chord Progressions - B♭

Fingerboard Notes on 2nd and 3rd String:

FRET	0	1	2	3	4	5	6	7	8	9	10	11	12
2nd string	D	D#E♭	E	F	F#G♭	G	G#A♭	A	A#B♭	B	C	C#D♭	D
3rd string	G	G#A♭	A	A#B♭	B	C	C#D♭	D	D#E♭	E	F	F#G♭	G

① ‖: B♭   F |E♭ |B♭   F |E♭   :‖

② ‖: B♭5 |E♭5 |D♭5 |G♭5   :‖

③ ‖: B♭ |A♭ |E♭ |E♭   D♭5 :‖

④ ‖: B♭5   D♭5 |E♭5 |B♭5   D♭5 | E5   E♭5 :‖

⑤ ‖: E♭m | B |B♭m |D♭   :‖

⑥ ‖: B♭m |A♭ |G♭ |F   :‖

⑦ ‖: B♭5 |A♭5 |B♭5 |F   :‖

⑧ ‖: B♭5 |D♭5 |E♭5 |G♭5   A♭ :‖

⑨ ‖: B♭5   G♭5 |E♭5 |B♭5   G♭5 |E♭5   F :‖

⑩ ‖: B♭5   D♭5 |B♭5   E♭5 |B♭5   D♭5 |B♭5   E5   E♭5 :‖

Rock Chord Progressions - B

Fingerboard Notes on 2nd and 3rd String:

FRET	0	1	2	3	4	5	6	7	8	9	10	11	12
2nd string	D	D#Eb	E	F	F#Gb	G	G#Ab	A	A#Bb	B	C	C#Db	D
3rd string	G	G#Ab	A	A#Bb	B	C	C#Db	D	D#Eb	E	F	F#Gb	G

① $\|:$ B   F# | E | B   F# | E $:\|$

② $\|:$ B5 | E5 | D5 | G5 $:\|$

③ $\|:$ B | A | E | E   D5 $:\|$

④ $\|:$ B5   D5 | E5 | B5   D5 | F5   E5 $:\|$

⑤ $\|:$ Em | C | Bm | D $:\|$

⑥ $\|:$ Bm | A | G | F# $:\|$

⑦ $\|:$ B5 | A5 | B5 | F# $:\|$

⑧ $\|:$ B5 | D5 | E5 | G5   A $:\|$

⑨ $\|:$ B5   G5 | E5 | B5   G5 | E5   F# $:\|$

⑩ $\|:$ B5   D5 | B5   E5 | B5   D5 | B5   F5   E5 $:\|$

Rock Chord Progressions - C

Fingerboard Notes on 2nd and 3rd String:

FRET	0	1	2	3	4	5	6	7	8	9	10	11	12
2nd string	D	D#Eb	E	F	F#Gb	G	G#Ab	A	A#Bb	B	C	C#Db	D
3rd string	G	G#Ab	A	A#Bb	B	C	C#Db	D	D#Eb	E	F	F#Gb	G

① ‖: C   G | F | C   G | F   :‖

② ‖: C5 | F5 | Eb5 | Ab5   :‖

③ ‖: C | Bb | F | F   Eb5 :‖

④ ‖: C5 Eb5 | F5 | C5 Eb5 | Gb5 F5 :‖

⑤ ‖: Fm | Db | Cm | Eb   :‖

⑥ ‖: Cm | Bb | Ab | G   :‖

⑦ ‖: C5 | Bb5 | C5 | G   :‖

⑧ ‖: C5 | Eb5 | F5 | Ab5 Bb :‖

⑨ ‖: C5 Ab5 | F5 | C5 Ab5 | F5   G :‖

⑩ ‖: C5 Eb5 | C5 F5 | C5 Eb5 | C5 Gb5 F5 :‖

168

Rock Chord Progressions - D♭ - C♯

Fingerboard Notes on 2nd and 3rd String:

FRET	0	1	2	3	4	5	6	7	8	9	10	11	12
2nd string	D	D♯E♭	E	F	F♯G♭	G	G♯A♭	A	A♯B♭	B	C	C♯D♭	D
3rd string	G	G♯A♭	A	A♯B♭	B	C	C♯D♭	D	D♯E♭	E	F	F♯G♭	G

① ‖: D♭   A♭ |G♭ |D♭   A♭ |G♭   :‖

② ‖: D♭5 |G♭5 | E5 |A5   :‖

③ ‖: D♭ | B |G♭ |G♭   E5 :‖

④ ‖: D♭5 E5 |G♭5 |D♭5 E5 |G5 G♭5 :‖

⑤ ‖: G♭m | D |D♭m | E   :‖

⑥ ‖: D♭m | B | A |A♭   :‖

⑦ ‖: D♭5 |B5 |D♭5 |A♭   :‖

⑧ ‖: D♭5 | E5 |G♭5 | A5   B :‖

⑨ ‖: D♭5 A5 |G♭5 |D♭5 A5 |G♭5 A♭ :‖

⑩ ‖: D♭5 E5 |D♭5 G♭5 |D♭5 E5 |D♭5 G5 G♭5 :‖

Rock Chord Progressions - D

Fingerboard Notes on 2nd and 3rd String:

FRET	0	1	2	3	4	5	6	7	8	9	10	11	12
2nd string	D	D#E♭	E	F	F#G♭	G	G#A♭	A	A#B♭	B	C	C#D♭	D
3rd string	G	G#A♭	A	A#B♭	B	C	C#D♭	D	D#E♭	E	F	F#G♭	G

① ‖: D A | G | D   A | G   :‖

② ‖: D5 | G5 | F5 | B♭5   :‖

③ ‖: D | C | G | G   F5 :‖

④ ‖: D5 F5 | G5 | D5 F5 | A♭5 G5 :‖

⑤ ‖: Gm | E♭ | Dm | F   :‖

⑥ ‖: Dm | C | B♭ | A   :‖

⑦ ‖: D5 | C5 | D5 | A   :‖

⑧ ‖: D5 | F5 | G5 | B♭5 C :‖

⑨ ‖: D5 B♭5 | G5 | D5 B♭5 | G5 A :‖

⑩ ‖: D5 F5 | D5 G5 | D5 F5 | D5 A♭5 G5 :‖

Rock Chord Progressions - E♭

Fingerboard Notes on 2nd and 3rd String:

FRET	0	1	2	3	4	5	6	7	8	9	10	11	12
2nd string	D	D#E♭	E	F	F#G♭	G	G#A♭	A	A#B♭	B	C	C#D♭	D
3rd string	G	G#A♭	A	A#B♭	B	C	C#D♭	D	D#E♭	E	F	F#G♭	G

① ‖: E♭   B♭ |A♭ |E♭   B♭ |A♭   :‖

② ‖: E♭5 |A♭5 |G♭5 |B5   :‖

③ ‖: E♭ |D♭ |A♭ |A♭   G♭5   :‖

④ ‖: E♭5   G♭5 |A♭5 |E♭5   G♭5 |A5   A♭5   :‖

⑤ ‖: A♭m |E |E♭m |G♭   :‖

⑥ ‖: E♭m |D♭ |B |B♭   :‖

⑦ ‖: E♭5 |D♭5 |E♭5 |B♭   :‖

⑧ ‖: E♭5 |G♭5 |A♭5 |B5   D♭   :‖

⑨ ‖: E♭5   B5 |A♭5 |E♭5   B5 |A♭5   B♭   :‖

⑩ ‖: E♭5   G♭5 |E♭5   A♭5 |E♭5   G♭5 |E♭5 A5 A♭5   :‖

Rock Chord Progressions - E

Fingerboard Notes on 2nd and 3rd String:

FRET	0	1	2	3	4	5	6	7	8	9	10	11	12
2nd string	D	D#Eb	E	F	F#Gb	G	G#Ab	A	A#Bb	B	C	C#Db	D
3rd string	G	G#Ab	A	A#Bb	B	C	C#Db	D	D#Eb	E	F	F#Gb	G

① ‖: E B |A |E B |A   :‖

② ‖: E5 |A5 |G5 |C5   :‖

③ ‖: E |D |A |A G5 :‖

④ ‖: E5 G5 |A5 |E5 G5 |Bb5 A5 :‖

⑤ ‖: Am |F |Em |G   :‖

⑥ ‖: Em |D |C |B   :‖

⑦ ‖: E5 |D5 |E5 |B   :‖

⑧ ‖: E5 |G5 |A5 |C5 D :‖

⑨ ‖: E5 C5 |A5 |E5 C5 |A5 B :‖

⑩ ‖: E5 G5 |E5 A5 |E5 G5 |E5 Bb5 A5 :‖

Rock Chord Progressions - F

Fingerboard Notes on 2nd and 3rd String:

FRET	0	1	2	3	4	5	6	7	8	9	10	11	12
2nd string	D	D#Eb	E		F	F#Gb	G	G#Ab	A	A#Bb	B	C	C#Db	D
3rd string	G	G#Ab	A	A#Bb	B		C	C#Db	D	D#Eb	E	F	F#Gb	G

① ‖: F   C |Bb | F   C |Bb   :‖

② ‖: F5 |Bb5 |Ab5 |Db5   :‖

③ ‖: F |Eb | Bb |Bb   Ab5 :‖

④ ‖: F5   Ab5 |Bb5 | F5   Ab5 | B5   Bb5 :‖

⑤ ‖: Bbm |Gb | Fm |Ab   :‖

⑥ ‖: Fm |Eb |Db |C   :‖

⑦ ‖: F5 |Eb5 | F5 |C   :‖

⑧ ‖: F5 |Ab5 |Bb5 |Db5   Eb :‖

⑨ ‖: F5   Db5 |Bb5 | F5   Db5 |Bb5   C :‖

⑩ ‖: F5   Ab5 | F5   Bb5 | F5   Ab5 | F5   B5   Bb5 :‖

Rock Chord Progressions - F♯ - G♭

Fingerboard Notes on 2nd and 3rd String:

FRET	0	1	2	3	4	5	6	7	8	9	10	11	12
2nd string	D	D♯E♭	E	F	F♯G♭	G	G♯A♭	A	A♯B♭	B	C	C♯D♭	D
3rd string	G	G♯A♭	A	A♯B♭	B	C	C♯D♭	D	D♯E♭	E	F	F♯G♭	G

① ‖: F♯   C♯ | B | F♯   C♯ | B   :‖

② ‖: F♯5 | B5 | A5 | D5   :‖

③ ‖: F♯ | E | B | B   A5   :‖

④ ‖: F♯5   A5 | B5 | F♯5   A5 | C5   B5   :‖

⑤ ‖: Bm | G | F♯m | A   :‖

⑥ ‖: F♯m | E | D | C♯   :‖

⑦ ‖: F♯5 | E5 | F♯5 | C♯   :‖

⑧ ‖: F♯5 | A5 | B5 | D5   E   :‖

⑨ ‖: F♯5   D5 | B5 | F♯5   D5 | B5   C♯   :‖

⑩ ‖: F♯5   A5 | F♯5   B5 | F♯5   A5 | F♯5 C5 B5 :‖

Rock Chord Progressions - G

Fingerboard Notes on 2nd and 3rd String:

FRET	0	1	2	3	4	5	6	7	8	9	10	11	12
2nd string	D	D#Eb	E	F	F#Gb	G	G#Ab	A	A#Bb	B	C	C#Db	D
3rd string	G	G#Ab	A	A#Bb	B	C	C#Db	D	D#Eb	E	F	F#Gb	G

① ‖: G   D | C | G   D | C   :‖

② ‖: G5 | C5 | Bb5 | Eb5   :‖

③ ‖: G | F | C | C Bb5 :‖

④ ‖: G5 Bb5 | C5 | G5 Bb5 | Db5 C5 :‖

⑤ ‖: Cm | Ab | Gm | Bb   :‖

⑥ ‖: Gm | F | Eb | D   :‖

⑦ ‖: G5 | F5 | G5 | D   :‖

⑧ ‖: G5 | Bb5 | C5 | Eb5 F :‖

⑨ ‖: G5 Eb5 | C5 | G5 Eb5 | C5   D :‖

⑩ ‖: G5 Bb5 | G5 C5 | G5 Bb5 | G5 Db5 C5 :‖

Rock Chord Progressions - A♭

Fingerboard Notes on 2nd and 3rd String:

FRET	0	1	2	3	4	5	6	7	8	9	10	11	12
2nd string	D	D♯E♭	E	F	F♯G♭	G	G♯A♭	A	A♯B♭	B	C	C♯D♭	D
3rd string	G	G♯A♭	A	A♯B♭	B	C	C♯D♭	D	D♯E♭	E	F	F♯G♭	G

① ‖: A♭   E♭ |D♭ |A♭   E♭ |D♭   :‖

② ‖: A♭5 |D♭5 |B5 |E5   :‖

③ ‖: A♭ |G♭ |D♭ |D♭   B5 :‖

④ ‖: A♭5   B5 |D♭5 |A♭5   B5 |D5   D♭5 :‖

⑤ ‖: D♭m | A |A♭m |B   :‖

⑥ ‖: A♭m |G♭ | E |E♭   :‖

⑦ ‖: A♭5 |G♭5 |A♭5 |E♭   :‖

⑧ ‖: A♭5 |B5 |D♭5 |E5   G♭ :‖

⑨ ‖: A♭5   E5 |D♭5 |A♭5   E5 |D♭5   E♭ :‖

⑩ ‖: A♭5   B5 |A♭5   D♭5 |A♭5   B5 |A♭5 D5   D♭5 :‖

CIGAR BOX GUITAR BOOK COLLECTION

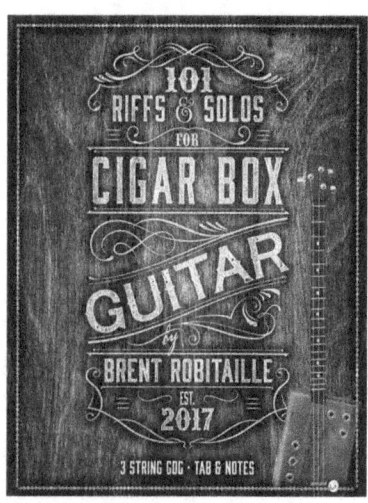

WWW.BRENTROBITAILLE.COM

More Great Music From Kalymi Publishing

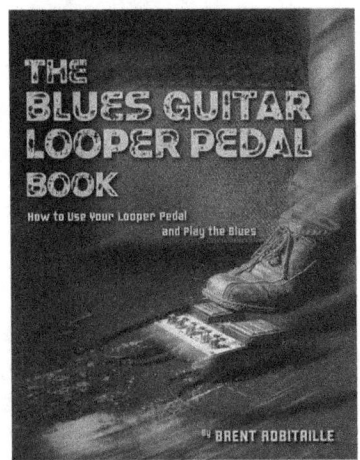

THE BLUES GUITAR LOOPER PEDAL BOOK

- 2, 4, 8, 12, & 16 Bar Blues Loops
- Riffs, Bass, Chords, and Rhythm for Each Loop
- 10 Tips for Making Great Loops
- 10 Tips for Better Guitar Solos
- Blues Scales & Fingerboard Charts - Slide Guitar Exercises
- Blues Progressions & Strumming Patterns
- Free Audio Tracks Online

Improve Your Guitar Chord Playing

- 12 Tips, tricks, and exercises to improve your chord switching
- Step by step chord switching exercises excellent for beginners
- 45 common chord progressions in pop, rock, folk, and blues.
- Barre chord tips with strengthening exercises
- Master the fingerboard with triangle patterns and diagrams
- Key and capo charts to transpose from key to key

Guitar - Mandolin - Fiddle - Ukulele

WWW.BRENTROBITAILLE.COM